W9-CPH-856

BORODIN

BORODIN

Photograph taken by Lorentz at St. Petersburg towards the end of 1880. A copy of this print, given to L. J. Schestakova by the composer in 1882, is preserved in the Rimsky-Korsakov family collection.

BORODIN

BY

SERGE DIANIN

Translated from the Russian

by

ROBERT LORD

LONDON
OXFORD UNIVERSITY PRESS
NEW YORK   TORONTO
1963

Oxford University Press, Amen House, London E.C.4

GLASGOW NEW YORK TORONTO MELBOURNE WELLINGTON
BOMBAY CALCUTTA MADRAS KARACHI LAHORE DACCA
CAPE TOWN SALISBURY NAIROBI IBADAN ACCRA
KUALA LUMPUR HONG KONG

English Translation
© Oxford University Press 1963

Printed in Great Britain by
Spottiswoode, Ballantyne & Co. Ltd.

CONTENTS

FOREWORD TO THE ENGLISH TRANSLATION   vii

BORODIN'S LIFE

1. BORODIN'S ANCESTRY. HIS BIRTHPLACE. CHILDHOOD AND
   YOUTH (1833–59)   2

2. VOYAGE ABROAD. MARRIAGE. MEETING WITH BALAKIREV.
   OPENING OF THE PERIOD OF MATURITY (1859–63)   23

3. THE FIRST SYMPHONY. 'THE VALIANT KNIGHTS.' BALLADS
   (1863–9)   43

4. 'PRINCE IGOR.' THE SEVENTIES (1869–79)   58

5. THE LAST YEARS (1880–7)   113

BORODIN'S WORKS

6. GENERAL OBSERVATIONS. BORODIN'S FIRST COMPOSITIONS.
   WORKS OF HIS CHILDHOOD AND YOUTH   158

7. THE SYMPHONIES   184

8. THE CHAMBER AND PIANO WORKS   229

9. THE SONGS   257

10. 'MLADA' AND 'PRINCE IGOR'   267

11. A FEW GENERAL CONCLUSIONS   327

APPENDIX A. LIST OF BORODIN'S WORKS   332

   B. BORODIN'S BIRTH CERTIFICATE, AND A FURTHER
   NOTE ON HIS ANCESTRY   344

   C. RUSSIAN TITLES OF PERIODICALS AND BOOKS
   REFERRED TO IN TEXT OR FOOTNOTES   348

   D. GENEALOGICAL TABLE

INDEX OF WORKS   349

GENERAL INDEX   351

B
B 736 d
Art

24 Je 64 C B 10.80 Cummings

345851

ILLUSTRATIONS

Borodin in 1880   *Frontispiece*

facing page

   I. Borodin at the age of fifteen   20

  II. Gitinsky, Borodin, Mendeleev, and Olevinsky   21

 III. Catherine Protopopova   36

 IV. The main building of the Academy of Physicians   37

  V. Balakirev   68

 VI. The organizers of the Russian Chemical Society   69

 VII. Stassov   84

VIII. The house in which Borodin lived during the summer of   85
1879

 IX. A general view of Soligalitch   116

  X. Rimsky-Korsakov   117

 XI. Louise, Countess of Mercy-Argenteau   132

 XII. Borodin in 1885   133

XIII. A. P. Dianin   148

FOREWORD TO THE ENGLISH
TRANSLATION

Music is one of the most effective and most beautiful means of communication between peoples. However characteristically national the music may be, it will penetrate to the hearts of all receptive listeners regardless of outlook, provided that it has real beauty.

Russian music stems from the genius of Glinka and reaches its full development in the works of the 'Kuchka' (the mighty Handful); it has long since become well known all over the world. It is only fitting therefore that a book on Borodin by a Russian musicologist should appear in English translation.

It was my good fortune to be born in the flat where Borodin spent most of his life, and into a family who had been intimately associated with him, though not in any way related to him by birth. My father studied chemistry under Borodin, and became one of his close friends; he succeeded him as Professor of Chemistry, and sorted out Borodin's affairs after his death in accordance with Borodin's own wishes and those of his friends. My mother was Borodin's adopted daughter and had grown up in his family; a second adopted daughter, Elena Guseva, also lived in our house. They were all passionate devotees of Borodin, both as a man and as a composer.

From my earliest years I have been used to hearing anecdotes about Borodin himself and about his various friends and acquaintances, and the various opinions he had on different topics. I was brought up in a home environment which was not very different from Borodin's own.

Luckily, I have managed to remember from my childhood days a vast assortment of hitherto unpublished facts relating to Borodin. I have long been wanting to publish this material, especially as I am keenly interested in music, but work on my other speciality, mathematics, and various other complications have so far prevented me from doing so.

I was finally persuaded to begin work on preparing this material for publication by the late Andrey Rimsky-Korsakov, who was much my senior as a musicologist and actually taught me a great deal about the history of music. When he learnt (sometime in 1922) that I had been working on the extant portions of Borodin's archives, and that there were a number of unpublished letters amongst this material, he strongly urged me to do something about getting them published.

I gave the matter a fair amount of thought before approaching the Musical Department of the State Publishing House with a view to bringing out a volume of Borodin's Correspondence, which would include as well all the surviving sketches and fragments. In seeing this project through, and in drawing up the contract for the first volume of the Letters, I was greatly indebted to the enlightened cooperation of the late H. Y. Myaskovsky and to a certain extent to B. P. Jurgenson.

Thus, in 1927, work was begun on the four-volume edition of *The Letters of A. P. Borodin*, edited by myself and completed in 1951. In all 1,284 documents were published together with a detailed commentary on each. I went through hundreds of books and manuscripts, and was given much friendly advice and assistance by friends and even by strangers. In the interests of scientific accuracy, I checked wherever possible the published texts in minutest detail against the extant autographs.

In addition to Borodin's own correspondence, I prepared for publication a number of letters and documents relating to Borodin (1948). There were 450 documents in all, but by 1961 only 161 of these had appeared in print.

From the time when I first began work on the publication of Borodin's letters, I had already decided that there was room for a definitive biography of Borodin. At first, I had intended to do nothing more than supplement the existing biographies with the unpublished letters and other documents, especially as I was working along these lines at the time, preparing a series of lectures on the life and work of Borodin for my seminars at the State Institute of the History of Art.

But when I came to look closer at the documents relating to Borodin and to check the facts with my mother and Elena Guseva, I found that I would not only have to supplement the existing material, but also to correct a number of details already given by earlier biographers. The immediately obvious mistakes were the date of his birth, the location of the house in which he was born, his ancestry, and a whole host of minor facts, especially those touching on his compositions.

To clear up all these uncertainties and inaccuracies, I was obliged to work on the archives, and to seek out various people who had known Borodin personally. These quests brought me into some strange situations, and if I ever have time I hope to be able to write about these expeditions (in Leningrad, Moscow, Vladimir, and Perov). I managed to finish all this work by the end of the 1920s, while at the same time doing a considerable amount of teaching and research in mathematical sciences.

It was at this time that I had the idea of writing a definitive biography; this was to have followed the publication of the complete collection of documents. I had in mind an extremely detailed, 'exhaustive' biography which would include an analysis of his compositions.

As things turned out, however, my calculations were upset, for even as late as 1955 I had managed to bring out only a fairly short account of Borodin's life, as the first part of my book on Borodin.

Nevertheless, this work, in my opinion, meets the basic demands of scientific research. All the facts given in it are corroborated by documents, references to which are given in the notes (in all I worked through about 2,000 manuscripts and published works, including the 1,734 documents in Borodin's archive).

It is this biography, with all its corrections and supplementary material, particularly the full details of his birth-certificate and his genealogy, which forms the first part of this book now appearing in English translation.

The second part of my book is an analysis of the compositions. Although it contains a considerable amount of general material dealing with Borodin's compositions, I have concentrated to some extent on one particular aspect. My research was determined on the one hand by the discovery of new facts about Borodin's themes, and on the other hand by the possibilities of tracing the origin of his compositions, which opened up as a result of my work on the archive material.

A chance conversation with an old peasant who was personally acquainted with Borodin led me (in 1928) to the discovery of the significance of motifs taken from the song 'The Sparrow Hills', which appear as 'concealed leit-motifs' in the opera *Prince Igor* and also as thematic material in the First Quartet.

This discovery was of two-fold importance: it suggested the existence of a hidden meaning (a meaning known only to the composer) in Borodin's themes, and it showed how the composer set about constructing his 'folk' themes.

And much more recently (after 1950) I managed to determine the way in which the 'Polovtsian' themes had evolved, which in turn threw some light on Borodin's use of the 'combination' method in constructing his themes.

It was also around this time that I received certain information from the musicologist A. N. Dmitriev, which drew attention to notes which Borodin had made of lays and folk-songs. He also explained Borodin's shorthand system of making his notes, which for the most part gave no indication of key signature, no note values and no words.

Thanks to N. V. Shelkov, I managed to obtain copies of the short-hand versions of three songs mentioned by Dmitriev, and when I compared them with certain themes in *Igor* and the First and Second Symphonies I was convinced that Borodin used these notes whenever he was creating new thematic material.

In the Second Part of this work on Borodin, therefore, I have devoted a great deal of space to the genesis of his themes. In addition to this, I have traced Borodin's development as a composer, giving all the details I consider relevant about the works of his early years, and a complete analysis of the works of his maturity. In the section devoted to *Prince Igor* I have singled out for special attention Borodin's adaptation of the original scenario, since no information relating to this aspect of the opera has so far been published.[1]

My study of the genesis of the themes and their formal structure, as well as a vast amount of detail of a biographical nature, have given me the opportunity to put forward plausible hypotheses as to the programme content of Borodin's compositions, for which no actual programme was indicated by the composer personally.

Finally, I have included at the end of my book a list of Borodin's compositions which contains a greater number of works than have previously been mentioned in the biographies. I have managed to date certain of the works mentioned in the list, and have also indicated where the original manuscripts may be found.

The reader, I think, will agree that this book represents a considerable step forward in the study of the life and work of Borodin. The work will have been justified if more people are drawn to Borodin's music and unique personality as a result of it. I also hope that the

---

[1] I was working on this as early as 1934. The material I used has been in the State Depository since 1950, but this does not prevent me from claiming priority in the investigation.

results of my research published here will be a contribution to musico-
logy as a whole.

In preparing and publishing this work, I am indebted to the
following: Professor Gerald Abraham, V. V. Danilova, A. N. and
O. A. Dmitriev, A. S. Lyapunova, V. N. and G. M. Rimsky-Korsakov,
N. F. Teplinskaya and N. V. Shelkov. I want to express my sincere,
heart-felt thanks to them all.

I wish also to thank the Oxford University Press for giving me the
opportunity to publish my book in one of the great languages of the
world, thus enabling me to see at least the partial fulfilment of a lifetime's ambition.

S. A. DIANIN

TRANSLATOR'S NOTE

There are many inconsistent conventions governing the transliteration of
Russian (Cyrillic) characters. In this book: (i) when previous translations
or critical biographies have adopted a particular transliteration of a proper
name, this has been taken as a precedent, e.g. 'Stassov' and not 'Stasov',
although the latter would be more correct; (ii) in other cases the convention
adopted by the *Slavonic and East European Review* (University of London)
has been taken as the model.

In general the English rather than the Russian style has been observed in
personal names. Thus patronymics and initials are normally omitted unless
there would otherwise be ambiguity, e.g. Catherine [Borodin], not Ekaterina
Sergeevna, Stassov, not V. V. Stassov

Dates. Owing to the fact that the reform of the calendar was delayed
until 1 February 1918, Russian dates in the mid-nineteenth century were 12
days behind other European countries. In this book: (i) for events outside
Russia the reformed calendar ('New Style') is used; (ii) for events inside
Russia the unreformed calendar ('Old Style') may be used (to get the 'reformed' date, add 12); (iii) if there is ambiguity both forms are given, e.g.
12/24 January, 1880, where 12 January is Old Style, 24 January New Style.

BORODIN'S LIFE

CHAPTER ONE

BORODIN'S ANCESTRY.
HIS BIRTH-PLACE.
CHILDHOOD AND YOUTH
(1833–1859)

Borodin's ancestors on his father's side were the Gedianov Princes, but we have only the scantiest information about them. According to documents preserved in the Leningrad section of the Central Historical Archives (formerly the Department of Heraldry), the first of the line of these princes was 'Prince Gedea'. There is a statement to the effect that 'he took the honourable course of defecting from the Horde and bringing his Tartars into Russia' and 'was baptized, by God's grace, in Moscow in the reign of Ivan the Terrible, having the title Prince Nicholas[1] conferred upon him at the sacred font.'

In this case, the term 'Horde' signifies nothing more than the region where the nomadic Tartars lived, since 'The Horde' was no longer of any political importance by the time of Ivan the Terrible. It is quite certain the Gedea was a Tartar by origin, very likely a Nogai from the northern Caucasus,[2] but in any case a Tartar.[3] It would appear that Gedea and his son, Stepan Gedianovich, lived for some time in Moscow; we know this for certain in the case of Gedea's grandson, Prince Ivan Stepanovich Bolshoi Gedianov.[4] Prince Ivan distinguished himself as a military leader in the defence of Moscow against the Poles in

[1] The heraldic deed of the governing senate No. 20: 'Concerning the incorporation of the coat of arms of the Princes Gedianov into the general book of arms of the nobility of the Russian Empire.' Begun 4 March 1825, completed 8 June 1827. Half-sheet No. 7.

[2] A. N. Samoilovich, the academician, suggested to me that this might be Gedea's origin. During the reign of Ivan the Terrible the term 'Horde' probably embraced the regions inhabited by the nomads. These Tartar encampments were concentrated mostly near the northern spurs of the Caucasus.

[3] Philological analyses confirm that the name Gedea is of Tartar origin. According to Samoilovich, this name is the beginning of one of the Tartar-Moslem names; hidajet-ulla (God's way) or hodie-ulla (God's gift). Samoilovich considers that the second name (hodie) is the more probable, basing his assertion on the phonetic laws of evolution by permutation of vowels.

[4] Called 'Bolshoi' to distinguish him from his brother John, called 'Menshoi'.

the reign of Tsar Michael (Romanov) in 1618. We know from a letter written by Tsar Michael to Ivan on 11 February 1631 that he was rewarded 'for his illustrious service to the Throne and to the whole of Moscow' and for 'having stayed with his Lord the Tsar throughout the siege . . . and having fought, without a thought for his own safety, in battles and assaults despite the favourable offers made to him by the Invader,[1] and the privations he had to undergo'; he was granted hereditary possession of estates in Vologda province, namely, the villages of Fedyaikovo and Khudodushevo in the county of Toshinskaya.[2]

The Gedianov Princes held these lands in Vologda Province until the beginning of the eighteenth century. We know how they came to lose possession of these domains from a 'petition' presented by Borodin's grandfather, Lieutenant Stepan Antonovich Gedianov. (A copy of this petition was presented to him on 6 February 1734.) The petition was addressed to the Governor of Bakhmut, and reveals that the last representative of the elder branch of Gedianovs, Prince Alexandr Gorbun-Gedianov, had surrendered these 'ancient domains in Vologda to the monastery of St. Sergius, the worker of miracles, as a token of remembrance for the souls of his wife, Princess Evdokia, and his daughter Praskeva'. With this went the estates belonging to Stepan Antonovich (a representative of the younger line of Gedianovs). He had done this 'not out of dishonesty or wickedness, but in sorrow for the death of his daughter and because his memory had faded through old age'. It was thus that Stepan Gedianov reconciled himself to the loss of these former lands of his.

It is also apparent from this petition that he was living at the time (in the seventeen-thirties) in the town of Bakhmut which is in the Ekaterinoslav Province.[3]

From the fragmentary knowledge we have of Borodin's ancestors on his father's side, it is clear that they were well-off, and that, apart from Ivan Bolshoi Gedianov, they did not distinguish themselves in any way. This also applies to Borodin's father, Prince Luka Gedianov, about whom we know rather more than in the case of his predecessors.

Luka Stepanovich Gedianov was born in 1774.[4] His father was

---

[1] The Polish Prince Vladislar, the son of Sigismund III.
[2] See the same heraldic deed, half-sheets 2–4.
[3] See the same heraldic deed, half-sheet 4, reverse.
[4] The date of his birth is established primarily from details in the genealogical book of the St. Petersburgh province (Vol. 8, 1821–7). In the passage where he is entered into the fifth part of the book (dated 29 September 1823) he is mentioned as being 49. My

already old and died shortly after his son was born. Judging by the portraits[1] and Borodin's own accounts, Luka Gedianov's features were distinctly oriental. This gives us reason to suppose that Luka's mother or grandmother were of eastern extraction. It is possible that through one or the other of them he was related to the ruling family of Imeretia; this would account for the tradition that he was descended from the 'rulers of Imeretia', which appears to be based on Borodin's own statements.[2]

Nothing is known of Luka's childhood. His education very likely left much to be desired. At the age of sixteen (18 May 1790) he joined the Velikolutsky Musketeer Regiment. Although a prince by birth, he was given a non-commissioned rank. He served in this regiment until 23 October 1797, when he went into retirement with the rank of lieutenant. During the course of his army service he 'took part in a number of battles with the enemy.'[3]

At the turn of the century, Luka Gedianov married Marya Ilinichna Isakova, the daughter of Ilya Ivanovich Isakov, and on 26 May 1804 she bore him a daughter, Alexandra.[4]

After his marriage, he lived in Tver Province, and later in Moscow and St. Petersburg. He owned an estate in the Staritsky district of Tver Province until 1818; later, in 1824 or thereabouts, he inherited more land in the Bezhetsky district of the same province; and in 1830 he came into possession of the village of Perovo on the outskirts of Moscow.[5] Perovo, as we already know, was in the middle of the eighteenth century the residence of the Empress Elizabeth and her

second source of information comes from the late B. L. Modzalevsky who had seen the inscription on Gedianov's grave in the cemetery of the Sergeevsky hermitage (near the station of Volodar on the Baltic railway). The year '1772' which is given as Gedianov's date of birth on the published portrait is therefore incorrect.

[1] I did have a water-colour portrait of Gedianov, dated 1836, in my possession, but unfortunately it was destroyed without being published. Also (as I mentioned in the preceding note) there is a large picture in oils painted by Denyer in the year 1840. This was reproduced atrociously in *The Russian Musical Gazette* for 1897.

[2] See also the 'Further Note on Borodin's Ancestry', p. 334.

[3] See the report on Gedianov's army service (as quoted in note 4, p. 3) made on the basis of Order No. 42951 of the State Military College on 23 October 1797.

[4] In the *Moscow Necropolis* (part II, p. 190) we come across a mention of Borodin's sister which reads: 'Alexandra Lukinichna Gedianova-Lukash. Born 26 May 1804. Died 23 February 1834. Buried in the Spaso-Andronyevsky Monastery.' Alexandra married N. E. Lukash, a 'lieutenant colonel and cavalier', on 2 April 1819 and had by him six male children (see 'Deed No. 882 of the Governing Senate of Heraldry in accordance with the reports of the Moscow College of deputies of the nobility').

[5] These details as to Luka's place of residence and the estates belonging to him are taken from the documents mentioned in note 1, p. 2, and note 4 above.

favourite, Count Alexei Razumovsky; the palace there is built of wood and was designed by Rastrelli.[1] It appears that Luka Gedianov bought Perovo from the last representative of the Russian branch of the Razumovskys, Count Peter Razumovsky, a squanderer and debauchee, who sold all his possessions in the 1820s. But Luka did not own Perovo for very long; by the end of his life, he had no land at all, and only a single summer residence in the suburbs of Petersburg, at Lesnoi.[2] He spent the last years of his life entirely in Petersburg.

We have only fragmentary and extremely limited information about Luka Gedianov. It is known that he led a fairly riotous life in his youth and went on the usual sprees, just like all the other well-to-do young people of his day. There is a certain amount of evidence that he was on friendly terms with Peter Razumovsky, and used to join him in the orgies which he arranged in Perovo and which won for themselves such a scandalous reputation.[3]

It is known too that Luka Gedianov was at one time drawn to Labzin's pietistic and mystical religious movement which eventually led to the foundation of the Bible Society. The aim of this society was to publish and distribute copies of the Old and New Testaments translated into every language in the world. However, despite the good intentions of this society, the reactionary Nicholas I found the movement dangerous (partly owing to its international connections), and got rid of it as quickly as possible by dissolving it.

There is only indirect information about Gedianov's part in the activities of the Bible Society,[4] but, although we know from Borodin that he joined the society, he was never on the board of directors, and it is doubtful whether he even took an active part in the society's activities. Nevertheless Gedianov took the Society very seriously, and in Denier's portrait, which was commissioned fourteen years after the liquidation of the Society, he posed holding a bible in his hands.[5]

By comparing the documents relating to Borodin's father with published information about the Bible Society, we are enabled to make a

[1] With regard to this palace, see the article by I. Bondarenko: 'Eighteenth-century palaces in the vicinity of Moscow', *Former Years*, 1911, Book 3, pp. 11–30.

[2] See 'Senatorial Declarations' for 1844, Vol. 2, No. 31, para. 5, rubric 17, concerning Luka's widow's acquisition of landed property upon her husband's decease.

[3] I was given this account by E. A. Guseva who often heard such stories from Borodin.

[4] Amongst the records of the Bible Society which are preserved in the Saltikov-Shchedrin State Public Library in Leningrad, I managed to find an account of a financial bequest made to the Society by A. L. Gedianov in 1817 (see 'News of the Affairs and Successes of the Bible Society', 1824, report No. 2, para. 7).

[5] See note 1, p. 4.

few inferences about his more intimate acquaintances. It would seem that his closest friends were Prince Peter and Prince Ivan Meshchersky, and various other members of this family.¹ Their influence was undoubtedly responsible for Luka's mystical leanings. The Meshcherskys were all involved in the activities of the Bible Society. They were, for these times, well educated and had connections with literary circles.² The only other friends we know of are the Golitsyns, who were in some way connected with the well-known adventuress of the time, Mme. Krüdener.³

Gedianov was not particularly happy as far as his family life was concerned. After the birth of his daughter he had no more children and for some time lived apart from his wife.⁴ Perhaps it was his unsatisfactory domestic life which led to his protracted love affair with Borodin's mother, Avdotya Konstantinovna Antonova. She was from Narva⁵ and 'the daughter of a soldier' (she was born in 1809). Her brother, Sergei Antonov (born 1804), was a civil servant in the War Department, at the Petersburg Ordnance House, and had risen high in the ranks. He became assistant superintendent of the building department of the Winter Palace, and later inspector of the French Embassy (which was housed in the unused half of the Winter Palace), and finally served on a committee concerned with the planning of a Roman Catholic Theological Academy. We know nothing of him after 1854. Their sister, Ustinya Konstantinovna, was married to an official in the St. Petersburg Finance Office.

¹ The members of the Meshchersky family are continually mentioned in official acts relating to the Gedianov and Lukash families, in the capacity of godfathers, witnesses, etc. See, for example, the 'Heraldic Deeds', Nos. 20 and 882, quoted in note 1, p. 2, and note 4, p. 4.

² Prince Peter Sergeevich Meshchersky was from 1818 one of the directors of the St. Petersburg committee of the Bible Society. On his personal intercession, Tsar Nicholas I allowed the Society to complete certain projects which had already been put into operation, after the organization had been suspended.

³ See the letter from Borodin's father to Princess A. S. Golitsina published on p. 337 of my Russian book, *Borodin* (2nd ed., 1960).

⁴ There is a reference in the letter referred to in the preceding note to his sorrow at being separated from his family (Luka was then in St. Petersburg while his wife, daughter, nephews, and nieces were in Moscow).

⁵ There is a note as to his origin in the service record of Avdotya's brother, Sergei Konstantinovich Antonov, which says: 'Son of a soldier from the department of Narva.' (See deed No. 1 of the court intendancy bureau relating to the promotion of Corporal Antonov to the rank of officer. Begun 12 March 1830, completed 5 December 1831. Half-sheet 5.)

According to the laws of the time, the term 'soldier's child(ren)' was applied to the sons and daughters of men who had spent not less than a certain number of years in the ranks. Thus Borodin's grandfather on his mother's side, Konstantin Antonov, was a

Avdotya Konstantinovna was very good-looking.[1] Luka Gedianov came to know her sometime during 1831 or 1832. I have been told that he saw her for the first time at a dance or at dancing lessons,[2] which were held apparently 'at the house where the department concerned with the Imperial Household had its offices'; it is possible that Sergei Antonov had his flat in this building at the time. This house (now No. 7 Gagarinskaya Street) was next door to the house belonging to a Mrs. Bulina (No. 9), where Gedianov had rooms at the time.[3] Shortly after their acquaintance Avdotya moved in there with him. His flat was on the first floor and had windows looking out on three sides. Avdotya gave birth to a son, Alexander,[4] on 31 October 1833 (O.S.).

soldier in the Russian army. The legend as to the mercantile origin of the Antonovs is not confirmed by any documents and probably arose through Borodin's being obliged to register with the merchant class (in order to qualify for the Academy). This was perhaps supported by D. S. Alexandrov, his brother, who wished to conceal his true origin.

[1] Many tales are told of her beauty in her youth. Up to 1942 her portrait, which was painted by Denier in 1840, was in the possession of her granddaughter L. E. Konopleva. True, it did not reveal her beauty, but it certainly gave a more favourable impression than the hideous reproductions made in the *Russian Musical Gazette*, 1897, where her portrait appeared with Gedianov's. I presume that this was the reason for Stassov's reference to Borodin's parents as 'those monsters' (see the unpublished correspondence between Stassov and N. F. Findeisen, preserved in the Public Library).

[2] E. A. Guseva and my mother (E. G. Dianina) often told me this. They in turn had heard it in their childhood from people friendly with Avdotya, and especially from E. E. Belzmann, her servant.

[3] Gedianov's address in the St. Petersburg directory for 1837 was kindly found for me by B. L. Modzalevsky who had this rare book in his possession. Bulina's house can easily be found by comparison of the address in the 1837 volume with that of later directories.

[4] For a long time Borodin's birth was attributed to 31 October 1834 (12 November, N.S.), and not to 1833. In my paper 'Concerning the Year of Borodin's Birth' (1925), I showed that this was a longstanding error. The incorrect date was even accepted by Borodin himself on the basis of information given him by D. S. Alexandrov and E. E. Belzmann on the occasion of his birthday (31 October 1873). He describes this in a letter to his wife dated 4 November 1873: 'They gave me a present (nothing of great importance to them, but one very dear to me), namely a year of my life. They showed me by counting that I was not 40, but 39. In fact, I had entered the Academy at 15, not 16, for in my case they did not insist upon my having reached the usual entrance age of 16. It is certain that I started there in 1850 and as it is now 1873, I must be 39, not 40' (see *Letters*, Vol. II, p. 68, note 217). Borodin instantly told all his friends of this 'present' with the result that the incorrect date appeared in his biography. Unfortunately, the reasoning upon which his theory of his entry into the Academy was based was false. One had to have reached the age of 17, and not 16, in order to enter the Academy (see the Regulations of the Academy, ratified on 18 December 1835. Chap. VIII, para. 87, added to the book, *History of the Academy of Military Medicine*, ed. Ivanovsky, St. Petersburg, 1898). Therefore he was not accepted by the Academy until the age of 17. Consequently, in the autumn of 1850 (at the beginning of the academic year) he was 16 years of age, but on 31 October 1850 he was 17 years of age. According to this reasoning, he was born not in 1834, but in 1833. This coincides with the details of his birth which appear in various documents, namely in the parish register preserved in the archive of the Academy

Gedianov registered his illegitimate son as the legal son of one of his servants, Porfiry Ionovich Borodin. In this way the boy was in effect the serf of his own father, but this was far from unusual for those times.

We know very little about Borodin's early years. It is extremely probable that Avdotya went on living with her small son in Gedianov's flat until 1839.[1] There is no doubt that he spent his early childhood with his father, for he could picture him very clearly and would often mimic him for a joke. When he was about two years old he struck his head on the parapet of the balcony[2]; the scar remained with him for the rest of his life. Avdotya was passionately fond of her little Sasha, although she never officially recognized him as her son, and always referred to herself as his 'auntie'.[3]

We do not know for certain how Gedianov looked on his son. I have heard it said, however, that the old prince not long after the birth of his son said he would like him to be apprenticed to a shoe-maker.[4] However that may be, we have no grounds for supposing that Borodin's early days were anything like as bad as one normally expects in the case of illegitimate children born of serfs. He had his nephews the Lukashes[5] as playmates, for they were about the same age as himself. He was also allowed to play with a girl called Marya Yurevich, the daughter of a rather 'superior' neighbour.[6] Moreover, his father

of Physicians ('Documents', No. 346), and in the archive of the former register for marriages of the Leningrad Province which I personally examined in the authentic parish register in the Church of St. Pantelemon in 1925. Both clearly state that he was born in 1833. See Appendix B.

[1] I.e. up to the time of her marriage (see p. 9).

[2] Borodin often showed this balcony (which was at the corner of Gagarinskaya and the former Sergeevskaya Street 'above a tea shop') to his friends, in particular A. P. Dianin and E. A. Guseva, saying that he was born in the flat there. E. A. Guseva herself pointed out the house to me, and as it corresponded with Gedianov's address given in the directory of 1837, I was fully convinced that this was the place of his birth. In 1910 its last owner, Baroness Büler, constructed another two storeys and converted the balcony into a verandah. In view of these facts, it is clear that the details given in D. S. Alexandrov's *My Reminiscences of my Brother* as to the place of Borodin's birth are incorrect (see Stassov's book on the composer, pp. 1–2).

[3] As Borodin addressed her in all his letters.

[4] The widow of Borodin's younger brother, V. A. Fedorova, told me this.

[5] This is seen from a letter of Borodin to his mother on 5/17 May 1860 (*Letters*, Vol. I, Letter 7, p. 48). In this letter he tells how pleased Elizabeth Lukash was to see him. From that time onwards he calls her brother (who was his nephew on his father's side) by the diminutive 'Serezha'. This corresponds to the relationship between Elizabeth Lukash and Borodin's mother. (In the same letter he sends her his warmest greetings.)

[6] Concerning M. S. Yurevich-Krasovskaya see, for example, Borodin's letter to his wife dated 10 July 1866 (*Letters*, Vol. I, Letter 32, p. 85). It is seen from the St. Petersburg handbook for 1854 that Semen Alexeivich Yurevich, father of Marya, was a 'court

was godfather to Borodin's first cousin, the daughter of his mother's brother.[1] In this way, there was no sharp line of demarcation between the 'noble' prince and the 'low-born' relatives of his illegitimate son.

In 1839, things changed in the life of Sasha Borodin. The old man Gedianov wanted to see Avdotya comfortably provided for before he died, and arranged for her to be married to a retired army medical man, Christian Ivanovich Kleineke,[2] who held a fairly high rank in the civil service. It appears that, to mark the occasion, Gedianov presented them with a four-storied house or at least gave her the money to purchase it.[3] This marriage was a purely legal arrangement; Borodin's stepfather left very little impression on his son and lived with him only for a very short time.[4] Gedianov kept up his friendship with Avdotya up to the time of his death. We know this from the portraits that Denier painted of them together, and the large number of articles that Borodin's mother kept from the Gedianov household and later passed on to Borodin.[5]

The first really valuable piece of information we have of Borodin relates to the period around 1840. As a child he was sickly and highly-strung, but at the same time very likeable. In the reminiscences which Borodin's wife dictated to S. N. Kruglikov, she writes: 'He was a wonderful child, attractive to look at, but of an unusually gentle and

lieutenant-general' who lived in his own house near the Gagarinskaya Quay, i.e. not far from Gedianov's flat.

[1] He was the godfather of S. K. Antonov's daughter Olga (born 5 October 1836). The godmother was Borodin's aunt Ustinya Konstantinovna.

[2] In the birth certificate of Borodin's cousin Elizabeth, which was issued on 28 May 1839, Borodin's mother (who was the godmother) is described as the wife of a 'retired civil servant, Christian Ivanovich Kleineke'. On the other hand, there is preserved in Borodin's papers a congratulatory acrostic commemorating the occasion of Avdotya's marriage, dated 27 July 1839. It seems therefore that she married Kleineke in the spring of 1839.

[3] It appears from the deed of the court intendancy bureau with reference to 'S. K. Antonov's dismissal' (1842–4) that neither he nor his parents had any property. Only Avdotya was a person of some means. Gedianov was a fairly wealthy man. From all accounts, he was very attached to Avdotya and wished to give her a definite 'position' in his declining years. The presence of a dowry in such a solid form as her own house was probably the motive behind the decision of Kleineke (who was then an old man) to marry the prince's former mistress.

[4] Kleineke must have died before 25 September 1841, as Borodin's mother, who was the godmother of S. K. Antonov's daughter Maria who was baptized that day, is described in the baptismal register as Kleineke's widow.

[5] Amongst the objects left Borodin's mother by Gedianov there was a small ikon of St. Nicholas which was painted (judging by its style) about the fifteenth or sixteenth century, belonging probably to Prince Gedea. This relic clearly shows that in the last days of his life Gedianov regarded Borodin as his heir, rather than his grandchildren, the Lukashes.

placid disposition.' His usual playmate at this time was his cousin Marie Gotovtseva, who was staying in his mother's house.¹ Little Sasha played at dolls with her, and used to imitate the organ-grinder. Another favourite pastime was to make up stage-settings and plays for his mother and her housekeeper, E. E. Belzmann, his only audience.

From a very early age Borodin had showed signs of musical talent. His first experiment in composition was apparently a Polka in D minor,² which he composed when he was nine years old. Also in her reminiscences, Catherine Borodin tells how this Polka coincided with Borodin's 'first love affair': 'Sasha fell in love for the first time when he was nine years old. The object of his passion was a lady called Elena. This Elena was tall and rather fat! When he danced with her, little Sasha was so tiny that he could not reach above her knees. How jealous he was when she danced with anyone else! It was in her honour that he composed a Polka which he called "Helène" . . .'

'Auntie' spoiled her Sasha terribly and was very affectionate towards him. She was an intelligent woman and saw to it herself that her son had a thorough educational grounding. She paid no attention to those relatives of hers who tried to persuade that she was overdoing his studies and might harm his health. She engaged a lady to teach him French, and the German housekeeper called Luischen, who lived with them, taught him German. Even at this early age Sasha was exceptionally studious and had an unusually good memory.

Borodin's father died on 21 December 1843.³ Before he died he granted freedom to his son. Shortly afterwards Avdotya⁴ became attached to another man, and she gave birth to a son Dimitri in the following year. (The only things we know of him come from his correspondence with his brother. His surname was Alexandrov.)

It was roughly about this time, or perhaps a little before, that Avdotya sold the house Gedianov had given her and bought another.

---

¹ About M. V. Gotovtseva, see *Letters*, Vol. I, Letter 54, p. 129: note 11 to this letter, and also note 31 to Letter 2.

² Stassov states erroneously (on p. 4 of his book and elsewhere) that this polka is in F major. The polka *Hélène* was first published by P. A. Lamm in 1946.

³ The date of Gedianov's death is found on the inscription on his tomb (see note 4, p. 3), this date coincides with the entry describing his widow's inheritance (as mentioned in note 2, p. 5). This paragraph is especially interesting as there is no mention in it of either Kleinecke or Borodin. Presumably Luka gave them part of his property during his lifetime.

⁴ According to V. A. Fedorova's description, this was 'Prince Volkonsky' with whom Luka was acquainted to a certain extent. For his son, D. S. Alexandrov, see *Letters*, Vol. I, p. 330, (note 38 to Letter 2).

Her new house was not far from the Semyonov Parade Ground, on Glazovskaya Street (Nos. 13–15).[1] She kept this house until 1870. Borodin spent part of his childhood and the whole of his adolescence there.

Soon after they had moved to Glazovskaya Street, Borodin started going to the Semyonov Parade Ground with their maid, Luischen, where he listened to the military band playing. He made friends with the bandsmen, studied the instruments they played, and picked out on the piano the tunes he heard when he came back home. Around this time he began taking flute lessons; his mother engaged a musician from the Semyonov Regimental Band to teach him.

Avdotya's next affair was with a retired teacher of German, Feodor Fedorov,[2] and it was through him that Sasha made a great friend. Fedorov introduced him to Mikhail Shchiglev, who was about the same age as Sasha and the son of a mathematics teacher who taught at the Tsarskoselo Lycée and the Gatchina Institute. Not long after this Misha Shchiglev came to live with Borodin's mother 'so that I would not have so far to travel to the college where they wanted to send me, and also so that I could do my lessons with Sasha Borodin.' Both boys were taught by 'teachers who were specialists in their particular subjects.'[3] It seems that all these tutors were engaged on R. P. Shchiglev's recommendation. The latter was thus responsible for Borodin's education for a time. It was probably Shchiglev too who recommended his piano teacher, 'a German by the name of Pormann, a very patient and painstaking man, but not very sensible when it came to teaching'.[4]

In their time the two boys played piano duets, and became acquainted with the symphonies of Haydn and Beethoven. They rather liked Mendelssohn, and went regularly to the symphony concerts at the University, conducted by Karl Schubert. In summer they used to go to the Pavlovsk to hear Johann Gungl. (From this and other indirect information, it is reasonable to assume that Borodin never went very far from Petersburg as a child, and perhaps the farthest he travelled was to the summer residential areas in the suburbs with his mother.)

---

[1] It is still the same house—No. 20 Borovaya Street. This house appears in the old directories as No. 14 Glazovskaya Street.

[2] He had a son by her at the end of the 1840's called Evgeny (Borodin's half-brother, Evgeny Fedorovich Fedorov).

[3] Taken from Shchiglev's reminiscences of Borodin which are cited here from Stassov's book (p. 5); the original manuscript has disappeared.

[4] Ibid., p. 5.

Borodin taught himself to play the cello. In the year 1847 or there-abouts he wrote a concerto for flute and piano and a Trio in G major for two violins and cello on a theme from *Robert le Diable*.[1]

Some time later, probably in 1849, he composed two piano pieces: *Fantasia per il piano sopra un motivo da J. N. Hummel*, and a study *Le Courant*. It is clear from a very complimentary review, written by F——ov (F. A. Fedorov?), and published in the newspaper *Severnaya Pchela* (No. 263) on 25 November 1849, that these pieces were subsequently published by Robert Gedrim (F——ov's review was discovered and brought to my attention by Olga Pavlovna Lamm).

Even before he met Shchiglev, Borodin had developed a passion for chemistry which equalled if anything his love of music. It began with attempts at making fireworks and other pastimes, but gradually developed into a more serious occupation. By the time he was thirteen or fourteen years old, Borodin had built up for himself a complete laboratory at home, using various corners of the flat for this purpose. This laboratory of his alarmed 'auntie' somewhat, and she had to put up with smells and run the risk of a fire.

As a boy Borodin also delighted in electrotype experiments and made his own water-colours, which he used himself for painting.[2] He read a great deal, mostly scientific books and journals, and he became so absorbed in what he had read that he gave the impression of being very absent-minded. In his memoirs D. S. Alexandrov wrote: 'If he was engrossed in anything or even merely busy, you had to repeat a question several times before he would reply.'[3]

In the summer of 1850, Borodin passed his matriculation examination at the Petersburg college. Apart from a not very good mark in the scripture paper, the results as a whole were 'outstanding.'[4]

In the autumn of that year, Borodin entered the medical faculty of the Academy of Physicians as an external student. But in spite of the work he was doing in his laboratory at home, he had not yet definitely decided whether he wanted to become a chemist.

[1] In all probability, the autograph of the D minor Polka in its arrangement for piano duet (for performance with Shchiglev?) derives from this time. The nature of Borodin's handwriting suggests that it is the work of a fourteen-year-old rather than a child of nine or ten.

[2] My mother had a few of Borodin's sketches, painted by him as a child.

[3] The original is preserved in the Stassov archive in the Pushkin House of the Academy of Sciences of the U.S.S.R. The passage in question is taken from Stassov's book (p. 6).

[4] Borodin's testimonials are in the archives of the Academy of Physicians, 'Documents', No. 346. (Now transferred to the Leningrad Archives of Military History.)

To make it easier for her son to study at the Academy, Borodin's mother moved to a flat in the Viborg district of Petersburg, and took with her the entire household (including F. A. Fedorov). The flat was part of a house belonging to a Doctor M. D. Charnoi, and was on Bocharnaya Street immediately opposite the Artillery School.[1]

Borodin threw himself wholeheartedly into his work at the Academy, and in every course he took he was consistently near the top. He completed his studies in 1855 'cum eximia laude'.

During his first two years at the Academy, Borodin had become more and more interested in chemistry through attending the brilliant lectures given by the gifted 'grandfather of Russian chemistry', Nikolai Nikolaevich Zinin, who was at that time Regius Professor of Chemistry at the Academy. In his third year he began work of an advanced nature in Zinin's own laboratory. 'Borodin, who was exceptionally shy and sensitive, could not bring himself to approach Zinin for some considerable time', writes Alexander Dianin, 'but now that he was in his third year, he at last went to see him, and explained that he would very much like to work in his laboratory under his supervision. Zinin was a little suspicious at first, but soon saw that he had not only a sound knowledge of chemistry, but also some acquaintance with experimental techniques. From that time onwards, he never ceased to be Borodin's teacher, friend, and guide.'[2]

While at the Academy, Borodin made a more than superficial study of botany, zoology, anatomy, and crystallography; he became so fascinated with botany that he spent some time on it each summer right up to the very last years of his life. In all these branches of the natural sciences, he found Zinin an expert guide, for his knowledge covered a variety of fields.

'I can vividly recall my country walks with him in the vacations', he wrote, shortly after the death of his teacher. 'These were highly instructive outings. N. N. [Zinin] was a keen and expert naturalist, and could find something interesting to discuss in each tiny leaf, pebble, tree, or blade of grass.'[3]

However fascinating his studies might be, Borodin could never forget his music. His friendship with Mikhail Shchiglev remained

[1] Bocharnaya Street has been renamed Komsomol Street, and the house in question stands opposite the Military College of Technology.

[2] A. P. Dianin's article 'Alexander Porfiryevich Borodin' in the *Journal of the Russian Physico-Chemical Society*, 1888. Vol. IV (April).

[3] A. P. Borodin and A. M. Butlerov: 'Nikolai Nikolaevich Zinin. Reminiscences of him and a Biographical Sketch', *Journal of the Russian Physico-Chemical Society*, 1880.

untouched, and they continued to make music together as before. In addition to this, he made the acquaintance of two musically-gifted people: Vladimir and Peter Kirillovich Vasilyev, the one a singer and the other a violinist.[1] He went with them to musical gatherings held in private houses, and, by doing so, greatly extended his knowledge of music. Sometimes he would actually perform himself.

Much later, he told his wife about a certain notary he once met; he 'once went to his house with Vasilyev (a singer) and did some playing'. He describes how, in his youth, 'he would go to choir practices where they sang such things as "Mia Letizia, Frapoco", songs by Gurilev, Varlamov's "Swimmers" and Villebois's "Men of the Sea".'[2]

The young musicians often played quartets. Kirillov played first violin and Shchiglev second; Borodin played the cello; and usually they had to engage a viola player to come and play. 'We let no opportunity pass of playing trios and quartets. We would play anywhere and with anyone we could get', says Shchiglev, 'Hail, rain, or snow, nothing would stop us. We used to cover enormous distances on foot, Borodin with his cello in a baize bag on his back, and myself with my fiddle under my arm; we might for instance walk the whole way from the Viborg to the Kolomna district, as we hadn't a farthing between us.'[3]

Borodin's favourite chamber-music gatherings were held at I. I. Gavrushkevich's flat, a wooden cottage built by Lisitsyn, which used to be 'on the Artillery Parade-Ground just by the Cathedral of the Transfiguration.'[4] He was a splendid host even if not a particularly outstanding cellist, and many musical people including A. N. Serov, I. K. Hunke, F. K. Drobysh, and N. Y. Afanasiev, used to meet there in the fifties. Usually 'there was a surplus of violinists and violists' and if possible they would play sextets, septets, and octets. For this reason their repertoire was not first class. They played string octets by Gade and Spohr, quintets by Boccherini, Gebel,[5] Onslow, and Feit.[6] Borodin was delighted to see the 'influence of Russian Moscow' on Gebel, and agreed with Serov who on one occasion was defending

---

[1] See M. R. Shchiglev's reminiscences (Stassov's book on Borodin, p. 9).

[2] *Letters*, Vol. I, Letter 91, pp. 193–4, and the note on p. 368.

[3] Shchiglev's reminiscences (Stassov, op. cit., pp. 9–10).

[4] Stassov's book, p. 10. The Artillery Platz is now called Ryleev Square.

[5] Franz Xavier Gebel (1787–1843), well known in his time as a composer. Lived as a music teacher in Moscow from 1817 till his death.

[6] A composer writing chamber music at the end of the eighteenth century.

Gabrushkevich's string octet arrangement of Glinka's 'Jota Argonesa' against the unfounded attacks perpetrated by 'the Germans'. At these musical gatherings Borodin only played if Drobish was unable to come, and even then only took second cello parts. His cello technique was very weak, but he had a good sense of rhythm and was always quick to grasp a work's qualities.[1]

According to Gabrushkevich and Shchiglev, Borodin continued writing music even while he was a student. He wrote several vocal works, including the ballad 'The Beautiful Fisher-maiden' to words by Heine, which he composed for Adelaida Shashina, an amateur singer and composer, and the songs 'My fair young maid no longer loves me', and 'Hear this ditty of mine, dear friends.'[2] As far as we know, Borodin never said anything about these works at Gavrush-kevich's musical evenings. According to the latter, he advised Borodin 'to take advantage of his acquaintance with Hunke, who was an excellent teacher of composition, and to have a shot at writing a quintet with two cellos'. But Borodin said: 'It is very difficult, because there are two main parts (the first violin and first cello), and I don't think I could write a cello part that would sound decent and suit the instrument'.

The archives however show that Borodin did in fact follow Gavrush-kevich's advice and sketched a string quintet in F minor with two cellos, but the manuscript is so incomplete that it is impossible to ascertain whether he finished the work or not. In any case, this early work of his was never performed at Gavrushkevich's.

In the mid-fifties, Borodin completed a string trio which took its theme from the song 'How have I offended thee'. As E. M. Braudo justly points out: 'In this trio there is a marked influence of the great master whom Borodin rated above all other composers and to whom he dedicated his *Igor*, namely Glinka. Indeed, I would go so far as to say that, if one did not know that Borodin was the composer, one could easily mistake it for an excerpt from *A Life for the Tsar*.'[3]

Another of his early works probably belongs to this period; the Scherzo in B flat minor, for piano. Unfortunately, there is no longer any trace of this work. According to Shchiglev, there was a distinct 'Russian idiom' in this piece. Thus, even at this early date, there was

[1] Stassov's book, p. 10.
[2] All these works, written for voice with piano or cello accompaniment, were first published in a collection of Borodin's songs published by Musgiz in 1947, ed. P. Lamm.
[3] *Alexander Porfiryevich Borodin* (Petrograd, 1922), p. 16.

evidence of the folk strain which was to assume such mighty proportions in his later music.[1]

His musical activities were viewed with disfavour by those who saw in him the makings of a brilliant chemist. Once, for instance, Zinin apparently said to him at one of his lectures: 'Mr. Borodin, it would be better if you gave less thought to writing songs. I have placed all my hopes in you, and want you to be my successor[2] one day. You waste too much time thinking about music. A man cannot serve two masters.'[3]

We have only a very incomplete picture of Borodin's student days, and it is not possible to present a coherent account. We mention here just a few details of his family life relating to this time.

It was in 1853 or thereabouts that their maid, Luischen, died; she had lived with them till the very end. Borodin always spoke highly of her, and it was under her tuition that he gained a mastery of German.[4]

About this time, 'auntie' began to find herself in straitened circumstances; income from the property left her by Gedianov had gradually diminished. She had never been very good at managing the housekeeping and accounts; and in addition to this fell into the clutches of a certain Timofeev who swindled her and ruined her financially. He was aided and abetted by Ekaterina Belzmann who was their housekeeper at the time.[5]

After graduating from the Academy of Physicians, Borodin was appointed medical practitioner at the Second Military Hospital on 25 March 1856.[6] There is a photograph of him which was taken at this

[1] D. S. Alexandrov informs us in his memoirs that Borodin composed many fugues in his fourth year as student at the Academy. Borodin himself informs us of his sonatas for flute and cello which he wrote in his youth (in a letter to the Countess de Mercy-Argenteau on 6 November 1884) (*Letters*, Vol. IV, p. 106). The same letter shows that he presented a full list of his musical works (including his youthful efforts) in applying for membership of the Paris 'Société des Auteurs'. If this list is still extant in the archives of this society, it might throw some interesting light on the number and character of his youthful productions. See also my monograph: 'Description of the Borodin collection in the Leningrad Philharmonic Museum made by N. F. Findeisen.' This account was delivered at a meeting of the historical section of the Department of Theory and History of Music of the Russian Institute of the History of Art on 16 June 1927.

[2] I.e. to the Chair of Chemistry in the Academy of Physicians.

[3] Taken from the reminiscences of I. I. Gavrushkevich written for Stassov (see his book on Borodin, p. 11).

[4] See the letters of Borodin quoted in note 1, p. 10. A. P. and E. G. Dianin also heard him praise Luischen highly.

[5] E. A. Guseva and E. G. Dianina heard Borodin describe the parts played by A. E. Timofeev and E. E. Belzmann in this.

[6] Now the hospital of the Military Academy of Medicine.

time.[1] He posed with his cousin, Marya Gotovtseva, to mark important events in both their lives: he had become a doctor, and his former
playmate had become engaged to Borodin's friend, Ivan Sorokin.
Borodin in this picture looks very handsome. His regular facial
features and certain oriental characteristics are reminiscent of the
physiognomy of saints and emperors to be found on Byzantine and
ancient Georgian frescoes and mosaics.

The first years after leaving the Academy (1856–9) were spent doing
work which was not congenial to him. He was in fact not at all suited
to medical practice.

Once, for example, the coachman of some high-ranking official was
brought into the hospital, and Borodin had to remove a bone that was
choking him. While he was operating, the rusty instrument he was
using broke in the patient's throat. But the young surgeon kept his
presence of mind, and after a few unsuccessful attempts, removed the
broken fragment of metal and the bone at the same time. Borodin tells
how 'the coachman went down on his knees before me, and it was as
much as I could do to restrain myself from doing likewise. Just think
what might have happened if the broken piece of forceps had stuck in
his throat! You can bet that I would have been court-martialled and
ended up in Siberia.'[2]

Another unpleasant occasion was when Borodin in the course of
his duty happened to see with his own eyes the cruelty of serfdom in
all its horror. D. S. Alexandrov gives the following account of the
incident: 'In his first year as house-surgeon at the hospital, my
brother happened to be on duty one day when they brought in six
serfs belonging to Colonel V . . . who had flogged them for locking
him in the stables because of the cruel way he treated them. Borodin
had the job of pulling out the splinters from their backs. He fainted
three times at the sight of the skin hanging in tatters from their backs.
In the case of two of them, their bones were visible.'[3]

During the time he was at the hospital, Borodin completed his first
piece of research. He submitted a paper: 'Recherches sur la constitution chimique de l'hydrobenzamide et de l'amarine' at the session of
the Mathematical Physics section of the Russian Academy of Sciences,
held on 5 March 1858, and was also working on a dissertation for the

---

[1] I published this portrait as a frontispiece in the first volume of *Borodin's Letters*.

[2] Based on the description by M. A. Guseva. Her mother lived in Charnoy's house
at the same time as Avdotya, who was then on excellent terms with the Gusevas.

[3] D. S. Alexandrov's reminiscences quoted in Stassov's book on the composer, p. 13.

degree of Doctor of Medicine. He had very little time for music, and the whole of his spare time was taken up with laboratory work.

At this time he was sharing a flat with his friend I. M. Sorokin who was also a relative of his. His first wife Marya Gotovtseva had died in childbirth at the end of 1856. They lived with 'auntie' in Klimov's house on the Samsonievsky Prospect.

It was at this time that he first met Mussorgsky. We have Borodin's own account of how they met: 'I was a raw recruit in the army medical service and was house-surgeon at the 2nd Military Hospital. M. P. was an officer in the Preobrazhensky Regiment, and looked very new to the job; he could not have been more than 17 at the time. We first met in the hospital, in the hospital orderly room. I was the duty doctor and he duty officer. The room was like any other of its type, and neither of us liked being on duty. Neither of us was reserved and we naturally started up a conversation, and very quickly became friends. That night we had both received an invitation to a party the next evening by Popov, the Head Doctor at the Hospital. He had a grown-up daughter, and it was for her sake that he frequently threw parties, and of course the duty officers and doctors had to be invited. It was pure politeness on his part. M. P. was scarcely more than a boy at the time, but a very smart and dapper young officer. He was wearing a brand-new and tight-fitting uniform, he stood well, and his hair was well-groomed; he manicured his finger-nails, and obviously took great care of his hands, just like a true aristocrat. He had the manners of a gentleman, and spoke through his teeth; he interlarded his speech with French turns of phrase, and rather flowery ones at that. There was just the least suspicion of foppishness. He was polite and unusually well-bred. The ladies fell for him. He sat down at the piano, and, lifting his hands coquettishly, played excerpts from *Trovatore* and *Traviata* and so forth, with much grace and delicacy; around him the chorus of murmurs "charmant, delicieux!" and so on. It was in these circumstances that I met Mussorgsky, three or four times at Popov's and when we were on duty together.'[1]

This story is a good illustration of Borodin's acute powers of observation and his ironic attitude towards the cult of the aristocracy and the 'beau monde' as reflected in the fashionable atmosphere of a 'salon' of his day where amateurs played badly music of poor quality.

[1] From Borodin's account of his friendship with Mussorgsky which he wrote at Stassov's request. See also Rimsky-Korsakov's memoirs, 5th ed., pp. 63–66, wherein he describes his acquaintance with Mussorgsky (cf. *Letters*, Vol. IV, p. 297).

In 1857 Borodin went abroad for the first time. He had been delegated to accompany the royal oculist, Ivan Ivanovich Kabat, to an international ophthalmological congress in Brussels. Borodin set out at the beginning of August 1857, and on the way stayed for a short time in Berlin and Frankfurt-am-Main. From there he travelled up the Rhine and spent a few days in Paris. For part of the time he travelled in the company of Kabat's 'well-to-do' lady patients, among them Borodin's distant relative (?) 'the Princess of Imeretia'.¹ Borodin gives none too respectful descriptions of his travelling-companions in a letter to his mother.² But there is not a mention of music in this letter. He restricts himself to impressions of his journey, and also tells her that he had a good look round Berthelot's laboratory. From an invitation card of 8 September 1857 (N.S.) we learn that Borodin was at a party given by the Committee of the Brussels ophthalmic congress. It was on this trip that he visited Italy for the first time, and possibly England as well.³

It was in 1858 that Borodin published his first paper on chemistry,⁴ as mentioned above, and on 3 May defended his dissertation for the degree of Doctor of Medicine, the title of which was 'on the like action of arsenic and phosphoric acids on the human organism'. This work had much to do with problems of a chemical nature. Shortly after this, in the summer of 1858, Borodin paid an official visit to the small town of Soligalich in Kostroma Province. It was on Zinin's recommendation that he had been invited by the well-known financier, V. T. Kokorev, to make a study of town's mineral waters. He spent the whole of the summer there and carried out the work assigned to him very thoroughly indeed.⁵

In the autumn of 1859,⁶ he again met Mussorgsky; this time at

¹ As may be seen from the 'Business of the State Dept. of Law', this was Ekaterina Sergeevna, the widow of the Imeretian Tsarevich Konstantin: 'Of the use of the title "his Highness" by the heirs of the descendants of the former Georgian Tsars', No. 25 (1865). On half-sheet 51 it states that E. Sergeevna received the sum of 3,000 roubles for her journey abroad in 1857.

² *Letters*, Vol. I, Letter 1, pp. 25–28.

³ Borodin mentions his trip to Italy in Letter 6 (*Letters*, Vol. I, p. 46). Whether he visited England on this occasion has never been confirmed.

⁴ In Vol. 17 of the *Proceedings of the Academy of Science.*

⁵ His report, *The Saline Mineral Waters at Soligalich*, was originally published in the form of an article in No. 130 of *The Moscow Gazette* for the year 1859, but was later issued as a separate brochure, a copy of which may be found in the Saltikov-Shchedrin State Public Library in Leningrad.

⁶ See Borodin's correspondence quoted in note 1, p. 18. Also Stassov's book, p. 15.

Professor Ivanovsky's. Borodin wrote about this as follows: 'Mussorgsky had already retired from the army. He had pretty well reached maturity, and had started to put on weight, and he had lost his military manner. He was just as smartly dressed, and still the perfect gentleman, but there was now no trace of foppishness. We were introduced to one another, but of course we immediately recognized each other, and went on to reminisce about the times when we first met at Popov's. Mussorgsky explained that he had gone into retirement because "his special interest was music, and it was somewhat complicated to combine a military career with music". The conversation automatically turned to the subject of music. I was still mad keen on Mendelssohn, and at that time hardly knew anything about Schumann at all. Mussorgsky was already acquainted with Balakirev, and had an eye for all the new things that were going on in the musical world, of which I had not even the slightest idea. When the Ivanovskys saw that we had found a common ground for our conversation, they suggested that we should play the piano-duet arrangement of Mendelssohn's A minor Symphony. Mussorgsky pulled an odd face and then said he would be delighted, as long as "he did not have to play the Andante, which was just not symphonic, but in place of this, one of the 'Songs without Words' arranged for orchestra" or something of that nature. We played the first movement and the Scherzo. After that, Mussorgsky began to rhapsodize about the symphonies of Schumann, which at the time I was totally unacquainted with. He to play me extracts from the E flat major Symphony of Schumann. When he came to the middle section he broke off with the words: "That's where the musical mathematics begins." It was all new to me and I liked it. Seeing that I was very interested, he played something else that was new to me. I also learnt that he was writing music himself. Naturally I was fascinated, and he began playing me a Scherzo of his (could it have been the one in B flat major?).[1] When he came to the Trio, he muttered: "Look, this is oriental", and I was astonished by this strange kind of music, which was like nothing I had ever heard before. I won't pretend that I was very much taken with it to begin with; I was a little perplexed by the novelty of it at first. But when I had heard a little more of it, I soon developed a taste for it.'

In this account of his meeting with Mussorgsky, his concluding

---

[1] Borodin's guess is quite possible as Mussorgsky had just finished his B♮ major Scherzo at that time.

I. BORODIN AT THE AGE OF FIFTEEN

The original oil painting, painted by Denière in 1848, no longer exists.

II. GITINSKY, BORODIN, MENDELEEV, AND OLEVINSKY

A copy of the photograph taken by Schulze at Heidelberg on 28 June 1860.

words about the pleasure 'the strange new elements' had given him is of particular interest. It is quite clear that the young Borodin's musical development was proceeding along lines which eventually made it easier for him—as one who admired the compositions of Glinka above all others—to accept the new music and appreciate the new ground that was being broken by his gifted friends.

We can take it that in the autumn of 1859 his student days came to an end, and that the main features of his personality and character were already visible.

To sum up, we shall make a few general conclusions. Borodin grew up in a mediocre middle-class environment, and was in contact with the narrow-minded and petty officialdom which flourished in the reign of Nicholas I. The landed gentry, to which his father belonged, might also have had some influence on him, but only while he was still very young. It was from his father's anecdotes that he developed his sense of the legendary and semi-fantastic, and it was these tales which perhaps gave the initial impetus to the sharp but good-natured satire which stands out in his comic opera *The Valiant Knights* and in his song 'Pride'.

The young Borodin's heterogeneous social background and his great gifts which raised him well above the people around him, led him before long to break with his milieu, and eventually made an 'intellectual' of him. Shchiglev's father was an important influence in this direction. R. P. Shchiglev was an educated and enlightened man, and as Borodin's teacher did much to stimulate in him a repugnance towards his environment, which was later reflected in his quizzical attitude to any kind of nonsense. His study of classical literature and critical articles, in particular, those of Belinsky, was a further step in this direction. There were also the many students he knew in his own year at the Academy who no doubt had an influence on him. Borodin grew up in the 'age of reform', and shared its passion for the exact sciences and desire for assertion of national independence; he was thus a typical avant-garde 'man of the sixties'.

His intense interest in science, his creative bent, and personal traits kept him from entering the political struggle; but this did not mean that he had no interest in social questions.

He had already read a good deal of the published work on chemistry and was adept at experimental technique. Also he had a sound knowledge of related fields. He knew a number of foreign languages and had an unquestionable talent for expressing himself clearly, vividly, and concisely. The young Borodin was clearly a man of promise.

If we compare the level of his musical development with his scientific achievements at this time, it is perfectly clear that the former was lagging behind. He says himself that his knowledge of music 'began with the old masters'[1]; by then, he was well steeped in the classics and Mendelssohn; but he had only the merest acquaintance with Berlioz, Liszt, and Schumann. He referred to himself as 'a keen Mendelssohnist'. He had a high regard for the music of Beethoven, but it was Glinka whom he admired most of all. He had composed very little himself, though he had already tried his hand at writing songs and chamber works. But it is the next few years which were really important in moulding his tastes and stimulating original musical ideas.

[1] Borodin's letter to L. I. Karmalina of 15 April 1875 (*Letters*, Vol. II, Letter 270, p. 89).

CHAPTER TWO

VOYAGE ABROAD.
MARRIAGE.
MEETING WITH BALAKIREV.
OPENING OF THE PERIOD OF
MATURITY

On 27 October 1859 Borodin went abroad as a delegate of the Academy of Physicians. Zinin had arranged this, insisting that Borodin should spend some time abroad to gain the necessary experience for the post of Adjunct-Professor of Chemistry which he would take up on his return. Thus it came about that Borodin was able to abandon a medical career, which had seemed to him in any case the wrong choice. It now became possible for him to pursue scientific research and, in addition, to prepare himself for teaching work, which to him seemed a most important activity.

We have Borodin's own detailed description of his journey from Petersburg to Heidelberg, which appears in a letter to his mother, dated 5 November 1859.[1] Here as always, Borodin displays his keen powers of observation and his acuteness. He left Petersburg in the evening by post-coach. He had taken a seat in the open, and, through this, his sensitive musical ear had to suffer several affronts during the course of the journey; he remarks about 'the conductor sitting behind a very thin partition, with his horn blaring mercilessly, and terribly out-of-tune at that.' In his own humorous way Borodin presents the details of the snail's-pace itinerary to the German frontier by way of Narva, Yuryev, Riga, Mitava, and Shavli to Taurogen; in all it took six days to reach Königsberg.

Being sociably inclined, Borodin soon got to know his travelling companions. In the letter just mentioned he speaks very warmly about one in particular: 'In Derpt another young fellow joined us. I would have taken him at first sight for a Derpt intellectual, but in

[1] *Letters*, Vol. I, Letter 2, pp. 28–34.

fact he proved to be Russian.[1] He went by the name of Borshchov[2]...
he was going abroad with the serious intention of furthering his
studies in the natural sciences. Borshchov ... as it turns out was a
very likeable young man, intelligent, and well-educated. He had
already specialized in botany (having had several papers published)
and geology, and had spent two years with Severtsev in the Kirghiz
steppes in the region of the Aral Sea, and so forth. In addition to this,
he turned out to be a very good musician, in sympathy with "our"
trend in music.'

In this same letter we learn something about the way in which
Borodin defined 'our' trend. He comments on the fact that: 'Borshchov is a passionate admirer of Glinka and knows the operas by heart
from cover to cover.'

After Derpt the pace became a crawl: 'The roads in Livonia ...
are foul. .... The ten nags, horribly badly shod, could scarcely drag
themselves along. The driver, a phlegmatic Lett, a boy of fifteen or
thereabouts, lashed the horses continually. Armed with two whips, a
small and a large one, the fellow systematically lashed the horses out
in front with the long whip, and then, putting this down, picked up
the small one and pitilessly whipped the rear horses. . . . We were
making about 4 or 5 versts an hour. To make matters worse, they put
on in place of fresh horses an extra driver. .... The two drivers, one
with a large, and the other with a small whip, were like uncle Mityaya
and uncle Minyaya in *Dead Souls*. In the end it became sickening. . . .'

After crossing the frontier at Taurogen on 1 November 1859,[3]
Borodin spent a few hours in Tilsit in the company of his fellow-
travellers, Borshchov and two German businessmen.

'We spent the time here very gaily: we had dinner and took a stroll
round the town. We finished up singing German part-songs.'

From Tilsit Borodin in the company of Borshchov set off via
Berlin to Heidelberg, where Zinin had directed him to work in the
laboratory of the famous German chemist, Bunsen.

'Stopping at the Badischer Hof we found ourselves in the hotel
where all the Russians living in Heidelberg dine. And, who should be
there but Mendeleev, Sechenov, and many others. After dinner we all

---

[1] At that time the students at the University of Derpt (Yuryev), now called Tartu,
were mostly German.

[2] Ilya Grigorevich Borshchov (1833–78), the gifted Russian botanist. Nikolai
Alekseevich Severtsev (1827–85) was the famous zoologist.

[3] This date is established from an entry in Borodin's passport which was in my possession.

made for Mendeleev's place; he has a delightful little laboratory, so neat and tidy, and even provided with gas.'

It is worth noting that this letter describing his journey to Heidelberg also contains a number of indications of Borodin's musical interests. There is nothing of this for example in the letter from Paris, referred to earlier. Immediately upon his arrival in Heidelberg, Borodin was not slow in making the discovery that the proprietress of the baths there hired out musical instruments. Borodin and Borshchov, while they were waiting for their bath, played through by heart the overture to *A Life for the Tsar*.

Borodin took rooms on the Friedrichsstrasse (No. 12) 'with an unrivalled view' of the Kanzelberg with its crown of towers. He immediately set about hiring a harmonium, at the same time joining a music lending-library. One of the first days there (between 5 and 13 November) he went to a concert given by the Symphonic Society. He wrote in a letter his impressions of this concert.

Borodin also at this time made the acquaintance of the people living there, Germans as well as Russians. There are some distinctly adverse comments about German philistinism; but about his fellow-countrymen he has the following to say: 'They fall into two categories: those who do nothing at all, namely the aristocrats . . . and those who do something, i.e. those pursuing various studies. My most intimate acquaintances are of course Mendeleev and Sechenov. The latter is a really remarkable man, extraordinarily simple and very sensible.'[1]

Sechenov, also, recalls in his autobiography the close friendship that grew up between them in Heidelberg. He describes the rooms Borodin had on the Friedrichsstrasse, and tells how he used to provide musical entertainment for his guests, 'modestly hiding the fact that he was a serious musician, by never playing anything serious, but merely songs of various kinds, or favourite arias from Italian operas, anything his audience cared to ask for. Knowing for instance that I was passionately fond of *The Barber of Seville* he used to entertain me with all the main arias in this opera, and in general surprised us all by playing everything we asked for, from memory and without music. . . .'[2]

In his *Autobiographical Notes* Sechenov tells also about his trip to Paris in the winter of 1859 with Borodin and Mendeleev. This trip lasted from 12 to 23 or 24 December[3]; and it was probably at this time

---

[1] *Letters*, Vol. I, Letter 3, pp. 36–37.
[2] I. M. Sechenov, *Autobiographical Notes* (Moscow, 1907).
[3] This date is also established from Borodin's passport.

that Borodin made the acquaintance of the distinguished French chemists Wurtz and Berthelot in Paris.

In accordance with Zinin's instructions Borodin was to work in Heidelberg in Bunsen's laboratory. But when he got to know the conditions under which he would have to work there, Borodin decided that it was unsuitable, and planned to carry out his research work elsewhere.

Soon after his return from Paris, that is, at the beginning of January 1860, Borodin began work in the laboratory of a young Privatdozent E. Erlenmayer. Earlier, in December 1859, Borodin had made a trip to Darmstadt to a manufacturer to secure a supply of reagents.

Although he had left the university laboratory and felt it was unnecessary to put in regular attendances at the lectures of the Heidelberg professors, Bunsen, Helmholtz, and Kirchhoff, which he found too elementary, Borodin nevertheless made use of the opportunity of seeing and hearing those great men of science, and of familiarizing himself with their manner of delivery and their research, e.g. with the investigations of Kirchhoff in the early sixties which produced spectrum analysis.

A few months after leaving Russia Borodin began to feel homesick; he jokingly tells about this in a mock letter to his 'dear auntie', dated 'the 31st March or maybe the 1st April' 1860: '. . . I have been depressed for some time now . . . it's quite simple, I feel I must get out of here. . . . Why not get to know people, make some friends, they tell me. What am I to say to them, if you please! . . .' But it is actually at about this time that the circle of Borodin's acquaintances in Heidelberg begins to widen. He starts visiting the family of Anna Pavlovna Brugger whom he refers to as 'that most sweet and kind Russian young lady'; he also becomes acquainted with M. A. Velinskaya-Markovich, the authoress,[1] and with T. P. Passek, a cousin of Herzen. Perhaps Borodin's interest in Herzen's activities is due to this latter friendship. It should also be mentioned that he frequents a certain German family, Kunz, which he describes as 'very musical'. He gives a humorous account of an evening-party given by this family in a letter to Sorokin.[2]

All this while Alexander Porfiryevich was busily at work in Erlenmaier's laboratory, and he moved to a new flat in the immediate vicinity (Karpfengasse No. 2). Outside his flat was a garden and open

---

[1] She published her works under the pen name Marko-Vovchok.
[2] *Letters*, Vol. I, Letter 5, pp. 41–45.

country, and from one side he had a view of the Neckar and the mountains.

Besides this, Borodin managed to keep up his music. 'I pass here for a musician,'[1] he writes. 'All my friends have got themselves pianos . . . some of them have even acquired cellos. . . . I played the flute at one musical gathering, and shall soon be playing quintets.' At the Bruggers' in particular he played piano duets and the cello. Scientific research and music absorbed him completely.

'I live well, though extremely quietly, and my health is good,' he writes in a letter to his mother dated 1 May 1860, 'I am perfectly satisfied with my position. . . . I work a lot and do it because I like it; I enjoy myself in fact. Besides this, three times a week or even more, I play piano duets and cello duets with a certain Mme. Stutzmann, a Russian lady permanently resident in Heidelberg. She is a good player. Tomorrow I shall be playing music for two pianos and eight hands with her and two English women called the Misses Barlow.'[2]

There are no indications from his letters written that year that he was engaged in composition. We can take it for certain however that the B minor Cello Sonata belongs to this period. This was written, in all probability, in the early summer of 1860 and is based on a theme of Bach's in D minor, originally for violin solo. The composer himself informs us that the sonata was inspired by a violinist in an adjoining flat who often played this Bach sonata. To this period also belong his transcriptions, for a group of instruments including cello, of three very early vocal pieces mentioned in Chapter I. Also the G minor string trio on the theme, 'What have I done to grieve you', was completed and possibly even revised.

In a letter dated 7 May 1860, Borodin tells his mother 'there will be a string quartet here this evening. Usually we play once a week.'[3] And in a letter of 20 June there is the remark: 'Regularly every week I play quartets and quintets at the house of the American (?). . . . In the museum, where I am a member, there are musical evenings and dances. I go to the former, but, it goes without saying, not to the latter.'[4]

Until July 1860 Borodin's life followed its regular pattern: the whole of his time was divided into laboratory research, music, and visits to friends. Borodin's work in chemistry at this time was yielding

---

[1] Ibid., Letter 4, p. 38.
[2] Ibid., Letter 6, p. 46.
[3] Ibid., Letter 8, p. 50.
[4] Ibid., Letter 9, p. 51.

results, and an article entitled 'The investigation of certain derivatives of benzidine' was published by him in 1860. Borodin made haste to publish this article since he had found out through Zinin that 'Hofmann in London was working in this same field'[1]; he did not want Russian chemistry to be deprived of any right to priority in the discovery of new facts on account of this man.

Among his acquaintances of this time, a niece and her brother, Lukash by name, should be singled out. His encounter with them brought forth a rather sharp comment about the Lukash family, and about 'the silly upbringing' the upper-class youth of those times received.[2]

On 26 June 1860, a sad event occurred in Borodin's circle of Heidelberg Russians; A. P. Brugger, in whose house the young Russian scholars had found welcome and sympathy, died of consumption. Borodin was pained by this loss, and, in order to relieve his gloom,[3] left Heidelberg and made a trip down the Rhine in the company of a beautiful young woman, the wife of a professor in applied chemistry. Her name was M. Y. Kitarry, and he had undertaken to accompany her as far as Bonn. In the course of this trip he visited a succession of towns in western Germany. Leaving his travelling-companion in Bonn, he travelled through Belgium and Holland as far as Rotterdam. Borodin looked round the chemistry laboratories whenever he happened to be in a university town.

In a letter dated 12 August 1860 he informed his mother of his return to Heidelberg. 'To my indescribable joy, I found Nikolai Nikolayevich [Zinin] there. He had returned straight from Paris. Now I am his constant companion, and we are only waiting for fine weather, and then we shall be off to Switzerland and Italy.'[1]

Somewhere around 22 or 23 August 1860 Borodin, Zinin, and Mendeleev set off on a short tour of southern Germany and Switzerland. (They did not go to Italy on this tour.) In the early part of their trip they spent a day in the Swiss town of Fribourg, admiring the picturesque scenery, and taking a look at the famous suspension bridge across the river. They also heard the large Fribourg organ. In the words of Mendeleev, 'this must be the largest organ in the world: its pipes are 32 ft. high (i.e. nine metres or so). People come and listen to

---

[1] *Letters*, Vol. I, Letter 10, p. 52.
[2] Ibid., Letter 7, p. 48.
[3] See note 1 above. This Madam Kitarry is the same 'Madam K.' whom Stassov mentions in his book on Borodin (p. 18). A large photograph of her is preserved in the Borodin archives in the State Institute of Drama and Music in Leningrad.

the organist who plays here. For a franc you have minutes of pleasure such as you will never forget. We went there one evening as it was growing dark. Inside the church only the organ was lit up, otherwise there was no light except that of a single lamp on the altar. In this romantic setting, sounds such as no orchestra could ever produce filled the whole church. Especially striking were the vox humana stops.'

Mendeleev left his companions for the time being after seeing Vevey, and went on his own to Chamonix. They all three met again in Geneva and from there went on to Zermatt.

After leaving Switzerland the three Russian chemists travelled to Karlsruhe to take part in an international congress of chemists, a very important event in the history of chemistry as things turned out. The meetings took place between 3 and 6 September. Despite the fact that Borodin was quite young and at that time little known, he was elected member of the congressional committee. While they were in Karlsruhe the three Russian chemists shared the same flat.[1]

After the congress, Borodin and Mendeleev returned to Heidelberg, where they stayed until the latter part of October, 1860. It is probable that during these six weeks Borodin shared a room with Mendeleev in a house in the Schulgasse (No. 2).[2]

The sketches for the D major Piano Trio as well as the D minor String Sextet were made, as far as we can tell, not later than October 1860,[3] and belong to the Heidelberg period. The same is true of Borodin's song, 'The Beautiful Fisher-girl'; this was performed by a singer called Vögeler at a public performance in Heidelberg.[4]

In a letter written between 16 and 28 October Borodin wrote to his mother as follows: 'I had thought of going to Switzerland again to

[1] The facts mentioned above describing the three Russian chemists' journey to Switzerland and their stay in Karlsruhe are taken from M. N. Mladentsev and V. E. Tishchenko's book entitled *Dmitry Ivanovich Mendeleev. His Life and Work*, Vol. I (Moscow-Leningrad, 1938), pp. 171, 180–2, 194, 250–8.

[2] In a letter to his wife dated 30 July 1877 (*Letters*, Vol. II, Letter 371), Borodin recalls the *Zimmer* (room) in Heidelberg 'where we lived with Mendeleev'. The address is given in the book *D. I. Mendeleev* in the note on p. 179. The probability that they shared rooms at this period is confirmed by examination of Borodin's letters to Mendeleev published in Vol. IV of *Letters*, pp. 243–4 and 251.

[3] This supposition is based on: (1) The fact that Borodin was not living in Heidelberg between 20 October 1860 and the end of May 1861. (2) The unlikelihood that Borodin would be occupied with the composition of large chamber works during his second Heidelberg summer (1861): during that summer he left Heidelberg fairly often and spent a great deal of time with his future wife.

[4] I was told this by Anna Ivanovna Mendeleeva who had learnt it from Mendeleev.

take a look at the places I haven't yet seen. But things have turned out differently. After loitering in Heidelberg for some time I learned that the autumn was too advanced for a trip to Switzerland.'[1] Instead he 'set out on a sudden impulse for Rome along with Mendeleev'. They went via Basle, St. Gotthard and Lake Maggiore to Genoa. 'We walked most of the way across the St. Gotthard. Goodness! How delightful it was! Nature at its most wonderful. And what harsh, bold scenery!—especially fine was the old road up to Andermatt: Streams cascade from the mountains and the river roars at your feet, swirling and foaming like a rough sea; the black, menacing slopes, with their summits lost in the clouds, soar right above your head; in the distance the blinding whiteness of the glaciers and snow peaks . . . sheer wonder!'[1]

Later on Borodin and Mendeleev had to pass through the province of Lombardy-Venetia, then belonging to Austria. At the frontier Borodin was arrested by the Austrian police. They had taken him for a political fugitive, who was active in the Italian revolutionary movement. While the Austrian police were searching Borodin and had not yet realized their mistake, the Italian they were actually looking for managed to get across the frontier on to Italian territory. As a result of this, Borodin and Mendeleev, who had unwittingly saved the Italian, were given a great ovation by the passengers on the Italian train in which they were travelling after Borodin's release.

The travellers then left Genoa by boat for Civita-Vecchia. 'We are travelling second-class as befits true democrats, of course, and needless to say, we aren't sorry; we have a very lively crowd here.' Borodin didn't especially like 'the cream of society' who packed the first-class deck on such boats.[2]

Mendeleev has given us a piece of information about the domestic side of this journey: 'We started out with very little luggage, with only a minute travelling-bag for two. We wore only blouses, so that we would look like artists; that's not a bad idea in Italy, because you can get along very cheaply that way. We took hardly any shirts with us, and had to buy new ones when the need arose; we gave these away to the waiters in place of tips. We absolutely let ourselves go in Italy, after the stifling cloistered life of Heidelberg. We spent the whole day rushing round the streets, looking at churches and museums; we liked most of all the small folk theatres, with their liveliness, gaiety, and

---

[1] *Letters*, Vol. I, Letter 11, pp. 53–55.
[2] See *D. I. Mendeleev*, pp. 174 and 198.

typical flavour, and the unbridled comedy that you find in any true folk performances.'[1] During their stay in Rome together, Borodin and Mendeleev visited St. Peter's and the Sistine Chapel, amongst other things. In the Sistine Chapel they had an opportunity not only of viewing the famous frescoes, but also of attending a magnificent mass celebrated by Pius IX with the cardinals in attendance.[2]

On this occasion Borodin spent one week in Rome. He left Mendeleev on 5 November[3] and made for Paris, where he stayed in the same hotel as the Russian chemist, Valerian Savich. Borodin remained in Paris until the spring of 1861, carrying out the studies he had planned in accordance with Zinin's 'instructions'.

We know very little about Borodin's life in Paris from 1860 to 1861; the only thing we know for certain is the following circumstance. At that time Borodin was assiduously set on enlarging his scientific knowledge and his pedagogical skill, by listening to distinguished scholars and readers in physics, crystallography, chemistry, bacteriology, and physiology. He studied the methods of exposition employed by the various lecturers with a view to preparing himself for his future professorial activity in the Academy of Physicians. He was lucky enough to see and hear gifted French scholars, whose names have remained immortal in the history of science. There was Claude Bernard, who was outstanding for his clarity of exposition, as well as Regnault, Sennarmon, Sainte-Claire-Deville, Dumas, and Pasteur. In particular, by means of personal recommendation, Borodin gained admission to the private lectures given by Sainte-Claire-Deville and Pasteur in the École Normale.

Borodin also undertook some practical research on polarization during that winter and practised the technique of glass-blowing. He became adapt at the latter technique during this time and was subsequently successful in teaching it to his own students of chemistry.

Borodin became a member of the Chemical Society of Paris; and while he was in Paris he read several papers outlining the results of the research which he had carried out in Heidelberg. Through this he gained a closer acquaintance with Wurtz, Reich, and Thénard the younger. During this time he was so busy that, in his own words, 'it was impossible to do any laboratory work anywhere, and even more impossible to carry out any independent chemical research.'

[1] See Stassov's book on Borodin, p. 17.
[2] See *D. I. Mendeleev*, pp. 174 and 198.
[3] See the passport mentioned in note 2, p. 24.

Despite all this activity, Borodin had of course some leisure time, whether days or hours. He spent his leisure partly in the company of Russian acquaintances; during that winter there were a good many of these Russian intelligentsia staying in Paris, who had come together in Heidelberg during the years 1859–60. Among them were N. N. Beketov, Bekkers, K. I. Lysenko, Marko-Vovchik, T. P. Passek, and E. F. Tolstaya. At this time too, Borodin made the acquaintance of Turgenev. In 1861 the young chemist P. P. Alekseev came to Paris, made friends with Borodin and Savich, and stayed in their hotel.

Borodin sometimes went to the theatre and to dances, and followed with interest the carnival revelries on the Paris streets.

I have no definite knowledge of Borodin's musical pursuits during this period from 1860 and 1861. It may however be mentioned that Borodin obtained from a Paris music shop two songs for voice and piano accompaniment; these were arrangements of Moorish melodies by Francesco Salvador-Daniel. These pieces were later to serve as material for some of the 'Polovtsian' themes incorporated in the opera *Prince Igor*. It is quite possible that in the season of 1860–1 Borodin worked from time to time on chamber works sketched earlier in the summer of 1860; for example, on the D major Piano Trio, and the D minor String Sextet.

On 11/23 March 1861, at a Senate meeting of the Academy of Physicians, it was agreed that Borodin's period abroad should be extended until August 1862.[1]

Around 10 or 11 April he left Paris for Italy.[2] The aim of this trip was that he should 'have first-hand experience of volcanic phenomena, and see the formation and mining of sulphur, boric acid, and so forth'. On this trip Borodin was in Turin, Genoa, and Leghorn, and then in Florence and Sienna. He visited the boric acid factory at Volterra. Finally he reached Naples; he explored the vicinity, the ruins of Pompeii, and Vesuvius, where he collected samples of lava for the Academy of Physicians. The greater part of his stay in Naples—

---

[1] For details of his life and work in Paris in 1860–1, see *Letters*, Vol. IV, pp. 241–57. For his Heidelberg acquaintances, see the book *D. I. Mendeleev*, p. 175. For his relationship with Turgenev, see Vol. IV (1953) of *The Literary Archives* (letter from Borodin to Turgenev, p. 392). Finally, the text of the Academy's decision to extend the length of his stay abroad is given in N. A. Figurovsky and U. I. Solovev's book, *Alexandr Porfiryevich Borodin* (Moscow-Leningrad, 1950), pp. 192–3.

[2] The date of his departure from Paris is established by a comparison of the visas in Borodin's passport with the letter to Mendeleev describing his stay in Italy from 1/13 April 1861 (*Letters*, Vol. IV, p. 249). As to the aims of his journey to Italy, see his account of the mission abroad (*Letters*, Vol. IV, p. 257).

twelve days in all—was marred by attacks of jaundice, from which he was suffering at the time.

On 14 May Borodin left Naples and set off for Heidelberg 'by way of Genoa, Arona, Lake Maggiore, St. Gotthard, Lake Lucerne, Lucerne, and Basle. . . . I travelled for six days on end, and was dog-tired'. Three days after sending P. P. Alekseev the letter from which this quotation is taken, Borodin wrote yet another letter to him, informing of the establishment of a Chemical Society in Heidelberg, and complaining of lack of money which had forced him to share lodgings with a friend, N. M. Yakubovich, who lived in the Schulgasse.[1]

A few days later (27 May) Borodin met his future wife, the young pianist Yekaterina (i.e. Catherine) Sergeevna Protopopova,[2] who had come to Heidelberg to be treated for tuberculosis. She was staying in Professor Hoffmann's pension in the Bergheimerstrasse (No. 14). Shortly afterwards Borodin moved there from Yakubovich's flat.[3] On the first day after her arrival it became known at the pension that Miss Protopopova was a talented pianist. For this reason a deputation of the Russians living there (Borodin, Lysenko, Maynov, and others) came to ask her to play for them. The young lady played the F minor Fantasia by Chopin, and Schumann's 'Schlummerlied'.

From the very start love of music brought Borodin and Catherine together. In later years she recalled her first meetings with the great composer. 'We were often together. His day was usually arranged as follows: From five in the morning till five in the afternoon he was in his laboratory; from five till eight we went for a stroll in the hills. What pleasant walks these were; we must have talked about every subject under the sun. From eight or nine in the evening until midnight we had music in the pension. And then six days later, Borodin said to me: "You know what, my dear Catherine, your Schumann is haunting me. It seems so fine when you play it."'

Love of music it certainly was that led to their intimate friendship.

---

[1] *Letters*, Vol. IV, pp. 249–51.

[2] She was the daughter of the staff-doctor of the Golitsyn Hospital, Sergei Stepanovich Protopopov, and Yekaterina Alexeevna Konstantinova, daughter of the hospital supervisor. Born in Moscow (in the Golitsyn Hospital) on 3 January 1832 she died in the village of Ramenskoe, near Moscow, on 28 June 1887. She was a very gifted pianist and studied under Dubuque, Schulhoff, Reinhardt, and Shpakovsky. In 1861, she went to Heidelberg to undergo climatic treatment for incipient tuberculosis. She raised the money for this by means of a piano recital which she gave in Moscow on 27 April 1861.

[3] Stassov's account (in his book on Borodin, p. 18) of Borodin's removal to Hoffmann's pension is taken from the memoirs which Catherine wrote at Stassov's request.

Catherine goes on: 'Once I went with Borodin to Baden-Baden to hear a concert. ... While the orchestra were playing a particular work, I turned to Alexander Porfiryevich: 'What a fine modulation there," I said. I could see that Borodin was astounded. "What! You mean to say you have absolute pitch? But that's quite unusual!" he exclaimed, and became lost in thought. But his face, his eyes at that moment were so bright and full of happiness. I didn't understand at that time what was going on inside him; it seemed odd he should be so surprised, since I couldn't see anything special about being gifted with such a musical ear. In the meantime on that very evening, so Alexander told me later, he had decided beyond doubt that he was deeply, irrevocably and for the rest of his life in love with me. ... And actually, it was that very evening that we both knew for certain, though we never admitted it to each other, that we were in love.'

Soon after this, some time about 10/22 August, on one of their walks in the outskirts of Heidelberg, near the so-called Wolfs-brunnen, Borodin proposed to Miss Protopopova, and they became engaged.[1] This was a time of perfect happiness for the young lovers. They continued their walks together, sometimes for whole days at a time; they travelled to Baden-Baden to the concerts, and also to Mannheim where they heard for the first time three Wagner operas, *Tannhäuser*, *Lohengrin*, and *The Flying Dutchman*. P. P. Alekseev,[2] Sorokin, the amateur chemist Prince Kudashev and his wife, and certain others of Borodin's friends were frequently with them on these trips and outings. Also the famous violinist Laub[3] used to see Borodin and his fiancée on informal terms. Catherine got to know him on one of their trips from Heidelberg to Baden-Baden, and she used to play duets with him. Laub saw that Borodin was a man of immense musical talent, and more than once told Catherine: 'Wissen Sie, Fräulein, dieser Borodin wird einmal ein grosser Musiker werden.' ('You know, young lady, one day this Borodin will be a great musician.')

The events just described form the most important biographical

---

[1] This description of Catherine's acquaintance with Borodin is taken from the above-mentioned memoirs. I have in my possession a sheet of paper headed by a date in the composer's handwriting, surrounded by a garland of tender names which Borodin used to call his wife.

[2] See the correspondence between Borodin and P. P. Alekseev (Vol. IV of *Letters*).

[3] Ferdinand Laub (1832–75), a native of Prague, spent his last years as a professor at the Moscow Conservatory. Tchaikovsky valued Laub's gifts highly, calling him 'a Titan among violinists' in one of his critical articles. Tchaikovsky's Third String Quartet is dedicated to his memory. References to his association with Borodin are taken from Catherine's memoirs.

information we have for the summer of 1861. Unfortunately we do not possess enough data to be able to present a systematic narrative. The most we can do is to add a few less important supplementary facts to what has already been said, though not in any particular chronological sequence. For this we have to make use of Borodin's account of his mission abroad, and this has already been cited earlier.

Let us begin with Borodin's residence in Heidelberg. In the course of the year 1861, he did not move at all. With the exception of his move from Yakubovich's to the Hoffmann pension, he made only one change; that was the time when he lived at No. 2 Karpfengasse, the same house he had lived in at the beginning of 1860. It is quite possible that these moves were connected with the programme he had been set by Zinin, which included visits to a number of towns in southern Germany. During the first half of 1861 Borodin spent two weeks in Würzburg, where he visited Scherer's laboratory. Later he went to Giessen to see Kopp's laboratory, and afterwards made a tour of the neighbourhood.

Leading such a nomadic life, and spending a great deal of time with his fiancée, Borodin almost certainly had very little time to devote to composition. He restricted himself to going to concerts and operas with Catherine, and to playing in orchestras and chamber ensembles. The D major Trio and the D minor Sextet, if in fact they were finished[1] by that time, were very possibly performed by one of these ensembles in which the composer himself would be playing. It is natural that Borodin, who was now on intimate terms with a gifted pianist, should feel the desire to compose works for piano duet. It is highly probable, therefore, that the unpublished D flat major Allegretto for piano duet was written during the summer or at the beginning of the autumn of 1861. We know for certain that the unpublished Scherzo in E major for piano duet was composed in August 1861.

About the middle of September 1861 Borodin again left Heidelberg to take part in a congress of German chemists and naturalists. It was at this congress that A. M. Butlerov gave his famous report on 'Aspects of the structure of chemical combinations', which was the beginning of structural chemistry.

On his return to Heidelberg Borodin learnt that his fiancée was

---

[1] We have no reliable data relating to the completion of these works, other than a single remark about the sextet made by Shchiglev in his memoirs. Only an autograph notebook containing two movements of the sextet has survived. The manuscript of the trio has no finale.

seriously ill. 'As soon as autumn and cold weather arrived', writes Catherine, 'I again became ill after a respite in the summer. I developed a heavy cough, and blood came from my throat. It seemed as though my chest was bursting; I grew paler and thinner, as pale as death. Borodin and Sorokin took me to see Professor Friedreich, a well-known Heidelberg doctor. He evidently made no bones about it: "She won't even see the month out, if she doesn't go to a warm climate. Pisa is warm at this time of the year; let her go there." What was to be done! We started off for the south together. A. P. (Borodin) left his laboratory for a few days to accompany me to Pisa and to see to everything there. An Italian October awaited us there; you simply couldn't compare it with Germany at that time of year. With the heat and the flies, it was the height of summer. I immediately found my breathing easier; and I felt myself coming back to life again. I felt I wanted to live then, more than at any other time. But the days just rushed by. Time was up, but Alexander could not bring himself to leave me. It was a time of moral torture for us both. I panicked at the thought of being left alone, all alone, with no one, in a foreign town, amidst strange people, who could understand neither my French nor my German. Alexander packed his things, and at the last minute had to go on an official visit to two well-known chemists in Pisa: Lucca and Tassinari. I was alone. I cannot describe how painful it felt to be left alone. I threw myself on to my bed and wept bitterly. Suddenly, I could not believe my ears; it was Alexander: "Katya, just imagine what has happened! I shall not be going to Heidelberg after all, but shall be able to stay with you here. Lucca and Tassinari gave me a very kind reception. They have a first-class laboratory, nice and bright, and very convenient. They said I could use it whenever I liked. . . . Things couldn't have worked out better: the fluoric combinations, that I'm just beginning to study, demand experiments carried out in the open. In Heidelberg it's too cold for that, but here I can work on them throughout the winter." It was too much for me. Again the tears flowed, but this time for a quite different reason. And how quickly I began to mend!'[1]

Borodin and his fiancée lived in the same flat, consisting of two bedrooms and a general work room. They had their rooms in the house of an Italian family, Centoni. They stayed there during the winter of 1861–2 and the spring of 1862. They both soon picked up a fluent command of Italian, and even acquired a small circle of acquaint-

[1] From Catherine's memoirs.

III. CATHERINE PROTOPOPOVA

The original, long since destroyed, was a daguerreotype made about 1857–9.

IV.   THE MAIN BUILDING OF THE ACADEMY OF PHYSICIANS

ances.[1] Borodin worked hard in the laboratory, spending the mornings and sometimes whole days there. He became friendly with Tassinari, who was in charge of the laboratory, and they often visited one another. Borodin's work in Pisa appears in three papers, printed in the journal *Il Nuovo Cimento* in the year 1862. Besides this, Borodin as usual sought the acquaintance of musicians. One of the first musicians in Pisa that he got to know was a certain Carrani. In the winter months Borodin and his fiancée got together amateur chamber groups; as well as this, Borodin played the cello from time to time in the opera orchestra.[2]

We may assume that Borodin, and certainly his fiancée, who at that time was attracted by the ideas of Herzen, did not remain indifferent to the revolutionary movement then growing up in Europe; they probably had some connection with its breeding-grounds. Unfortunately we have no specific knowledge of this beyond a fragmentary note which appears in Catherine's diary.[3]

In their spare time Borodin and his fiancée went to see the towns around Pisa—Leghorn, Pescia, Viareggio; and they were often at the theatre. In Pisa they heard Bellini's *Beatrice di Tenda* and *Norma*; they also saw comedies of Goldoni, Molière's *L'Avare*, and Cornelio's *Tsar di tutte le Russie*, as well as a number of vaudevilles.

Taking advantage of the fine Italian spring, Borodin and Catherine often went for walks around the town at night, listening to folk-songs, and sometimes even taking part in the impromptu choruses, which, as everyone knows, are an integral part of the Italian way of life.

On the 20 March at Carrani's they were introduced to the director of the Menocci music school. From this time onwards they were often at the house of this elderly violinist, who arranged chamber groups with them. They played sonatas for piano, with violin and cello obligato, piano trios, quartets and quintets. Amongst other things they performed the Kreutzer Sonata, some Beethoven trios, and the

---

[1] Several details of this period in the life of Borodin are taken from Catherine's diary which is preserved in the Borodin archive. The entries were written partly in the margins, partly on the clean sheets of an account book for the year 1862, starting from the beginning of February. The entries at the end of March are more detailed, and the last insertion was made on 5 June (of the same year).

[2] In her memoirs, Catherine says that Borodin 'played the cello in the orchestra of the Pisa theatre where they often gave performances of Donizetti'. In her diary we find only a mention of his being unable to take part in a general rehearsal of *Norma*.

[3] In the margins of one of the pages of her diary (against the entry for 30 March) is the phrase: 'I wrote a letter to the part. com.' (*sic*). This letter might well have been an attempt to get into touch with some revolutionary circle.

F major Trio and the Quintet, op. 87 of Hummel. Menocci was filled with admiration for his gifted new acquaintances. He recommended Catherine to his friends as 'una straordinaria bravissima pianista'. Borodin filled him with amazement when he composed a short fugue in the space of half an hour.

Thanks to Menocci, Borodin and his fiancée were granted permission to play the organ in Pisa cathedral. Catherine tells how she produced an especially powerful effect on the congregation 'when on one occasion, I played Bortnyansky's "Heavenly Powers" during the Offertory'. Also through Menocci, she managed to be present at the first performance of a mass by Pacini, which was directed by the composer himself in Pescia.[1] The not particularly flattering comment on this mass that we find in the young pianist's diary, is evidence of the fact that the Russian musicians were quite critical of musical activity abroad.

During the Easter holidays, when the laboratory was closed, Borodin and his fiancée went to Florence, and stayed there from 19 to 24 April 1862, with one Sacchetti, in a house opposite the Strozzi palace. Catherine has described the days she spent in Florence with Borodin and his friend P. A. Khlebnikov. They went round the Pitti and Uffizi galleries, the churches of Santa Croce and San Lorenzo; they went to the Niccolini and Borgo ognissante theatres, where they heard Fioravanti's opera *Columella*. On 22 April they 'hurried from one theatre to another and eventually decided to take a box in the "Della piazza vecchia" to see *La austuria e la bonta di Stentarello*. At the close of this play one of the actresses appealed to the nation in a lively speech, shouting "Viva Garibaldi!" After that came another vaudeville. We listened with great delight.'

Borodin certainly had 'Garibaldian' sympathies, as a note in his fiancée's diary for 1 June shows. That evening the unification of Italy was celebrated by festivities. Borodin and his fiancée 'went to the Luminara at nine o'clock, music was being played in three places, the town was illuminated, and the crowd was shouting furiously, "Viva Garibaldi!", "Viva il re galantuomo!", "Viva l'Unione, Venezia e Roma!", and so on. Tears began to roll from dear S.'s [Sasha's] eyes, and he had to turn away so that we wouldn't notice.'

The spring of 1862 produced a number of compositions from Borodin: as well as the fugue already mentioned, he wrote a tarantella

---

[1] Giovanni Pacini (1796–1867) was an Italian composer and follower of Rossini. The influence of the latter is clearly apparent in all his 73 operas. He also composed masses, oratorios, and cantatas.

in D major. Evidently it came to birth on the evening of 16 April (soon after the time Catherine mentioned in her diary that they had been talking about tarantulas). A note runs as follows: 'S. was at home, playing the piano. He was writing something for piano.' Judging by the manuscript, this tarantella was written quite impromptu.

From 22 May onwards, the entries in Catherine's diary tell how Borodin was working intensively on the C minor quintet. The entries are as follows:

22nd May. 'S. did not go to his laboratory this morning, but spent the whole morning writing the quintet . . .'

23rd May. ' . . . S. is still playing and writing his quintet. . . . In the evening we went to the Menocci's, but they didn't play any quintets, only a trio (F major) by Hummel and one of Beethoven's Adagios. . . . As soon as we came home, S. sat down at the piano and didn't stop writing until one o'clock in the morning. . . .'

26th May. 'S. spends the whole time writing his quintet, and never goes out. . . .'

27th May. ' . . . S. is still writing his quintet. . . .'

After 28 May people began to go off to their villas. Borodin worked for days on end in his laboratory but completed his work by 2 June. The following day Catherine and he moved to the villa region of Viareggio. Viareggio is by the sea. We know how much they liked the place from the following entry in Catherine's diary: 'After dinner S. took the chairs on to the slope overlooking the sea; we sat there, wallowing in the sand, and then had coffee—and at twilight we sat there by the very edge of the sea until it was quite dark; the sea was calm, the moon was out; all four of us[1] sang Italian songs. It was lovely. S. is enjoying himself.'

Other than this entry made on 5 June 1862, we have at our disposal only extremely scanty information relating to the time Borodin and his fiancée spent in Viareggio. We know from a few remarks in Catherine's account book that she got the local people to tell her stories, and listened to strolling singers, and that on occasion they went to Lucca, Pisa, and Leghorn.[2]

[1] The two others were someone by the name of Cenci and a girl called Ida.

[2] . . .

	7 June	For the story-teller, bread and butter	1.50
	30 June	To Barbari, the story-teller	.40
	13 July	To a good singer	.60
		To an eccentric singer (*sic*)	.20
	19 July	Journey to Pisa and back	5.60
	22 July	Journey to Leghorn and back	2.20
	23 July	Journey to Lucca	2.20

On 17 June 1862 Borodin put the finishing touches to his quintet, the last work to fall in the 'pre-Balakirev' period.

We do not know the exact date of their departure from Italy. The only thing we know for certain (from Catherine's diary) is the date of their arrival in Berlin (16 August), and the date they crossed the Russian frontier at Verzhbolovo, 20 September.[1] In any case Borodin arrived in Petersburg not in November as the biographies have it, but at the end of September.[2] On her return to Russia, Catherine went to her mother's home in Moscow.

Immediately after his arrival in Petersburg, Borodin became taken up by various activities as Zinin's assistant in the Academy of Physicians. He was appointed to the post of adjunct-professor on 8 December 1862, and began lecturing to the students of the Academy in organic chemistry. Among his audience at these lectures was Alexey Petrovich Dobroslavin, who subsequently became one of Borodin's close friends. In a report written for Stassov, Dobroslavin vividly describes the impression produced on students by Borodin's lectures and his brilliant, fascinating personality.

In the late autumn of 1862, there occurred one of the most important events in the life of Borodin: he became acquainted with Balakirev at Professor Botkin's house.[3] Balakirev was already a fully developed musician in his own right, and was the head of a circle of young composers which at that time consisted of Mussorgsky, Rimsky-Korsakov, and Cui. As regards his musical development, Borodin had one point in common with these young active musicians; they were Glinkians or, to quote a term used by Borodin, 'Ruslanists'. The Borodin piano quintet, like all his other early works, is indisputable evidence of the fact that his close rapprochement with the Balakirev circle grew up as a result of his awareness of the immense problems facing Russian composers. They believed they had a vocation to assert the originality of their national art music, and to carry on the work begun by Glinka.

'Balakirev wanted to acquaint me with the music of their circle and above all with the symphony of their "absent one".[4] Mussorgsky sat down at the piano with Balakirev (Mussorgsky was playing primo,

---

[1] In Borodin's passport, there is an entry to show that he arrived at Verzhbolovo (the frontier station) on 20 September 1862.

[2] This clearly follows from the date of his arrival at Verzhbolovo. With the railways as they were then, he could travel only to St. Petersburg.

[3] Sergei Petrovich Botkin (1832–89), the celebrated Russian doctor and social worker.

[4] I.e. the First Symphony of Rimsky-Korsakov, who in the middle of October 1862 had bade farewell to his friends to go on a long sea voyage abroad.

and Balakirev secondo) . . . I was struck by the brilliance, the sensibility, and the energy of their playing, and by the great beauty of the work itself. They played the Finale of the symphony.'[1] This comment of Borodin's on Rimsky-Korsakov's symphony clearly shows that he immediately took to the music of this Balakirev circle; he found it so close to his own both in content and in the mode of expression.

That is why we cannot look on Borodin's final maturity as the outcome of a sudden revolution; even though it was attained through the influence of Balakirev.[2] The significance for Borodin of this meeting with Balakirev lay not in any sudden, imaginary 'revolution', but in the experienced Balakirev's recognition of his true musical vocation and of the powers hidden within him.

'Our acquaintance', wrote Balakirev to Stassov, 'has had a special significance in that he had regarded himself before only as a dilettante, and had not taken seriously his own efforts at composition. It appears that I was the first to point out to him that his real vocation was—composition.' This was all the more important for Borodin when we consider that he was occasionally over-self-critical. His powerful intellect and deep critical sense at times got in the way of his creative work.

The influence of Balakirev brought about a powerful creative upsurge in Borodin. He began to entertain the idea of writing his own first symphony. At the end of December 1862 he played 'the first Allegro of his symphony almost in its entirety' to Catherine, probably when he saw her in Moscow, after making a special journey there. While he was composing this symphony, he found Balakirev's critical advice quite invaluable. It is doubtful if he had any need to explain 'the form of a composition' to Borodin, as he done earlier to Mussorgsky in 1858, but the critical comments of such a man must of course have been highly beneficial. 'Every bar he wrote was submitted to me for criticism', relates Balakirev, 'and this succeeded in

---

[1] See Borodin's account of his acquaintance with¦Mussorgsky (*Letters*, Vol. IV, p. 298).

[2] Such an opinion, for instance, is expressed in Catherine's memoirs; it will suffice to recall the often quoted sentence: 'His recent acquaintance with Balakirev soon bore fruit; the effect was fabulous. I could not help but notice the change. Even as early as December this Westerner, this "ardent Mendelssohnist", was playing me nearly the whole of the first Allegro of his E Flat major Symphony. . . .' Surprise at Borodin's 'transformation' at this period is also expressed in Stassov's book on Borodin (pp. 27–29). But, one may ask, did not Borodin's Piano Quintet already border closely on the aesthetic of the 'Handful' in its content, despite its belonging to the genre of chamber music that Balakirev 'condemned'? Moreover, as is now known, there is reason to suppose that the Quintet, judging by the composer's comments, was intended for orchestra (see Lamm's preface to the first edition of the Quintet in 1938).

developing a critical feeling for his art, which in the end determined his musical taste and sympathies. . . .' Such criticisms, of course, were important not so much for their technical aspects but rather for their ideological content. 'The whole tendency . . . of the mode of composition' pursued by the followers of Balakirev was formed through discussion in which all members of the circle participated.[1]

It was not for nothing that Borodin became a member of the Balakirev circle; for he became aware of his own potentialities as a result, and saw clearly from then on that it was his task to help create a Russian musical idiom, and to overcome Western influences. This event in Borodin's life is not so much a turning-point as the natural outcome of earlier stages in his musical development. As a composer, he was now sufficiently mature to retain his individuality in face of the powerful influence of Balakirev.

On 17 April 1863 Borodin was married to Catherine. Their marriage took place in Petersburg,[2] where they had to spend the whole of the summer, as a result of Borodin's being involved in the fuss over the completion of the new chemistry laboratory, and for other reasons connected with his work in the Academy.[3] That autumn the Borodins moved to a new flat in a new building belonging to the natural history section of the Academy, at the corner of Nizhegorodskaya Street and Pirogovskaya Embankment. Their flat was on the first floor. Borodin lived here, with the exception of comparatively short absences, for the rest of his life.

[1] See Balakirev's letter to Stassov which is reproduced in the latter's book on Borodin (pp. 26–27).

[2] From the information preserved in Deed No. 155 of the Academy of Military Medicine: 'Record of Associate-Professor Borodin's Service' (commencing 28 December 1862, terminating 1 March 1887), it is seen that Borodin married Catherine on 17 April 1863 in the chapel of the agricultural college in the Udelnaya. One of the witnesses was a laboratory assistant attached to the Chair of Chemistry in the Academy of Physicians, N. K. Siebert.

[3] See *Letters*, Vol. I, Letters 12 (p. 57), 13 (pp. 58–59).

CHAPTER THREE

THE FIRST SYMPHONY.
'THE VALIANT KNIGHTS.'
BALLADS
(1863–1869)

Borodin's first years after his return from abroad, as professor in the Academy of Physicians, were peaceful, happy, and fruitful. He dedicated himself wholeheartedly to teaching chemistry and to research. He showed a lively interest in all that went on around him, and found time to do some serious playing and some composition as well.

Not long after he had made friends with Balakirev and had met his old friend Mussorgsky again, Borodin acquired three more acquaintances: first Stassov, then Cui (around 1864), and finally, in the autumn of 1865, Rimsky-Korsakov, who had returned a short while before from his round-the-world voyage.

The Balakirev circle was now in its hey-day. The sixties produced 'great, new, Russian music, quite unprecedented, undreamt of even.'[1] These words of Stassov would apply to the group as a whole, and to their aims which were identical with the common urge of the more advanced Russian public of the day, and with the ideals of Belinsky, Chernyshevsky, Dobrolyubov, Herzen, and the other leading lights of the movement for progress and democracy.

Different as the members of the Balakirev circle were in their social status and approach to composition, they were all united by a burning passion for the authentic and the national in art, and for realistic truth, which their 'mighty handful' wanted to use against the Westernist circles. The latter were in sympathy with the Court and supported a reactionary art which was remote from the people and its problems. 'The Most August Protectress' of the Russian Musical Society, the grand duchess Elena (who was satirized in Mussorgsky's *Peep Show*

---

[1] Taken from a letter of Stassov's to Balakirev, 13 February 1861. *Balakirev's Correspondence with Stassov* (MOSCOW, 1935), p. 91.

as the 'Muse Euterpe'), was the ringleader of the 'German party' and opposed the 'Handful' in their struggle for national independence in Russian music. The term 'German party' was used by the Balakirev group for all those hacks who were trying to hold the entire development of music down to a few outworn procedures, originally fostered in the Leipzig conservatory, a place that Liszt poured scorn on. It was naturally to be expected that the Russian and the European conservatives would be hostile to the democratic tendencies of the great Russian masters. Once, for instance, Borodin wrote to his wife: 'I will mention one fact that is typical: the German party in Belgium (things are quite as bad there as here) has tried every conceivable means of preventing my second symphony from being performed in Antwerp.'

Their common interests and their struggle for the lofty ideals of 'the new Russian School' closed the ranks of the Balakirev group. Borodin, in particular, formed lasting friendships with every member of the group at this time, which none of their subsequent changes of outlook and disposition could shatter. Despite the disparity of their ages, Borodin and Rimsky-Korsakov became especially close friends.[1]

Borodin spent that winter in Petersburg at his flat in the Natural History block of the Academy of Physicians. This flat was quite spacious but not very convenient as it was dispersed among official premises. The kitchen was in the basement, and those parts of the flat actually on the ground floor were separated by a corridor leading to laboratories and studies; for this reason, there was a constant stream of students and officials going and coming. This was only one of the inconveniences. There was no quiet, secluded place at home where Borodin could work; and he did not even possess a private laboratory of his own, though he managed to have one equipped for himself at a later date. Catherine nearly always had one or another of her relatives or dependents staying there. This made things awkward for the Borodins, and they sometimes actually suffered privation, since they felt obliged to help all those in need.

In spite of all these upsets, Borodin at this time was nearly always in a bright, light-hearted frame of mind, showing constant enthusiasm for his work whether in the lecture room, in the laboratory, or at the piano.

Rimsky-Korsakov remembers Borodin as 'a most sincere and highly cultured man; a pleasant and, in his own way, a witty conversationalist. When I went to see him, I would often find him at work in the

---

[1] See, in particular, Chap. VI of Rimsky-Korsakov's *Chronicle of my Musical Life.*

laboratory next door to his flat. When he had finished what he was doing, he would come back with me to his flat, and we would play together or talk. Right in the middle he would jump up and rush back into the laboratory to make sure nothing had burnt or boiled over, all the while making the corridor echo with incredible sequences of successive ninths or sevenths; when he came back we used to pick up the music or conversation from where we had left off.'[1]

Rimsky-Korsakov was not the only member of the Balakirev group to visit Borodin; the whole circle sometimes gathered in his flat, for he was at this period the most active of the 'mighty handful'.

In the spring of 1864 Borodin had been planning to go abroad with his wife. On 12 May 1864 he wrote to his wife to tell her he 'would have to compose by next Saturday a flowery report which would have to contain a poetical exposé of our reasons for wanting to go abroad.'[2] But this trip never materialized, and Borodin, it seems, spent the summer of 1864 in Moscow.

In all probability the Scherzo of the First Symphony was composed in the course of that summer; this agrees with a remark of Catherine's in her memoir already referred to, and also with her husband's custom of devoting the whole of the summer vacation to composition.

On 26 May 1865 (O.S.) the Borodins did go abroad, spending the summer holidays in Graz in southern Austria. They went to the local theatres and wandered in the mountainous surroundings of Graz; in short, their life was not very different from when they were first together. According to Catherine, her husband actually composed the middle section of the Andante to the First Symphony on one such outing. 'Alexander returned from an excursion in the mountains round Graz. He was walking by some arbour in the grounds of an old castle when the D flat major middle section of the Andante came into his head; especially those rising and falling sighs in the accompaniment which go so well there. I can see him now, sitting at the piano.'

The Borodins returned to Russia on 18 August.[3] Soon after this, in the autumn (1865), Rimsky-Korsakov too came back to Petersburg. In December, Borodin was present at the first performance of his First Symphony (originally in E flat minor) given in a concert of the Free School of Music.[4]

---

[1] Rimsky-Korsakov's memoirs, 5th ed., p. 61.
[2] *Letters*, Vol. I, Letter 15, p. 60.
[3] The dates of Borodin's departure and return are taken from entries in his passport.
[4] Rimsky-Korsakov's E flat minor Symphony was first performed in orchestral form at a concert of the Free School of Music on 19 December 1865 (see his memoirs, 5th ed.,

We have in our possession somewhat more detailed items of information relating to Borodin during the following year (1866), thanks to his correspondence with his wife in the spring and early summer of that year. From their letters, for instance, we get to know more about Borodin and his friends of the Balakirev circle. We may surmise indirectly that at the end of May 1866 Borodin was busy putting the finishing touches to the finale of his First Symphony.[1] We find also in these letters some biographical information, and his indignant reactions to the die-hard behaviour of the President of the Academy, Dubovitsky, who was introducing a heavy-handed barrack-like way of doing things into the Academy.[2]

Also from this correspondence we know something of the endless trouble Borodin put himself to on behalf of his brother-in-law, A. S. Protopopov, who was suffering from an eye disease. After this time-consuming business was all settled, he went in June of the same year (1866) to Moscow, where he spent the entire summer. The letters he wrote in June and July to his wife, who had gone back to Petersburg, are overflowing with tenderness and inexhaustible good humour. One of these letters contains a description of a drive to the country-estate of Sviblovo just outside Moscow, quite near Ostankin.[3]

In the autumn of 1866 Borodin travelled to a place called Khilovo in the district of Pskov, with a view to carrying out some research on the mineral waters there. This prepared the way for the establishment of the now-famous health resort. Borodin was there from 6 to 17 September, after which time he returned to Petersburg.[4]

Apparently, soon after this (in the late autumn of 1866 or during the holidays)[5] his First Symphony was brought to completion; he had been working on it for some five years.

Borodin spent the summer of 1867 with his wife in Moscow. But towards the end of the year he fell ill, and was prevented from returning

p. 62). There is an entry in Catherine's account book against a list of expenses for this date which reads 'Lom(akin's) Con(cert)', showing that the Borodins were present on this occasion. (G. Y. Lomakin as is well known, was one of the founders of the Free School of Music, and during the first few years of its existence the concerts were colloquially referred to as 'Lomakin's'.)

[1] See *Letters*, Vol. I, note 3 to Letter 19, p. 337.
[2] These reactionary measures were connected with the general tightening up of regulations following Karakozov's attempt on the life of Tsar Alexander II.
[3] *Letters*, Vol. I, Letter 33, p. 87.
[4] This is learnt from a note in Catherine's account book.
[5] See *Letters*, Vol. I, notes 2 and 3 to Letter 35, pp. 342–3.

to Petersburg until 24 September. In the summer Borodin began work on the music to a farce by V. A. Krylov entitled *The Valiant Knights* (*Bogatyri*). The music was originally intended as a parody of the 'grand' operas of Meyerbeer, Rossini, and other Western European composers, and of Serov's *Rogneda* as well.

At first it had been the intention that Borodin should write original music in the manner of a burlesque, but this plan had to be dropped as Krylov wanted to stage *The Valiant Knights* at the Moscow Opera very soon.

In a letter to Krylov, written in August or early September 1867, Borodin reckoned that preparation of the score would take 'more than seventy days strenuous, concentrated work, to the exclusion of everything else. And don't forget either', he continued, 'that this estimate is correct only if I achieve perfection at the first go; it does not allow for blots, corrections, alterations, or even for copying—actually this is hardly possible. If you add to this the fact that composition is more than a purely mechanical process; the themes, melodies, harmonic combinations, and vocal and instrumental effects cannot be produced daily on demand. . . . From all this it is clear that, even if I were to devote the whole of my time exclusively to the operetta, I still wouldn't have finished it in three months even.' Borodin also points out that for him 'music is a pastime, a relaxation from more serious occupations' and hence he could not 'write on an average more than two pages of full score or more than four pages of piano score a day. . . .' Borodin concluded that he would need almost a whole year to compose completely original music to the opera.

After mature consideration, Borodin warned Krylov in the same letter that, if he was in a hurry to stage his opera, he had better take the music 'from the existing theatrical repertoire.'[1]

Presumably after receiving this letter, Krylov thought of asking Borodin himself to go ahead and undertake this. Borodin agreed, but at the same time wrote a certain amount of original music. This, combined with wittily chosen excerpts from well-known operas, made excellent pastiche of the conventions of grand opera. It is apparent from Borodin's letter to Savitsky that the music to *The Valiant Knights* was ready by 13 October 1867.[2] The operatic farce was produced at the Bolshoi Theatre on 6 November 1867, for the benefit of the stage-manager, Savitsky; it was not a success however. Both

[1] Ibid., Letter 39, pp. 95–97.
[2] Ibid., Letter 40, pp. 97–99.

the general public and the theatre critics completely failed to understand that the music was intended as burlesque; the Moscow music-
lovers saw in it simply a collection of rehashes of their favourite tunes,
borrowed by a composer who had chosen to conceal his identity under
the three asterisks appearing on the poster.

But events took a curious turn. N. M. Panovsky,[1] an acquaintance
of Borodin and a contributor to the *Moscow Journal*, had let it be known
in one of his articles, published shortly before the performance of the
opera, that the farce would refer to a scandal which had taken place
recently in a restaurant in the Moscow suburbs. It is quite likely that
in his own way the writer in question simply wanted to do Borodin
a good turn by stirring up interest in *The Valiant Knights*. But it had
the reverse effect. The people who had come to the first night expressly
to see the staging of some scandal were extremely upset at the complete
lack of connection between the libretto and this particular scandal, and
apparently gave rather violent expression to their annoyance.

The opera was taken off after only one performance. There was a
proposal for producing the opera in Petersburg, and the score was sent
there; but nothing came of this.

B. V. Asafyev drew attention to the fact that Borodin's parody was
in fact 'the only Russian operetta' in existence.[2] He justly remarked:
'*The Valiant Knights* may seem no more than a piece of good-
humoured leg-pulling, but, to my mind, it deserves the attention
of any student of Borodin's work which, I repeat, might have looked
very barren had it not been for his own inimitable way of poking fun
and his flashes of buffoonery. Who knows; perhaps Skula and
Eroshka in *Prince Igor* would not have been the rich characters they
are, if Borodin had not involved himself much earlier in such an
apparently absurd undertaking as *The Valiant Knights*.'

It is important to emphasize also that the point of Borodin's 'piece
of good-humoured leg-pulling' was aimed simultaneously at the
conventions of western-European opera and at what the Balakirev
group called the 'pseudo-Russian' style of *Rogneda*; it was on the
subject-matter of this opera that Borodin's pastiche was based. (In his
memoirs, Rimsky-Korsakov writes: '*Rogneda* was the continual
laughing-stock of the Balakirev circle.')

The action of *The Valiant Knights* takes place, 'up to a given

---

[1] See *Letters*, Vol. I, note 6 to Letter 26, p. 340.
[2] Igor Glebov (B. V. Asafiev), 'From the forgotten pages of Russian music', *Musical Chronicle*, Vol. I (Petrograd, 1922), p. 61.

moment', in the dukedom of Kurukhansk on the river Kaldyk, which is ruled by Prince Gustomysl (Fathead).

In the first act,[1] Solovei Budimirovich, a knight from distant lands, swears to Gustomysl's son, Prince Zadir, 'with the whole of the people as his witness', that he will steal his sister Zabava (Amusement).

In the second act Solovei fulfils his intention. During a solemn sacrifice to the god Perun, attended by the prince and all his subjects, he abducts Zabava, after lulling the whole assembly to sleep with his singing. When they come to, Prince Gustomysl's knights begin long preparations for a campaign against the abductor.[2] The chief knight himself, Foma Berennikov, out of cowardice stays behind to defend the capital.

The third act takes place in the private chamber of Gustomysl's wife, the Princess Militrissa Kirbityevna. The central moment is the appearance of a chorus of pilgrims. They bring news of the approach of a numberless host of female warriors, who are advancing on the city with the amazon Amelfa at their head. Foma sets forth to defend the capital.

In the fourth act we have the single combat of Foma and Amelfa. Foma emerges victorious from this contest, but only with the aid of treachery and good fortune combined. At the start of the fight, trembling all over and screwing up his eyes through fear, Foma begins to steal up on Amelfa. The latter, supposing Foma's action to be some special stratagem, does exactly the same as he. But Foma notices this, and seizing the moment when her eyes are tightly closed, tilts her crown, which contains the secret of her power, and knocks it off her head.

But Gustomysl, who has been hiding all through the battle, now comes forward and takes the full credit for the victory. Solovei wants to marry Zabava whom he abducted earlier, and sends emissaries to make overtures to the prince with a view to obtaining his 'parental blessing'. Gustomysl graciously accedes.

The fifth act is devoted to Solovei's wedding feast, in which the entire cast takes part; the banquet ends in wild dancing ('the bacchanalia of Kurukhan').

The music to the opera consists of 22 separate musical items and has

---

[1] On the poster, *The Valiant Knights* was divided up into acts, whereas the score indicates scenes.

[2] Raoul's well-known aria from Meyerbeer's *Les Huguenots* is parodied here; he repeats the word 'run' several times but stays where he is.

a very important part to play, in that it accompanies the action from start to finish almost without a break. The opera does not consist entirely of singing; there is a fair amount of speech: for example, Gustomysl's 'foolish speech' in the last act. It begins with the customary introduction to be found in every liberal speech of the period: 'At the present time, when . . .' This speech was included in the libretto at Borodin's suggestion.

In order that the reader should have a brief and clear picture of the music to *The Valiant Knights*, I reproduce below a table compiled by Lamm.[1]

Musical Numbers of 'The Valiant Knights'	Name of individual scenes and numbers	Number of bars of original or parodied music	Name of borrowed sources	Number of bars of borrowed music	Total number of bars
	SCENE 1. A HEROIC WOOING				
1	Chorus of Maidens: Solovei's Song	34	MEYERBEER. *Robert le Diable*, Act I, No. 1	13	
		—	ROSSINI. *Barber of Seville*, Act III, Trio	16	
		—	OFFENBACH. *Bavard et Bavarde*, Act II, No. 10	54	148
		—	ROSSINI. *Barber of Seville*, Act III, Finale	31	
2	Solovei's Cavatina	—	OFFENBACH. *Barbe-bleue*, Act II, Sc. 2, No. 16	42	42
3	Solovei's Burlesque Aria	8	OFFENBACH. *Barbe-bleue*, Act II, Sc. 1, No. 14 (Finale)	42	50
	SCENE 2. A FAIRLY CONSIDERABLE ROBBERY				
4	Gustomysl's Procession	92	Theme of an Austrian Military March	—	92
5a	Gustomysl's Aria (with chorus)	13	CAVOS. *The Invisible Prince*, No. 4 (March)	17	30
5b	Militrisa's Aria (with chorus)	45	—	—	45
5c	Duet and Scene	14	MEYERBEER. *Robert le Diable*, Act I, No. 1 (after the ballad)	30	44

[1] See *Soviet Music*, 1934, No. 1.

Musical Numbers of 'The Valiant Knights'	Name of individual scenes and numbers	Number of bars of original or parodied music	Name of borrowed sources	Number of bars of borrowed music	Total number of bars
6	Sacrificial Scene	32	ROSSINI. *Barber of Seville*, Act III, No. 15	27	150
		91	Melody of the Folk-song: 'Kak u nashikh u vorot'	—	
7	March of the Valiant Knights and Chorus	72	OFFENBACH. *La Belle Hélène*, Act I, No. 7 (twice), the Couplets des Rois	160	232
8	Perun's Dance, Chorus and Scene	56	Theme from SEROV's *Rogneda*, Act I, No. 3, Sacrifice to Perun	—	56
9a	Solovei's Slumber Song	42	SEROV. *Rogneda*, Act II, No. 9, Fool's Tale	8	50
9b	Melodrama (scene of Zabava's abduction)	1	OFFENBACH. *Barbe-bleue*, Act III, No. 23, Melodrama	29	30
10	Finale (of the second scene)	240	—	—	454
		63	Theme from SEROV's *Rogneda*, Act I, No. 3, Sacrifice to Perun	—	
		—	VERDI. *Ernani*, Act II, No. 12, Terzetto	151	

SCENE 3. THE PRIVATE CHAMBER OF MILITRISA KIRBITYEVNA

Musical Numbers of 'The Valiant Knights'	Name of individual scenes and numbers	Number of bars of original or parodied music	Name of borrowed sources	Number of bars of borrowed music	Total number of bars
11	Chorus of Maidens and Scene	49	SEROV. *Rogneda*, Act IV, No. 16, Prelude and Women's Chorus	32	162
		50	Theme from *Rogneda*, Act IV, No. 17, Recitative and Izyaslav's Song	—	
		31	Melody of the Folk-song; 'Kumanechek, pobyvai u menya'	—	
12	Kostryuk's Burlesque Couplets (repeated several times)	30	—	—	30

Musical Numbers of 'The Valiant Knights'	Name of individual scenes and numbers	Number of bars of original or parodied music	Name of borrowed sources	Number of bars of borrowed music	Total number of bars
13	Beggars' scene	43	MEYERBEER. *Le Prophète*, Act I, No. 3, Chorus of Anabaptists	21	
		—	MEYERBEER. *Robert le Diable*, Act I, No. 1, Ballad	17	
		29	Theme of the Song: 'Sredi doliny rovniye'	—	158
		—	OFFENBACH. *Barbe-bleue*, Act I, No. 1, Floretta's Song	48	
14	Quartet	—	OFFENBACH. *La Belle Hélène*, Act II, No. 12, March of the Geese	64	64

SCENE 4. FOMA THE VICTOR

15	Alyosha's Love-song	—	Music by Y. Gerber	—	
16a	Chorus of Valiant Knights and Scene	—	OFFENBACH. *Bavard et Bavarde*, Act I, No. 1, Chorus. Music by K. Valts	193	193
17	Kseniya's Burlesque Aria	4	OFFENBACH. *Barbe-bleue*, Act I, No. 7, Chorus	66	70
18	Chorus of Valiant Knights and Amazons	3	Freely adapted from OFFENBACH. *Barbe-bleue*, Act III, No. 22b, Ballad	69	72
19	The Single Combat of Foma and Amelfa	34	MEYERBEER. *Robert le Diable*, Act III, No. 9, Prelude	135	
		—	HEROLD. *Zampa*, Act I, No. 4, Quartet	70	169
		—	Ibid., Act II, No. 10, Finale (after the Rondo)	16	
20	Finale of Scene 4	1	ROSSINI. *Semiramide*, Act I, No. 9, Chorus of Priests	169	170

SCENE 5. SOLOVEI'S FEAST

21	Chorus of Greeting and Burlesque (couplets)	22	OFFENBACH. *Barbe-bleue*, Act III, No. 21a, Marriage Chorus	38	
		—	OFFENBACH. *La Belle Hélène*, Act I, No. 3 Burlesque (couplets	84	144
22	Finale of Scene 5	157	—	—	157
		1,256		1,642	2,812

Lamm's table shows that 44 per cent of the music to the opera was either Borodin's own, or had been adapted by him to fit the sequence required by the libretto. In a few cases the orchestration has been changed, but this is the work of the conductor, E. N. Merten.

It should be mentioned in conclusion that here, as indeed in some of his other works, Krylov has introduced more than one hint of social criticism. The characters themselves make this quite obvious; one need only mention the phenomenal stupidity of Prince Gustomysl, or the greed for money and hypocrisy shown by Kostryuk the priest. The censor however took exception to only one of the very numerous allusions to contemporary personages and events, when he deleted the name Dlinnorukov given to one of the characters on the grounds that it had a fairly obvious connection with Dolgorukov who was at the time Governor-General of Moscow. (Both names mean literally 'Long-arms'.)

It can safely be said that Borodin never completely forgot *The Valiant Knights*; long afterwards he used to let his friends hear bits of it. Nikolai Dianin, for instance, who entered the University, and made Borodin's acquaintance about the middle of the 1870's, knew all the main characters of the opera, and a few of the tunes besides.

It is well known that the second half of the sixties brought with it a whole series of operatic projects from the Balakirev circle. It was in opera particularly that they were striving to establish their principles of nationalism and realism in opposition to those operatic conventions they had ridiculed in *The Valiant Knights*.

Mussorgsky was working on *Boris Godunov*, Rimsky-Korsakov on *The Maid of Pskov*, and Borodin himself was entertaining the idea of writing a serious opera. Stassov tells us that, around 1867, Borodin had Mey's historical drama *The Tsar's Bride* suggested to him by Balakirev as a possible subject for an opera. With this opera in mind Borodin wrote several 'first-rate scenes and choruses (the most outstanding was the chorus of wild, revelling life-guards), but Borodin soon lost interest in the subject and finally dropped it.'[1] The autograph originals of *The Tsar's Bride* are missing from the Borodin's archives. But, as regards the music, we know something of the material he used, as the Leningrad Conservatory possesses transcriptions of songs made by Borodin himself, in particular the lay 'The Terrible Tsar Ivan Vassilyevich'. These transcriptions, made in 'abridged form' without any indication of key, were discovered amongst archive material by A. N. Dmitriev.

---

[1] Stassov's book on Borodin, p. 33.

But, even if Borodin's work on his first operatic idea (subsequently, as we know, carried out by Rimsky-Korsakov) was not a success, he was nevertheless achieving a great deal in other directions, for he had composed 'The Sleeping Princess' and 'The Song of the Dark Forest'. Although we do not know exactly when these ballads were written, it is worth noting that Catherine congratulated her husband on his name-day, 28 August 1867, calling him her 'new Glinka'. If anything had prompted her to call him this, it would have been his 'Sleeping Princess' which the Balakirev circle frequently compared with Glinka. Therefore, 'The Sleeping Princess' was composed not later than August 1867.

Balakirev had been invited that autumn to take up the post as conductor of the Russian Musical Society. On 24 February 1868 he arranged for a private performance to be given in the hall of the Mikhailov Palace, at which Borodin's First Symphony was played, along with other new works by Russian composers.[1] But the performance did not go well, since the parts, which had been copied in a hurry, contained a number of mistakes. In spite of this, Rimsky-Korsakov says: 'one could form some idea of the symphony's greatness and its splendid orchestration.'[2]

In the spring of 1868 Dargomizhsky joined the Balakirev circle. Every week Balakirev, Borodin, Cui, Rimsky-Korsakov, Mussorgsky, Stassov, and others of the 'new Russian school' met at his house. At these gatherings extracts from Dargomizhsky's recently composed opera *The Stone Guest* were played, and other works besides, including Borodin's songs.[3] Among the performers were the Purgold sisters— Alexandra Nikolaevna (her married name was Molas) and Nadezhda Nikolaevna (who later married Rimsky-Korsakov). Borodin also got to know here Anna Nikolaevna, the sister of the composer Lodyzhensky (her married name was Kalinin). The Borodins very quickly made the acquaintance of other members of the numerous Lodyzhensky family. They were invited by two of the brothers to spend the summer of 1868 in the Kashinsky district of Tver province on the estate of 'Makovnitsy'[4] belonging to Ivan Nikolaevich Lodyzhensky.

[1] I established the date of this rehearsal from an entry in Catherine's account-book (cf. *Letters*, Vol. I, note 4 to Letter 61, p. 354).

[2] Rimsky-Korsakov's memoirs, 5th ed., p. 81.

[3] On the page containing Catherine's entries for 7, 8, and 11 May 1868, there is the note: 'At Dargom[yzhsky's] were performed *Radcliffe* [*sic*] and the Princess.'

[4] For part of the summer Borodin and his wife also stayed on the estate of Turovo, which belonged to N. I. Kalinin. That year they left St. Petersburg early—around 15 May.

That summer, Anna Kalinina (*née* Lodyzhensky) fell in love with Borodin. He told his wife of his affair with her in a letter dated 25 October 1868: 'My feelings towards her do not alter the way I feel towards you, and I am giving only that which I cannot give to you; it is nothing more than that 'feeling of mine towards children', in her words, towards weakness, youth, hopes, and the future. . . .' It was the influence of Anna that led him to compose the ballad 'The Sea Princess' to his own words, in July 1868, and later 'My Songs are filled with Poison' ('Otravy polny moi pesni') and 'The False Note'; these reflect what he was going through and reveal the slight element of tension in his relations with his wife.

Soon after returning to Petersburg (September 23) Borodin paid a visit to Cui, only to find Mussorgsky and Rimsky-Korsakov there as well. On that occasion Cui played part of his recently completed opera *Ratcliffe*; Rimsky-Korsakov gave a few extracts from his *Maid of Pskov* that he had only recently begun work on; and Mussorgsky played through the first act of his opera *The Marriage*.

Borodin was very favourably impressed by *Ratcliffe*,[1] but was in raptures over *The Maid of Pskov*: 'There is such fragrance there, such youthfulness, freshness and beauty. . . . I was simply overcome with delight. What a colossal talent this man has! And the ease with which he composes!'

He felt otherwise about *The Marriage*, sharing the opinion of Cui and Balakirev, which was one of reserve: 'After that, Mussorgsky played us the first act of his opera *The Marriage*, based word for word on Gogol's text. The piece is uncommonly bizarre and paradoxical; it is full of innovations and in places very humorous, but on the whole —this is une chose manquée—it is quite impossible to perform. In addition to this, the work shows signs of having been written in a hurry.'[2]

Although he participated to the utmost in the activities of 'the Handful' and abounded the whole time in new ideas, Borodin still kept up his work at the Academy and achieved a reputation as a scientist and public figure. In early December 1868, for instance, he took part in the foundation meeting of the Chemical Society.

'This was a very nice and happy occasion for me. The second session has been fixed for 9 January,' he wrote in a letter to P. P.

---

[1] 'Cui showed me the latest numbers he had written for his opera *Ratcliffe* and the orchestration of the entire opera as well. It's a sheer delight!'

[2] *Letters*, Vol. I, Letter 45, p. 109.

Alexeev. It is clear from this same letter (dated 23 December 1868) and from other sources as well,[1] that Borodin was very fully occupied with research at the time. He was working on the products of condensation of valerian aldehyde, and also carrying out some experiments of a physico-chemical nature; on the attraction of water by deliquescent substances, for instance, and on the evaporation of aqueous solutions.

We also gather from Borodin's letters to Balakirev that, in December 1868, he was revising the score of the First Symphony and correcting the parts in preparation for its first public performance at a concert of the Russian Musical Society.[2] This was work requiring great accuracy and precision and, judging by the letters mentioned above, provoked sighs of exasperation from the composer: 'What a devil of a lot of mistakes! It's a general rule that you never know where you are with a symphony until it is performed. We all had our works played at the Free School concerts, and only mine was a flop. They got their performances through in good time, but I had to wait three years for mine. Haman did the copies for the others, but some real son of a bitch has done mine. It wouldn't surprise me if they bombard the composer with rotten apples.'

After he had made all the necessary corrections Borodin sent the score of the symphony to Balakirev and wrote: 'You've never seen such a bungled job in all your born days. . . . Apart from the intentional harmonic peculiarities, I came across most extraordinary sequences of minor seconds, diminished fifths, clashes of major and minor, and the devil only knows what. . . . Well, old chap, I never realized correcting parts could be such a hellish business.'

The First Symphony 'of a composer seeking oblivion', as Borodin put it, was given its first performance at a concert of the Musical Society under the direction of Balakirev on 4 January 1869. Balakirev recalls[3] that 'the first part was received coldly by the audience; there was little applause at the end of it, and even this soon died down. I was unnerved by this and went straight into the Scherzo; but this went splendidly and brought long applause. They called for the composer, and insisted on an encore. The rest of the symphony simply captivated the audience, and after the Finale, they called for the composer again and again. Even F. M. Tolstoy, a music critic of those days

[1] See, for example, A. P. Dianin *A. P. Borodin*, p. 6 (separate offprint).
[2] *Letters*, Vol. I, Letters 60, 61, and 62, pp. 139–42.
[3] In a letter to Stassov. See Stassov's book on Borodin, p. 35.

and an enemy of the new Russian music, found good words for the Finale and had obviously not expected so much. Dargomizhsky, who was on his death-bed, waited impatiently to hear how the concert had gone, but unfortunately none of us called to break the news to him for fear of disturbing him so late at night. The only one who called was his friend K. N. Velyaminov, but he was unable to give him full details. But by the following morning Dargomizhsky was no more; he had passed away from an aneurysm at 5 in the morning of January 5.

. . . But more pleased than anyone with the performance was Borodin himself, for this had been for him a decisive moment. Its success had a powerful effect on him, and almost immediately he set to work on the B minor Symphony, feeling now that his true vocation lay in music.'

It was just at this time that the antagonism between the Balakirev group and the other musical circles reached its highest pitch. This is no surprise, since those critics who were hostile to 'the Handful' were refusing to acknowledge the success of Borodin's symphony; this is to be seen, for instance, from Serov's well-known comment.[1]

But, even if the symphony with all its success was not yet universally acclaimed, its first performance was indeed an important landmark in the life of the composer. Borodin felt himself inspired by his success and was eager to achieve new things.

The critical articles written during 1868–9 give us some insight into the composer's views on music at the time. These were published in the *St. Petersburg Journal*, on which Borodin was temporarily taking the place of Cui who was busy with rehearsals for *Ratcliffe*. These reviews, which give us the broad outline of Borodin's views at that time, are printed in Vol. IV of his *Letters*.

[1] 'A symphony by someone called Borodin gave little satisfaction. Only his friends called and applauded him with any enthusiasm' (in the newspaper, *The Voice*, for 1869).

CHAPTER FOUR

'PRINCE IGOR.' THE SEVENTIES.

(1869–1879)

The 'Sleeping Princess' and 'The Song of the Dark Forest' brought to the fore one of Borodin's most powerful musical attributes; his ability to create musical epic full of rich and original tone-colours. This tendency found new embodiment in the late sixties and early seventies.

It was the success of his songs and the First Symphony that led him to write the preliminary sketches for a new composition in a similar vein: The Second ('Heroic') Symphony. At this time also he was coming back to the idea of writing an opera on a subject taken from Russian life. He told his friends 'he would like his next composition to be an opera and not a symphony;' more than once he approached Stassov to see if he could give him any new ideas.

In April 1869 Stassov suggested an historical epic *The Lay of Igor's Campaign* (Slovo o polku Igoreve). On 20 April Borodin received the scenario for the opera from Stassov, who had used the original epic and the Ipatyevsky Chronicle. Borodin wrote back immediately to say that he would be delighted to use the scenario.

Here is the text of the scenario as it was first published by E. M. Braudo in his monograph on Borodin.

FIRST ACT

No. 1. The private chamber of Princess Yaroslavna. She comes on to the stage alone, looking thoughtful and sad. She is worried because there is still no news of her husband who has gone off to fight the Polovtsi. The peculiar and wanton behaviour of her brother, Prince Vladimir, disturbs her. He has been their guest now for two years, ever since he was banished from Galicia by his father, and at the moment is plotting some mischief with the boyars of Novgorod-Seversk and Putivl. Not only this but she is haunted by a terrible and ominous dream she had during the night.

No. 2. Just then, her brother bursts into her room. He is drunk and obstreperous. He tries to make out that he is the master there, and tells her she must take orders from him now; it was no use waiting or living in hopes of her husband's return, for he had either been killed in battle or taken prisoner by the Polovtsi along with his retainers and boyars. Prince Vladimir also lets it be known that he is tired of being without a throne, and that he has persuaded the Putivl and Novgorod-Seversk boyars to make him ruler in place of Igor.

Princess Yaroslavna is terrified and cannot believe her ears—surely her brother must be joking or trying to make fun of her in his coarse, drunken way. She reminds him that Igor, her husband, had not begrudged him shelter after he had been banished by his father, and at a time when none of his family dared or even wanted to take him into their houses. She also asks him to remember that he has been living in Putivl for the past two years as an honoured guest, allowed to do as he likes and to come and go as he pleases, with all his violent behaviour and outrages forgiven him. But Vladimir will not listen, and in a drunken fury warns her that if she does not obey him and hold her tongue, he will send her to a nunnery.

No. 3. Shouting and a disturbance can he heard off stage. The Princess's ladies-in-waiting come rushing in to tell her that new arrivals (merchants) have just come on horseback, and that they might be able to tell her something about Prince Igor and his followers. Princess Yaroslavna bids them be brought in. They enter along with princes, noblemen, Russian men and women, and foreign supporters and friends of Vladimir as well. The merchants begin their tale (interrupting one another) and start by saying that everything is lost, the Russian army destroyed, and Igor and his son taken prisoner. Yaroslavna collapses when she hears this and weeps and weeps until she gathers enough strength to command them to tell her how it all happened. Then they go on to tell her how they took their caravan near the river Kayala and were involuntary witnesses of the battle. The Polovtsi let them go, after telling them that the battle had already been going on for three days and would certainly end in disaster. Not only this, but an eclipse had occurred right at the outset of the campaign (there follows a long quotation from *The Lay of Igor's Campaign* relating to this eclipse). But Prince Igor and his retainers hurled themselves against the foe, and at first the Polovtsi actually got the worst of it, and withdrew. Igor rode out some way ahead of his men and received a wound in his left arm. His warriors were long since exhausted, and lost sight of him; so they turned tail and fled. Thereupon Igor took off his helmet and dashed back to his men hoping that they might recognize him. But it was too late. The Polovtsi surrounded them and rounded them up. This story is interrupted by shrieks of terror and loud sobs from Yaroslavna and the other men and women in turn.

The Germans, Venetians, Greeks, and Moravians who were among Vladimir's supporters sing the praises of Igor's father Svyatoslav, for he had always been victorious against the Polovtsi, and immediately begin cursing and jeering at Igor. Prince Vladimir joins in the sneering and accuses Igor of flippancy and recklessness—so much for his gallantry! Vladimir said it was just as he had expected. Igor was now a prisoner, but they were no worse off for that! Now there was an end to the matter, and he would never return. From now on Vladimir would be lord and master!

Obsequiously the foreign travellers sing the praises of Vladimir. Even the Russian princes and noblemen submit to his rule, but in the meantime the women, weeping and sobbing, have made off in various directions to their homes to take with them their unhappy tidings. The rest follow shortly after.

No. 4. Princess Yaroslavna is left alone. She abandons herself to mourning, despair, and hopeless terror; she has no idea to whom she can turn for help. Her grief is not so much for the loss of her throne as for the loss of her husband. Just then, she remembers Ovlur and orders him to be brought to her without delay. While they are fetching him she flings herself about the stage in despair; her only consolation is the thought that this prisoner, although a Polovtsian, has a Russian mother and belongs heart and soul to Russia, and is devoted to Igor and herself. 'Ovlur', she exclaims as soon as he arrives, 'have you heard already, tell me, have you heard what has happened. I am no longer your princess, my husband is dead, and my princedom has been taken from me—I have lost everything. But an idea came to me out of the blue that you might still be able to help me; you and only you could do anything at this stage to help us. Will you do what I ask?' Ovlur assures her of his affection and devotedness, whereupon she bids him go to the Polovtsian camp. They would receive him with open arms, thinking he had managed to escape from the Russians. He would have to act like a true Polovtsian and deceive Konchak and his followers; he must without fail get an opportunity of speaking to Igor, to tell him what is going on in Putivl, and, after that, help him to escape from the Polovtsi. She begs and pleads with him, reminding him of all that Prince Igor has done for him. Ovlur joyfully consents. He had always wanted to do something great and noble for Russia, and for the Prince and Princess too. They discuss their plan of action, and the Princess gives the order for Ovlur to be let out of the city.

SECOND ACT

No. 5. The Polovtsian camp. Igor's son, the young Prince Vladimir, and Konchak's daughter are sitting together in the Khan's sumptuously decorated tent. A love scene. Vladimir tells the princess that he is ready to forgo everything and to forget everything for her. If his father does not agree to their marriage, he will go over to their faith and become a Polovtsian, so that she can be his wife and he can be with her always. They hear the sound of a horn and leave.

No. 6. Prince Igor has been out hawking and now returns accompanied by a member of his fellow-Russians and a few Polovtsians who make up his escort. Igor is gloomy and down-hearted; hunting and other pastimes no longer gratify him, and he can no longer find any diversion in them. He is constantly reproaching himself for his lack of forethought, his arrogance and over-confidence, as a result of which he brought the Russian army to disaster and had lost, perhaps for ever, his beloved Yaroslavna. His escorts are unable to distract him from his gloomy thoughts.

No. 7. Khan Konchak arrives and reproaches him in a mild and friendly fashion for being sad and home-sick. 'What more do you require?' he asks, 'I've surely done all I can for you. Here are you an enemy who brought a whole army against us, and I treat you well and don't torture you like the other prisoners.' Russia has known for a very long time what a terrible man Khan Konchak can be; he has drowned whole villages and towns in blood, and wields his flaming sword from one end of Russia to the other. And see how differently he treats Igor, making a special exception for him; he has given him permission to come and go as he likes, and to do as he pleases. And why? Because of their old friendship. Six years ago when his father, Prince Svyatoslav, had wanted the princely throne of Kiev instead of the throne of Tchernigov, Igor came to ask Konchak for assistance, and assistance he gave. He went with his hordes to Kiev and put to flight the old Prince, and seated Svyatoslav on the throne in his place. Nothing interfered with their friendship until quite recently. 'Do you remember how you and I set out together to fight Prince Rurik, son of Rostislav? Do you remember how they defeated us and took my two sons prisoner and killed my brother Eltut, and how we both leapt into a boat and narrowly escaped being captured by Rurik? We shared the same joys and sorrows, the same successes and mishaps, and I have never forgotten this. You are a brave warrior; only a short time ago you put many of my men to death, but brave men such as we should not be enemies. After the battle I saved you from the fury of the Polovtsi, I gave you my guarantee, and did the best I could for you. Take heart then! Look on the brighter side of things and give yourself some peace! Is there anything more you desire? Is it worth while reminding yourself of Russia and your wife? Be one of us. Choose a wife from among the slave beauties and the Polovtsian girls; as you can see, they are no worse looking than your Russian women. Then we can live a gay life together here, a life of danger, fit for any warrior of mettle! The lion will walk with the leopard, and share and share alike.' Later he makes another attempt to persuade Igor to let his son marry his daughter, Konchakovna. This would strengthen their friendship still further, and the youngsters are in love anyway.

Igor thanks Konchak, declares his love and devotion to him, but he is not prepared to accept a single one of his offers and thinks only of Russia, Putivl, and his wife. Under no circumstances will he let his son marry Konchak's daughter.

No. 8. Konchak scowls and grows angry, saying that they can do without his permission. 'With a wave of his hand' he summons the whole of his court into the tent. The entire Polovtsian court enters, Vladimir and his bride-to-be as well. There is dancing and singing. Slave girls jingle Russian gold and make fun of the Russians (this is allowed now because the Khan is angry with Igor). Igor bitterly resents such taunts and the disgrace that is being brought on the Russians. He becomes even more restless and gloomy. Vladimir is oblivious to everything, and has eyes only for the princess. There enters a crowd of Polovtsians just back from a campaign. They tell how they captured and sacked Pereyaslavl, and how they laid waste everything with fire and sword, struck down and murdered young children, took the women captive, and led away the cattle. The whole crowd of Polovtsians goes wild with delight. Konchak is happy and in high spirits, but Igor becomes even more sullen and depressed. He reproaches himself yet again. There is more dancing and singing. Vladimir and the princess eventually leave with the crowd.

No. 9. Igor is left alone with his son and the Russians. In his despair he curses life and prays that God may let him die, if he is never to be able to do anything for his wife and country.

At that moment a man detaches himself from the Polovtsian escort and directs his comrades to stand farther off near the entrance to the tent. He comes up to the prince and tells him his name is Ovlur. The prince recognizes him, but at first does not believe what he has to tell him about his wife Yaroslavna and Putivl, but in the end has no choice but to believe him. Ovlur, seeing that he is overwrought, reckons that this is an opportune moment to suggest escape. Igor replies that he will never consent to anything so shameful. But Ovlur plays on his love of honour and glory with tales of renowned Russian heroes; he reminds him of Mstislav the Brave Prince Tymutarakansky, the son of Vladimir the Blessed, and of how he killed the Kososh Khan, Rededu, in single combat, thereby saving his country from disaster. Then there were the exploits of his grandfather, Roman Svyatoslavovich, and finally his father, Svyatoslav, who fought many battles against the Polovtsi. Igor's Russian companions also try and persuade him to escape; eventually he decides to do so and then and there settles with Ovlur how the plan of escape is to be carried out.

No. 10. The fringe of the Polovtsian encampment; there is a tent on one side and the forest on the other. In the background is a river. It is night. The Polovtsi, drunk with koumiss, are lying here and there among the tents, gambling and making merry; gradually they all drop off to sleep. Igor enters with his son Vladimir and tries to persuade him to escape with him. Ovlur is already waiting on the other side of the river with a horse and the Russian prisoners. In a few minutes they will hear his whistle, which means that everything is ready and the road clear. Vladimir is in fact also pining, but his infatuation for the princess holds a greater sway over him, and he remains undecided. At that very moment the princess comes running in. She already knows Igor's intentions in part, but the rest she guesses. She throws herself at Vladimir and refuses to let him go. Vladimir offers only weak resistance, but he listens despite everything to his father's exhortations and entreaties. Just then, Ovlur's whistle is heard from the direction of the forest across the river. Igor makes a final appeal to his son but Konchak's daughter holds him in her passionate embrace, kisses him and lures him towards the Khan's tent. Igor makes off towards the forest, but at that moment the alarm is given. Konchak and the Polovtsi make a furious dash after him into the forest. His warriors go in pursuit of Igor and they have been given orders to shoot in the direction of the runaway prisoner. He gives furious expression to his rage and despair when they bring back the news that Igor, Ovlur, and the other Russian prisoners have outridden them.

THIRD ACT

No. 11. The scene is set at the top of the watch-tower in Putivl. It is early morning. Princess Yaroslavna is sitting alone and weeping. There follows an extract from *The Lay of Igor's Campaign* known as Yaroslavna's Lament'.) All of a sudden there is a sound of horses' hooves in the distance. Yaroslavna starts with joy. Intuition tells her it must be her husband. The thunder of hooves grows nearer. The riders come to a halt, right beneath the tower. She runs to the edge of the tower, looks down, and recognizes her husband. They exchange a few words in hushed voices, and a second later Igor has made his way unnoticed into the city square. The scene is one of rejoicing. They exchange a few rapid, fragmentary accounts of what they have been doing, and then they consider what should be their next move. Igor and his wife reach agreement as to what should be done; they count on those Putivl noblemen who have remained faithful and true. Igor takes his revenge on his enemies in Putivl, and then goes off to fight the Polovtsi.

No. 12. A sumptuous princely banquet chamber in Putivl, two years later. A magnificent wedding ceremony is being performed. Prince Igor and Princess Yaroslavna are marrying their son, Vladimir, to Konchak's daughter. The young couple have left the Polovtsian camp. During the festivities and wedding songs, it is announced amongst other things that Igor has gaoled Vladimir Galitsky and has dealt with his own treacherous followers according to their deserts. There is a final chorus; the words are: 'Towns and countries rejoice, sing to the old princes and then to the young. Sing the praise of Igor, son of Svyatoslav, of Vsevoloda and Vladimir Igorevich. Glory to the princes and their faithful retainers who fought for the Christian cause against the heathen host, and vanquished them. Glory to the princes and their faithful retainers, Amen!'

The subject of *The Lay of Igor's Campaign* made a strong appeal to Borodin,[1] and, with a view to preparing himself for the task of writing the opera, he began to study with enthusiasm the various historical sources, folk narratives, and Russian epic ballads. Stassov proved particularly helpful.

In the summer of 1869, Borodin completed his somewhat unusual preparations by making a trip with his wife to a place which, though not actually the site of Putivl itself, was very similar both in character and location.

The Borodins were spending the summer on the estate of their close friend, Prince N. I. Kudashev, in Alyabyevo in Kursk province, some twenty versts from Kursk itself. Their host was a typical feckless landowner who had come down in the world. Borodin arrived there before Catherine. Astonished by the way things were run there, he wrote to his wife to tell her about it. He wrote that Kudashev's house was on an island, and that he lived there in total isolation. Whenever Kudashev needed anyone's services, he blew a whistle and somebody came from the other side of the river in answer to his call; this curious individual 'lives in absolute chaos. All his things are thrown together in a heap: tobacco, linen, papers, revolver, slippers, books, candles, cigarette ends, flowers, remnants of food, and so on—all scattered pell-mell on tables, chairs, book-cases, the fireplace, and on the floor of course.' The Borodins did not have to live in this chaotic repository, but had their rooms in a small extension of the house situated on the other side of the river. Part of the summer was spent in Kursk itself where Kudashev had a flat. As far as one can judge from Borodin's memoirs and subsequent letters, they spent a very happy and quiet summer there.

At the beginning of August the Borodins left for Moscow; here Borodin saw Balakirev, and was invited to Tchaikovsky's place.[2] Catherine's health however left much to be desired; she kept on having severe attacks of asthma, which made it necessary for her to stay in Moscow.

The usual routine of hard work awaited Borodin on his return to Petersburg (6 or 7 September). In addition to lectures and tutorial work, he managed to carry out some intensive research and to get down to serious work on his opera. Writing to Catherine on

---

[1] *Letters*, Vol. I, Letter 64, p. 142.
[2] Ibid., note 2 to Letter 68, p. 355; also M. I. Tchaikovsky's book *The Life of P. I. Tchaikovsky*, Vol. I, p. 330.

September 21, he mentions that he has just finished 'Yaroslavna's Dream':

'Notwithstanding my many activities, and extremely hectic ones at that, I have actually managed to finish the first number of the First Act, but that's all as yet. So far, I haven't shown it to anyone. . . .' A little later he writes to say that his piece has 'gone down well' with my musical friends, and that '"Yaroslavna's Dream" has delighted them.'[1]

In all probability this Arioso, sung by Princess Yaroslavna, was conceived during that same summer but was written down not earlier than September 1869. In the same letter, Borodin also states that he is 'caught up in lab. work'. It was at this time that Borodin received news that the German chemist Kekulé was working in a field closely related to his own. He had always sought to uphold the leadership of Russia in science, and this drove him to step up the pace of his work in order to bring it at least to partial completion and to publish the results to date of the research he had begun in 1865 on the products of condensation of valerian aldehyde.

All these various activities took up nearly the whole of his time. In one of his letters, written about this time, he claims: 'at the present time I am involved in the most feverish and varied activity. . . . When Saturday comes, you wonder where on earth the week has gone.' More particularly: 'I managed to get the laboratory accounts done[2] . . . Then I have to write a couple of memoranda for the bulletin of the Academy of Sciences, and finish off some laboratory work; I really must do something about this laboratory of mine. . . . Of course I expect I shall have to see to everything myself. But then the place will look a treat. We shall be able to work twice as quickly as before and was to get twice as much done.'

Even with all this concentrated research, and administrative and tutorial work as well, Borodin still found time to keep in touch with 'the Handful' and followed with keen interest the tussle Balakirev having with the Petersburg branch of the Musical Society.

We hardly need point out that all Borodin's sympathies were with Balakirev. In his correspondence with his wife, for example, we find caustic comments by Borodin about the Musical Society's programme

[1] Ibid., Letters 70 and 71, pp. 150–1.
[2] Ibid., Letter 73, p. 154. In the same letter, Borodin describes how he succeeded in exposing tremendous frauds in the matter of chemical laboratory equipment, and how he was able to place the authorities in such a position that they decided not to reduce the laboratory allowance, fearing a public scandal.

of concerts, together with a few stories about the way these programmes were put together.[1]

In yet another letter to Catherine, he makes a sharp distinction between the type of audience and concerts of the rival camps. About one such concert presented by the Musical Society on 1 November 1869 he writes: 'There was quite a large audience, and all the fashionable people were there: horseguards, pages, young men from the Lyceum, lawyers, the entire entourage of Elena Pavlovna, girls from boarding-schools, their headmistresses, and other music-lovers. Everything about the concert put one in mind of a salon: Italian coloratura singing, such as one finds in the *Barber of Seville*; a Moroccan March that one often hears played in the Pavlovsky pleasure-gardens; epaulettes, sabres, shockingly low-necked dresses, and so on and so forth.'

The audience of the Free School concerts, given in the same hall, provided a complete contrast with this upper-class 'beau monde': 'It was quite fantastic that immediately afterwards in the very same hall there was a rehearsal of a Free School concert, despite the late hour. The hall was suddenly transformed as if by magic. The epaulettes and low-cut gowns had vanished. Mili was on the rostrum. On the front row were myself, Korsinka, Bach [Stassov's nickname], and other supporters of the Free School. Instead of the Moroccan March and Artôt's coloratura which had scarcely died away, the air was filled with the tremendous sounds of Berlioz's *Lélio*. The concert the next day, the second of the season, was a huge success. The hall wasn't quite full, but at least there were no shoulder-knots, no directors, no headmistresses, no girls from boarding-schools, no pages, and no bare-shouldered ladies. But there certainly was a full complement of serious musicians.'[2]

From the records available, there appears to be no further information relating to his work on *Prince Igor* in the later months of 1869 after the composition of 'Yaroslavna's Dream'. It seems that he restricted himself to attempts to making adaptations for *Prince Igor* of some of the sketches he had made earlier for *The Tsar's Bride*.

All through the autumn and winter of 1869–70, Borodin had been living in hopes that his wife would be able to return to Petersburg, but the unusually bad winter of that year and the dislocation of railway traffic caused by an accident on the Moscow–Petersburg line near Msta

[1] See the letter referred to in the preceding note, pp. 154–5.
[2] *Letters*, Vol. I, Letter 76, pp. 161–2.

made it impossible for her to come. During the winter vacation Borodin himself made the trip to Moscow to see his wife. The few restful days he spent there produced a ballad 'The Sea', which he originally called 'The Fisherman'. He played excerpts from this new work to Rimsky-Korsakov, who was in Moscow at the time with Balakirev.[1]

Borodin's varied activities kept him constantly busy throughout the later part of the winter and early spring of 1870; as always, music was relegated to the background since he had so little time to spare for it. He still went on with his strenuous programme of research. A chemist with whom he kept up a regular friendship at this time was A. M. Butlerov.

Borodin's work on the condensation of valerian aldehyde was very close to that of Kekulé, and it was this that made the latter accuse Borodin of borrowing his ideas. Borodin was furious when he heard about this. He wrote to his wife on 9 March 1870 to say that 'Kekulé (in Bonn) is claiming that my work on valerian aldehyde (which I am doing now) has been borrowed from him (that is to say, not so far as the factual side is concerned, but the very idea itself). He has printed this accusation in the *Berichte* of the Berlin Chemical Society. This compelled me there and then to make a statement of the true facts of the case, and to prove that I have been working on this problem since 1865, whereas Kekulé entered the field only as late as August last year. So much for German honesty! Although our Chemical Society is fully aware of all this, I have nevertheless thought it necessary to make a statement so that it will be brought to the notice of the Berlin Society by the usual procedure.'[2]

At first Borodin was not content with the statement he issued at the meeting of the Chemical Society, and wanted to write a polemical article condemning Kekulé, but he soon thought better of it.

'I have decided not to take up the matter with Kekulé', he writes to Catherine on 20 or 21 March, 'but simply to get on with my work. Let him go on thinking that he has in actual fact scared me with his statement. When the work is finished, perhaps I'll slip in a remark about Kekulé in passing, though with rather more tact.'[3]

In addition to his own research, he had to spend some time analysing soils and rock strata for the amateur geologist, the Duke of Leichtenberg. He undertook this work at Zinin's request. In connection with this, there is one humorous remark which gives us some idea of

[1] Ibid., Letter 92, p. 197.   [2] Ibid., Letter 96, p. 202.
[3] Ibid., Letter 98, p. 211.

Borodin's attitude to rank in general; this occurs in one of his letters to his wife: 'Kozlov and the rest are becoming somehow more deferential towards me, as though I give off the odour of a grand duke, which clings to me as a result of the visits of our exalted guest.'[1]

Borodin's musical friends expressed their annoyance at his meagre musical output, and this had created a certain amount of ill-feeling. In a letter dated 9 March 1870, for example, Borodin remarks: 'Our musicians never stop abusing me. They say I never do anything, and won't drop my idiotic activities, that is to say, my work at the laboratory, and so forth.'

It was only after a number of reminders that Balakirev managed to persuade Borodin, 'on his word of honour', to send his definitive versions of the three songs: 'The Sleeping Princess', 'The False Note' and 'My Songs are filled with poison' to Jurgenson's publishing house in Moscow. This was in February, and the songs were published around the end of March.[2] Apparently Borodin had promised Balakirev that he would send the rest of his songs as well. When he did not keep his promise, he was accused of being insufficiently serious about his music, and so forth.

Also in February he put the finishing touches to his ballad 'The Sea', the words of which he had written himself. Stassov has it that the words in the published text are different from the ones originally intended. According to Stassov, the text was rejected by the censor; 'it depicted a young exile banished from his country for political reasons. Full of impassioned and burning hopes he returns home only to meet a tragic death in a storm within sight of the shores of his native land.'

'The Sea' received a tremendous ovation from Borodin's musical friends.[3] He wrote to his wife: 'This work is rated very highly indeed by "the severest of critics". Many, including Balakirev, regard it more highly than "The Princess"—and that's saying quite a lot. The fact is that it's a good piece; it has charm, fire and sparkle, and is tuneful as well. Everything in it "rings true" from the musical point

---

[1] *Letters*, Vol. 1, Letter 95, pp. 199–200. This letter was first published in Stassov's book on Borodin, pp. 73–75, but the passage referring to 'the odour of a grand duke' was omitted, probably as a result of censorship.

[2] In the first edition of the ballad 'My Songs are Filled with Poison' we find the note: 'Passed by the Censor, 17 March 1870.'

[3] See Stassov's book on Borodin, p. 32. Stassov memorized the text of this passage and related it to B. V. Asafiev. Unfortunately, he could not remember it exactly and for a long time was unable to find it in any written form.

V. BALAKIREV

Reproduction of a photograph taken between 1863 and 1867. The original is preserved in the Rimsky-Korsakov family collection.

VI. THE ORGANIZERS OF THE RUSSIAN CHEMICAL SOCIETY

Reproduced from a photograph taken on 5 January 1868. Borodin is fifth from the left, in the back row.

of view. I must confess however that I had my doubts about it. I kept feeling it sound awkward and clumsy, etc. I was quite astonished that it came off so well.' Owing to the satisfaction of the composer himself and his friends, the song very soon appeared in print; it came out in October 1870.[1]

It was at the same time as this display of musical activity that he distressed his friends, Stassov in particular, by his categorical refusal to give any more thought to *Prince Igor*.

There were several reasons for this decision on the part of Borodin. On the one hand, so Stassov tells us, Catherine was not in favour of the subject matter. She held the view that an opera or a drama for that matter, should be based on present-day life and events.[2] On the other hand, Borodin himself was not altogether happy about the subject either. However suitable it was for musical treatment, it was doubtful whether it would appeal to the general public. There was too little drama, and almost no stage movement whatsoever.

Fearing that he would not be able 'to make a libretto which would satisfy both musical and scenic requirements', he also made the point that 'an opera (undramatic in the strict sense) was an unnatural sort of thing anyway'. Thus it would appear that epic opera did not seem to Borodin at that time a suitable medium for him to attempt.

Finally, his attempts at adapting old material for the opera and his 'Yaroslavna's Dream' had not led to the creation of any basic themes and leitmotifs, which might convincingly counteract the dampening reflections and conversations of those around him.

It is natural that in such circumstances Borodin should turn again to the composition of his B minor Symphony. Very soon he became reconciled with the dissatisfied 'critics'.

In the period immediately following the composition of 'The Sea' there was a great deal to distract Borodin from music. In his free time he liked visiting friends, going to concerts and attending meetings of learned societies. Moreover, at this time (the end of winter and the spring of 1870) he used to visit from time to time his recently acquired acquaintances, the Makovskys. Konstantin Makovsky and his wife, Elena Timofeevna, were artists. It was Elena who painted his portrait at this time.[3]

---

[1] On the specimen copy of the first edition of 'The Sea' we find the note: 'Passed by the Censor, 12 October 1870.'

[2] Stassov's book on Borodin, pp. 37–38.

[3] It is now to be found in the State Central Museum of Musical Culture in Moscow.

During the spring vacation, in April Borodin went on a short visit to Moscow. During this trip he composed most of the first Allegro of the B minor Symphony. Rimsky-Korsakov was the first of Borodin's musical friends to hear about this work. Borodin tells how he 'played him this new symphonic essay' once when he was at his flat, and how 'old Korsakov raved about it and said it was his best and most effective thing yet'. When he heard about this work, and even though he had not yet heard it personally, Balakirev dropped his feelings of resentment against his pupil.

Borodin has given us a comic description of the scene of his meeting with Balakirev, who was clearly in a radiant mood:

'Mili [i.e. Balakirev] was too funny for words!' runs the account, 'I have already said in my letters that he'd been sulking at me for some time, and that he was off-hand, angry, and at times captious. I turn up at Liudma's[1]—and there was Mili; you'd hardly recognize him. He softened, melted, and gazed at me with loving eyes. In the end, at a loss as to how he could express his affection, he gently took me by the nose between two fingers and gave me a resounding kiss. I couldn't help but laugh! You must have guessed the reason for this change, of course. Korsinka has told him that I'm trying my hand at another symphony and played him a bit of it.'[2]

Borodin left Petersburg that year at the end of May. The Borodins spent the summer in the village of Davydkovo about six or seven kilometres from Moscow on the road to Mozhaisk. This summer was not very productive for Borodin as far as music is concerned. Catherine, who had always tended towards hypochondria, was terrified of the cholera that was raging in Moscow; this mood of hers had a depressing effect on Borodin. But there was a piano at his disposal,[3] which he may have used.[4]

On his return to Petersburg around the middle of September, Borodin moved into his old friend Professor Sorokin's flat; he felt he would miss his wife too much if he stayed at home for Catherine was once again staying in Moscow, this time to undergo treatment for her asthma. Sorokin's flat was in Furstadt Street (now Petr Lavrov Street) 'near the Kusma and Demyan Square in Kononov's house'.

Borodin was worried the whole of that autumn about Catherine's

---

[1] Liudmila Ivanovna Shestakova, Glinka's sister.
[2] *Letters*, Vol. I, Letter 102, pp. 221–2.
[3] From 4 July 1870.
[4] *Letters*, Vol. I, Letter 105, p. 228.

health, and was afraid that living with her relatives, the Stupishins, would have an unhealthy effect on her physically and mentally. 'It seems to me', he writes, 'that this Moscow atmosphere and the surroundings as a whole are having a bad effect on your nerves. It's so stuffy and oppressive. Living there one is obliged to contemplate the vicissitudes of people leading very sad lives, without any prospect of a good way out. . . . An impressionable person like yourself could not help but be influenced by it, when even I, who am in any case less susceptible to Moscow influences, on occasion feel stifled in this atmosphere.' In passing, Borodin strongly emphasizes the fact that Catherine's home surroundings are quite alien to him. 'It was not only the sense of misfortune and suffering that induced morbidity in me there, but the narrow bourgeois set-up, their way of thinking and life generally, Alexei's whole entourage,[1] and so on. The prejudices, the petty jealousies, bred by Moscow loose-living, the superstition, etc. All this had a killingly depressing effect on me. Perhaps you don't even feel a small fraction of this; you have grown up in this atmosphere, and you have grown accustomed to it all. . . . But all the same it will leave its mark on you unconsciously, whether you like it or not.'

With a view to extricating her from this milieu, Borodin wanted to transfer her to Tsarskoe Selo, but for various reasons nothing came of this plan.

The autumn passed, Borodin becoming involved in one thing after another at the Academy. He did little work, partly on account of the fact that he felt unsettled living in someone else's house, and partly on account of his eye trouble. At this time Borodin saw his musical friends quite often and continued to show an active response to what went on in the circle. A letter to Catherine shows his deep sympathy for Balakirev after his concert in Nizhniy Novgorod had been a complete failure. We learn from the same letter that Balakirev was unable to organize any concerts at the Free School that season.

It is with great delight that he announces that there is to be a concert, in aid of raising a monument to Glinka, on 14 November under the direction of Balakirev.

In a letter of 19 November, which was sent by hand in order to avoid censorship, he made a scathing attack on the Grand Duchess, Elena Pavlovna, giving a detailed account of the scandal perpetrated by this 'august' personage, which arose over one of Cui's criticisms of the Musical Society. He concluded his description with the query:

[1] Catherine's brother.

'How can the old woman not be ashamed? She's making a fool of herself.'[1]

At the end of November Catherine made the decision to return to Petersburg. He was overjoyed that she was coming back, after having been away for a year and a half, and spent the early part of December working hard to get the flat ready for her return. At the same time as this, he had to spend hours writing up one report after another in connection with his academic work. 'As a result of all this I never go anywhere', he wrote in a letter dated 16 December 1870. 'I missed two Mondays at Ludmila Ivanovna's and finally received an invitation from her for last Monday; this was accompanied by a host of regrets and complaints that I was forgetting the dear old soul.'[2]

At last, but only after everything conceivable had gone wrong, and after wasting a great deal of time, Borodin had everything ready for Catherine's arrival. In the second half of December she returned to Petersburg accompanied by her adopted daughter Lisa, who had been living with her in Moscow.[3]

Sometime during the winter of 1870–1, Borodin composed the song 'From my Tears' (Iz Slyoz Moikh) to the words of Heine, and dedicated it to M. S. Stupishina.[4] In the spring of that year the piano score of the first movement (Allegro) of the B minor Symphony was ready, but he had already sketched it out a year before. It also appears that he had already made sketches of the Scherzo and the Andante.[5]

---

[1] *Letters*, Vol. I, Letter 128, p. 272.

[2] Ibid., Letter 135, p. 283.

[3] Lisa—Elizaveta Gavrilovna Dianina (*née* Balaneva)—my mother. She was adopted by the Borodins and lived with them till their death.

[4] The date of this song may be determined with reasonable accuracy from the following: Firstly, the song is dedicated to M. S. Stupishina who lived in St. Petersburg and often visited the Borodins up to the summer of 1871. They met each other at Davidkovo in the summer of that year, but after the autumn Borodin seems to have seen her but rarely. Therefore, bearing in mind the fact that the song 'From My Tears' was published in June 1873, it seems probable that it was composed not later than the summer of 1871.

Secondly, Borodin did not possess a great number of poetical anthologies until the end of the seventies and relied on the suggestions of friends for the selection of suitable texts for his compositions. My mother recalls that he was particularly fascinated by a copy of Heine's *Buch der Lieder* which was given to him by Balakirev. Eventually Balakirev took it back. (This fact was indelibly inscribed on my mother's memory, for she was especially fond of this book which had a beautiful red cover.) Bearing in mind that Balakirev did not visit the Borodins from the spring of 1871 till the summer of 1880, that my mother lived as a boarder in the Helena Institute, and that she clearly remembered Balakirev personally collecting the *Liederbuch* before she moved to the Institute, it seems fairly certain that the song was written in 1871.

[5] This is all the more probable if one remembers that, according to Rimsky-Korsakov, the first bars of the *Scherzo* (the modulation from B minor into F major) were written

The Borodins again spent the summer (1871) at Davydkovo. At first Borodin had intended to go with his wife to Kiev to attend a conference of naturalists,[1] but he had to change his plans, most probably owing to Catherine's indisposition. This year his summer holiday enabled him to orchestrate the first movement of his B minor Symphony.

Once again, in the autumn Borodin left his wife behind in Moscow so that she could undergo treatment for her asthma, and returned to Petersburg on the 13 or 14 September with his adopted daughter, Lisa. On his return Borodin found that relations between Balakirev and the other members of the circle had changed considerably. This had some connection with the serious mental crisis which had beset Balakirev, and Borodin already knew something about the situation from the letters he had received during the summer.[2] Another important piece of news was that Rimsky-Korsakov had been offered the post of Professor at the St. Petersburg Conservatoire.

In his letters to his wife, Borodin says what he thinks about these changes, very objectively and with real sympathy towards all his friends.[3] The members of the group were still on friendly terms and still visited one another; they discussed among themselves the works they had written that summer. His letters also tell us that *The Maid of Pskov* and *Boris Godunov* had been performed at their gatherings, and that they were delighted to see the score of the first movement of the B minor Symphony.

Feeling relaxed after his summer holiday, and finding himself again in the thick of his friends' musical activities, Borodin began to feel a strong creative urge. By the end of September he had finished the greater part of the Finale of the B minor Symphony. In a letter to his wife, dated 4 October, he writes:

'I had Modya, Korsya, and Nikolai Lodyzhensky round the other day; they all fell for the Finale of my symphony. There's only the

by Balakirev. As Balakirev broke off his association with his musical friends in the autumn of 1871, the *Scherzo* must have existed before this time. The *Finale* of the Second Symphony was composed in the autumn of 1871. There is very little likelihood that the *Finale*, which follows the previous movement without a break, was written before the latter. Therefore, the sketches of both the *Scherzo* and the *Andante* must have been made by the spring of 1871.

[1] There is a reference to Borodin's intention of staying in Kiev with Alekseev in a letter from Borodin to Alekseev dated 24 June 1871, which was written in Davydkovo (*Letters*, Vol. IV, Letter 137a, p. 293).

[2] *Letters*, Vol. I, Letter 138, pp. 285–6.

[3] See, for example, *Letters*, Vol. I, Letter 150, pp. 310–13.

last few bars still to finish. The middle part couldn't be better. I'm very pleased with it; it's full of life and power, and it's dashing, lively, and very effective.'[1]

He completed the Finale in October of the same year; we know this from a letter to his wife, dated 24–25 October, where he mentions that Cui came to see him specially to hear 'the end of the Finale'.

Borodin was eager to bring about a reconciliation between Balakirev and his friends, and with this in view, he made use of some opportune business to pay a formal visit to him. Here is the full account of his meeting with Balakirev, which he sent to Catherine shortly after. This account is of great interest as it shows clearly the full creative maturity of Borodin and his new critical attitude towards Balakirev's views:

'On Friday [15 Oct.] I went to see Balakirev. He sends you his kind regards and was terribly pleased to see me. He was interested in the symphony and, as usual, immediately began asking me to make certain alterations here and there. It was just typical—he told me exactly the opposite to what he had suggested last spring. (For instance, when I wanted originally to put the whole of the second subject in G major the second time, he raised fierce objections and kept trying to convince me that it would have to be in E flat major, and only some of it. But now when I play this section, he starts asking me why I have done that, and why I haven't repeated "the whole theme in, say, G major, and not as before in E flat major, which doesn't go at all well here." That's exactly what I had been saying in the spring. What a fantastic fellow!) My real reason for going was to retrieve the score of the First Symphony which he has been hesitating to return to me under various pretexts for the past year. Meanwhile, Nadyezhda Purgold keeps pestering me. She wants to make a piano arrangement of the work. Balakirev won't have this, but keeps saying he will do the arrangement himself. Of course, he'll never get round to this. It turns out that he has been keeping it all this time simply so that he can make various comments about the alterations and reorchestration he thinks necessary.

'And would you believe it; the score is absolutely covered with remarks, such as "give to the clarinets" or "cellos", "double here", and so forth. And what do you think; that's exactly as I had done in the first place; it was only at Mili's insistence that I rescored clarinet parts for bassoon, and gave certain parts to the violas instead of to the cellos; the doubling was there, and everything. It's a very odd thing

[1] *Letters*, Vol. I, Letter 147, p. 303.

indeed! It's as if he's literally recommending me to do the exact opposite to what he had wanted before. Reluctantly he gave me back the score and then only on condition that I took serious note of his corrections.'[1]

Before Catherine arrived home in the middle of November, Borodin had to face the usual complications at the Academy; he made various alterations to his flat and laboratory, had to find a suitable school for his adopted daughter, Lisa, and so forth.

During the autumn, two women chemists, Miss Dannenberg (?) and Miss A. N. Lukanina, were working in Borodin's laboratory. This small contribution towards assisting women in their attempts to secure higher education was very soon destined to grow into a major social undertaking, when Borodin took part in organizing medical courses for women.

Shortly after her return home, Catherine and several of her friends hit upon the idea of organizing private dances. The first dance was to be on a 'sharing expenses' basis and was arranged by the Borodins in conjunction with the Dobroslavins and other Professors of the Academy; it took place on 6 January 1872.[2] It was held in the pharmacology lecture-room, just next door to the Borodin's flat, and this room was chosen for future occasions. Most of the guests wore fancy dress. Borodin himself seems to have favoured the garb of 'King Menelaus' as he appears in *La Belle Hélène*, but sometimes dressed up as a Chinaman.

It was towards the beginning of 1872 that Borodin contributed his share to the composition of the fairy opera *Mlada*. It was based on the life of the western Slavs (Polabians) and was taken from the scenario by S. A. Gedeonov,[3] who was at that time Director of the Imperial

[1] Ibid., Letter 149, pp. 307–8.

[2] In a letter from Catherine to Borodin dated 27 October 1873, she mentions that 6 January 1874 will mark the second anniversary of the founding of their fancy-dress balls. A rather amusing incident took place after one of these dances some time in 1872. On the day following the dance, M. V. Dobroslavina visited Borodin in order to work out the distribution of the evening's expenses. During the conversation, Borodin for a joke put on the theatrical crown of King Menelaus which was lying on the table. They were suddenly interrupted by someone announcing that a young doctor was asking for him on business. At that time, Borodin was deputising for the secretary of the Academy, I. M. Sorokin, who had been taken ill, and all kinds of people called upon him to obtain his signature for various reasons. Borodin went out to attend to his visitor with the crown still upon his head and was extremely surprised when the young doctor, instead of stating his business, stammered out a few incoherent phrases and hurriedly withdrew. The visitor decided that the professor had taken leave of his senses and that flight was the most fitting course of action. This anecdote was told me by M. V. Dobroslavina.

[3] See Stassov's book on Borodin, p. 38.

Theatres. The libretto was written by V. A. Krylov. Stassov was seeing a great deal of Gedeonov at the time for one reason or another, and it was through Stassov that he approached the four members of 'The Handful', Borodin, Cui, Mussorgsky and Rimsky-Korsakov, and proposed that they should write all the music with the exception of the ballet scenes (which Minkus was to write). Stassov was quite surprised when all four willingly agreed.

According to Rimsky-Korsakov, work on *Mlada* was opportioned according to what it was thought each could do best.

'The First Act, the most dramatic of the opera, was given to the most dramatic composer—Cui; the Fourth, a mixture of the dramatic and the elemental, was given to Borodin; the Second and Third Acts were allocated to Mussorgsky and myself jointly, only certain parts of the Second Act and the whole first half of the Third, the flight of the phantoms and Mlada's apparition, were for me; Mussorgsky took on the whole of the second half himself. It was his intention to incorporate *The Night on the Bare Mountain* which so far he had not been able to find any use for.'[1]

Borodin set about his allotted task with considerable enthusiasm, since it was just what he had been looking for as regards musical epic and fantasy. He made himself familiar with the history of the Baltic Slavs, and in an exceedingly short time produced wonderful, sublime music for the Fourth Act of the opera.[2]

He was working on the opera in March and April 1872, and seems

[1] Rimsky-Korsakov's memoirs, 3rd ed., p. 128.

[2] In Rimsky-Korsakov's memoirs (3rd ed., p. 128), he mentions that: 'Borodin, who had been somewhat disappointed in writing *Prince Igor*, now took much of the suitable material from it, composed some new music also, and thus wrote almost the whole draft of Act IV.' This statement is questionable. In the first period of his work on *Igor*, Borodin composed nothing apart from 'Yaroslavna's Dream', and several re-arrangements of choruses from *The Tsar's Bride*, but he threw aside this work in the early spring of 1870. It is only in this way that the theme:

Ex. 284

(which is related to the Finale of the B minor Symphony) could have appeared in the scene of the Chorus of Idol Worshippers in *Mlada*, from whence it was returned to the Prologue of *Prince Igor*. Generally speaking, the whole of the Fourth Act of *Mlada* was based on original music written by Borodin in 1872.

to have composed first 'The Chorus of Sacrifice to Radegast'; thematically this is related to a certain section of the Finale of the Second Symphony and the Prologue to *Prince Igor*. On the manuscript copy he presented to Stassov, containing part of this Chorus, we find the date '5 March '72'. After this Chorus came the remaining items, the duets of Yaromir with the High Priest, and Yaromir with Voyslava must have been ready by the end of March; the second of these Duets carries the date 12 March. The remarkable scene of the 'Apparition of the Phantoms' was composed at the end of the month, and after this came 'Voyslava's Address to Morena'. The final versions of both these, as well as the end of the Fourth Act ('Flood, Storm, Destruction of the Temple, Mlada's Apparition and Apotheosis') were completed by April 14.

Borodin's creative powers were high at the time when he was working on *Mlada*. In Stassov's own words:

'At this time . . . I was seeing a good deal of him, and I frequently found him of a morning standing in front of his high writing-table actually engaged in composition. He looked inspired; his eyes were on fire, and he looked transformed. One occasion I remember in particular. He had not been very well, and had been staying at home for the past two weeks; but during the whole of that time, he had scarcely left the piano. It was then that he was composing the most monumental and amazing moments of *Mlada*. Whenever I turned up, he immediately played and sang everything he had just written with most extraordinary fire and enthusiasm.'[1]

In writing the Fourth Act, Borodin was eager to keep as accurately as possible to the timings allotted for each number in the scenario. The duration of each number (to the nearest half minute) is clearly indicated above the manuscript autographs.[2]

As we already know, Gedeonov's *Mlada* was never actually produced; the most likely explanation for this is that the Director of the Theatres had to give up the idea of producing the opera owing to lack of funds. When it became clear that the *Mlada* project had fallen through, Borodin, according to Stassov,[3] returned to work on the B minor Symphony, the greater part of which was still in rough; only the first movement had been orchestrated.

The Borodins spent the summer of 1872 abroad. Catherine wrote

[1] See Stassov's book of Borodin, p. 39.
[2] Borodin also used this system for *Prince Igor*.
[3] See Stassov's book of Borodin, p. 41.

on a scrap of paper, now in the Borodin archive, that they left Petersburg on 17 June and travelled by way of Königsberg to Berlin. From there they went on to Jena (where they stayed in the Hotel Adler), and after that spent a few days in Dresden. They went finally to the Austrian health resort of Gleichenberg where Catherine caught severe bronchitis.[1]

It would appear that at this period Borodin was showing an interest in the German chemical industry; there is a letter of recommendation from Wiechelhaus, the Secretary of the Berlin Chemical Society, addressed to a German factory-owner (S. Martins) asking permission for Borodin to look round his factory.

The Borodins set out for Moscow on 27 August and, after spending about three weeks there, returned together to Petersburg on 15 September.[2]

The autumn of 1872 brought yet another addition to the many-sided activities already taking up the whole of Borodin's time. Under the modest title of 'Course in Obstetrics' an advanced medical course for women was inaugurated, the first of its kind in Russia. At first this course was housed in the Academy of Physicians. Borodin was the professor of Chemistry on these courses from the very start, and he took a keen interest in helping with their organization and in seeing that they had the necessary equipment. He also organized help for poor students.[3]

Borodin still continued to work fairly intensively on his research in organic chemistry; in 1872 no less than three articles of his appeared in the *Journal of the Chemical Society*. Over and above this a woman student, A. N. Lukanina, who had been working under Borodin's direction, had an article published in the *Bulletin de l'Academie des Sciences de St. Petersbourg*.

He kept up his friendly connections (as before) with the members

[1] These details of the Borodins' trip abroad in 1872 are taken from Catherine's memoirs, and from references to Jena in her letters to Borodin and A. P. Dianin in the summer of 1877. In these letters she reveals that she suffered from an acute attack of bronchitis in the course of one of her journeys abroad, whilst staying in the Austrian health-resort of Gleichenberg. (In consequence she referred to every successive attack of this ailment as 'a Gleichenberg'.) We can only determine the year of her visit by a process of elimination. The Borodins spent the summer of 1865 at Graz; they could not have stayed in Gleichenberg in 1862, when they travelled from Berlin to Italy without any protracted stops; therefore, it must have been during their third journey abroad in 1872.

[2] These dates are taken from Catherine's expense book.

[3] According to a document preserved in the philharmonic museum, Borodin was appointed instructor of the Women's Medical Course of Obstreticians on 11 October 1872.

of the Balakirev circle. From time to time he had been making efforts to coax Balakirev back among them, since he seemed to have cut himself off completely from the musical world. Borodin's efforts were of no avail, but Balakirev remained on friendly terms with him as before. One of the things he did was to send on to Borodin, in January 1873, four supplementary verse couplets to his ballad 'The False Note'; Balakirev had received these from an unknown writer in the Caucasus through a woman singer by the name of L. I. Karmalina. These verses were worse than banal, and needless to say they were not used in the revised edition of the ballad which appeared in 1885; they are however to be found in the archive.

In the early part of 1873 two important events in the history of the circle took place; the first stage performance of *The Maid of Pskov* on 1 January, and of three scenes from *Boris Godunov* on 5 February. Both these productions were a great success, and Borodin himself was present at both premières.[1]

Towards the spring, the piano score at least of the B minor Symphony seems to have been ready. We have reason to believe this from the various indirect references to it in one of Stassov's letters to his niece: 'Once again last night we heard the symphony by Borodin, a composer of athletic strength—a leonine work.'[2]

If the symphony had not been played in its entirety, Stassov would certainly have remarked on the fact. His comment, as it stands, implies that the symphony existed as a complete whole.

Also at this time three of Borodin's songs were being engraved by Bessel's:[3] 'From My Tears', 'The Sea Princess', and 'The Song of the Dark Forest' (otherwise entitled 'An Old Song').

According to A. P. Dianin, there was a certain amount of difficulty in getting 'The Song of the Dark Forest' past the censor. He had found it 'seditious' and was not going to pass it. With Rimsky-Korsakov's help, Borodin found a way round this. The former placed 'The Song of the Dark Forest' between two of his own songs which were quite innocuous in this respect. The censor, who had been accustomed to passing Rimsky-Korsakov's songs without even looking at them, did likewise in this case and gave his signed permission for the publication of Borodin's ballad. (On the specimen copies of the

---

[1] In Catherine's expense book there is an entry under 1 January 1873: 'Cab to Pskovit. 1.25.'

[2] Letter to Zizi Stassov dated 21 May 1873 (partly quoted in V. Karenin's book, *Vladimir Stassov*, Part II, p. 409).

[3] This can be deduced from the censor's comments on the first editions of these songs.

first edition of all three of Borodin's songs the censor has written the identical remark: 'Passed by the censor, St. P. 13 June 1873.')

The Borodins spent the beginning of the summer of 1873 in Sokolniki, in the outskirts of Moscow, at the country house of Catherine's brother, Alexei. In the middle of July Borodin received a telegram asking him to return at once to Petersburg; his mother was seriously ill after an attack of apoplexy. For six days on end he was at his mother's bedside until her death on 23 July. Although there are no clear indications of his state of mind in his letter to Catherine (dated 18 July), but even a mention of a trip to Pargolovo to see Rimsky-Korsakov when there was a temporary improvement in his mother's condition,[1] we know nevertheless that the death of his mother affected him very deeply. One entry in Borodin's papers is of interest in enabling us to assess his reaction to this sad event; in it he meticulously records the whole course of the later stages of his mother's illness, the full details of treatment given, her last night of suffering, and, finally, the very moment of her death. His notes are written in a nervous, distorted handwriting and contain many errors—even spelling mistakes.

Shortly after his mother's funeral, Borodin left for Kazan to represent the Academy of Physicians at a conference of doctors and naturalists. He arrived in Kazan a considerable time before the conference was due to open,[2] and accordingly decided to spend his unexpected free days with his brother-in-law, Sergei, in Samara. After a pleasant rest at Samara, Borodin returned to Kazan to take an active part in the proceedings of the conference of naturalists; he was elected a member of the committee. During his stay in Kazan, he was the guest of Professor Zaitsev, and shared a room with Mendeleev.

On the whole Borodin was received very well at this Kazan conference. 'You can't imagine the attention I'm getting here,' he wrote, 'they give me a cordial reception wherever I go, and at every step I am greeted with most flattering marks of respect and esteem.'[3]

Borodin stayed in Kazan for the whole of the conference. The time he spent there was, as he wrote himself, both happy and profitable. He not only took an active part in the special discussions of the chemists at which he gave as many as seven reports on his experimental

[1] See Borodin's letter to Catherine dated 18 June 1873 (*Letters*, Vol. II, Letter 193, p. 29).
[2] *Letters*, Vol. II, Letter 196.
[3] Ibid., Letter 199.

work[1] and on one occasion presided, but also made several speeches at the formal dinners. One of these speeches was devoted to higher education for women, and a second touched on the question of setting up a magnetic observatory in Kazan.[2]

He also took part in musical evenings there. 'This evening', he wrote on 24 August, 'I have been invited to a musical evening; there the chief interest centres around my music.' In his last letter from Kazan, Borodin had, amongst other things, the following to say: 'Now something about myself. I found here all-round admiration, even for my music. They laid on two musical evenings for me where they played string quartets; it was nothing special, but not bad really. There is also a keen supporter of our circle here, who is acquainted with every single one of our works, even Mussorgsky's latest opera, which I don't even know thoroughly myself. . . . Today there is a concert, for those taking part in the conference, at the noblemen's club; they are playing Hummel's Septet, and a Chopin concerto, etc.'[3]

Borodin left Kazan on 30 August and set out for Moscow where he spent about two weeks with Catherine. He returned to Petersburg on 15 September and at once plunged into his usual work at the Academy.[4] In his flat he found the usual chaos. He wrote to his wife about this on 16 September as follows: 'The disorder was in exactly the same order as I left it; the chaos hadn't been touched; the dust, the fleas, the empty tables; everything where you can't find it, and things left lying about exactly as when I left. Ekaterina Yegorovna[5] is fussing about trying to be helpful.'

The moment he arrived back, Borodin was besieged by callers of every conceivable sort. He was kept so busy with all the fuss that he did not even find time to collect the specimen copies of his three ballads, recently published by Bessel.

Until later in the autumn Borodin's musical interests apparently had

---

[1] Consisting of three reports on his works, and four on the activities of his pupils (P. G. Golubev, A. P. Dianin, Lobanov, and M. I. Shalfeev). See Agenda of the Kazan Congress of Natural Scientists and Doctors, 1873. Minutes of the joint meeting of the chemical, mineralogy, geology and palaeontology sections, 22 August 1873.

[2] The Kazan town council were very unwilling to give financial assistance for the founding of this observatory. Borodin, giving the impression that he knew nothing of this, congratulated the council on their generosity and their willingness to co-operate. Needless to say, this greatly embarrassed the members of the town council, but delighted the supporters of the scheme.

[3] Letter to Catherine dated 28 August 1873 (*Letters*, Vol. II, Letter 200).

[4] Letter to Catherine dated 15 September 1873 (*Letters*, Vol. II, Letter 201).

[5] His mother's former housemaid, E. E. Belzmann (see *Letters*, Vol. I, note 33, p. 2).

to take second place. The only thing worth noting is that he had frequent discussions with Rimsky-Korsakov on the question of orchestration and, in particular, on the use of chromatic brass in the orchestra. Both composers at this time had practical experience of such instruments and were delighted at the new prospect of being able to give freer scope to the brass. Rimsky-Korsakov tells us that, as a result of their conversations, they both overestimated the possibilities of scoring for brass, and that this made for a certain heaviness in the orchestration of the B minor Symphony which might have been avoided.[1]

In the first weeks of October 1873 Borodin was suffering from boils on his foot; for almost a month, until 20 November, he was unable to leave the house. He spent the time copying music in the main; in all probability he was making the final transcripts of the orchestral parts of the Second Symphony. He has something to say about this in a letter to Catherine of 22 October. 'These past two days and the whole of last Sunday, while young Lisa was here, were spent copying music. All the time I was copying, she was reading aloud for me. . . . But I'm very glad to have someone to read to me, and I get on very rapidly while she is reading.'[2]

He also spent some of the time studying the instruments of the orchestra: 'While I have been having this foot trouble, I have been absolutely deluged with visitors, dropping in to see how the invalid is getting along: first Sorokin, then Sokolov, Reshetin, Zinin, Cui, Stassov, and even Shcherbachev; and to keep me occupied Korsakov kept bringing one instrument after another—first a flügelhorn from a military band, then a bassoon, and finally some special sort of clarinet. I enjoyed myself immensely playing these instruments, but I don't think my audience did one bit.'[3]

On 28 October Borodin added his signature to a telegram of congratulation which the Balakirev circle were sending to Liszt on the occasion of his fiftieth year of musical activity. Liszt, as we know, replied to say that he was not unfamiliar with their music and that he wanted to do all he could to help in making their music more widely known in Western Europe. Thus began the close relationship between Liszt and the 'New Russian School', which Borodin himself did so much to foster in later years.

[1] See Rimsky-Korsakov's memoirs, 3rd ed., pp. 155 and 197.
[2] *Letters*, Vol. II, Letter 213.
[3] Ibid.

Catherine returned to Petersburg around the middle of November. With her arrival a peculiar way of life began for them. Catherine was in the habit of going to bed about three or four o'clock in the morning; up to that hour neither she nor anyone else in the house could get any sleep, least of all her husband. She usually got up very late, around three or four o'clock in the afternoon. As a result of such an existence, Borodin began to suffer from lack of sleep. This disruption of his life made him unsystematic and slack in other matters as well. Quite frequently the Borodins did not have their dinner before midnight. The harmful effects of this routine were cumulative, and were one of the factors affecting his health; they undoubtedly hastened the onset of the heart disease which led to his death.

The winter of 1873–4 was not a productive one for Borodin as far as music was concerned. Apart from further work on the orchestration of the Second Symphony, he did no composition.[1] He continued to keep up his lively association with the members of the Balakirev circle. At the end of November his circle of musical acquaintances was further widened; L. I. Karmalina, the singer, visited the Borodins before she left Petersburg and produced a great impression on them with her singing.

There was one great event for Borodin's musical friends that winter, when the whole of *Boris Godunov* was staged in the Maryinsky Theatre. Borodin was present at the first performance of *Boris* and wildly applauded the success of his dear and intimate friend Mussorgsky.[2]

In May 1874 the members of the Balakirev circle, and Borodin in particular, arranged to meet Turgenev. Stassov has recorded[3] that Turgenev agreed to meet the members of the group at Stassov's place, and to hear a performance given by Rubinstein, who had earlier consented to play for Stassov and his friends. They were all there that evening with the exception of Balakirev who never went anywhere in those days. Turgenev arrived rather earlier than Rubinstein. The

[1] There is a possibility that the first sketches of the A major Quartet were made during this winter, but there are no details to confirm this.

[2] Mussorgsky often used to stay with the Borodins during these years and frequently played his compositions to them, *Boris Godunov* in particular. Usually several of the piano hammers were broken at the end of his performance. On one occasion, Borodin's mother, who was not especially musical, was so overwhelmed by an exceptionally brilliant rendering of *Boris*, that she embraced Mussorgsky when he had finished playing (reminiscence of E. G. Dianina).

[3] In 'Twenty Letters of Turgenev and my Acquaintance with him', *Severny Vestnik*, 1888.

latter, when he arrived, wanted the performance to start immediately. He played the C major Sonata of Beethoven, a few pieces by Chopin, and then Schumann's 'Variations' and *Carnaval*; his magnificent performance produced the usual tremendous impression on the audience. After a short interval, during which Rubinstein left, the second part of the concert, devoted to works by members of the Balakirev circle, was about to commence when Turgenev had a severe attack of arthritis. Borodin, being the only doctor present, gave him first aid. Turgenev's condition was so serious that he was obliged to return home.[1] And so it was that Turgenev never heard these composers playing their own music.

The Borodins spent the summer of 1874 in a very quiet corner of Vladimir Province. They were invited there by a student on one of the medical courses, M. A. Miropolskaya, who had made arrangements for them to stay with her friends, the Kulomzins, on their estate in the tiny village of Rozhnovo; this was in the Suzdal district between 55 and 60 kilometres from Vladimir. The Borodins went there with Lisa on 19 June. They travelled by rail as far as Vladimir, and from there by post horse. During the latter part of the journey, the carriage in which they were travelling overturned. Luckily they escaped with a few slight bruises.

In Rozhnovo the Borodins lived in a tiny, ramshackle house; it had once belonged to the globe-trotter Kruzenstern, and was furnished with nothing but the bare essentials. The only company they had there, apart from their hosts who lived a number of miles away, was Miss Miropolskaya, and later A. P. Dianin who spent the greater part of the summer with them. For the past year and a half Dianin had been studying chemistry under Borodin. In addition the Borodins made the acquaintance of a number of the local inhabitants—village school-teachers, neighbouring landowners, summer residents, and so forth.

There was hardly any forest there, but it was picturesque and very healthy, and Borodin spent much time walking in the surrounding countryside. He went bathing regularly in the River Urshma, near Rozhnovo, which abounded in cold springs. He also made a trip to Suzdal where he did some sightseeing.

Little is known of his musical activities during the summer. All we

---

[1] We know that, shortly after Rubinstein's death, an article about this occasion was published by M. Y. Goldstein (pseudonym Muge). In it some quite fantastic details are given (see V. Karenin, *V. Stassov*, Vol. I, pp. 379–80).

VII. STASSOV

Reproduced from a photograph taken between 1877 and 1879. The original was given to
L. J. Schestakova and is now preserved in the Rimsky-Korsakov family collection.

VIII. THE HOUSE IN WHICH BORODIN LIVED DURING THE SUMMER OF 1879

A photograph taken in 1954 by the painter O. A. Dimitriev.

know is that he had at his disposal some old-fashioned piano or harpischord.[1] As far as I can tell, the only thing he composed that summer was a humorous waltz for piano.[2] As far as serious composition is concerned, it is feasible that he had already begun work on the A major Quartet, although this cannot be known for certain.

The Borodins left Rozhnovo on 12 September; on the way back Borodin left Catherine at her mother's in Moscow, and he and Lisa went on to Petersburg, where he immediately became immersed in academic work. 'Like a cavalry horse answering the bugle,' wrote Borodin on 18 September in a letter to E. A. Kulomzina,[3] 'I pricked up my ears and plunged with regained strength into the fray of academic activity.'

On arriving in Petersburg, Borodin went to a gathering of his composer friends at Rimsky-Korsakov's. It was impossible for him at this time to take any active part in music; there are ironical remarks to this effect in a letter to Catherine, dated 25 September 1874[4]: 'They all played something in turn: A. P. some of his works and the sonata "Adieu, Absence et Retour"; Ira did the F minor Sonata of Beeth[oven], op. 2; and Idka the first movement of the C sharp minor Sonata. But as for me, I did nothing.'[5]

But very shortly, after an interval of four years, Borodin's thoughts turned once more to the opera *Prince Igor*. According to Stassov,[6] one of Borodin's favourite pupils, Doctor V. A. Shonorov, who had come to Petersburg that autumn, talked him into doing this. Doctor Shonorov was a great admirer of Borodin's music, and the first thing he asked was how *Igor* was getting along; when he learnt that Borodin had given up all idea of writing this opera, he instantly began pleading with him to reconsider his decision, and in the end Borodin acquiesced. If we can accept this story, then we ought to consider it probable that Borodin himself at this time was entertaining the idea of recommencing work on his opera. It could well have been the impressions remaining

[1] There is a mention of this instrument in Borodin's correspondence with A. P. Dianin over the summer of 1878.

[2] I was told of this waltz, together with many other details of Borodin's stay in Rozhnovo, by M. A. and I. A. Kulomzin, the sons of E. A. Kulomzina. The waltz was called *Kuchki*. (*Letters*, Vol. II, Letter 283, note 6, p. 242.)

[3] *Letters*, Vol. II, Letter 256, p. 80.

[4] Ibid., Letter 257, p. 81.

[5] These were the people living in his flat at the time and using his piano. A. P. are the initials of A. P. Dianin; Ira is Irinarkh Polikhronyevich Skvortsov, Idka is Iraida Alexandrovna Skvortsova.

[6] His book on Borodin, p. 41.

from his tour of ancient Russian cities the previous summer, and perhaps even the songs he heard there, that provided the impetus in this direction. However that may be, on 15 October 1874 Borodin made it clear to Stassov that 'he was starting work again on his opera *Prince Igor*'.

Stassov goes on: 'We spent almost the entire evening working out how he might be able to utilize the parts of *Mlada* that had originally been intended for *Igor*.[1] . . . Borodin did a fair amount of playing, and got so worked up that, when we[2] left at half past two in the morning, he came with us almost as far as Kirochnaya Street despite the rain, and talked the whole way about his opera. Tonight [18 October] I am taking round the history of Karamzin and, *The Lay of Igor's Campaign*[3] . . .'

This upsurge of interest in *Igor* was accompanied by all the usual disorder he had to put up with in the autumn and winter after Catherine's return on 2 November.[4] It meant going back once again to the mode of life that did so much harm to his health and interfered so disastrously with his work.

It appears that during this period he preferred to concentrate on those parts of the opera where the action takes place in the Polovtsian camp. It is very likely that his chief interest at this time was in the possibility of getting hold of some authentic Polovtsian melodies. In connection with this, he approached the ethnographer V. N. Mainov, on Stassov's recommendation, and asked him if he knew anything about Polovtsian music. Mainov told him that according to the celebrated Hungarian scholar and traveller, P. Hunfalvy: 'The Polovtsians in Hungary today are in no way different from the rest of the Magyars, except for a few archaisms in their speech. . . . Thus there is no need for you to bother looking for Polovtsian songs, for they are identical with Magyar, but if you like I will send you a few pieces.' After this quotation from Hunfalvy's letter, Mainov added: 'Since Konchak ruled both the Polovtsi and the Kumans (the latter for certain were Turks, that is, Altai Turks who are related to our Chuvash, so Hunfalvy says in his letter) then Polovtsian music (if you

---

[1] This seems to refer primarily to the motive of the Chorus of Idol Worshippers from *Mlada*.

[2] Stassov and Shcherbachev.

[3] Letter to D. V. Stassov, extracts of which are printed in V. Karenin's book on Stassov, Part II, p. 418.

[4] There is the following entry in Catherine's expense book: [18] 74 Left Peter[sburg] 19 June. I arrived with Alex. Pavl. [Dianin] on 2 November.'

will kindly permit me my profane opinion) must have consisted of a mixture of purely eastern motifs (and nothing like those graceful melodies of the kind that Glinka and Balakirev have written, the Persian kind, since the Altai Turks had not yet reached this stage; we have evidence of this in their descendants the Chuvash, Bashkirs and Kirghiz); these must have consisted of guttural, strident sounds, and subsequently have served as a basis for the great mass of czardas and other dances that we find in Liszt and elsewhere.'[1]

It seems that, after reading this letter, Borodin decided he must have the Polovtsian songs mentioned by Hunfalvy. With a view to acquiring them, Stassov approached Mainov, and the latter sent him a list of Hungarian folk-song collections, citing at the same time the title of a special collection of Polovtsian songs.[2] We do not know as yet to what extent Borodin made use of actual Polovtsian tunes, but the information passed on to him by Mainov was undoubtedly taken into account.

The first number for his opera, which he wrote in the winter of 1874–5, was the Polovtsian March; this was inspired by a reading of a description of an execution ceremony in pre-reformed Japan. On the original manuscript is given the date 16 December 1874. This was followed a little later by Konchakovna's Arioso and the Chorus of Polovtsian Women, and in addition the preliminary sketches of the Polovtsian Dances.

Finally, during the winter or early spring of that year, and certainly not later than 15 April,[3] Borodin composed 'Yaroslavna's Lament', though not in exactly the same form in which it has come down to us. While working on his opera, he not only composed completely new material, but also did over again some of the music he still had from *Mlada*, *The Tsar's Bride*, and other things. He used parts of the Finale of *Mlada* for his 'Lament'.

In addition to this, Borodin was probably devoting some time to his First String Quartet. As I have already pointed out, it is not as yet possible to ascertain the precise date on which he first had the idea of writing this quartet, but we know from Borodin's own words that the

[1] Undated letter to Borodin. See Russian edition of my book *Borodin*, 2nd ed., pp. 200–1.

[2] This letter of V. N. Mainov to Stassov is reproduced in Karenin's book, Part II, p. 415, and in the text of my book *Borodin*, Russian 2nd ed., p. 338.

[3] This is learnt from references to the composition of 'Yaroslavna's Lament' in Borodin's letter to L. I. Karmalina, dated 15 April 1875 (*Letters*, Vol. II, Letter 279, p. 88).

sketches were completed by April 'much to the horror of Stassov and Modest [Mussorgsky].'[1] All this intensive work on *Igor* did not interfere with his scientific work; in the years 1874 and 1875 Borodin had ready for publication a treatise entitled 'On Nitrosoamarine'. It is also worth noting that he brought out, early in 1875, a piano-duet edition of the First Symphony.

No account of Borodin's life at this period would be complete without taking into consideration the unfavourable conditions under which he had to live, and at the same time to work. In addition to having to put up with Catherine's peculiar ways, Borodin had to face complications in his work and professorial duties of a rather unusual nature; Zinin had at long last retired, and Borodin was saddled with all the administrative work. Nevertheless, despite almost insuperable difficulties of every kind, Borodin took over the responsibility for the laboratory and even managed to have it enlarged; now, according to A. P. Dianin, 'anyone who wished could work in the laboratory.' As well as this, Borodin felt it was his duty to keep an eye on the women's medical courses, and to help in running charity concerts in aid of impoverished students.

The Academy was going through a very difficult period. It was proposed that the Ministry of Education take over control; this necessitated a large number of administrative changes and created a good deal of confusion. There is hardly any wonder then that Borodin sometimes complained of having insufficient time for his music. 'Even if I do have free time occasionally,' he wrote to L. I. Karmalina on 15 April 1875, 'there is never any time when I am free from worry; I must have calm if I am to get on with my music. My mind is full of other things.'[2]

As far as music was concerned, Borodin placed all his hopes in the coming summer. And actually, the summer of 1875 proved to be one of his most fruitful periods from the point of view of composition. As always, the Borodins were very casual about arrangements for their summer holiday. They had originally intended to spend their vacation once again in the district of Suzdal on an estate not far from Rozhnovo; it would have been impossible for them to stay as before in Rozhnovo without carrying out major repairs on the dilapidated house they had lived in the previous year.

Borodin wrote to Mrs Kulomzina to explain matters: 'Owing to the fact that I have to be back in Petersburg some time in the summer to

[1] *Letters*, Vol. II, Letter 279, p. 89.   [2] Ibid., p. 88.

see to the major repairs which were going to be carried out on my laboratory and study, I have been compelled to drop the idea of travelling very far, and have decided to stay in Moscow.'[1]

Borodin reached Moscow on 16 June, and spent a few days with Catherine's relatives (the Stupishins and Protopopovs). It was at this time that he wrote the treatise on nitrosoamarine, mentioned above; he also went to a good deal of trouble arranging accommodation in a flat belonging to N. I. Stukovenko, the head doctor at the Gloitsyn Hospital, which was vacant for the summer. Their friend N. T. Zakharov, the hospital inspector, and K. K. Zenger, the head doctor's assistant, made arrangements for the flat to be let to them and even provided the necessary furniture. Catherine's mother, Ekaterina Alexeevna, lived in the same block. The Borodins moved into this palatial and comfortable apartment (there were twenty-one rooms at their disposal) on about 20 June. Towards the end of the month they even had a piano.[2]

The Golitsyn Hospital was an old building and was surrounded by a large garden; it was not very far from their beloved Neskuchny Park and the Moscow River. Borodin spent a happy and peaceful summer there, and found there the 'spiritual calm' which he felt was so necessary for him if he was to do any composing. He put the finishing touches to the piano arrangement of the B minor Symphony, did some further work on the A major Quartet, and composed a whole string of fresh additions to his opera, including Konchak's arias, the Polovtsian Dances,[3] and the Chorus in the First Act (Vladimir Galitsky's carousal). He also sketched the outline of Igor's arias, the themes and harmonies of which were taken from *Mlada* (they are to be found also at the beginning of the overture to *Prince Igor*).

This period, which had proved to be such a god-send as far as *Igor* was concerned, came to an end about the middle of September when Borodin was obliged to return to Petersburg to resume his usual duties at the Academy. Catherine stayed behind in the Stukovenko's flat, where she spent the rest of the autumn.

When Borodin arrived back, he found his flat in utter chaos as

---

[1] Letter of 29 July 1875 (*Letters*, Vol. II, Letter 283, p. 93).

[2] All the details relating to the arrangements of the Borodin's flat in the Golitsinskaya hospital are taken from the unpublished letters of Catherine to A. P. Dianin which were written during the summer of 1875.

[3] The sketches of the Polovtsian Dances were made some time before this. See the letter of 15 April 1875 where he writes: 'I have composed . . . something for the dances (in an oriental manner, for the Polovtsi were an Eastern people).'

repairs were in full swing. On 19 September 1875 he wrote: 'Up till now I have just about managed to put up with the loathsome and disgusting state of everything around me here, but I don't think I can go on much longer. . . . There's dust and lime everywhere; the stench is unbearable; there are howling draughts from the corridor where the wall has been knocked out . . . and the noise, you simply can't get away from it! And as for our rooms and hall, you would think there had just been a fire; our furniture . . . looked as though it had been hauled from a blaze. . . . You simply couldn't move. Everything was covered in a thick layer of dust, and there presiding over everything was Alexandra Andreevna, like Marius amid the ruins of Carthage, muffled up to the eyes in shawls and dispensing the secrets of the art of midwifery.'[1]

There is little wonder that, things being as they were, he quickly became inundated with hundreds of irksome trivialities. All the same, he still found time to see his composer friends. The composition he had achieved during the summer won their full approval. 'I must admit, I never expected the music I wrote in Moscow would create such a sensation,' Borodin wrote a few days later, 'Korsinka is delighted, and so is Modest; Ludmila Ivanova has invited the Petrovs specially to hear them. What surprised me most of all was their enthusiasm for the first Chorus [of the First Scene of Act One]. We even sang it with all the parts, and, I say it in all humility, they found it terrifically effective, dazzling even, and cleverly put over from a dramatic point of view. Konchak, it goes without saying, went down just as well as I had hoped, apart from a few awkward places—purely vocal—(which will need to be put right). The setting is fine. Korsinka especially likes it. Both he and Modest are frightfully pleased with the savage, oriental dancing which I wrote last of all in Moscow. Do you remember the lively bit in 6/8? Of course it's only a repetition by the chorus over and over again; I wrote it like this to get it over as quickly as possible, as it was the last, so that I wouldn't have to put it off till another time.'[2]

For various reasons, Stassov did not get a chance to hear Borodin's new compositions until much later. This provoked two letters from him; in the letter of 17 September Stassov wrote, amongst other things: 'Yesterday evening . . . the following people were at Rimsky-Korsakov's: Nikolai Adreevich [Rimsky-Korsakov], Nadezhda

---

[1] *Letters*, Vol. II, Letter 285, p. 97.
[2] Ibid., pp. 98–99.

Nikolaevna [his wife], Cui, myself, and someone whose name I don't know [Shchiglev].

'The fact of the matter is that a certain fellow by the name of Borodin, who is adored by all of us (especially me), promised to be there that evening at Rimsky-Korsakov's with his latest compositions, but *Prince Igor*—the Devil knows how much we are interested in it— was suddenly snatched from our grasp.

'But we all waited for you and went our separate ways, our heads cast down. Two misses in two days! The day before yesterday you weren't there (I went with Shcherbachev) and yesterday you forgot your promise!!'

In a letter dated 19 September, Stassov expressed an equally impatient desire to hear the new sections of *Igor*: 'Once again we waited for you yesterday evening and . . . we waited impatiently.

'I have a horror that I shall never get a chance to hear "Igor", and the Roman [Rimsky-Korsakov] goes into ecstasies about it!'[1] Finally, on 21 September Borodin visited Stassov; he mentioned this to his wife:

'I was at Stassov's. It goes without saying, he was just bubbling over with enthusiasm, and quite beside himself; and do you know what he liked most of all? That wild, Lesgian-like dance which I composed at the very end of my stay in Moscow. It's just as I had expected.'[2]

On 24 September his new additions to his opera were performed at L. I. Shestakova's, and the singers, the Petrovs, were there; 'they were very favourably disposed' towards these fragments of his opera, 'especially towards Konchak, who was always a great success.' The Petrovs prophesied 'a great future on the stage' for *Igor*.[2]

Heartened by the general enthusiasm for his new compositions Borodin tried to find time, even in Petersburg in the dreadful autumn of 1875, to write something more for his opera, notwithstanding 'all kinds of petty annoyances.' He had second thoughts about 'certain parts of Yaroslavna's Lament' and 'made alterations' accordingly, but everything in Petersburg was against him and his hectic routine soon put an end to this. The year 1875–6 was just as difficult for Borodin as the preceding one. In addition to all his other duties, he gradually became involved in the 'Society for the Assistance of Students attending the Women's Medical Courses', at which he was elected treasurer. His academic duties were thus not lessened.

[1] *Borodin*, Russian 2nd ed., p. 201.
[2] Letter dated 26 September (*Letters*, Vol. II, Letter 286, p. 101).

It was very gratifying to Borodin that the entire Balakirev circle, and others associated with it, were unanimous in their enthusiasm for his new opera. The unanimity gave him fresh encouragement, but surprised him a little in view of the divergent opinions which were becoming apparent at this time within the circle.[1]

'If people think we are on bad terms with Balakirev, then they are mistaken. We are all as deeply fond of him as ever, and spare no pains in trying to maintain our former relations with him.[2] ... And as for the rest of us, we continue to take an interest in each other's latest compositions. If it so happens that any one of our works is not completely to the liking of the rest, what is so extraordinary about that? Tastes and opinions are bound to differ. And besides, even in the case of an individual, his tastes and opinions will also be different at various stages of his development. There's nothing you can do to alter this.'[3]

This deep and accurate understanding of the differences within the group, and his own excellent relations with all the members without exception, together with a favourable response on their part to his compositions, made Borodin at this time the unifying factor in the circle. In this respect, he could have become the true 'leader of the new Russian school' (as musicians in the rest of Europe later actually called him), if music had been his sole interest.

Borodin's views on art matured during the time he was working on his opera, and he arrived at certain principles that he intended to incorporate.

'I should point out,' he wrote at this time, 'that in my approach to opera I have always been at variance with many of my friends. A purely recitative style goes against the grain, and doesn't suit me anyway. My leaning is towards aria and cantilena, and not towards recitative at all; although, in the opinion of those who ought to know, I am not too bad at the latter. Not only this, but I am given to the rounder, more perfect, but less restricted kind of form. My whole manner of dealing with operatic material is quite different. As I see it, superfluous detail has no place in opera. Everything should be drawn in bold strokes, as clearly and vividly as is practically possible for voice and orchestra. The voices should take first place, and the orchestra second. How far I shall succeed in my intentions is for

[1] Letter to Stassov dated 19 October 1875 (*M. P. Mussorgsky, Letters and Documents*, ed. A. N. Rimsky-Korsakov, 1932, p. 327).

[2] In the winter of 1875-6, Balakirev was showing signs of a musical reawakening, and started composing again (with a view to finishing *Tamara*).

[3] Letter to L. I. Karmalina dated 1 June 1876 (*Letters*, Vol. II, Letter 308, p. 108).

others to judge, of course, but I can say this much: my opera will be nearer in spirit to *Ruslan* than to the *Stone Guest*.'[1]

It is interesting to note that these views on opera are in keeping with those embodied in Rimsky-Korsakov's *May Night*, which is chronologically nearest to this letter of Borodin's. The *May Night* is highly melodic and consists of concerted numbers throughout. There is much in common between the two great masters, even if they evolved separately. The link between Borodin and Rimsky-Korsakov in the years 1875 and 1876 was evident in other respects. Borodin took an active part in helping Rimsky-Korsakov to compile Russian folk-songs. It was through Borodin that he came across a number of ancient songs;[2] and Borodin himself began to make himself more widely acquainted with Russian folk-song. This was reflected in the last number of *Igor* to be composed, the Chorus of Praise. As Borodin himself tells us, this chorus was composed during the Christmas holidays, when he was obliged to stay in bed with influenza. This Chorus, in accordance with Stassov's scenario, was originally to have been the epilogue to the opera, and had been conceived on rather a large scale.

In the middle section of the Chorus (beginning with the words 'From the Mighty Don') the following two bars:

are undoubtedly a variation on a part of the tune of 'The Vorobiev Heights' which appears in Prokunin's collection, edited by Tchaikovsky.[3]

Shortly after writing this wonderful Chorus, Borodin gave a hand in organizing a benefit concert in aid of needy students at the Academy. Miss Miropolskaya introduced him to S. I. Taneev, who offered his services as pianist on this occasion. Borodin and Taneev remained close friends from that time onwards.

The Chorus of Praise did not take Borodin long to orchestrate and

---

[1] *Letters*, Vol. II, Letter 308, p. 109.

[2] Borodin personally assisted in the transcription of A. E. Vinogradova's song 'Zvon-Kolokol', and also the songs of Catherine and A. P. Dianin.

[3] It is not impossible that Borodin used a number of variants of this song earlier in the same opera, in 'Yaroslavna's Lament'. But in any case there is no doubt that he made use of it for the theme of the Andante of the First Quartet.

was ready for performance at a concert in the Free School on 23 March 1876 which was conducted by Rimsky-Korsakov. The Chorus received a huge ovation, and was warmly acclaimed by Stassov and Cui.

Cui deemed this Chorus 'unsurpassable', and said he thought 'the magnificent themes were brilliantly worked out and developed. The harmonization was original and beautiful throughout, and powerful too.' He liked the end of the Chorus in particular. He even had praise for the orchestration; the only fault he could find was some slight misuse of the woodwind. At the same time he expressed doubts as to whether the Chorus would be successful on the stage, and could not help but laugh at the archaic-sounding names of Igor's confederates: 'What solemn names these people have! I am deeply indebted to Mr. Borodin for bringing ethnographical material into his programme, but God forbid that he should bring it into the music as well.'[1]

In a letter of 30 March 1876, Stassov described Borodin's Chorus of Praise as 'a work of genius', and at the same time came down heavily on Cui's article; Stassov was angered by the latter's coldly formalistic approach to the Chorus, particularly the allusion to the ethnographical element and his reference to the weak middle section of the Chorus. But actually Stassov was misrepresenting Cui, who merely thought that it might seem too mild on the stage and not sufficiently heroic.

The composer himself felt that the success of his Chorus imposed upon him a moral obligation to carry on and finish the opera. In a letter to Mrs Karmalina he wrote: 'The Chorus of Praise was performed at the Free School and was a great success. It had a special significance as far as the fate of my opera is concerned. But I ought to point out that on the whole I am a composer in search of oblivion; and I'm always slightly ashamed to admit that I compose. That's not too difficult to understand. For the others it's a simple matter, a vocation, an end in life; but for me it's a recreation, an idle pastime which provides diversion from my real work, my work as professor and scientist.... It is for this reason that, although I want to carry my opera through to the end, I nevertheless have qualms about getting too involved, lest it should tell on my other activities. But now that my Chorus has been performed, everybody knows that I am writing an opera. There's no getting away from it; now I shall have to finish the opera whether I want to or not.'[2]

[1] See No. 87 of the *St. Peterburg Gazette*, 28 March 1876, p. 3.
[2] Letter dated 1 June 1876, p. 109.

The Borodins spent the summer of 1876 at a place not very far from Moscow. They arrived in Moscow at the end of May and shortly after moved on to the village of Staraya Ruza,[1] which is quite near the small town of Ruza. They had been invited there by one of Catherine's brother's friends, who was a teacher in the village school there; he had made arrangements for them to stay in the house of the village priest, A. Miroliubov, high above the Moscow River. The Borodins occupied one half of the house, comprising entrance hall, reception-room, drawing-room, study and bedroom. All these tiny apartments were heated by a single stove set right in the centre of the building. The bedroom and entrance-hall were like dark closets. The furniture consisted of three tables, four chairs and one bed.[2]

The countryside around was quite picturesque, but almost treeless. Borodin spent a good deal of time walking and gathering mushrooms, which grew in abundance there. He was passionately fond of doing this and took a special delight in paring them from the stalk with a pocket-knife. If one of his fellow-gatherers found a mushroom, he would exclaim: 'Don't touch, please don't touch it! Let me cut it myself, or you'll damage the stalk.'

We have very little concrete information about Borodin's musical activity during the summer, apart from his rather vague remark: 'Only in the summer could I make the slightest progress.'[3] According to Catherine, Yaroslavna's recitative, 'How dreary is everything around me', was composed before the end of the summer.

'September is already here, and Alexander had to get back to Petersburg', writes Catherine. 'He set off, but was held up by the Moscow River, which suddenly and quite unexpectedly burst its banks. To cap everything, a strong wind blew up, and made it impossible to get across. Alexander waited some time on the bank. Just there the bank is very steep, and he had a dismal view of the raging torrent, and the sad grey waves leaping and surging below him. So he came back, and was not sorry to be able to spend an extra day with us. But he couldn't shake off the impression of that sombre scene. He sat down at the piano, and the whole of Yaroslavna's Arioso "How dreary is everything around me" simply poured out of him.'[4]

It is possible that other parts of the Fourth Act were composed not

[1] Nine versts from the railway station of Shelkovka on the White Russian-Baltic Railway.
[2] These details are taken from a letter of A. Mirolyubov to Borodin.
[3] Letter to L. I. Karmalina dated 19 January 1877 (*Letters*, Vol. II, Letter 347, p. 122).
[4] Stassov's book on Borodin, p. 42.

long after this, namely, the Duet of Yaroslavna and Igor, and the Final Chorus in G major. It is more likely however that these belong to the period immediately following his return from Ruza to Petersburg.[1] During the autumn his work on *Igor* proceeded by fits and starts, since he had learned on his return that the B minor Symphony was due to be performed early in the new year at a concert of the Musical Society, with Napravnik conducting. The orchestration was already complete,[2] but the parts had to be gone through and checked. When he came to do this, however, he discovered that the originals of the first movement and Finale of the symphony were missing; he 'must have shoved them away somewhere'. He was therefore obliged to reorchestrate these movements. Owing to inflammation of his leg, Borodin was unable to go to work, and thus managed to complete this task.

About this time also, the first edition of the piano-duet version of the B minor Symphony appeared. On 18 January 1877, Borodin presented Marya Dobroslavina with an autographed copy of this work, bearing the following inscription[3]:

> 'A gift from a friend to a friend;
> The printed harmony
> Of his Second Symphony
> Your protegé dares to commend.'

At the end of January, Borodin found himself in a position 'that no Professor of the Imperial Academy of Physicians had ever been in before'. His two symphonies were due to be performed in the same week. But in actual fact, this never happened. Rimsky-Korsakov did conduct a performance of the E flat Symphony at a concert of the Free School on 25 January; but it was not until a month later, on 26 February, that his B minor Symphony received its first performance, under Napravnik, at the fifth concert of the Russian Musical Society season.

It is a well-known fact that the B minor Symphony contains some

---

[1] The G major chorus was performed at a concert of the Free Music School on 27 February 1879. As it could not possibly have been written in the summer of either 1877 or 1878, it must therefore belong to the autumn of 1876.

[2] It seems that the orchestration of the B minor Symphony was completed not later than December 1875, and possibly even earlier, some time during the previous summer.

[3] Taken from M. V. Dobroslavina's reminiscences. I have a copy of this inscription, made by A. P. Dianin (see *Letters*, Vol. II, p. 121).

rather heavy scoring, particularly the Scherzo, which Napravnik found he could not take at the proper tempo. To make matters worse, there was a large number of people at the concert who were unfavourably disposed to the music of 'the Handful' as a whole, and, according to Dianin, who was in the audience, 'there was a regular hullabaloo; you would have thought you were at a cat's concert'.[1]

The composer, by nature sensitive, retiring, and lacking in self-confidence, was terribly upset by the symphony's failure. His friends tried to console him; Glinka's sister sent him a very heart-warming letter, in which she prophesied a glorious future for the Symphony and compared its poor reception with that of *Ruslan*, which was a fiasco at the first performance.[2]

The spring of 1877 brought nothing new with it in the way of science or music as far as Borodin was concerned. He rested all his hopes upon the coming summer, when he thought he would be able to make great strides with his opera. In a letter to L. I. Karmalina, dated 19 January 1877, he wrote:

'I am an incurable poet at heart, and I am cherishing the hope of one day getting to the end of my opera, though I can't help laughing sometimes. The work is progressing slowly but surely, albeit at somewhat irregular intervals. . . . Perhaps it will all come to nothing. I would like to have it finished by next season, but this seems too much to hope for.'[3] It is apparent from this that Borodin was hoping to be able to write the remainder of his opera between February and September 1877 (for the most part, of course, in the summer months), although this amounted almost to two whole acts.

But his calculations were completely upset by complications arising during the summer which he had not foreseen the previous winter. It turned out that he had to make the necessary arrangements for two of his favourite students to spend some time abroad, and this disrupted his plans. One of these students was Dianin, whom he called 'his son in spirit if not in flesh'; the other was M. Y. Goldstein. Both these young students had started out in medicine, but under the influence of the fascinating lectures given by Borodin and Zinin they had decided to specialize in chemistry. They had come up against a great deal of opposition to their studies in Russia, and had decided to

---

[1] Taken from an unpublished article by A. P. Dianin on the thirtieth anniversary of the composer's death.
[2] See my *Borodin*, Russian 2nd ed. p. 208.
[3] *Letters*, Vol. II, Letter 347, p. 122.

read for their degrees in Germany without more ado. Borodin was intent on helping them, and, having been given several commissions by the Academy which necessitated a journey abroad, he accompanied them personally as far as Jena.

He arranged for Catherine to go to Moscow, finished off his various end-of-term jobs, and on 13 June the three of them set out together from Petersburg. After a short stay in Berlin they went on to Jena, arriving there on June 15. Borodin had to stay on for some time in Jena waiting for the Professor of Chemistry to recover from an illness, as he wanted to see him personally to discuss his 'boys'' doctorate examinations and dissertations.

He happened to read by chance in a local newspaper (June 30) that a concert of church music was to be given in Jena cathedral, and heard by some means or other that Liszt might possibly be coming specially from Weimar to hear it. Borodin had for a long time been intent on seeing Liszt in person, one of the reasons being that the famous maestro was sympathetic towards 'the new Russian music'; Borodin knew about this from Cui, who had brought word back from Bayreuth to this effect in 1876. It was his natural shyness that made him 'keep procrastinating and putting off' his proposed visits on such occasions. But this time he overcame his hesitation and on the very next day (1 June) he set off for Weimar.

After locating Liszt's house and inquiring about his visiting hours, he went off to see the sights of Weimar to fill in the time. He very much admired the houses where Goethe and Schiller had lived, and the memorial erected in their honour, which the German humorists called 'Schultze und Müller', and finally arrived at Liszt's house.

The great musician seemed very glad to see Borodin, and the latter wrote to his wife about his visit.[1] When Borodin modestly remarked that he was 'strictly a Sunday musician', Liszt said: 'Aber Sonntag ist immer ein Feiertag. . . . You have good cause for celebration. . . . Never be afraid of being original; remember that exactly the same advice was given to Beethovens and Mozarts in their time, and they would never have become great if they had taken it into their heads to follow such advice.'

Liszt had nothing but praise for the B minor Symphony, when Borodin showed it to him; he found it 'excellent' and even performed the Scherzo in its piano-duet version (with the pianist Zarembsky) at one of his musical matinées. He saw that Borodin had 'a colossal musical

[1] *Letters*, Vol. II, Letters 366–70, pp. 130–60.

technique'. He made him promise to go on composing, and to ignore unfavourable comments and people who could not understand: 'Go on working, even if your works are not performed or published, even if they get bad reviews. Believe me, they will make their own way, through their own merit; you are immensely gifted and most original.' Liszt emphasized that he was being completely sincere: 'I am not merely paying you compliments; I am an old man, and it would not become me to say other than what I think.'

During the course of July, Borodin met Liszt and some of his pupils on more than one occasion: on 2 July in Jena, and at Liszt's own house in Weimar on 9, 14, 15, and 21 July.

He took his final leave of Liszt on 21 July, and made his way to Heidelberg, travelling via Marburg and Bonn (where he probably met Kekulé); he arrived at the end of July. From Heidelberg he wrote Catherine a most poignant letter, full of reminiscences of the time when they first met. This letter clearly reveals how young and light at heart Borodin had remained.

As they came nearer to Heidelberg, Borodin 'became so excited, and so worked up that I did not even notice that it was already dusk. . . . I was taking in everything, every hillock, every lane, every house, every village—everything brought back at once memories of those happy times. . . . I pressed my face against the window to hide my tears, and gripped the handle of my umbrella to prevent myself from crying like a small baby.'[1]

When he arrived at the Badischer Hof Hotel Borodin 'took a room there, and when I was alone I couldn't control myself (incurable sinner) from crying like a child. . . . I can't describe to you the torrent of feelings which engulfed me.'

He visited those very places where, seventeen years before, he had strolled with his fiancée. 'I found it difficult to believe,' he wrote, 'that I was not really in a complete dream when I was wandering around these familiar places. I actually touched the walls of the houses, and the door-handles of those porchways we used to know so well.'

After spending two or three days in Heidelberg wandering about the place and visiting various people, Borodin went on to Munich, where he saw his old friend Professor Erlenmeyer. On 7 August he returned to Jena. He finally settled all his students' affairs in two or three days, and departed for Russia. After staying for a very short time in Vilna with his two brothers who lived there, he continued his

[1] Letter of 30 July 1877 (*Letters*, Vol. II, Letter 371).

journey to the village of Davydovo in Vladimir Province, where his wife had been staying since 24 June as the guest of A. P. Dianin's father, Pavel Afanasievich Dianin. Borodin reached Davydovo on 5/17 August.

Borodin was quite delighted with this peaceful spot set amidst picturesque and varied surroundings. 'I can't tell you how delighted I am with Davydovo,' he wrote to Dianin. 'How lovely it is here! What wonderful coppices, woods, pine forests, meadows and lakes there are here! And what air! From my very first day here the place took a hold of me and completely drove thoughts of abroad out of my mind. If it were not for the material proof that I had been abroad, I would have sworn that it had all been a dream. . . . I often think of you, my dear Alexandrushka, when we go out looking for mushrooms (it's rather too early yet, though) as we used to do in Rozhnovo and Staraya Ruza. . . . The weather couldn't be better, and I can really *feel* the summer, I can feel it in my bones.'[1]

Shortly after his arrival, around 13 August to be precise, Borodin worked on his A major Quartet. On 18 August Catherine wrote to Dianin: 'Sasha has got down to work on his quintet (*sic*), and goes on playing from morning till night. He has propped his writing desk up against the crockery cupboard right beside the piano (in the second room), and there he is busy writing.' Apart from his work on the quartet, we have no further information as to what he was composing during the summer of 1877; in particular there is no mention of any work on *Igor*.[2]

His holiday in Davydovo seems to have done him a great deal of good. 'It's wonderful here in Davydovo, perfectly delightful!' he wrote in a letter to his Jena students, on 24 August. 'I have been in quite a number of country places in my time, but I can confidently say that I have never come across a more healthy spot. And as for the woods and pine forests you could never get tired of walking in them and drinking them in, even if you spent the rest of your life here.' Also in this letter, he told them how he had got together a small chorus on the occasion of the departure of Nikolai Dianin: 'We sang the Hunter's Farewell,[3] Katya sang the first tenor part, and I sang the

---

[1] Letter of 13 August (O.S.) 1877 (*Letters*, Vol. II, Letter 373).

[2] In view of the thematic relationship between the Andante of the A major Quartet and the *a cappella* Chorus from the Fourth Act of *Igor*, there is a strong likelihood that both these compositions were written simultaneously, but this theory is contradicted by A. P. Dianin, who says he was in Davydovo when the *a cappella* chorus was being composed. But in 1877, A. P. Dianin spent the whole summer in Jena.

[3] A Chorus by Mendelssohn.

second, Fyodor sang first bass, and Nikolai the second.[1] We sang everything we knew.' These choral exercises were a great pleasure to the local inhabitants, who 'nearly climbed out of their windows' with curiosity.[2]

The Borodins left Davydovo on 16 September. Borodin stayed two days in Moscow at his mother-in-law's and then went on to Petersburg on 19 September, leaving Catherine behind to spend the autumn as usual in Moscow.

On arriving in Petersburg, Borodin immediately set about tidying up his flat which was in the usual mess after the vacation repairs. Until his wife came back a month or so later, he was on his own, but for the two students, Olga Ispolatovsky and Fedor Dianin who were staying there and Lisa, his adopted daughter, who came to stay when she was on holiday from school.

In view of the fact that his private assistant, Alexander Dianin, was away in Germany, Borodin was obliged to spend a great deal of time and energy supervising the students' practicals in the laboratory. Not a little of his time was taken up in visits to the Nikolayevsky Military Hospital (on the Suvorovsky Prospect), where the women's medical courses were now held, after having been transferred there from the Academy of Physicians. He continued to help in raising funds for impecunious students of both sexes, by organizing benefit (charity) concerts, and so forth. Owing to the vast number of matters of every kind that he had to cope with, Borodin made a habit of getting up at six o'clock every morning.

On 22 October Borodin went to Moscow to fetch his wife. They returned to Petersburg on 24 October.

Also at this time Borodin was in correspondence with Turgenev. He asked Turgenev if he would kindly be of assistance to an ex-pupil of his, A. N. Lukanina, who had made her début as writer during the year. In his reply to this letter Turgenev mentioned, in passing, that the B minor Symphony had greatly pleased Viardot, who was now giving it some publicity in Paris. As might be expected this piece of news was very welcome to Borodin, who still had bitter memories of its unfortunate first performance eight months previously.

On her return to Petersburg, Catherine showed some of her friends the letters containing Borodin's accounts of his meetings with Liszt.

---

[1] Nikolai and Fyodor Dianin were Alexander Dianin's brothers.
[2] *Letters*, Vol. II, Letter 374, p. 166.

Stassov thought the descriptions were superb and so clear that he
insisted there and then that certain passages from these letters together
with a copy of Liszt's portrait should appear in the next issue of the
journal *The Bee.* Despite Stassov's frequent insistence, he could not
persuade Borodin to go over the texts of these letters with him for
some considerable time. Towards the end of 1877, or possibly in
the early part of 1878, the following episode took place. What we
know of it is based on a rather vague and incomplete description of
events in Catherine's memoirs. It seems that a young girl fell in love
with Borodin, and it was only with great difficulty that he managed
to keep the whole thing on a platonic basis, or, as his wife puts it,
'in treating her as a daughter.'[1] But it seems as though this episode
acted as an impetus eventually leading to the composition of Prince
Vladimir's Cavatina, belonging to the Second Act of his opera
('slowly the day has died away'). And according to the information
we possess, this was followed shortly after by the Duet between
Prince Vladimir and Konchak's daughter.[2]

It was about this time that Borodin had a new idea for a work
entitled 'Paraphrases'; this was to be a collection of short pieces on a
fixed motif:

Ex. 1

'As far as I can remember,' writes Rimsky-Korsakov, 'it was I who
first had this idea of writing, in conjunction with Borodin, a set of
variations and short pieces on this fixed theme. And I managed to get
Cui and Lyadov interested in the idea too. I seem to remember that
Borodin was at the outset quite opposed to the idea, and preferred
instead to publish a polka he was writing on this theme; but he was
not long in joining us.'[3]

By the early summer of 1878, a fair amount of material had accumulated; and 'Paraphrases' was ready the same year. As regards performances of Borodin's works in the 1877-8 season, a fact worth mentioning
is that a plan was afoot for putting on the First Symphony at the Erfurt
Music Festival. Liszt was behind this, and it was he who prompted

[1] See Catherine's account as given in Stassov's book on Borodin, pp. 42–43.
[2] This may be seen from an examination and comparison of the rough sketches of the
words of the cavatina and the duet, which were preserved in my archives.
[3] Rimsky-Korsakov's memoirs, 3rd ed., p. 211.

K. Riedel, the President of the All-German Musical Society, to write to Bessel asking him for the score. It is clear from Bessel's letter to Borodin, dated 22 April 1878, that this performance was to have taken place in the spring. The manuscript of the symphony was sent off to Riedel, but the work was not actually performed that year.

The Borodins once again spent the summer in Davydovo, and arrived there in June. They stayed with P. A. Dianin until the end of the month. During the early weeks of his summer vacation, Borodin was without a piano; for he had departed from his usual practice of taking his brother-in-law's piano with him, in view of the fact that the owner was not too pleased about the damage to the instrument the previous year. In addition to the usual walks and relaxation, Borodin was quite busy compiling material for an article he was writing about Liszt and himself, which Catherine called 'The Lisztiad'; it was to be based on the correspondence already mentioned, and on a few other sources. But Borodin's *My Memories of Liszt* were not published during his lifetime.

At the end of June 1878, their peaceful life in Davydovo was disrupted by a terrible fire, which gutted part of the village. The fire broke out in a neighbouring village about four o'clock in the morning, and the wind was so strong that the blaze spread very quickly to Davydovo. The Borodins, P. A. Dianin and the rest of the household had barely managed to escape from the house, when it too caught fire and collapsed in flames. Owing to the fierce heat, they had to take refuge in a near-by field, where Catherine had an attack of agoraphobia. Before morning, Borodin and the Dianin brothers managed to find temporary shelter for Catherine and the servants in a neighbouring village. As for Borodin and Alexander Dianin, they spent the night sleeping in coffins which were stored in a shed by the church porch. This was indeed a weird state of affairs, but Borodin despite everything never lost his sense of humour: 'I'd never have thought, Shashenka, that I would ever have to shake down for the night in a place of eternal rest.'

On 30 June Borodin made a trip to Moscow where he bought a Sturtzwage piano at Kampe's store for a hundred roubles. It was on this piano that Borodin composed much of the music to *Igor*, and all his later works. After spending several days in the neighbouring village of Filyandino, the Borodins rented a place in the undamaged part of Davydovo with a peasant woman named Volodine. Here Borodin finished work on his article of reminiscences about Liszt. During the first few weeks Borodin and Catherine composed a poem about the village night-watchman and his dog; they used to sing this humorous ballad as a chorus to music improvised by Borodin.

After the terrifying night of the fire, Catherine was afraid to go to bed at night, and kept everyone else in the house up as well. They were allowed to go to bed at dawn, and only after some peasant-woman whom she nicknamed 'the stately woman', had gone by the house on her way to milk a cow. It was their three adopted daughters who suffered most from these whims of Catherine's.[1] Borodin at least managed to find the opportunity to rest at other times during the day.

The Sturtzwage piano he had bought in Moscow was eventually delivered on July 16, and Borodin got down to work without delay. We have, unfortunately, no precise information about his work during the summer of 1878. But in one of Catherine's unpublished letters to Alexander Dianin, dated 28 July, she reports that 'Sasha goes on playing till two in the morning', and there is also a mention of some outstandingly beautiful music he had recently begun to write. This must have been the music to a ballad, although we do not know which, for Catherine confines herself to say that the words seemed very suitable, but that she could not make up her mind as to whether she would suggest a text of her own choice or not. Borodin himself is rather sceptical about his music at this period. In a letter to Alexander Dianin, dated 30 July 1878, he describes his mode of passing the time as follows:

'If you want to know what else I do, apart from my service to Apollo which between ourselves is rather slack just now, I dip into the [chemical] journals, gather mushrooms and, for exercise, I occasionally take on the kind of agricultural work I think I can manage; for example, I do some hay-making, help with the loading of sheaves, threshing, and carrying straw. As a rule I do the sort of jobs usually given to tiny boys and girls not yet experienced in working in the fields'.[2]

But a short time after this, in the early part of August, his 'service to Apollo' took a more serious turn; he composed the elaborate choral scene (Prince Galitsky's feast) and the 'princely song' for

---

[1] During the summer of 1878, the Borodins had three girls staying with them—E. G. Balaneva, E. A. Guseva, and Ganya Litvinenko, who was adopted by Catherine's mother. Ganya finally stayed with the Borodins until 1884.

[2] *Letters*, Vol. III, Letter 418, p. 42.

Skula and Eroshka, which form part of the first scene of the First Act of *Prince Igor*. This composition marked the beginning of a great creative upsurge in Borodin. Catherine tells us how he used to go on playing till three in the morning.[1] Borodin himself wrote[2]: 'I am already anticipating Stassov's hum of approval, and a kiss from Mussorgsky. This scene has turned out very well indeed, both as regards the music and, I trust, the staging as well. If the performance is satisfactory, it should have plenty of sparkle and movement.'

On 12 August Borodin went to Moscow for three days and took with him E. A. Protopopov's adopted daughter Ganya Litvinenko, who had been staying with him for the summer; from there he sent his two adopted daughters on to Petersburg.

The Borodins left Davydovo early in September, and Borodin himself made straight for Petersburg; whereas his wife stayed behind as usual in Moscow, and did not leave there until 25 September.

It was in the winter of 1878 and 1879 that Borodin began what was to be his last piece of scientific research, when he set about constructing a method for determining the nitrogen content of urea. But for the present his work amounted to little more than the supervision of work being carried out by his students and attending meetings of the Chemical Society; the greater part of his time and energy was devoted to lecturing, administration, and attendance at meetings and committees.

After an interval of more than a year, Rimsky-Korsakov again organized a series of concerts at the Free School, which were to take place between 16 and 23 January and 20 and 27 February 1879. The concerts were to include performances of the new fragments of *Igor*, namely, Konchak's Aria, the final G major Chorus from the Fourth Act, and the Polovtsian Dances with chorus. A great deal of time would have to be spent on revising the score and on orchestration, since all three numbers were still no more than rough sketches. In his memoirs, Rimsky-Korsakov has a number of interesting things to say about this.[3]

Work on Konchak's Aria went very well, and he managed to do the entire orchestration himself.[4] But the same could not be said for

---

[1] Letter to A. P. Dianin relating to the beginning of August 1878.
[2] Letter to A. P. Dianin dated 12 August (*Letters*, Vol. III, Letter 419, p. 45).
[3] 3rd ed., pp. 217–18.
[4] Judging by a note from Borodin to Rimsky-Korsakov dated 5 January 1879, the score of Konchak's aria was ready by this date and was sent to Rimsky-Korsakov for inspection.

the Polovtsian Dances and the G major Chorus. On 18 January[1] Rimsky-Korsakov asked Borodin to let him have 'as much of the Polovtsian Dances as is ready (preferably the D major section in 3/4,[2] but if that is not possible, never mind). It would be most convenient if I could have them tomorrow, in time to send them in for copying, which would mean that I could start rehearsing them the following week.'

By the end of January the Chorus of Prisoners ('Fly away on the wings of the wind') was being rehearsed at the Free School under the composer's supervision[3]; but the orchestral scores of this chorus, the Polovtsian Dances, and the Final Chorus were nowhere near completion.

'But in the meantime,' writes Rimsky-Korsakov, 'these works were down on the programme and we had already put in a fair amount of rehearsal on them. It was high time the parts were copied. In despair I reproached Borodin. But he was none too happy either. In the end, I gave up hope of the parts ever being ready, and offered to give him a hand with the orchestration; so he came along in the evening and brought the first part of the score of the dances. The three of us, that is Borodin, Lyadov, and I, took a section each and got on with the orchestration as quickly as possible. To save time we wrote in pencil and not in ink. This kept us going till very late at night. When we had finished Borodin coated the pages of the score with liquid gelatine to prevent the pencil from rubbing out; and to get the pages dried out as quickly as possible, we hung them about my room on lines like washing.[4] The number then was ready and went to the copyist. I orchestrated the Final Chorus almost single-handed, as Lyadov was not available for some reason or other.'[5]

On top of all this, Borodin had to hurry with the score of the B minor Symphony which was to be performed at a Free School concert on 20 February 1879. After its unfortunate first performance under Napravnik, Borodin and Rimsky-Korsakov thought it would be necessary to simplify the orchestration. The latter states that their craze for brass had dwindled, and that Borodin went through the

[1] In a letter dated 18 January 1879, which is preserved in the Stassov archive of the Pushkin house. See the Russian 2nd edition of my book, *Borodin*, p. 213.
[2] I.e. the complete score up to the 'dance of the little boys', *Presto*.
[3] Borodin's letter to Stassov dated 31 January 1879 (*Letters*, Vol. III, Letter 453, p. 54).
[4] Judging by M. M. Ippolitov-Ivanov's reminiscences, Borodin often used gelatine to preserve scores written in pencil (*Fifty Years of Russian Music*, Moscow, 1934, p. 34).
[5] Rimsky-Korsakov's memoirs, 3rd ed., p. 218.

score reducing the preponderance of brass in the Scherzo. As a result of this, Rimsky-Korsakov could manage the Scherzo at the correct tempo. The performance went quite smoothly this time, and the symphony was well received.

After all the troubles the Polovtsian Dances had undergone during composition, that and the Final Chorus were performed on 27 February at the final concert of the Free School season; they were well received.

Evidently Rimsky-Korsakov's persistence had a lasting effect on Borodin. According to a letter which Rimsky-Korsakov wrote to Borodin on 12 April 1879,[1] it appears that Vladimir's Aria was sung by a member of the Bolshoi Theatre company at a concert of the Philharmonic Society in Moscow on 9 April 1879, conducted by Rimsky-Korsakov. 'Bartsal sang beautifully,' writes Rimsky-Korsakov, 'he even took the B flat; the audience called for him again and again.' It was Rimsky-Korsakov who had prevailed on Borodin to knock his Aria into shape for this performance. As I have already mentioned, it was probably composed in December 1877, but did not receive its first performance until this concert.

The 'Paraphrases', composed largely in the previous year, made their appearance in print in the spring of 1879. Stassov had been insisting that Borodin should send Liszt a copy of the first edition. A copy was finally sent in May, and Liszt went into raptures about this collection of short piano pieces and even went so far as to compose his own variation on the fixed theme, a facsimile of which appears in the second edition.[2]

Rimsky-Korsakov had of course been taking considerable interest in the progress of Borodin's opera all along, and could hardly wait to see it finished. So, before he left for his summer retreat in the country, he persuaded Borodin to give him the beginning of the First Act so that he could edit it. This section of the opera had been composed as early as 1875, but was still 'in a complete muddle; some sections needed shortening, others had to be transposed into another key, and the chorus had to be fitted in somewhere. But in the meantime, no progress had been made.' Borodin 'was always on the point of doing something about it, but could never make up his mind; instead he procrastinated and the work was getting nowhere. . . . I wanted to

---

[1] Reproduced on p. 215 of my book *Borodin* (Russian 2nd ed.).

[2] Liszt's letter of 9 June (O.S.) 1879 with its reference to *Paraphrases*, was first published by Stassov in the journal, *The Voice* (1879, No. 277).

help him, and accordingly offered my services as musical secretary—anything in fact that would bring this wonderful opera nearer to completion. After persistent refusals, Borodin gave in and I took the score of this scene away with me on holiday.'[1]

That year, Borodin left Petersburg for Davydovo in the middle of June, and travelled with his two charges, Elizavita Balaneva and Elena Guseva. Catherine followed a few days later but, on the way there, stayed for three weeks at her mother's in Moscow.

On arriving in Davydovo, Borodin stayed with Pavla Dianin, but after a few days took rooms in Mrs. Volodina's house, where he had stayed after the fire in the summer of 1878. He found Dianin's new house, which he had had built since the fire, rather small and cramped, and there were so many people staying in the house that life was not exactly comfortable. In his new rooms Borodin did not find everything ship-shape, though his piano was in good condition, and he came across all kinds of things he had left there the previous year including 'papers, sketches for "Igor", and one thing and another.' He wrote to Catherine complaining that 'the furniture here is very inadequate. All the chairs without exception are broken. There is only one intact, and even this has a hole in the seat; I have even put a board on it instead of a cushion. . . . We all sleep on the floor. The stove isn't working as usual. Today the grandmother and the small children had their dinner at eight o'clock in the morning (!) and nearly choked us with the smell of bread, cabbage-soup and onions; in short, it smelt just like a barracks . . .'[2] In addition to all these discomforts, the weather was unusually rainy and cold; it poured for two weeks on end.'[3]

Despite these minor setbacks, Borodin found the peaceful country life very congenial. On 23 June he wrote to Catherine to say that he was thoroughly rested and 'had really got down to some music'. At that time he was working simultaneously on his opera and on the score of the A major Quartet. In particular, he was making alterations to parts of the scenario of *Igor*, and putting the finishing touches to the Scherzo of the quartet, which earlier had been 'very much in the air'.[4] These modest efforts gradually flared up into powerful inspiration. In the month of July alone, Prince Galitsky's song ('O to regain my

[1] Rimsky-Korsakov's memoirs, 3rd ed., p. 223.
[2] Letter dated 21 June 1879 (*Letters*, Vol. III, Letter 465, p. 60).
[3] E. G. Dianina gave me a vivid description of the depressingly bad weather of 1879 and of the pains Borodin took to prevent the girls becoming bored.
[4] Letter to Catherine dated 1 July 1879 (*Letters*, Vol. III, Letter 467, p. 64).

honour') in the first scene of Act One,[1] and a whole host of numbers for the second scene in this act (including the scenes of Princess Yaroslavna with the young girls of Putivl, and Princess Yaroslavna and Galitsky) were composed. In early August, Borodin began work on the Finale of Act One, and it was about this time that he finished the score of the First Quartet.

While he was staying in Davydovo, Borodin received two letters from Rimsky-Korsakov, who was proposing to make certain changes in the first scene of Act One. It is evident from Borodin's reply to this letter, and also from a comparison of the published text of *Igor* and the manuscript, that he took some of Rimsky-Korsakov's advice seriously and rejected the rest.

He wrote most of this music in the back garden of the house where he was staying, and sat at a tiny table or at a collapsible home-made desk beneath the trees; he called it his 'luxurious and spacious study,' and it had 'a huge green carpet, with magnificent trees dotted about, and the deep blue vault of the sky for a ceiling.'[2]

Borodin decided to incorporate the tune of the song 'About the Sparrow Hills' in the Finale of the First Act. With a view to refreshing his memory, and perhaps also in the hope of coming across a new variant of the tune, he asked the peasants he knew to introduce him to someone who knew this song. One of his Davydovo acquaintances, a peasant from the village of Novskoye called Lapin, brought his cousin Vakhrameevich to see him. He was an old man and he knew many ancient folk-songs; he was able to sing for Borodin the theme he was looking for.[3]

As far as it is possible to judge from information available, the Chorus

---

[1] It is quite clear from Borodin's letters to Stassov and Rimsky-Korsakov dated 4 August 1879 (*Letters*, Vol. III, Letters 469 and 470) that the song of Vladimir Galitsky was written in July 1879. The statement in Rimsky-Korsakov's memoirs that the song was composed at an earlier date is incorrect (*Chronicle of My Musical Life*, 3rd ed., pp. 202 and 217).

[2] Letter to A. P. Dobroslavin dated 15 August 1879 (*Letters*, Vol. III, Letter 472, p. 71).

[3] I was told this personally by I. P. Lapin in 1928, with whom I spent some time when returning to Davydovo from Vladimir. When the conversation turned to Borodin, Lapin told me that the composer had been most anxious to hear the sad old Russian folk-song 'Pro Gori Zhiguli', which he needed 'for a theatrical production'. Lapin accordingly brought his first cousin Vakhrameevich, who was a very old man with an expert knowledge of folk-songs, from the village of Novaya Bykovka. As soon as Vakhrameevich had sung a little of the folk-song, Borodin thanked him, saying that he was satisfied and could remember as much as he would need. He bought the singer a glass of vodka and rewarded him with a 'red' (i.e. a ten-rouble note).

of Boyars and the Scene of Princess Yaroslavna and the Boyars seem to have been composed at this same period.[1] It is also fairly certain that he composed, some time in July or August, the beautiful Chorus of Villagers 'a cappella' in the Fourth Act. This Chorus is also linked thematically with the folk-song 'About the Sparrow Hills'.[2]

The weather took a turn for the better towards the end of the summer; as Borodin put it, 'the autumnal months of June and July gave way to a truly May-like August.' The result was that he could find added enjoyment walking in the idyllic countryside around and enjoying the harmonious blend of colours. This time Borodin was loth to leave Davydovo; it was as though he sensed that he would never come back to this little corner of Vladimir Province to which he had grown so attached. In a letter to A. P. Dobroslavin, the Secretary of the Academy of Physicians, he asked what was the latest date he would have to be back in Petersburg, and wrote: 'Well, that's good-bye to freedom, to the peasant shirts, trousers and top-boots, which I used to walk everywhere in, for miles on end, through forest, thicket and marsh, without the least fear of bumping into professors, students, officials or porters.'[3]

It was unfortunate that, just at the time when his music was streaming forth in great profusion, he had to return to Petersburg even earlier than usual, by 25 August. Immediately on his return, he was overwhelmed by the tasks and problems of one kind or another in store for him; lectures were due to begin on 3 September. He wrote to Catherine: 'I have to attend committee meetings of every conceivable kind, and see to other things as well; in short, I'm up to my neck in everything except my research. And I haven't written a note

[1] My father gave me quite a number of details as to Borodin's activities in Davydovo in 1879, which were fully in accordance with the letters referred to in note 1, p. 109. At the same time, we discovered a number of sketches relating to the choral scene depicting the 'mob' and the rebellion of Vladimir Galitsky, on the reverse side of the rough draft of a letter at the end of the summer of 1880 (*Letters*, Vol. III, note 7 to Letter 592, p. 333). This would seem to imply that the composition of the music to the 'mob' scene also relates to 1880.

[2] With reference to the date of composition of this chorus in the summer of 1879, there is in existence a document preserved in a file of Borodin's entitled, 'Libretto of Igor and Musical Matters'. On one sheet of paper were the words of the chorus of boyars and the chorus of which we are speaking. We have an indirect allusion to the effect that the *a cappella* chorus was written during Borodin's stay in Davydovo provided by A. P. Dianin who was staying in the same village as Borodin in July 1878 (when he was not writing music), and in the summer of 1879.

[3] This letter is found in *Letters*, Vol. III, Letter 472. Borodin's companion during these walks was usually A. P. Dianin.

of music.'[1] Nevertheless, the success he had had with the work on his opera during the summer led to a performance of his new compositions at a Free School concert on 13 November 1879.

Rimsky-Korsakov observed in his memoirs[2] that the items included in this concert were: 'Yaroslavna's Lament', Prince Galitsky's Song, and the Scene of Princess Yaroslavna with young girls of Putivl, all orchestrated this time by Borodin himself.[3] In the last week of December 1879, Borodin was involved in a conference of naturalists and doctors, held on this occasion in Petersburg. Attendance at the meetings of this conference prevented him from hearing a performance of his Prince Galitsky's song at a concert of Russian operatic music. The singer was Fyodor Stravinsky and the performance was a huge success.

[1] *Letters*, Vol. III, Letter 473, p. 73. It is interesting to observe one extraordinary phrase, which, if it is not intended as a joke, is an example of absentmindedness exceptional even for Borodin. He writes; 'When you come, tell me what you need and I will send it to you'. (I.e. 'when you come to St. Petersburg,' where he actually was at the time!).

[2] 3rd ed., p. 229.

[3] It is interesting to note that the chorus of girls including the 5/4 section, 'O have pity on us' was performed at this concert as may be seen from the programme. The incorrect statement taken from Catherine's memoirs, that this chorus was composed in the summer of 1880 in the village of Sokolovo, has been repeated in all the biographies on Borodin. I think it necessary therefore to reproduce the programme of this concert:

TUESDAY, 13 NOVEMBER 1879

PROGRAMME

of the first subscription concert of the Free Music School given under the August patronage of the Crown Prince

I. 8th Symphony (F major) . . . . *Beethoven*
    (*a*) Allegretto vivace e con brio: (*b*) Allegretto scherzando;
    (*c*) Menuetto; (*d*) Allegro vivace.
II. Selections from the opera, *Pskovityanka* (1st performance) . *Rimsky–Korsakov*
    A. Scene in the Pechersky Monastery

Cast:

TSAR IVAN . . . . *Matchinsky*
NIKOLA SALOS . . . . *Stravinsky*
    (*a*) Introduction.
    (*b*) Song of the Wandering beggars.
           [*followed by verses about St. Alexis*]
    (*c*) Entry of the Tsar's hunt.
           [*followed by verses*]
    (*d*) Storm and song of maidens.
           [*followed by verses*]
        B. Cradle Song (from the Prologue)
           [*followed by verses*]
         C. Final Chorus
           [*followed by verses*]

III. Fantasia on a theme from *Rigoletto*, for piano . . . . . *Liszt*
   Played by Mme. T. A. Yakubovich.
IV. Aria from the opera, *The Demon*, by B. Shelei.
   Rendered by Matchinsky.
V. Selections from the opera, *Prince Igor* (1st performance) . . . *Borodin*

Cast:

YAROSLAVNA . . . . *Madame Velinskaya*
PRINCE VLADIMIR . . . . *Stravinsky*
   (*a*) Lament of Yaroslavna.
[followed by text]
   (*b*) Song of Prince Vladimir Galitsky.
[no verses in the programme]
   (*c*) Scene of Yaroslavna and maidens.
[followed by the text]*

VI. Overture to the opera, *Benvenuto Cellini* . . . . . . *Berlioz*

The orchestra and chorus will be conducted by
N. A. Rimsky–Korsakov

Piano provided by Herman Koch & Co.

Commencing at 8.00 p.m.

* Corresponding with a few minor differences to No. 4, as it appears in the Belyaev vocal score, Leipzig, 1889.

CHAPTER FIVE

THE LAST YEARS

(1880–1887)

It was in the first weeks of 1880 that Borodin composed his symphonic sketch *In the Steppes of Central Asia*. According to Rimsky-Korsakov, this work was composed at great speed, but it very soon achieved great popularity not only in Russia but in Western Europe generally.

On 6 February 1880, Borodin's beloved teacher and friend, Nikolai Zinin, died. This was a great loss to Borodin, even though he had seen comparatively little of him in recent years, mainly at the meetings of the Chemical Society. He had never lost his deep and sincere attachment to Zinin, and the death of this close friend left him grief-stricken, although it came as no surprise. Borodin helped with the funeral arrangements for 'the grandfather of Russian chemistry', and made a heart-felt and impassioned speech at the graveside to the crowd of young students gathered there. In addition to this, he and A. M. Butlerov compiled a short biography shortly after the funeral, and Borodin himself headed a commission set up for raising the necessary money for a monument to his late teacher to be erected in the Academy of Physicians. But, besides the public expression of his feelings towards his departed friend, Borodin went to a great deal of trouble to see that suitable provision was made for Zinin's illegitimate daughter, who was left penniless by her father's death.[1]

Shortly after this, Borodin was involved in a concert organized by D. M. Leonova, the opera singer. She asked Borodin if he would give permission for his 'Polovtsian March' or 'his work, written for tableaus vivants' (i.e. *In the Steppes of Central Asia*) to be performed. Borodin agreed to a performance of the latter, and Leonova's concert

---

[1] As a proof of the origin of this girl, her mother sent Borodin the letters which Zinin had written to her. These letters were kept by Borodin in a special envelope entitled; 'Letters of N. N. Z. to M. M. M.'

took place in the Kononov Hall on 8 April 1880; Rimsky-Korsakov conducted.[1]

[1] There are a number of inaccurate details given in Rimsky-Korsakov's memoirs (3rd ed., p. 232) as to the nature of this concert. I reproduce here the programme of this concert, a copy of which is preserved in the Borodin archive:

KONONOV HALL

On Tuesday, 8th April 1880

CONCERT BY D. M. LEONOVA

with the orchestra of the Russian Opera under the direction of *N. A. Rimsky-Korsakov*

PROGRAMME

PART ONE

1. Overture to the opera, *Maid of Pskov* . . . *N. A. Rimsky-Korsakov*
   Orchestra

2. Closing scene of Marfa, the Old Believer, from the final act of the folk-drama. *Khovanshchina* (1st performance) . . . . . *M. P. Mussorgsky*
   D. M. Leonova and Orchestra

3. Song, 'The King of Thule' . . . . *Liszt*
   D. M. Leonova

4. Musical picture in 'Central Asia' (1st performance) . . . *A. P. Borodin*
   Orchestra

   (In the silence of the monotonous deserts of Central Asia are heard for the first time the strains of a peaceful Russian song. From the distance we hear the approach of horses and camels and the melancholy notes of an oriental melody. A caravan emerges out of the boundless steppe, escorted by Russian soldiers and continues safely and fearlessly on its long way, protected by the formidable military power of the conquerors. It slowly disappears. The tranquil songs of conquerors and conquered merge in harmony, echoes of which linger on as the caravan disappears in the distance.)

5. Mephistopheles' song from Goethe's *Faust* (1st performance) *M. P. Mussorgsky*
   D. M. Leonova

PART TWO

6. 'Tarantella' . . . . *C. Cui*
   Orchestra

7. Dramatic scene from the opera, *Mary Tudor* (1st performance) *P. I. Blaramberg*
   D. M. Leonova and Orchestra

8. 'The Persians' (music and dances of the Persian girls at the feast of Prince Ivan Khovansky). From the folk-drama, *Khovanshchina* . *M. P. Mussorgsky*
   Orchestra

9. (*a*) 'Southern Night', Song . . . . . *N. A. Rimsky-Korsakov*
   (*b*) 'Spirits of Heaven and the Sky', Song . . . *M. A. Balakirev*
   (*c*) 'The Charming Maid', Mazurka . . . . . *Chopin*
   D. M. Leonova

10. Waltz-Capriccio, 'Letter after the Ball' . . . . *D. M. Leonova*
    D. M. Leonova

The piano accompaniment will be provided by *M. P. Mussorgsky*
Piano supplied by Schroeder
Commencing at 8.00 p.m.

One of the main reasons for Rimsky-Korsakov's organizing this concert was a determined desire to make Borodin settle down to work on *Igor*. Leonova's request to perform

One further detail relating to this period should be mentioned; in the winter of 1879 and 1880, he was Chairman of the committee of 'The St. Petersburg Circle of Music Lovers', which met in the Hotel Demut. His old friend Shchiglev was at that time associated with this circle as conductor.

In the spring of 1880, Borodin received a letter (dated 8 April, N.S.) from the President of the All-German Musical Union, Karl Riedel, asking him to send the score of the E flat major Symphony, as they 'would like to perform it some time between 19 and 23 May at the Baden-Baden musical festival'. Despite the fact that this symphony was not performed after he had taken the trouble to send Riedel the score the previous year, Borodin did not hesitate to let him have it a second time. This time the symphony was actually performed at a concert, given on 8 May, under the direction of Vendelin Weissheimer. Its success was so astonishing that he could hardly wait to tell Borodin the news, and even went so far as to call it a 'triumph'.

Remembering that Balakirev had always shown a particular interest in the E flat Symphony, which was written in fact under his supervision, Borodin wrote to him the very next day to tell him the news.[1] When he received this letter, Balakirev went round to see the Borodins; this was his first visit in nine years.

The spring of 1880 was a very difficult time for Borodin. 'I can't remember a time when I had so much urgent and priority work on my hands,' he wrote to Marya Guseva (sister of his adopted daughter Elena), in a letter dated 27 June 1880. 'It happens fairly often nowadays that I don't get to bed before two or three in the morning, and have to be up again at four or five.'[2]

The summer of that year was no less trying for Borodin. Catherine was emphatically against going to Davydovo and did not want to go there ever again. After much discussion, they eventually decided to stay at the country-house belonging to a family named Khomutov, at the invitation of A. A. Stolyarevsky. The estate was called Sokolovo, situated on a big hill overlooking the Volga not far from Kineshma.

Borodin managed to wind up his affairs by 19 June, and set out from Petersburg with his two adopted daughters. They arrived at Sokolovo

the 'Polovtsian March' from the opera was probably a result of Rimsky-Korsakov's prompting in the hope that Borodin would orchestrate it. The same applies to 'Konchak's Daughter's Aria' and again to the 'Polovtsian March', which are discussed below in connection with another concert of Leonova.

[1] Letter of 19 May 1880 (*Letters*, Vol. III, Letter 579, p. 100).
[2] *Letters*, Vol. III, Letter 587, p. 105.

on 22 June. They found a spacious and fairly well-furnished apartment at their disposal; there were five rooms, a large drawing-room and a balcony, and the furniture was ready for use. The place was very picturesque and much to Borodin's liking. 'We are at the top of a high, steep slope, and below us unrolls a monstrous coil of the Volga,' he wrote to Stassov the day after his arrival in Sokolovo. 'It stretches out for thirty versts or more before our eyes in a single huge sweep; a panorama of sandbanks, steep slopes, grassy foreshores, meadows, woods, villages, churches, country-houses, all merging into blue, infinite perspective. It's such an entrancing view that I simply can't take my eyes away from it! It's nothing short of a miracle!'[1]

In the same letter, he regretted the fact that 'the pianos here have been making a valiant effort to render the audaciously illicit sounds of modern music, but all we got was a hoarse rattle, and then silence; they proved quite unequal to the task.' It was for this reason that Borodin had to send for his own Sturtzwage piano which had been in Davydovo since the previous summer. Transport was slow and it was already the middle of July before it arrived.

But for a variety of reasons Borodin did only a limited amount of work on his opera during the summer. On the one hand, the strain of his work in the previous academic session was now telling on him, and on the other hand, he came across all kinds of hitches which prevented him from concentrating. It seems that nothing beyond the initial sketches of the final scenes of Act One was written that summer: the scenes of rivalry in Putivl, and the revolt of Prince Galitsky's supporters during the Polovtsian siege of Putivl. We know of course that Borodin later rejected these scenes.[2] (According to Alexander Dianin, Borodin at one time had intended to make use of every bit of material he had written for *Igor*, and eventually to make it stretch to two complete operas: *Prince Igor in Captivity* and *Prince Igor at Home*, which were to form part of the same cycle. He gave up this idea later, and made a careful selection of the music he would be using.)

Borodin's summer respite in Sokolovo came to an end on 19 September. Catherine had left three days earlier and had gone to her mother's in Moscow, where she stayed until the beginning of October. Borodin found the coming autumn no exception to the rule; there were

---

[1] *Letters*, Vol. III, Letter 586, p. 102.
[2] Sketches of 'the quarrel-scene' are preserved in the manuscript section of the Leningrad Public Library and in the Library of the Leningrad Conservatoire.

IX. A GENERAL VIEW OF SOLIGALITCH

X. RIMSKY-KORSAKOV

Reproduced from the copy given to L. J. Schestakova in 1882 by Rimsky-Korsakov.
The original is in the Rimsky-Korsakov family collection.

the usual medical courses, the various committees, the administrative work, and of course 'The Music Lovers' Circle', and so forth.

In September he received a letter from the conductor Leopold Damrosch, who wanted Borodin to let him have the score of the E flat Symphony 'about which he had heard so many glowing reports,' for a performance in New York. But the composer, as far as one can tell, had to turn down this request as the score of the symphony was still in manuscript.

A second performance of *In the Steppes of Central Asia* was given on 18 October 1880 at the second concert of the Petersburg branch of the Russian Musical Society, and was conducted by Napravnik. It was also at this time that Borodin was asked by Nicholas Rubinstein and Jurgenson if he would care to write an orchestral or choral-orchestral work for performance at the Moscow Exhibition, which was to be held in celebration of the Silver Jubilee of Tsar Alexander II. The suggestion was that the composition should by its title have some connection either with the Silver Jubilee or with the dedication of the Cathedral of Christ the Saviour. Borodin refused to write a work of this nature but had no objection to composing something for the Exhibition.

About this time it was decided to perform Borodin's A major Quartet at a chamber music concert of the Russian Musical Society in Petersburg either at the end of December or in January. The work of copying the parts was begun in November. Finally, in the same month, Rubinstein, who represented the Moscow branch of the Russian Musical Society, asked Borodin to send the score of the B minor Symphony for a performance in Moscow. This meant a great deal of work for Borodin who still had to put the final touches to the score before it could be sent.[1]

On 4 November 1880, Borodin was present at a gathering of his musical friends at Filippov's, when Mussorgsky's recently completed *Khovanshchina* was played in its entirety.[2]

On 15 December, Borodin set out for Moscow to hear a performance

---

[1] *Letters*, Vol. III, Letters 650–7, pp. 131–4. In all probability, in the alterations made to the orchestral score of the B minor Symphony prior to its performance in 1879, new pages were inserted in place of the old ones, besides normal manuscript corrections.

[2] This fact is established from T. I. Filippov's letter to Borodin, and the rough sketches of the latter's replies (*Letters*, Vol. III, Letter 629, p. 124; also p. 245 of the Russian 2nd ed. of my book, *Borodin*). By the term 'completion' of *Khovanshchina*, one should understand that the music already existed in Mussorgsky's mind, although it had not yet been committed to paper in its entirety.

of his B minor Symphony. The Moscow musical world gave him a
warm welcome. On 18 December he was present at the rehearsals of
his symphony, and heard a special performance of Tchaikovsky's
'Liturgy' at a symphony concert of the Russian Musical Society; he
was also at a banquet given by D. V. Razumovsky, the well-known
scholar and expert in old Russian liturgical music. His B minor
Symphony was performed on 20 December. A letter to Catherine
gives the following account of the performance[1]: 'The Symphony
went well, and to my amazement there was applause (but only slight)
after each movement. But at the end there was long and loud applause,
and twice I had to go out on to the stage and take a bow. The
orchestra also joined in the applause. The professors of the Conservatory congratulated me and showered me with compliments.'

Borodin returned to Petersburg on 25 December, and found a letter
waiting for him from N. V. Galkin, the first violinist of the Musical
Society String Quartet. He was writing to let Borodin know that
there would be a final rehearsal of the A major Quartet, and did not
omit to say that they were 'simply delighted' with the work. The first
public performance took place on 30 December 1880.

During the course of January and February 1881, Borodin wrote
two vocal items for Leonova's proposed Jubilee Concert. He composed 'a little piece based on an Arabian theme'[2] but then decided
that it would be unsuitable for such an occasion, and wrote instead a
song to words by Nekrassov, 'At Home among Real People'.[3] The
composer himself orchestrated the accompaniment. Borodin apparently wrote very little in the way of music during the spring of 1881.
He most likely did some more work on his opera, though in a rather
piecemeal fashion, and carried on rewriting certain parts of the
scenario. He also edited Konchak's Daughter's Aria, which he had
written some time before.[4]

In March, Mussorgsky became seriously ill. Borodin and Stassov
managed to get him into the Nikolaevsky Military Hospital, where he
was well looked after and frequently visited by his friends. Borodin
saw Mussorgsky for the last time the day before his death, which
occurred during the night of 16 March 1881. Borodin helped with the

[1] Letter of 22 December 1880 (*Letters*, Vol. III, Letter 666, p. 137).
[2] *Letters*, Vol. III, Letter 706, p. 148.
[3] Ibid., Letter 707, p. 148.
[4] For details of these alterations to Konchakovna's aria, see Rimsky-Korsakov's
memoirs, 3rd ed., p. 202. The final modification to this aria was made by Rimsky-
Korsakov after Borodin's death, when a few choral passages were inserted.

funeral arrangements, and in cooperation with Cui and Rimsky-Korsakov wrote a letter to the editor of *The Voice* expressing their gratitude to the staff of the hospital, and to Dr. Bertenson and the nurses in particular, who had been so devoted to the great composer during the last days of his life.[1]

On 18 April, a concert was arranged at Leonova's house by her admirers on the occasion of the thirtieth anniversary of her début. This took the place of the public celebration originally planned, which was now out of the question owing to the public mourning for the Tsar, Alexander II. At this concert Leonova sang Konchak's Daughter's Aria.

On 26 May, Borodin set out from Petersburg for Germany. Officially he was going as a representative of the Military Medical Academy, but actually his real purpose was to see Liszt and to visit the Music Festival organized by the All-German Musical Society in Magdeburg. He was slightly delayed in Berlin, but arrived in Magdeburg on 28 May (O.S.). He learned from a porter at the station that Liszt was already there and was staying in Koch's Hotel. 'Within half a minute I was at Koch's Hotel, ensconced in room No. 34, and half a minute later I was in Room No. 1, Liszt's apartment. His Montenegrin valet recognized me immediately, and seemed delighted to see me, greeting me profusely in Italian; he threw open the doors and a moment later my hands were fast in Liszt's iron grip.'[2]

Borodin stayed in Magdeburg until 2/14 June and went to all the concerts.[3] None of Borodin's works were actually being performed at this Festival; the only major Russian work to be heard was Rimsky-Korsakov's *Antar*. This was performed on 30 May (O.S.). The conductor was the extremely young, though already promising musician, Arthur Nikisch. Borodin conveyed to the conductor and orchestra the composer's own directions as to how he would like *Antar* to be played. He later gave a detailed account of the performance in his letters to Rimsky-Korsakov's wife and Cui.[4]

Borodin left Magdeburg on 2 June for Weimar, since he wanted to spend a little more time in Liszt's company; he was also attracted by

---

[1] A list setting out the duties and placing of wreaths at Mussorgsky's funeral, written in Borodin's hand, is preserved in the Borodin archive. The letter in question appeared in *The Voice* on 20 March 1881 (*Letters*, Vol. III, note 3 to Letter 714, p. 360).

[2] Ibid., Letter 740, pp. 156–7.

[3] A copy of Borodin's own programme of the Magdeburg Music Festival is still preserved. The margins are covered in a series of comments in his own hand.

[4] *Letters*, Vol. III, Letters 741 and 749, pp. 157–60, 179–82.

a production of Goethe's *Faust* which was to be given in its entirety on two successive evenings (19 and 20 June).[1] While he was staying in Weimar, Borodin showed Liszt the score of his *In the Steppes of Central Asia*. The Weimar maestro was so taken by it that Borodin dedicated the work to him. It was through Liszt that he made an arrangement for a piano duet of his symphonic sketch; they performed it together at a private concert given at the house of Princess Wittgenstein.[2] At Catherine's request, he wrote to Lodyzhensky, asking him if they might avail themselves of his kind offer and saying that they would be glad to spend the latter part of the summer at his estate in Zhitovo, in the Province of Tula. Nikolai Lodyzhensky wrote a very kind letter in reply (on 14/26 June) which he sent, at Borodin's request, to his Moscow address, the Golitsyn Hospital where Borodin would then be staying with his wife. Two further details relating to Borodin's stay in Weimar should be mentioned; he made the acquaintance of Hans von Bülow, and went to Jena to hear the annual concert of church music given in Jena Cathedral (nicknamed the 'Wurst-Konzert').[3]

Borodin gave an account of his protracted stay in Weimar to Alexander and Evgeny Dianin, in a letter which he wrote on 18/30 June: 'I expect you want to know what your pseudo-papa has been up to; well, as you can see, he got stuck in Weimar. And like a certain Tannhäuser, I found my Venusberg and my dear old, white-haired Venus, Liszt. But I drew the line at following Tannhäuser's example to the extent of calling on the Virgin Mary to rescue me. If there is any one who can rescue me, it will of course be my own patron Saint Catherine the Martyr, my Petersburg prophetess.'[4]

Borodin did not get out of his 'Venusberg' before the end of June, when he went to Leipzig in the hope of hearing a performance of *The Ring* which was going to take place there. He was disappointed, as the production of this operatic cycle had been postponed until the autumn. In Leipzig he stayed with Karl Riedel and his family, and became good friends with them.

He returned to Moscow on 7 July, and four days later he was in Zhitovo looking round the premises that Lodyzhensky had placed at

[1] A poster advertising this performance is preserved in the Borodin archive.

[2] See Borodin's letter to his wife dated 7/19 June 1881 (*Letters*, Vol. III, Letter 743, pp. 162–3).

[3] These concerts acquired this nickname among Liszt's pupils from the fact that they all used to visit Liszt's friend K. Hille after the concert and eat hot sausages (*Wurst*). See Borodin's letter to Catherine dated 3 July (N.S.) 1877 (*Letters*, Vol. II, Letter 366).

[4] *Letters*, Vol. III, Letter 744, p. 164.

his disposal, and making them suitable for habitation. When Catherine heard that the place was satisfactory, she set off to Zhitovo on 15 July to join her husband, bringing their adopted daughter Ganya with her. Lodyzhensky's country-house in Zhitovo was small and on a modest scale. They lived in an old wooden house with a large garden. Borodin started work on his compositions soon after their arrival. Catherine was quite satisfied with her summer residence, but she none the less suffered from her usual insomnia, and, as in the past, would not let the rest of the house sleep. But this did not prevent Borodin from having a good rest. It was there that he composed the Second String Quartet and orchestrated Konchak's Daughter's Aria.

The Borodins did not leave Zhitovo until 7 September, when they went on to Moscow. Borodin travelled on alone to Petersburg, and arrived there on 11 September. Shortly after his return, he became involved in two musical controversies. In the first place, he had to settle the dispute between M. R. Shchiglev and the committee of the St. Petersburg Circle of Music Lovers, which had led to the former's resignation from the conductorship of the orchestra. He used his influence on the directors of the Circle and managed to have 'Shchigliusha reinstated as conductor.'[1] Secondly, Borodin had to help in settling the question as to who should be the head of the Free Music School. In September Rimsky-Korsakov had turned down the offer, and the School Council had approached Balakirev asking him to accept the post a second time. But they were afraid that Balakirev would refuse, and Milanov, a member of the Council, asked Borodin if he would give them his support. Milanov's letter, now part of the Borodin archive, runs as follows: 'We, the members of the Council, have invited Balakirev to take over. Please help us, our much-esteemed Alexander Porfiryevich, to settle this matter once and for all, in the true spirit of the School tradition; we need your support. The Council will be meeting in Balakirev's flat on Friday, 25 September, at 8 p.m. Could you possibly be there?'

Owing to his other commitments Borodin was unable to attend this meeting, but sent Balakirev a letter in which he pleaded with him not to abandon 'what was nearest to his heart, for even if it caused him a good deal of worry and trouble, and brought with it difficulties and heart-breaks, it would nevertheless win him honour and glory, and bring him joy and happiness; and what is more, he would be serving

[1] Letter to Catherine dated 27 September 1881 (*Letters*, Vol. III, Letter 768, p. 201).

the cause of Russian music'.[1] As we know, Balakirev agreed to the Council's proposition, and Borodin took this to be a sign of his musical 'renascence'; a return to his former active musical life as a composer.

During the whole of this period, Borodin had his time taken up with administrative work both at the Academy and in connection with the medical courses for women. Since the beginning of the session that autumn, it had looked as though Borodin might be appointed Principal of the Academy. It was a great relief to him when the present Principal decided not to retire, and this unwelcome prospect vanished.

Catherine returned to Petersburg early in October. Her brother Alexey, who was living in straitened circumstances at the time, came with her; and Borodin, in addition to the numerous other pressing matters on his hands, had to set about finding a job for his brother-in-law with a certain amount of assistance from Balakirev and T. I. Filippov.

On 28 October, Borodin went to Bessel's to hear a performance of Rimsky-Korsakov's recently-completed *Snow Maiden*. This opera at once became one of Borodin's favourites.

The late autumn of 1881, as far as Borodin's musical friends were concerned, was devoted to musical events commemorating the recent death of Mussorgsky. A concert of his works was given on 8 November, and half of the proceeds went towards a memorial stone for his grave. This concert brought back vividly to Borodin's mind the memory of his recently departed friend, who had, like his bride-to-be before him, come to such an untimely end. It was in this sombre mood that Borodin composed his ballad 'For the Shores of a Distant Homeland'.[2] He did not at this time possess a copy of Pushkin's works, for the very likely reason that one of his friends, as was very often the case, had borrowed the edition he originally had, and never returned it. But Catherine knew the words of the poem by heart,[3]

[1] *Letters*, Vol. III, Letter 767, p. 199.

[2] E. G. Dianina told me that she was present during a conversation between the Borodins when they were discussing the death of Mussorgsky's fiancée. Catherine quoted Pushkin's lines 'For the shores of a distant homeland' and suggested that Borodin should make a setting of it. Cf. Ippolitov-Ivanov's account of this song in his book, *My Memories of 50 Years of Russian Music*, p. 35.

[3] The departure from the words of the Pushkin poem seem to be the result of Catherine's faulty memory. There is no foundation whatsoever for E. M. Braüdo's suggestion (op. cit., p. 120) that the deviation is deliberate.

and she wrote down the text from memory on a sheet of paper which is now in the Borodin archive. This ballad of course was not to the liking of most of his friends, Stassov in particular. It is possibly for this reason that Borodin never published this work. It also probably explains why the departures from the original words of the poem, as written down by Catherine remained uncorrected.

It was about this time that he wrote or, to be more precise, completed the final version of Prince Igor's famous aria, 'Neither sleep nor rest for the weary spirit'.[1]

The date of Leonova's jubilee concert, which had been repeatedly postponed for various reasons, was finally settled in December 1881. Borodin had promised to let them have Konchak's Daughter's Aria for this concert, as well as the 'Polovtsian March' which he had written quite some time before, but had not yet orchestrated. But he was unable to keep his promise, and accordingly wrote to Leonova to explain matters: 'My most sincerely and deeply esteemed Darya Mikhailovna, do with me what you will, for I am guilty, I have let you down. My Polovtsian March is not ready.'[2]

The copying of the parts for the song 'At Home with Real People', which was going to be sung at the concert, and possibly the rehearsals as well, stimulated much discussion of Nekrassov's poetry among

---

[1] The approximate period of the composition of this aria may be established from the following facts and reasoning. Many sketches for various parts of the libretto are written on the reverse side of government forms and other dated documents. These are preserved in Borodin's file: 'Libretto of *Igor* and Musical Matters.' In particular, one may learn the following with regard to Igor's aria:

(*a*) One of the sketches of the text of this aria (which is much at variance with the printed version) is written on the reverse side of a note which contains the text of the words of the 'quarrel-scene', and was therefore written after 1880.

(*b*) The scenario of that part of the Second Act which features Igor's aria, is written in pencil on the rough copy of a letter to Balakirev describing Rimsky-Korsakov's resignation from the Free School, i.e. not earlier than the last days of September 1881.

(*c*) A sketch of this aria, closely resembling the final version, is written on the back of an official letter from the Military Academy of Medicine, dated 27 October 1881.

Therefore, the aria took its final shape not earlier than November 1881. On the other hand, in a note from the Musical Society to Borodin dated 10 May 1882, the composer is asked about the score and parts 'of the aria Prince Igor' [*sic*]. It seems that Borodin intended to finish orchestrating the accompaniment to this aria by the spring of 1882. A comparison of the details given above leads us to the conclusion that the aria was written in the course of autumn and winter 1881. The references in Rimsky-Korsakov's memoirs to the effect that Igor's aria was composed at a much earlier date are probably explained by the fact that Rimsky-Korsakov was alluding to the principal motifs of this aria, i.e. leitmotifs which had been composed long before this, especially those taken from Gedeonov's *Mlada*.

[2] *Letters*, Vol. III, Letter 785 (and also 786), p. 206.

Borodin's friends. Catherine presented her husband with a volume of Nekrassov's poems which had just appeared in a new edition.[1]

Leonova's jubilee concert took place on 22 January 1882, and was conducted by Lyadov. The only works of Borodin to be performed in these concerts have already been mentioned.[2] At Leonova's request,

---

[1] I reproduce here *in extenso* Catherine's verses which were written by her in connection with this present.

> *Poem penned by a home–bred versifier, on the occasion of the presentation of a complete edition of Nekrassov's poems to the talented composer of Igor. 2nd edition, published by Pypin, due to appear in print, and obtainable in the second half of January 1882.*

In spirit, in your metier, in your powers of expression
You are akin to the Poet;
And your wonderful song makes us cry and rejoice,
You know how to present your song in a form both powerful and truly Russian,
And to the Russian ear, the song is their own.
You express Russian daring, Russian sorrow, sometimes merged with drunkenness,
The peasants' revelry or the Princess's pain at separation,
The charm and dreams of youthful love
And the thoughts, the passions, exaltations, torments—
In voicing all these things, you have given expressions to the Russian soul.
And so these poems of the sorrowful poet of the Russian land [i.e. Nekrassov]
May I have the honour to present to you, the Russian Bayan—
And please pardon the poor expression of my good thought.

31 December 1881.

The original is written in very bad irregular verse, the gist of which would be difficult to express in English. This is a literal line-by-line translation. 'Bayan' refers to a traditional reciter of the medieval epics. [Tr.]

[2] I reproduce here the programme of this concert, which is preserved in the Borodin archive.

Friday,* 22† January 1882

HALL OF CITY CREDIT COMPANY
CONCERT BY D. M. LEONOVA
with the orchestra of the Russian Opera conducted by *A. K. Lyadov*

PROGRAMME
PART I

1. Overture on Russian themes   .   .   .   .   *N. A. Rimsky-Korsakov*
Orchestra

2. 'Ah, not for me . . .', song of Vanya from the opera, *A Life for the Tsar*
M. I. Glinka

3. 'Gopak of the merry lads'
Orchestra

4. Song of 'Khivrya' [2, 4] (1st performance)
D. M. Leonova and Orchestra

Selections from the new opera, *Sorochintsy Fair* (orchestrated by A. K. Lyadov), by *M. P. Mussorgsky*

PART II

5. 'Night in Madrid', fantasia on Spanish themes   .   .   .   .   *M. I. Glinka*
Orchestra

Borodin wrote a notice giving details of her jubilee and the celebration concert,[1] for publication in a German musical journal.

A few days after this concert (on 26 January) Borodin's D major Quartet was given its first performance at a chamber music concert of the Russian Musical Society.[2]

6. 'Konchakovna's'‡ arioso from the new opera, *Prince Igor* (1st performance)

A. P. Borodin

D. M. Leonova and Orchestra

7. 2 Mephisto-Walzer (1st performance) . . . . . *F. Liszt*

Orchestra

8. (*a*) 'Forgotten', ballad to the words of Count A. A. Golenishchev-Kutuzov

M. P. Mussorgsky

(*b*) 'At home among real people'. Song to the words of *N. A. Nekrassov* (1st performance) . . . . . . *A. P. Borodin*

D. M. Leonova and Orchestra

9. Songs: (*a*) 'Svitezyanka' . . . . . *N. A. Rimsky-Korsakov*

(*b*) 'She sings and the sounds melt away' . . . . *C. A. Cui*

(*c*) 'It is all the same to me' . . . . . *A. S. Dargomïzhsky*

(*d*) 'The Charming Maid', Mazurka . . . . *Chopin*

D. M. Leonova with piano accompaniment

Piano provided by Schroeder

Commencing at 8.00 p.m.

* Corrected in pencil to 'Thursday'.

† Altered to '21' (also in pencil).

‡ Placed in inverted commas in the original.

[1] *Letters*, Vol. III, Letter 812, p. 211.

[2] In view of the fact that the D major Quartet of Borodin was performed in 1882 and that this is contradicted by Stassov who attributes it to the end of the composer's life (see his book on Borodin, p. 53), I consider it necessary to reproduce here the programme in which the Quartet was first performed. (The programme is preserved in the Borodin archive.)

THE IMPERIAL RUSSIAN MUSICAL SOCIETY

ST. PETERSBURG SECTION

1881/82 SEASON

FOURTH QUARTET MEETING

(Third Series)

26 JANUARY 1882

PROGRAMME

1. Quartet for two violins, viola and cello in D major. No. 2 (Manuscript) (1st performance) . . . . *Borodin*

1. Allegro moderato.

2. Scherzo; Allegro.

3. Nocturne; Andante.

4. Finale; Andante, Vivace.

Performed by: *Galkin, Degtyerev, Rezvetsov, and Kuznetsov.*

2. Sonata for violin and piano in G major, op. 9, No. 3 (1st performance) *Godard*

Performed by: *Kross and Galkin.*

In the spring of 1882, two concerts given at the Free School and conducted by Balakirev were absorbing Borodin's attention. The first of these was given in honour of Balakirev's return to musical life.[1] In the second concert, which took place on March 17, the E major Symphony of the young Glazunov received its first performance. Borodin warmly congratulated the young and talented composer whom he had met only a short time before.

The early years of Alexander III's reign were marked by violent reactionary measures. There were mass arrests of students and Borodin, who had always been closely linked with student life, shared the burden of their misfortune, and did all he could to help those who had been arrested. M. M. Ippolitov-Ivanov has it that, one night in February (1882?), Borodin turned up at the amateur singer, V. N. Ilyinsky's flat at two in the morning 'covered in snow and frozen to the marrow; it transpired that he had been going about in a cab, since eight o'clock that morning, and had been from one institution to another, enquiring after someone who had been arrested.'[2] Borodin, did not restrict himself to enquiries and investigations, but even went to the length of destroying any material that might have compromised his students.

One of the first effects of this reaction was to interrupt the medical courses for women that meant so much to Borodin. The newly-appointed Minister of War, P. S. Vannovsky, announced that such

3. Quartet for two violins, viola and cello, op. 59, No. 2 . . . *Beethoven*
    1. Allegro.
    2. Molto Adagio.
    3. Allegretto.
    4. Finale; Presto.
Performed by: *Galkin, Degtyarev, Rezvetsov, and Kuznetsov.*

Commencing at 8.00 p.m.

The Bechstein piano is from the Herman and Grossman depot.

The Management of the St. Petersburg Section kindly request patrons to refrain from entering or leaving the hall during the performance.

[1] On 1 January 1882, T. I. Filippov sent Borodin a letter in which he asked him to arrange for Liszt to send Balakirev a congratulatory telegram 'on the occasion of his return to society'. It appears that Borodin wrote to Liszt with the result that Balakirev received a very cordial letter from Liszt congratulating him on his 'apparition' in the musical world.

[2] *My Memories of 50 Years of Russian Music*, p. 34. I note also that, according to E. A. Guseva and A. P. and E. G. Dianin, Borodin often made use of the official position of his brother. D. S. Aleksandrov, who was then Assistant to the Warden in charge of offenders awaiting trial, in order to get information about students who had been arrested.

courses could no longer be held in the Nikolaevsky Hospital. With a view to keeping the courses running, proposals were put forward for them to be brought under the jurisdiction of the City Council or the Ministry of Education. Borodin, as one of those most actively concerned with these women's courses, and a few of the other professors did all they possibly could to ensure their continuation. This made no small demands on his time, and was a great strain on his nerves. Not only this but other matters connected with his work were beginning to wear him out. Finally Catherine's abnormal routine was beginning to tell on him.

If things went on like this, his hopes of finishing his opera would be gone for ever. Balakirev, who understood the situation better than anyone, wrote in a letter dated 15 April 1882 to suggest that Borodin should employ a nurse he could trust to look after Catherine, so that 'he would have free time to work on the opera, which must be finished at all costs'. But this suggestion, not to mention the continual reproaches of Stassov and Rimsky-Korsakov, had no effect whatsoever on Borodin. Catherine, who was a permanent invalid, did not so much need medical care, as the companionship of those near to her. It was for this reason that she always had a house full of people, but she did not understand that they were interfering with Borodin's work. In addition to the usual people living with them, there were at this time two extra guests staying in their flat, A. V. Gotovtseva and A. A. Stolyarevskaya, not to mention his constantly impoverished brother-in-law, Alexey Protopopov. To make matters worse, Borodin's sister-in-law, Alexandra Alexandrova, who had been living apart from her husband, was beginning to show signs of mental disorder. Borodin, who had not failed to notice this, went to her summer cottage in Lesnoye to keep an eye on her, and consulted a doctor about her illness. Her husband had been seriously ill not long before this, and Borodin often had to consult with medical people and send him by post details of the treatment they recommended.

But he did not drop his music entirely, and managed to spin out his time sufficiently to enable him to prepare the score of the E flat major Symphony for publication, and to read the proofs.

The Borodins were intending to spend the summer of 1882 in Zhitovo, where they had had quite a pleasant stay the previous year. But thanks to Catherine, their preparations for moving there were extremely slack; she kept putting off their day of departure until almost the end of June. Towards the end of June, however, Catherine again fell ill and, by the time she had recovered, they felt it was too late to go there, and began instead to make plans for a visit to Moscow where a series of concerts were being held at the Exhibition of Industry and Fine Arts.[1] But these plans too came to nothing. By the beginning of July, his sister-in-law's mental condition had become so critical, that Borodin felt obliged to get her into a mental asylum. He had to invent a fantastic story to persuade her to enter the asylum, and he had to look after her affairs in the meantime.[2] The treatment she received was successful, and there was soon a marked improvement in her condition; she was discharged not long afterwards. Borodin let her stay in his flat for the time being. He had settled all outstanding matters by 10 August, and he left that very day for Moscow to hear the concerts being given at the Exhibition. He had to leave Catherine at home as she had been taken ill again.

Borodin spent the first few days after his arrival in Moscow with his various musical acquaintances, some of whom, like P. I. Blaramberg, and S. N. Kruglikov lived in Moscow, whereas others, including Rimsky-Korsakov had come specially from Petersburg, like Borodin, for the concerts. He spent two nights at Blaramberg's flat, as he was afraid of disturbing his aged mother-in-law. He turned up regularly at the rehearsals of the concert in which his *In the Steppes of Central Asia* was going to be played. This particular concert took place on 15 August at two o'clock in the afternoon, and was conducted by Rimsky-Korsakov.[3] The performance was a success, and the composer was twice called on to the platform. At this concert Borodin met many people he knew, including D. V. Stassov, Lodyzhensky, and Anna Kalinina.

On 17 August Borodin fell a victim to the epidemic of gastro-enteritis which was raging in Moscow at that time. He had to spend several days in bed in his mother-in-law's tiny flat, whilst the other

---

[1] In a letter of Catherine's to A. P. and E. G. Dianin dated 7 July 1882, she writes: 'It seems that we shall not get there now [i.e. to Zhitovo], but only as far as the Moscow exhibition.'

[2] We learn a great deal of Borodin's activities from a number of rough drafts of his letters to her mother and sister, and also to his brother, D. S. Aleksandrov. It can be seen from these rough drafts that Borodin was very upset by what had happened and was obliged, as usual, to write several versions of a letter before being satisfied (*Letters*, Vol. III, Letters 863–74, 877–9). Obviously Rimsky-Korsakov had this in mind when, in her memoirs, he speaks of Borodin's relatives going mad (*Chronicle of My Musical Life*, 3rd ed., p. 204).

[3] See Catherine's letter to Borodin dated 21 August 1882. In this, she reproduces part of a newspaper criticism. She says, with reference to this review, that M. M.

two women living there were suffering from the same complaint. This indisposition prevented him from going to the rehearsals for the

Koryakin sang poorly from the musical point of view, but was popular on account of his magnificent voice.

Here is the programme of the exhibition concert, given on 15 August 1882.

THE IMPERIAL RUSSIAN MUSICAL SOCIETY

MOSCOW SECTION

INDUSTRIAL ARTISTIC EXHIBITION, 1882

Sunday, 15 August

SEVENTH SYMPHONY CONCERT

Conducted by *N. A. Rimsky-Korsakov*

Commencing at 2.00 p.m.

PROGRAMME

1. 'Antar', 2nd Symphony for orchestra (based on Senkovsky's Arabian fairy-tale)
   N. A. Rimsky-Korsakov
   [*followed by the Programme of 'Antar'*]

2. 'The Night Watch' . . . . *M. I. Glinka*
   M. M. Koryakin
   Interval of 15 minutes

3. Concerto (4th) for pianoforte, op. 70 . . . . *A. G. Rubinstein*
   (*a*) Moderato.
   (*b*) Moderato assai.
   (*c*) Allegro.
   N. S. Lavrov

4. 'In the Steppes of Central Asia', musical picture for orchestra (1st performance)*
   A. P. Borodin

   In the silence of the monotonous sandy steppes of Central Asia are heard the foreign strains of a peaceful Russian song. From the distance we hear the approach of horses and camels and the melancholy notes of an oriental melody. A caravan emerges out of the boundless desert, escorted by Russian soldiers, and continues safely and fearlessly on its long way under the armed protection of Russia. It slowly disappears. The tranquil songs of the Russians and of the native population merge into a common harmony, echoes of which linger on as the caravan disappears in the distance.†

5. Konchak's Aria from the opera, *Prince Igor* (1st performance)‡ . *A. P. Borodin*
   M. M. Koryakin

6. *Tarantella* for orchestra (1st performance)‡ . . . . *C. A. Cui*
   Piano provided by Bekker

The management kindly request patrons to refrain from entering or leaving the hall during the performance.

The Eighth Symphonic Concert will be held on Sunday, 22 August.

* I.e. first performance in Moscow.
† I have deliberately repeated this quotation in full, because it contains significant variants, omitting the words 'Conquerors' and 'Conquered'. (This same variant is found also in printed editions.)
‡ I.e. first performance in Moscow.

last concert (the eighth) of the series. But he did manage to be present at the concert itself, which took place on 22 August with Rimsky-Korsakov conducting. Two days later, Borodin left for Petersburg.[1]

The autumn of 1882 brought with it the usual burden of commitments. One thing worth mentioning is that his D major String Quartet was given a second performance at one of the chamber concerts of the Russian Musical Society on 11 December. Also his song 'At Home with Real People' was sung by A. A. Bichurina at a concert of Russian operatic music on 26 December. It was about this time that Borodin started going to chamber music evenings held at M. P. Belyaev's house, which later became known as 'The Belyaev Fridays'. It was probably for one of these 'Fridays' that he composed his well-known D major Scherzo in 5/8 time, which was later to form part of the Third Symphony.[2]

This was a very unproductive time as regards his opera, and at the close of the year 1882, it was no nearer to completion. 'It's a damned shame about my opera!' he wrote to Glinka's sister on 3 January 1883.[3] As usual he was up to his neck in everything but music. He spent February and part of March organizing a nation-wide subscription for a memorial to Zinin. It was his job as chairman of the appropriate committee to send out hundreds of letters and subscription forms.[4] Meanwhile he was still trying to save the Women's Medical Courses, whose existence in the face of increasing opposition from the authorities was becoming even more precarious. Borodin and the other professors came up against complete indifference in official circles. Borodin himself had the impression that everyone was busy with preparations for the coronation of Alexander III, and seemed to have no time for any other business.

At the beginning of 1883, Borodin was working on the manuscript parts of the First Symphony which had to be ready for a performance

[1] This date is established from a phrase in a letter of A. V. Gotovtseva to A. P. Dianin on 24 August 1882: 'We are expecting Alexander Porfiryevich in Petersburg tomorrow.'

[2] On one of the pages of Borodin's account book containing a list of published and manuscript music passed on by him to other people, there is one entry where he claims on 24 October to have entrusted Belyaev with the 'Scherzo 5/8, the D-major 4tet and the Quintet.' This list most probably refers to 1882 as it comes immediately after similar lists dated 1882, and immediately before lists relating to the very end of 1882 and the beginning of 1883.

[3] *Letters*, Vol. IV, Letter 968, p. 9.

[4] A large number of the rough drafts of these letters are preserved in the Borodin archive. This applies to letters 982–8, etc. (*Letters*, Vol. IV.)

to be given on 3 February at a Free School concert which was to be
conducted by Balakirev. On 7 March Borodin was at another such
concert in which Balakirev's *Tamara* received its first performance.
In April it turned out that Borodin had to send the full score and parts
of the First Symphony to Karl Riedel in Germany. It was from him
that Borodin learned that Rimsky-Korsakov's F major Quartet was
due to be performed there. Riedel did his utmost to persuade Borodin
to come to Leipzig, where a Music Festival was going to be held that
year. Borodin did not need much pressing, and had in fact made up
his mind to go to Germany, when he found at the very last moment
that he could not afford it.[1] Borodin's symphony was performed at
the Leipzig Festival on 4 May, and once again the conductor was
Nikisch.

The summer of 1883 was an even greater disappointment than the
previous one, as far as Borodin was concerned. He had hoped to get
away fairly early to his summer residence in Zhitovo, and to spend the
whole of the summer there, but as it happened there were still many
urgent matters which had to be settled even as late as June.

He gave the following description of this chaotic state of affairs:
'First of all, we had to drop the idea of going to Zhitovo through no
fault of our own. After that, we had to hunt around for other possibilities. We came across about five such places. But of course, as soon
as we think we have found somewhere, we immediately start looking
for excuses for not going there. . . . At long last, Kate plumped for
Lesnoye, and, now she is here, she says she has never been to a better
spot.'[2]

In Lesnoye the Borodins stayed at a cottage which Anna Kalinina
rented there, since they had been unable to find their own accommodation. Judging from his remarks, this summer was no rest for Borodin:
'Last summer was fine, and I was able to bathe [in the Neva]. But this
year it is neither one thing nor the other.'

Borodin felt so worn out by all the confusion that his remarks
about the kind of life he had to put up with are even more scathing
than usual. For example, he wrote on 31 August: 'Instead of getting
on with more urgent matters,[3] we go for a drive every single day to
Sosnovka to "start the day off", which for us of course, unlike normal

[1] This is seen from the letters of Catherine's mother addressed to her daughter,
relating to 1883.
[2] Letter to A. P. and E. G. Dianin dated 22 August (*Letters*, Vol. IV, Letter 1010,
p. 32).
[3] Seeing to repairs to their flat.

people, begins in the afternoon; you must know who is at the back of all this. Just now, as I am running off this letter to you, Kate is still in the arms of Morpheus and it is already nearly two. We had a picnic and everything arranged for a trip to Sosnovka at 12.0. But I am confident that we shall be able to make it even yet before "the morning" is out.'[1]

It is of course obvious that work was difficult under these conditions. Even as late as the second half of the summer Borodin was still studying various historical sources[2] and working on the scenario of his opera. But as a result of the work he actually did, he reached the stage of writing the Prologue. For this he made use of material he had written earlier. For the Introduction he used the Chorus of Idolaters in the temple of Radegast. He also drastically readapted the C major Chorus 'Slava' which had originally been intended for the Epilogue, and the 'Scene of the Apparitions'. All three were taken from the material he had written earlier for *Mlada*.

The routine repairs to the Borodins' flat were completed in September. On 30 September, Catherine left for Moscow to spend the rest of the autumn there with her mother. Borodin became once more inundated by his usual lecturing and administrative work at the Academy and in connection with the Women's Medical Courses. Nevertheless, life was much calmer as long as Catherine was away, and he could actually get down to work again on his opera. He managed this by getting up at five every morning, and working on his opera until ten. He wrote to his wife on 4 October 1883[3]:

'Yesterday I started work on *Igor* very early in the morning; it was just like the old days. And then at ten o'clock drove to the Nikolaevsky Hospital for a committee meeting . . . which dragged on till three in the afternoon. . . . I spent the morning disclosing the various swindles and embezzlements perpetrated by Vilchkovsky[4] and later, in the afternoon, his sharp practices in administrative matters. Fortunately, they managed to catch him, and even if they don't hang him, at least the guilty parties will be shown up, and this will do the students a

[1] Letter to A. P. and E. G. Dianin dated 31 August (Letter 1011, pp. 33–34).
Several lines further on in the same letter, Borodin announces that Catherine has woken up but has decided not to go to Sosnovka but to the zoological garden.
[2] At this time, Borodin was particularly interested in Vol. II of Karamzin's *History of the Russian State*, and in *The Kiev Chronicle*. See his letter to Stassov on 4 August (*Letters*, Vol. IV, Letter 1008, p. 31).
[3] Ibid., Letter 1014, pp. 35–36.
[4] Governor of the Nikolaevsky Military Hospital.

XI. LOUISE, COUNTESS OF MERCY-ARGENTEAU

The original photograph was taken between 1880 and 1885. This copy was given by the Countess to Rimsky-Korsakov.

XII. BORODIN

A photograph taken in the autumn of 1885 by Sobolev at St. Petersburg, and
given by Borodin to the author's mother.

good turn.' The day described here was in no way extraordinary but quite typical of Borodin's day-to-day routine at this time.

He spent the few free moments he had to spare rearranging the furniture in his study. He had thought of refurnishing it in oriental style, and he acquired a few inexpensive carpets with this end in view. He also made use of a tapestry (with an inscription from the Koran) which Anna Kalinina had given him, and installed instead of a bed, a Turkish style low sofa covered with a carpet. For a time Borodin was so carried away by the furnishings of his own little nook that he used to lay awake at night for hours on end trying to decide which carpet would go best with the sofa, and what kind of cushions to put on it.

He spent the whole of October working systematically on the Prologue, devoting his early mornings to it. 'I get up terribly early', he wrote to his wife on 15 October, 'at five or six, and get down to work on *Igor*, so you see, the old thing is getting along quite well after all. I sleep disgracefully little, five hours a night perhaps, six at the very most[1] . . .'

The Borodins carried on their usual lively correspondence. Catherine's stay in Moscow this year was not a very happy one. Her relatives, that is, her brother Alexey and his family, were still in serious financial difficulties. In addition to this, the Golitsyn Hospital authorities threatened to evict Catherine's mother from her flat. All these troubles inevitably had an adverse effect on Borodin's health. He was kept busy seeing and writing to various people to find out if anything could be done to prevent his mother-in-law's eviction, and he had to come to the rescue once again of his brother-in-law, offering him accommodation in his already overcrowded flat. But, unlike his wife's continual illness and insomnia, none of these worries upset his equilibrium, and he continued to work without interruption on his opera. In a letter to Catherine, dated 31 October, he tells her: 'Today I got up at six, and got down to *Igor* without even bothering to wash.' We learn from this letter that on the evening of 31 October he had been making corrections to the printed orchestral parts of the First Symphony.[2] G. O. Dutsch was helping him.

About the same time Borodin was informed that they were intending to perform his First Symphony in Belgium. He received a letter from

[1] *Letters*, Vol. IV, Letter 1018, p. 43. This shows how hard Borodin worked—the same composer whom Stassov once called 'lazy and idle' in a letter to I. E. Repin.
[2] Ibid., Letter 1022, p. 50.

Jadoul, the Belgian musician, which was very enthusiastic about this symphony; he asked Borodin if he might dedicate one of his ballads to him.

Meanwhile Borodin continued working on his opera during the early mornings, until almost the end of November. The Prologue was most likely finished by 21 November. He held a large party that day by way of celebration; among the guests were Rimsky-Korsakov and his wife, Lodyzhensky, Lyadov, Glazunov, F. Blumenfeld, and Stassov.

'Our musical fraternity,' he wrote to Catherine the following day, 'came along to hear my Prologue.'[1]

But very soon after this party, his work on *Igor* came to a halt. On 3 December, he wrote to his wife with the news that 'Igor is temporarily out of action, owing to lack of time.'[2] His mornings had to be spent preparing reports for various committees.

In the same letter Borodin broke it to his wife that 'I have been elected Director of the Musical Society. . . . My musical friends are somewhat peeved that I have become involved in this.' We learn also that Borodin's nomination was put forward by K. Y. Davydov, who was at that time Director of the Conservatory. Borodin supposed that, as Director of the R.M.O. he would be in a position to do something to promote Russian music; also he did not want to offend Davydov who had always been friendly towards him. Shortly afterwards, Borodin went to a musical party at Davydov's. The latter played Chopin's Cello Sonata specially for Borodin, and the pianist D'Albert gave a beautiful performance of both the Borodin Symphonies, which he played from the piano-duet arrangements.

Catherine came back to Petersburg early in December. In the same month his *In the Steppes of Central Asia* was given its first performance abroad, at the third of a series of Academy concerts in Jena.[3] Also at this time, Borodin received, through Riedel a request from the Dresden conductor, Wullner, to send the score and parts of the First Symphony for performance at one of his concerts.

From January 1884 and for a considerable time, work on *Igor* was completely at a standstill. The life Borodin was leading made further

---

[1] *Letters*, Vol. IV, Letter 1027, pp. 58–59.

As we see below, not all the numbers of the 'Prologue' had yet been committed to paper at this time.

[2] Ibid., Letter 1030, p. 62.

[3] A poster of this concert is preserved with a congratulatory inscription by Liszt and Hille (see *Borodin*, Russian 2nd ed., p. 265).

progress on his opera impossible. Not only this, but the work still to be done consisted mainly of editing and revising and this could never engage his interest completely. He began to have ideas for other compositions. It was probably in the winter months of 1883 and 1884 that he conceived the outlines of his Third Symphony and the notion of adapting the Quartet Scherzo movement for the Scherzo of this symphony, the trio of which was to be based on the theme of 'The Merchants' Tale'. (This had originally been intended for *Igor*, but Borodin changed his mind in 1879.)

A number of performances of Borodin's works were given that winter. It was in the spring of 1884 that Russian music caught on in Belgium, and Borodin received a succession of enthusiastic letters from Jadoul. It was his efforts and the patronage of Countess Louise de Mercy-Argenteau that made possible a performance of *In the Steppes of Central Asia* at a concert in Liège on 17/29 March 1884. In view of the work's enormous success, it was given a repeat performance on 19 April (1 May N.S.).[1] Jadoul informed Borodin that plans were afoot for a special concert of Russian music which would be held the following season in Liège, and asked him to send the score and orchestral parts of either one of his symphonies.

There was a sharp deterioration in Borodin's health later in the spring, accompanied by loss of strength and fits of nervous irritability, which were surprising in a man of such gentle and amiable disposition. He was saddled with a load of bureaucratic business, such as the notorious 'Commission for investigating the cost of drugs', could not get enough sleep on account of his wife, and was unable to indulge in his favourite pursuit. It is not surprising that it took Borodin all his time to put up with the usual fuss Catherine made in deciding where they would spend the summer.

This time, their summer residence was suggested by their recently acquired friend, the famous botanist S. G. Navashin, who at that time had only just entered on a scientific career. Navashin was intending to spend the summer in Pavlovskoye, which is in the Zvenigorod Province and within easy reach of Moscow, and he invited the Borodins to join him there. After a certain amount of hesitation they decided to accept the offer.

On 18 June Borodin saw his wife off to her mother's in Moscow, and he himself set off for Pavlovskoye with Elena Guseva, to get the

[1] The programmes of the first and third concerts of the *Société libre d'émulation*, in which *In the Steppes of Central Asia* was performed, have been preserved.

place ready for Catherine's arrival. His irritability and weariness show up clearly in a letter he wrote to his wife on 18 June; he was complaining of all the bother he was put to both by his own and other people's affairs: 'God knows, I am expected to be Glinka and Semyon Petrovich,[1] scientist and committee-man, artist, official, benefactor, father of adopted children, doctor and invalid, all rolled into one. . . . But it won't be long before I am nothing more than the last of these, to the exclusion of all the other roles. I would go anywhere just to get away from here, to the country, anywhere, to the devil even.'[2]

The worn-out composer could see still more troubles looming up ahead. He even had to 'acquire an instrument' before he could finally relax and get down to his music again. When he had settled everything at Pavlovskoye, he left Elena with the Navashins, and set off for Moscow to fetch Catherine. It turned out that she was suffering from a severe bronchial attack, and feeling very depressed. The description he gave her of Pavlovskoye (the thick vegetation, the heavy morning and evening dews, and the setting of the cottage which was in a hollow) put her off completely, for she thought it would be disastrous for her health. So Borodin had to look for some other place. He eventually found a cottage at Pechatniki in the Moscow suburbs. Unfortunately, there was a report in the newspapers that a gang of thieves had recently been rounded up and arrested in the vicinity. When Catherine read about this, she simply refused to go there. In the end, the Borodins decided to give Pavlovskoye a trial, if only 'for five days'. As a result of all this, Borodin spent the greater part of the time in Moscow in his mother-in-law's 'hen-coop' of a flat, and was so concerned about his wife's illness and so taken up with negotiations for summer cottages that he did not even manage to find a piano. As regards music, the only thing worthy of mention is his correspondence with the Countess de Mercy-Argenteau, who had become overnight a devoted admirer and active propagandist on his behalf. In his first letter to her, dated 29 June, he promised to orchestrate his ballad 'The Sea' for the forthcoming performance of this work at Liège, and to send her three solo numbers from *Igor* (Konchak's Aria, Prince Vladimir's Aria, and Prince Galitsky's Song).[3]

The Borodins settled down quite well in Pavlovskoye, and stayed

---

[1] Catherine's uncle by marriage. He is taken as a typical example of an official.
[2] *Letters*, Vol. IV, Letter 1046, p. 70.
[3] Ibid., Letter 1048, p. 72.

there for the remainder of the summer. Catherine had persuaded the Navashins to let them have their house, which was on higher ground than the one originally offered to Borodin, and the Navashins moved to another cottage. Thus the Borodins found themselves with a fair-sized house at their disposal. Borodin's own study turned out to be better than any of the rooms he had used in previous years.

Their house looked out on to a large meadow; and beyond this meadow was a cemetery with two very attractive shrines. Borodin also liked the countryside around. The most serious disadvantage was that Borodin had no piano there. He told A. P. and E. G. Dianin how he felt about this, in a letter of 2 August:

'It is true that I can use my neighbours' piano if I like, but that is not quite the same thing as having one's own; it makes me feel embarrassed.[1]

There is hardly any doubt at all that this factor, on top of his extreme exhaustion, contributed towards keeping Borodin's music that summer down to a minimum. It would seem that he spent most time on the Third Act of *Igor*, and in particular, the words sung by Konchak's daughter in the Trio. For this, he had decided to use Voyslava's theme from *Mlada*, which figures in the latter's duet with Yaromir.[2] In addition to this, Borodin was still going on with the orchestration of 'The Sea', which he had transposed into E minor.[3] And lastly, it is quite likely that he worked out the central theme of the Andante of the Third Symphony, which of course was never written down.

Borodin was given to observing local customs and writing down whatever songs he happened to be attracted to. In Pavlovskoye the situation was ideal for this, and he gathered some rather curious material. A number of 'bes-popovtsy', whose sect was opposed to any form of priesthood, were living in the district. In his own peculiar humorous style, he gives several descriptions in his letters of the various inhabitants of Pavlovskoye. But he did not come across any really interesting folk-music there: 'The lads and lasses here go about

[1] *Letters*, Vol. IV, Letter 1051, p. 76.
[2] One of the sketches of the text of Konchak's Daughter's vocal part in the trio in Act III has been preserved in the file 'Libretto of *Igor* and Musical Matters'. It was written on the back of a draft of a letter to V. A. Manassyein on 9 August, 1884. See *Letters*, Vol. IV, note 4 to Letter 1052, p. 337.
[3] Borodin described his alterations to the song 'The Sea', when orchestrating it, in a letter to the Countess de Mercy-Argenteau dated 6 November 1884 (*Letters*, Vol. IV, Letter 1074, p. 106).

singing pseudo-popular songs, in bad taste; such sentimental trash as 'The footprints of my dear one on the golden sand".'[1] Nevertheless Borodin unearthed some interesting liturgical music. With a view to finding out more of these melodies, he made several visits with Elena Guseva and one of the local women to a meeting-house of the priestless sect. He found that they sang 'most interesting hymns of considerable antiquity, resembling in some way Liszt's "Danse Macabre", and the "Dies irae, dies illa".'

Borodin made a note of the tunes he liked best of these:

Ex. 2

He based the following C minor theme on one of these tunes; it is marked Andante and is written on the same scrap of paper:

Ex. 3

Borodin later used this theme in the Andante of the Third Symphony.[2] It is probable that the composer had intended to use it as such right from the start.

In so far as the 'wicked' cold summer permitted, Borodin indulged in the usual walks and mushroom-gathering expeditions. By the beginning of September, both he and Catherine felt much better. Early that month, they travelled to Moscow together. Borodin had to keep prodding Catherine, who put off their departure more than once; as Borodin saw it, they were all the while 'getting ready to make a start on getting their things together.'[3]

[1] Letter to E. G. Dianina on 2 August 1884 (Ibid., Letter 1051, p. 75).
[2] These sketches of ritual songs together with the theme of the Andante were handed to E. A. Guseva with instructions to look after them carefully. I obtained the sketches from her in 1923.
[3] Letter to E. G. Dianina on 2 September 1884 (*Letters*, Vol. IV, Letter 1057, p. 82).

Borodin went on to Petersburg on 14 September; Catherine stayed behind in Moscow until November.

This autumn Borodin led a more regular life; he rose early as usual and went to bed around midnight. Almost every day was taken up by lecturing and committee work of all kinds. It is possible to assume that he composed the overture to *Igor* either shortly before he left Pavlovskoye or soon after he returned to Petersburg. We base this assumption on Borodin's reference to a meeting with his composer friends. He wrote:

'They are all pestering me about the overture. Glazunov and Dutsch have taken it upon themselves to copy the parts, if only I will do something about having it ready for the Musical Society concert.'[1] We can only surmise from this either that Borodin played them a few snatches of the overture, or that he had composed the whole thing by that time.

As we already know, Borodin had entered into correspondence with his Belgian admirers, T. Jadoul and the Countess de Mercy-Argenteau. This let Borodin in for new complications.

For instance, he received a letter from the Countess enclosing a translation of his ballads, made by her and the poet Paul Collen jointly, and further translations of the solo numbers[2] from *Igor*.[3] Borodin felt he had to make certain corrections in these translations which contained several 'howlers'. The following examples might be given: the Countess had given an entirely literal translation of 'to sit as Prince on Putivl' (which means 'to become ruler of Putivl') thinking that 'Putivl' was some kind of 'Georgian mare called Pultiva'; not only this but a number of absurdities had appeared in the translation of Prince Galitsky's Song, such as 'ambrosia', 'polkas and quadrilles', and so forth. There were also unfortunate mistakes in the translation of 'The False Note', and a glorious blunder in 'The Sleeping Princess' when the wood-goblins turned up in translation as satyrs. Borodin was extremely tactful in the manner in which he made all these corrections. Negotiations were also in progress for publishing the ballads with bilingual French and Russian texts, as well as for a French edition of 'The Three Igors'. In order to secure copyrights,

---

[1] Letter to Catherine dated 23 September 1884 (Ibid., Letter 1062, p. 87).
[2] Known to her as 'les trois Igors'.
[3] See Madame d'Argenteau's telegram to Cui on 9/21 October 1884, and also Lamoureux's letter to Madame d'Argenteau dated 8/20 October of the same year (*Borodin*, Russian 2nd ed., pp. 339–40).

he was obliged to become a member of the French performing rights society in December 1884.

He also had to discuss with his Belgian correspondents which of his two symphonies should be performed at a concert of Russian music to be given in Liège; he eventually decided on the First Symphony.

Reports from France and Belgium which proved that 'the new Russian music' was gaining an international reputation were now becoming more and more frequent as time went on. On 7/19 October, *In the Steppes of Central Asia* was well received in Paris at a concert conducted by Lamoureux.

About this time a committee for publicizing the new Russian music was formed in Liège; this organized weekly concerts at which were performed new works and anything else that was of particular interest to the members. At one of these meetings the E flat major Symphony was performed as a piano-duet. It went down very well with the director of the Verviers Conservatoire, who happened to be there on that particular occasion, and he took away with him the score and orchestral parts and performed it in Verviers[1] on 17 October 1884. A little later Lamoureux expressed a desire to perform the B minor Symphony in Paris.

During the Christmas holidays of 1884–5, he composed the ballad 'Pride of Place' for Anna Bichurina, the opera-singer, and probably also several movements of the 'Miniature Suite' for piano, which he dedicated to the Countess de Mercy-Argenteau.[2]

The first concert of music by Russian composers was given in Liège in January. Jadoul conducted a performance of Borodin's First Symphony, and the whole concert was well received. The Symphony in particular was such an outstanding success that, in response to popular request, it was given a repeat performance later in January. The most successful item, after the symphony, was the ballad 'The Sleeping Princess'.

At the end of January the A major Quartet was published by Rahter. This quartet was not long in gaining popularity in Europe, and later in America.

Early in February Borodin received a letter from Brunot, the President of 'The International Composers' Association' in Paris, asking

---

[1] See Jadoul's letter to Borodin on 13/25 October 1884 (*Borodin*, p. 279).

[2] See Borodin's letter to Madame d'Argenteau on 18 January 1885 (*Letters* Vol. IV. Letter 1087, p. 111).

him to send the score and parts of the First Symphony for a performance at the Association's festival.

Meanwhile reports continued to pour in of the successes Russian
music was having in Belgium. A third concert of Russian music took
place in Liège on 28 February. The works performed were: Borodin's
First Symphony, Prince Galitsky's Song, 'The Sea Princess', and
'The Sleeping Princess'[1]; Lel's song from Rimsky-Korsakov's *Snow
Maiden*; the Chorus of Marina's servants from *Boris Godunov*;
Glazunov's Piano Suite (on the theme of 'Sascha'); Dargomyzhsky's
Slavic Tarantella; Cui's song 'Enfant, si j'etais roi'; extracts from his
opera *The Caucasian Prisoner*, including the Circassian Song, Chorus,
Sextet, and Circassian Dances; and, finally, Cui's Andante and Scherzo
for violin and piano, and his Tarantella. 'The whole concert was a huge
success.'[2]

The 6 February 1885 was the fifth anniversary of the death of
Nikolai Zinin, and a memorial to him was unveiled on that day. This
was largely the work of Borodin, who had done much towards gathering the necessary funds; the memorial was housed in the Natural
History block of the Academy. In fact, the nation-wide appeal for
funds had raised such a sizeable sum of money that the surplus went
towards endowing a Zinin Scholarship for needy students.

For the remainder of the session Borodin continued to direct the
student orchestra, which had been founded by him in 1883. At this
period he was putting the finishing touches to his Miniature Suite and
to the A flat major Scherzo which he had dedicated to Jadoule. In an
attempt to stir Borodin to further work on his opera, some time in the
spring, Rimsky-Korsakov began preparing the piano arrangement for
Igor.

'I am doing the preliminary piano arrangement for *Igor* and at the
same time putting it into shape. I am also adding and cutting out bars
here and there, filling in the recitatives, numbering the modulations,
transposing where necessary, improving the part-writing, and so forth.
I have already finished the Prologue and the first scene of Act One,
and I think, if all goes well, the opera will be ready by the autumn,
and we shall then be able to get down to the orchestration; it should be

[1] Performed as an encore: the ballad was not on the programme.
[2] The programme of this concert is reconstructed from Van der Boorn's review which
appeared in the Liège paper, *La Meuse*, in early March 1885. It is learnt from this review
that the song of Vladimir Galitsky was performed with piano accompaniment. This was
contrary to the wishes of Borodin, who had sent them the orchestral score of this number
long before.

ready for performance by next spring. It is my fond belief that Borodin won't be able to resist doing something to the opera himself when he sees what I have done; I need his advice on the Third Act, because there is quite a lot still missing there.'[1]

But as far as we can tell, Rimsky-Korsakov did not get any further than the second scene of Act One.

At the end of June, Borodin suddenly went down with a mild form of cholera. The attack was so severe that he would have died but for an injection of a saline solution which proved successful.[2] His healthy constitution was soon able to grapple with the disease, and after a few days he was able to describe his illness to Anna Kalinina in a humorous piece of verse.[3] There is however no doubt at all that this illness seriously overtaxed his health and was one of the major causes of his fatal heart disease which appeared not long after.

Some time after 20 July Catherine left for Moscow to spend the summer in Ramenskoye, a residential area in the outskirts of Moscow, with a very old friend of hers, the amateur violinist Y. S. Orlovsky. A few days later, on 27 July to be precise, Borodin went abroad.[4] Still suffering from the after-effects of his illness, and perhaps as a result of increasing pain due to the onset of heart-disease, Borodin felt it would be advisable before he left to leave a note, which in the event of his death might provide useful information and instructions for the use of his friends and next-of-kin.[5]

Previous to this, Borodin had already completed all seven of the piano pieces comprising the 'Miniature Suite', which he had dedicated

---

[1] Quoted from Rimsky-Korsakov's memoirs, 3rd ed., p. 276 (footnote). Whilst Rimsky-Korsakov was working on this, he also jotted down the scene of the eclipse in the Prologue. This had been sketched out in the form of a series of modulations. [I printed this series of modulations in my article 'On the rôle of the feeling for tonality in Borodin's creative process', *De musica*, 1927, No. 3.] So well did Rimsky-Korsakov normally recollect Borodin's improvisations, and so well could he reconstruct a whole passage from a simple set of modulations, that he was able to re-write Borodin's music so accurately that, according to A. P. Dianin, when the composer examined such 'restorations' he did not find it necessary to alter a single note.

[2] According to E. G. Dianina, Dr. V. P. Dianin rendered Borodin this assistance, having just entered the laboratory when the composer was seized with this horrible attack.

[3] The date of Borodin's indisposition from this mild form of cholera can be definitely established from A. N. Kalinina's two letters to the composer (dated 14 July and 16 August 1885). E. M. Braüdo (op. cit. p. 87) incorrectly gives the date of the illness as 1884.

[4] The date of Borodin's departure abroad is established from entries in his passport for 1885. According to this document, Borodin passed through Verzhbolovo on 28 July. Hence, it is seen that he left St. Petersburg on 27 July.

[5] *Letters*, Vol. IV, Letters 1120 and 1121, pp. 123–4.

to the Countess. The Suite was programmatic in form; we know this from a sub-title 'Petit poème d'amour d'une jeune fille' which, although it does not appear in the published work, may be seen in the manuscript together with a rough sketch of the programme.[1] The 'Miniature Suite' and the Scherzo dedicated to Jadoule were published by Bessel; Borodin corrected the proofs of these works while travelling.

He arrived in Germany towards the end of the summer, but neither in Berlin nor in Leipzig did he find any of the people he really wanted to see. In Weimar however he saw Liszt again, but he did not know that this was to be their last meeting. The composers were of course delighted to see one another, and Borodin spent a whole evening with the maestro at Meyendorf's, when Liszt played the 'Miniature Suite' and the Scherzo from the proofs; he was 'terrifically pleased' with them.[2]

After saying farewell to Liszt, Borodin went on to Liège arriving on 5/17 August. He stayed in the Countess's chateau which was about thirteen kilometres from the town itself, and was given a small separate apartment all to himself. Borodin was impressed by the beautiful setting of the chateau, and by the warm welcome he received.[3]

Borodin was touched by all this, and, composing his last ballad 'Septain' to words by Georges Collen, dedicated it to the park, the chateau, and the gracious lady who lived there.[4]

After he had been a few days in Liège, he made a short visit to Antwerp, but this turned out to be a waste of time since the concerts due to take place at the Exhibition in Antwerp had been postponed until September, and all the musicians seemed to be away.

From Antwerp Borodin went on to Paris. He stayed there until 6 September.

While he was in Paris, Borodin did not come across a single one of his Russian acquaintances resident there. He spent the greater part of his free time in the company of the violinist, P. Marsick, whom he had met in Liège, and other French musicians. It was also about this time that he made the acquaintance of Bourgault-Ducoudray and Saint-Saëns. He also received an invitation from the Association of

[1] *Letters*, Vol. IV, Letter 1107, pp. 119–20.
[2] Ibid., Letter 1124, pp. 127–8.
[3] Ibid., Letter 1125 and 1126, pp. 129–32.
[4] As may be seen from Borodin's letter to his wife dated 27 March 1886, he brought back several copies of his song 'Septain' from Belgium in 1886 where it had been published in Liège, and sent Catherine one of these. Hence, it seems certain that 'Septain' was written abroad, and that Borodin did not bring the original manuscript back with him when he returned to Russia.

Antwerp musicians to conduct concerts of Russian music at the Antwerp Exhibition. It was through this that he learned that his First Symphony was to be performed, in addition to *In The Steppes of Central Asia*, the Second Symphony, and ballads already scheduled for performance. Borodin firmly declined the offer on the grounds that he was not accustomed to conducting large orchestras, but he certainly had no intention of missing the three concerts, which were all a magnificent success; his own works received a great ovation. *In the Steppes of Central Asia* was played at the first of these concerts; the B minor Symphony at the second, under the direction of Huberti; and the E flat Symphony at the last of the three concerts, with Radoux as conductor. Borodin became a close friend of both these conductors.

Borodin left for Russia the day after the third concert, that is on 8/20 September. He went by way of Leipzig and saw Riedel and his family for the last time. Borodin reached Petersburg on 14 September (O.S.) and shortly afterwards went to Moscow for a few days to see his wife. Catherine had decided, on the advice of her doctors, to spend the winter in Moscow. She was staying with Doctor M. V. Uspensky, an old friend and former colleague of Borodin who lived in a government flat at the Cadet Corps Headquarters in Lefortovo.

After seeing that all was well with Catherine there, Borodin returned to Petersburg on 24 September and resumed his normal work. The medical courses for women had been discontinued,[1] and as a result, Borodin's work as lecturer was now restricted to the Military Academy of Medicine. But, in addition to this, he was involved in several committees connected with the Ministry of War. One such committee was drafting proposals for providing the army with disinfectants. He was chairman of a number of these bodies.

In November 1885, Borodin, to satisfy his friends, resigned from the board of governors of the Russian Musical Society.

It was about this time that a new musical organization came into being; its aims were to provide a series of Russian symphony concerts. The organization was the idea of Belyaev, and the musical direction of these concerts was carried out by the musicians who used to meet at Belyaev's home. They called themselves 'the Belyaev circle'. Borodin was present at the first concert which took place on 23 November 1885.

---

[1] The abolition of the medical courses took place in 1885. A. P. Dianin describes in his *Biographical Sketch* how deeply Borodin was affected by this misfortune. When they were obliged to transfer the equipment of the chemical laboratory back to the Academy of Medicine, Borodin could not contain himself and burst into tears.

The programme included the B minor Symphony; according to Borodin, this 'went off very well and was well received.'[1]

Four days after this concert, a memorial to Mussorgsky was unveiled at a ceremony held at the composer's graveside in the Alexandro-Nevsky cemetery. 'At Stassov's insistence' Borodin himself paid tribute to Mussorgsky by making the opening speech at the ceremony.[2]

On 1 December he conducted a concert given by the amateur orchestra he had founded two years earlier at the Academy. The concert went well, and the overture to *Ruslan and Ludmila* was encored. The press drew attention to Borodin's talent as a conductor.[3]

In the course of the season, Hans von Bülow and the violinist Marsick visited Petersburg. Bülow conducted a few concerts of the Russian Musical Society, and included Borodin's First Symphony in one of the programmes (21 December 1885).

Early in the winter, Borodin and Cui received invitations from Belgium to visit Liège and Brussels at the end of December. Works by Borodin and other Russian composers were to be performed there, and there was to be a production of Cui's opera *The Caucasian Prisoner* at the theatre in Liège. The composers left Petersburg on 21 December (O.S.) and arrived in Liège on 25 December.

Borodin's last visit to Belgium lasted until 12/24 January 1886. The whole time was spent going to rehearsals, concerts, performances of *The Caucasian Prisoner*, and of course in official and informal visits of one kind or another. Borodin once again heard fine performances of his two symphonies, a number of his ballads, and selections from his opera. He made a number of new acquaintances, including Habets, his future biographer, and Dupont, the conductor from Brussels. Dupont was charmed by the bits of *Igor* he had heard, and asked Borodin to let him have a French translation of the libretto together with the full score of the opera, which he was determined to stage in Brussels. This time, the concert-goers gave the Russian music an even more enthusiastic reception than ever before, Borodin's works in particular.

Borodin returned to Petersburg, a tired but contented man; and immediately upon his arrival (16 January) he was plunged up to the eyes in routine work of every sort. An alarming amount of work had

---

[1] Letter to his wife dated 30 November 1885 (Letter 1160, p. 156).

[2] Letter to his wife dated 3 December 1885 (Letter 1162, pp. 158–9).

[3] A review signed 'A. Sk.' appeared in No. 325 of the paper *Novosti* (3 December 1885) (*Letters*, Vol. IV, p. 158).

accumulated during his absence. The whole of his time was taken up, and he was even obliged to cut down his normal hours of sleep.

In his letters to Catherine, written during January and February, we see Borodin sharing with her his dreams of a summer holiday, and hoping that one day he would be able to rid himself forever of all his administrative and official duties: 'I keep on dreaming of next summer, of a summer cottage, of life in the country; I am looking forward to the time when I can put on my red shirt, and go bathing and walking whenever I like! Lord knows, that's not much to hope for, but somehow it doesn't always turn out just like that! But time still rushes by, absolutely flies, and here's me thirty years a professor, and all the time slaving away. I can tell you, that's no joke! ... And what the devil could I do about it, even if I wanted to break off my official appointment to go and live as I pleased! After all, one has to eat. My pension won't cover everything, and you certainly can't make a living out of music. If I were a painter, that would be a different matter altogether! Makovsky's picture "The Marriage" went down no better than my Symphony in Antwerp; I would even go so far as to say that mine was even more successful. His picture brought 15,000, but my Symphony not a bean! That's music for you!'[1]

In the middle of February Borodin spent a few days in Moscow. On his return, his Petersburg composer friends made yet another concerted effort to persuade him to finish *Igor*. Borodin wrote to Catherine telling her about a musical evening at their flat on 9 March: 'Last Sunday we had visitors: Glazunov, the Korsakovs, Belyaev, the two Blumenfelds, V. Stassov, Ilyinsky, Moiseyenko (you remember, Ilyinsky's friend, one of our staunch supporters) Kurbanov, Marya Vasilievna [Dobroslavina], and Alexandra Alexandrovna [Alexandrova] were all there. *Igor* was the only thing they played, and everybody went mad with delight. All this was a prearranged plot to make me get on with my opera; even Pavlych [Dianin] knew all about this, but he didn't want to let on! Belyaev, who was also a party to this and who also has his own publishing firm in Leipzig, took me completely by surprise and offered me 3,000 roubles on the spot for the publishing rights of the opera! Bessel would give no more than 600, at the most 1,000 (if that!). Not only this, but Belyaev is in a different class altogether from Bessel; his editions comprise full-score and piano arrangement, whereas Bessel couldn't afford this sort of

---

[1] Letter to Catherine dated 1 February 1886 (Letter 1182, p. 180).

thing. Finally, Belyaev offered to pay cash down, which of course Bessel would never dream of doing! So things have turned out rather better than I expected.'[1]

He asked Catherine to keep this information about Belyaev's offer secret. But he was not very strict about it himself, for he wrote the news to Marya Guseva only two days later, and was not long in telling his Belgian friends as well.[2]

Borodin now realized that he would have to finish his opera if he wanted to avoid a breach of contract: 'I really must get some serious work done on my opera this summer',[3] he wrote to Catherine on 27 March.

Apart from the various letters he had to write to his musical contacts, Borodin was occupied right through to the summer with just about everything except music. There were the Spring Examinations at the Academy, and the usual miscellaneous committees and commissions. In early April he was re-elected Professor for a further five-year term of office.[4]

The Easter holidays fell in April, and Borodin took the opportunity to go and see his wife in Moscow. He rented a cottage in Ramenskoye in the suburbs, and they spent their short holiday together there. During this time he made friends with two young French women named Judith and Delphine, who were living almost next door to Catherine in the Lefortovo Headquarters. Judith (whose married name was Raquint) was a talented pianist, and her unmarried sister was both singer and violinist.

Soon after he returned to Petersburg, he received a telegram asking him to go again to Moscow at once as his mother-in-law was seriously ill. But he managed to combine this visit with a number of matters he had to attend to in Moscow. In a letter dated 6 May 1886, he wrote: 'I have been driving all over the place, on personal as well as official business; I suppose one of these days I shall be back again in Petersburg.'[5] He did actually return to Petersburg in the middle of May.

Meanwhile Catherine herself took a turn for the worse. Swellings began to appear as a result of dropsy. At the beginning of June her condition became so serious that Alexander Dianin, who happened

[1] Letter dated 15 March 1886 (Letter 1184, p. 183).
[2] Ibid., Letter 1185, p. 185.
[3] Ibid., Letter 1187, p. 188.
[4] Letter to Catherine dated 5 April 1886 (Ibid., Letter 1189, p. 189).
[5] Letter to P. P. Alekseev dated 6 May 1886 (Ibid., Letter 1191, p. 191).

to be there at the time, sent a telegram (June 3) to Borodin asking him to come at once.

The next four days were nerve-racking for Borodin, and he hardly slept at all, expecting that his wife might die at any minute. These bitter experiences came as a severe strain on his already worn-out frame, and seriously aggravated the heart disease which probably already existed. On 8 June Catherine began to show signs of recovery, and Borodin himself came back to life. But even after they had settled in their summer cottage at Ramenskoye and Catherine had improved in health considerably, Borodin none the less found he had no free time to himself and was therefore unable to do any composing.

It was not until the end of July that Catherine recovered a more normal state of mind and Borodin was able to relax a little. But this was not to last long. Suddenly Catherine's mother became fatally ill and died on 6 September 1886. It was on this account that the Borodins had to give up their cottage and move into Moscow. They took a flat as near as they could to where Catherine's mother was living.[1] Borodin lived here until the end of September, and it was at this time that the Third Symphony, which he had had in mind for some time past, began finally to take shape. He composed the first subject of the first movement, and worked with a will on the movement as a whole.[2] It is very probable too that he was working on *Igor* at this time, making a number of sketches for the Third Act and editing the Second Act. But we know nothing about this for certain.

Borodin came back to Petersburg on 5 October, leaving Catherine behind in Moscow in the hands of two servants and a private nurse. This autumn was no exception as regards pressure of administrative work and lecturing. Yet Borodin tried to put aside as much time as possible for music; it was though he sensed that his end was near. He had rehearsals and concerts of Russian music to attend, correspondence to keep up with musicians abroad, and the student orchestra to conduct, but he still managed to devote a certain amount of his time each day to composition; the early mornings came in useful for this. Early that autumn the proofs of B minor Symphony score began to arrive batch by batch from the publisher's. Borodin worked pains-

[1] She lived in the Golitsinskaya Hospital, the Borodins in Bolshaya Kaluzhskaya Street (house No. 43).

[2] My mother told me that Borodin taught my late brother Boris to play the theme of the first movement of the Third Symphony on the piano, during the month of September 1886, when A. P. and E. G. Dianin and their son were staying with the Borodins in Kaluzhskaya Street, while moving from Davydovo to St. Petersburg.

XIII. A. P. DIANIN

A photograph taken at Davidovo in September 1897.

takingly on these, and made a great number of minor alterations to the orchestral score.[1] His mornings were devoted to new work on *Igor* as well as to proof reading, and he eventually finished the editing of the Second Act. It was at this time that he wrote the Chorus of Polovtsian Patrol Guards ('The sun is going to rest behind the mountain'), the conversation between Igor and Konchak, and probably also the 'Chorus of Russian Prisoners', which was still in the form of an improvisation, and had not yet been put into shape.[2] In a letter of 20 November he wrote to tell Catherine: 'I have at last finished the Second Act of Igor.'[3]

Also this autumn, Borodin contributed towards a joint composition with other composers of a quartet based on the notes B flat, A, and F. It was being written for Belyaev on the occasion of his name-day which took place on 23 November 1886. We find the following details relating to this work in the letter of 20 November just mentioned:

'Korsakov did the first movement, Glazunov the Finale, Lyadov the Scherzo, and I have been writing a Spanish Serenade for the slow movement; it is a very odd piece of music indeed but it sounds all right. . . . I worked out a charming little Spanish tune on the three-note sequence B flat, A, F, and counterpoint for the other instruments. The whole thing is delightfully original and witty in the extreme, but at the same time very musical. I dashed it off at one go, and it is the height of spontaneity.'[4]

The autumn of 1886 therefore was a period of great creativity for Borodin. But his low state of health prevented him from making the best use of it. Quite early in the autumn Borodin had begun to feel occasional pains in the region of his heart, and he sought the advice of Alexander Dianin and several doctors whom he knew personally, asking them to give him a thorough examination. The diagnosis was that he was suffering from a serious heart disease. It goes without saying, however, that the diagnosis was withheld from the patient.

Dianin was afraid Borodin would not last long, and promised Rimsky-Korsakov and Glazunov that he would give them immediate news of anything Borodin was writing, so that they could take advantage of Glazunov's phenomenal memory, in case of necessity,

---

[1] As is generally known, Borodin did not live to see the score of his Second Symphony appear in print; some of the proofs were corrected by Glazunov and Rimsky-Korsakov after his death.

[2] Glazunov later wrote down this chorus from memory.

[3] *Letters*, Vol. IV, Letter 1218, p. 217.   [4] Ibid.

and thus be able to reconstruct even the bars of music that had yet to be written. The whole of December and right up to the Christmas vacation, Borodin was enmeshed in useless and most tedious official business. On 18 December he wrote to Catherine: 'I am dashing off this note in a great hurry, as I am up to my neck in stacks of screed for various committees, scrawling ink in liberal quantities over all kinds of reports, notifications, memoranda, recommendations, decisions—a heap of utter rubbish. Lord! When will it all end. . . .'[1]

In the latter half of December, Borodin made use of the Christmas vacation to go and see his wife in Moscow. He stayed there until 7 January 1887. He spent his last few days with his wife composing; he was working on the first movement of the Third Symphony.[2]

The train back to Petersburg was packed, and this made him very tired; but on his return he immediately got into stride on his multifarious activities. In a letter dated 3 February 1887, he was delighted to pass on to Catherine the news that his First Symphony had been well received in Amsterdam at a concert conducted by Julius Röntgen. In the same letter was the information that S. Blumenfeld had made a piano duet arrangement of the D major Quartet, followed by the remark: 'As you know, I have a Third Symphony in mind, but it is hardly likely to see the light of day for some time yet, as I have a lot still to do on Igor, which is going very slowly indeed.'[3]

We do not know what in fact his last work on *Igor* was. The only thing we know for certain is that Borodin continued to make sketches for the Overture and Act 3. But the conception of the Third Symphony now maturing in his mind distracted him from his work on the opera. In the very last days of his life Borodin was in the throes of the slow movement of this symphony. A few details of this we know from Marya Dobroslavina's memoirs.[4] She has it that one day he came to her house for dinner and arrived in a very gay mood. 'Seeing that he was in a very cheerful mood, we talked about Igor. As usual this eventually proved to be an unpleasant topic of conversation, and he began to lose his temper. "See now, I have come to play you

[1] *Letters*, Vol. IV, Letter 1224, p. 223.
[2] A sheet of music with the Moderato theme from the Third Symphony written on it was left on the stand of the piano in Catherine's room after Borodin's departure. When A. P. Dianin went to break the news of her husband's death, he found the sheet of paper in the same place where it had been left by the composer.
[3] *Letters*, Vol. IV, Letter 1233, p. 231–2.
[4] These reminiscences were written by M. V. Dobroslavina at my request. I discovered a number of inaccuracies in her account which I have corrected in Chapter V of the present volume. Cf. *Borodin*, Russian 2nd ed., pp. 343–7.

something," he went on, "and you are simply tormenting me with Igor instead. I'm damned if I'll play."'

'We asked his forgiveness, and promised never to mention the matter again; we begged him to play for us. And he finally agreed. He played what turned out to be the Andante of the Third Symphony. It would appear that, apart from my husband and myself, no one has yet heard this Andante.[1] He said himself that he had not shown it to anyone else, because it was not fully written down yet. It was in fact never written down, and was lost forever to Russian music. . . .

'The work took the form of a theme and variations. The theme was stark, "a song of the old believer" as he put it.[2] I do not remember how many variations there were; all I know is that they went in one terrific crescendo and, if I may use the expression, with a fanaticism all of their own.

'The final variation struck us with its power and impassioned cry of anguish.

'I am not particularly fond of this musical form. It feels studied and artificial, and thus, more often than not, tedious and dull. But the way Alexander Porfiryevich had used it, the result was such that my husband and I just looked at one another in astonishment and sheer delight. He could see that his work was making an impression on us, and played all the more, pointing out the scoring he had in mind as he went along. . . .'

This fresh outburst of creative energy which brought this Andante into being had a remarkable effect on Borodin's frame of mind during the last days of his life. His last letters to Catherine, dated 3, 9, and 14 February, are full of optimism and high spirits. He badly wanted to see her again so that he could share his joy with her. He had been planning to go to Moscow and to take advantage of the shrove-tide holiday, but this trip never materialized owing to the fact that he had

---

[1] In Dobroslavina's reminiscences, she mentions that this *Andante* was also known to my father (A. P. Dianin). This is untrue. My father heard the improvisation of the Finale to the Third Symphony, but if Borodin played the Andante in addition to the last movement that morning, my father certainly did not know of it.

There is a tradition that the Andante of the Third Symphony was also heard by Glazunov, but that he was unable to remember the theme around which the variations of the Andante were centred. I mention this story which I heard from B. V. Asafiev about 1925 and which was current in musical circles, without accepting its authenticity.

[2] Evidently, this was the same theme, or a similar variant, as that which we mentioned in the description of the summer of 1884. But M. V. Dobroslavina could not detect any resemblance between the theme shown to her and the music which she had heard in 1887. What struck her most about Borodin's performance of the Andante were the harmonies.

to appear as a witness in connection with Anna Lukanina's court case.

Sometime around 10 February, Borodin apparently did not feel too well for a little time, and he experienced something in the nature of a vague presentiment of impending death. This we know from what A. P. Dianin says. One day he found Borodin in the 'room with the open-fire' throwing bundles of letters into the grate; among these Dianin noticed particularly a number of wads of letters from the Countess which were easy to recognize from their black-bordered notepaper similar to that used in letters of mourning. When Dianin asked him what on earth he was doing, Borodin declared: 'Well, you see, my dear fellow, I am making quite sure that all this does not fall into the hands of some journalist after I die. I am afraid someone might have the bright idea of publishing the lot.'

But this phase probably did not last very long, since a large number of these personal and intimate letters are still in existence. It is possible too that he was diverted from the task of burning his letters by some urgent piece of business.

A. P. Dianin has told me more than once that on 12 and 13 February he was working in the Chemistry laboratory at the Academy, and listening to Borodin playing and composing in the room next door. This music left a very deep impression on Dianin. He says himself that he had never known any of Borodin's music to be so impressive and so beautiful as this, though this did not mean that he in any way underrated the rest of his music. The music that Dianin heard was quite different in style from any other that Borodin had written.

'He thundered away for quite a long time playing this tremendous music of his, and then he stopped. A few minutes later he came into the laboratory in a state of excitement and joy; there were tears in his eyes.

'"Well, Sashenka," he said, "I know that some of the things I have written are not bad. But this finale! . . . What a finale! . . ." As he said this, Borodin covered his eyes with one hand and gesticulated with the other. . . . But not a single bar of this finale has survived; unfortunately, he never got as far as writing it down.'[1]

Dianin did not forget his promise to Rimsky-Korsakov and Glazunov, and felt he ought to tell them as soon as possible of this new work of Borodin. But Dianin did not have the chance to arrange

---

[1] Among Borodin's musical manuscripts which were presented by Glazunov to the St. Petersburg conservatoire, there are a number of short sketches (of 1–2 bars) with the heading, 'For the Andante'. There were no sketches for the Finale.

for them to visit Borodin, since the latter was busy making arrangements for a fancy-dress ball to be held in the immediate future.

Borodin wrote to Catherine about this ball on 14 February 1887; it was his last letter. The ball was to be in grand style: 'il y aura de la bougie, such as one finds in Murget's *La Bohême*. Today we engaged a woman to play the piano. . . . The ball is going to be in the Sushchinsky lecture room.'[1]

Marya Dobroslavina tells how Borodin 'came to see us on 14 February and invited us to the ball on the following day; he said his idea was to provide entertainment for his "young things".[2] It was carnival time and he asked us to dress ourselves up if that was not too much trouble, for he wanted it to be as gay and informal as possible. I managed to concoct some kind of Russian folk costume. . . .

'After leaving us, he called on Prof. Yegorov, and begged him to come and bring his wife to the party; he assured them that they would have an interesting time and see things they would never see the like of again.'

Just as the ball was about to commence, the girls started quarrelling over nothing. Borodin was always upset by any kind of bickering, and this proved to be no exception, leaving him with a slight feeling of irritation and unpleasantness.[3]

He appeared at the ball dressed in a dark-red woollen shirt in Russian style and dark-blue baggy trousers.[4] Dobroslavina writes: 'They were all there at the appointed time. There were not many people, but the place was packed. Everyone was in high spirits. Not long after the dancing began, A. P. had a waltz with someone, I don't remember who, and then came over to me. We were standing there talking when Prof. Pashutin arrived and came across to greet us. He had come from a dinner and was in evening dress. Borodin asked him why he was looking so smart. I remarked that of all male attire I liked evening dress the most; it seemed to suit everyone and always looked elegant. A. P. declared with his usual mock gallantry that if I was really so fond of evening dress, he would in future always wear his frock-coat whenever he came to see me, so that I should never have any cause for displeasure.

---

[1] *Letters*, Vol. IV, Letter 1235, p. 236.   [2] His adopted daughters.

[3] My mother used to tell me with great sadness, that she met Borodin already dressed for the ball, and that the last words which she heard him utter before it started were an expression of reproach or displeasure on account of this quarrel.

[4] My mother kept this costume in Borodin's bureau, but I have no idea what happened to it subsequently.

'These were his last words. He spoke them indistinctly as though his tongue had grown numb, and it seemed to me that he was swaying. I stared at him, and I shall never forget the look on his face; a helpless, pitiful and frightened look. I hardly managed to cry "What's the matter?" before he fell full length on to the floor. Pashutin was standing right next to us, but failed to break his fall. . . .

'My God! How terrible this was! And the cry that went up from everyone! They all rushed towards him and, without lifting him up from the floor, tried to bring him round. Every doctor and professor in the Academy was soon there. For almost a whole hour they tried everything possible to revive him; but it was no use. I shall never forget the despair of one of the doctors, who was sitting with his head in his hands saying again and again that he would never forgive himself for not applying bleeding treatment at the start.

'And there he was, lying on the floor before us, and we all standing round him in our fools' costumes, afraid to admit to each other that this was the end.

'I remember that the last to come was Prof. Manassein, but all hope had been abandoned by that time. He leant over him and listened to his heart; with a wave of his hand he said: "Lift him up."

'And they lifted him up, and carried him out. It was all over.'

The post-mortem examination was carried out in the very same room in which the last dance had been held. The autopsy showed that the cause of death was a burst artery in the heart; the artery wall had become so fragile that it could not support the pressure of the blood. In falling he had struck his temple against the corner of the stove where he had been standing. This caused a minor haemorrhage in the brain. According to Professor Vinogradov, who was conducting the post-mortem examination, it was surprising that Borodin had lasted so long with his heart in such a condition. In circumstances such as these, death could have occurred at any minute.

There was an exceptionally large crowd at Borodin's funeral. A large number of people of all professions and walks of life, whom he had known and helped in one way or another, assembled at his grave-side to pay their last respects. Students from the Academy bore his coffin all the way to the cemetery. Shchiglev, the close friend of the deceased, was in tears as he conducted a student choir at the funeral. Borodin was buried in the cemetery adjoining the Alexander Nevsky Monastery, next to the grave of Mussorgsky and not far from Dargomizhsky. A memorial was erected above his grave. Stassov was responsible for this, and a large part of the funds were donated by Belyaev, whose contribution was 3,000 roubles, the sum which he put aside every year as an award to Russian composers.

His friends, Rimsky-Korsakov and Glazunov, took it upon themselves to edit and publish the unfinished works Borodin had left behind. In the spring of 1887, the two movements of the unfinished Third Symphony were edited by Glazunov, who had written down the whole of the first movement from memory. A trio was added to the Scherzo, and was based, in accordance with the intentions of the late composer, on the 'Merchants' Tale' which he had earlier rejected from *Prince Igor* in 1879.

The task of editing *Igor* went on throughout the summer and autumn of 1887; Glazunov did the Overture,[1] and then finished and edited the Third Act, whilst Rimsky-Korsakov worked on the orchestration of the remainder. The French and German translations of the libretto were the work of Alexandra Alexandrova, Borodin's sister-in-law. The full score and piano arrangement of *Igor* were published in 1888.[2]

Catherine heard the terrible news from A. P. Dianin who made a special journey to Moscow. The shock was too much for her; she was already very weak and this proved to be the last straw. For the rest of the winter and early spring she was seriously ill. Then she recovered a little and devoted her returning strength to compiling material for the biography of her husband which Stassov was writing.

---

[1] In his notes on Borodin, which were compiled at Stassov's request and published in *The Russian Musical Gazette* for 1896, Glazunov says that the overture was worked out by him '*roughly* in accordance with Borodin's intentions'. On the other hand, Rimsky-Korsakov states in his memoirs (*Chronicle of My Musical Life*, 3rd ed., p. 282) that when he and Glazunov divided between them the editorial work on the musical material left by Borodin at his death, Glazunov was entrusted with the task of writing down from memory the overture which had been played many times by the composer'. Stassov, in his book on Borodin (p. 55), confirms that Glazunov wrote down the overture to *Igor* entirely from memory.

Apropos of this, I heard the following story from my father. Borodin told him that Glazunov once asked him to play the overture to *Prince Igor*. Borodin refused, saying: 'Please excuse me, old fellow, I'm so tired of it.'—'In that case, Alexander Porfiryevich, perhaps you would allow *me* to play it?'—'With pleasure.' Whereupon Glazunov sat down at the piano and played the overture, which, according to Borodin, was accurate 'to the last note'.

Upon reviewing these details, one comes to the conclusion that Glazunov remembered perfectly the composer's improvisation of the overture, and that his modest disclaimer merely reflects his meticulous honesty, together with the fact that certain minor alterations were introduced into the work in its final formulation.

[2] See Rimsky-Korsakov's memoirs, 3rd ed., pp. 287, 288, and 294.

This was dictated in note form to S. N. Kruglikov and then sent to Stassov.

In the late spring of 1887, Catherine moved to the cottage at Ramenskoye. Here she had a relapse, and with the swift onset of dropsy her condition became hopeless. She died on 28 June 1887, with Dianin and his wife at her bedside.

Catherine had stated in her will that Dianin should be sole executor, and act as trustee of income received from performance of Borodin's works.

Ten years after the death of Borodin, royalties and other income from *Igor* alone amounted to 50,000 roubles. Dianin, not without the assistance of Balakirev and Filippov, arranged for this sum to be donated to the Petersburg Conservatoire, in the form of a Borodin Scholarship for young composers.

BORODIN'S WORKS

GENERAL OBSERVATIONS. BORODIN'S FIRST COMPOSITIONS. WORKS OF HIS CHILDHOOD AND YOUTH

Any exhaustive study of the works of a great composer is difficult, even when, as in this case, the number of compositions is small. It is not my aim here to depart from strict analysis, but I intend to explore the available material as thoroughly as possible. I shall not however allow my own personal feelings or bias to obscure the objective picture of the facts, and for this reason I have been obliged to limit the scope of the present study.

My analysis of Borodin's music will be restricted in the main to the thematic content of his works. Wherever sufficient evidence allows, I shall endeavour to determine his sources, and, in particular, the extent of folk influence.[1]

This work is by no means exclusively for musicologists and folklorists, and will consequently examine the structure of Borodin's compositions, including the thematic material he incorporated in them. There is a risk that much of this will make for dry reading, but there is no question that this analysis will serve a useful purpose.

Owing to the large amount of work I have done on Borodin's biography, I have been tempted to advance certain hypotheses, since in some cases works appear to conform to a programme where none has been indicated by the composer.

I have devoted relatively little space to the harmonic structure and orchestration of Borodin's works; this is not due to any oversight on my part, but simply to the enormous difficulties besetting any musicologist who cares to probe the matter. An enquiry such as this would have to make use of the comparative method. As I see it, a comparison would have to be made between the harmonic treatment of Glinka,

---

[1] From this analysis, one can well assess the value of his technical mastery as a composer, and his place in the history of music.

Dargomizhsky, and the 'handful' on the one hand, and the European classical and romantic treatment on the other; and, even then, only certain aspects would lend themselves to this approach.[1] The same applies to a certain extent to the problem of Borodin's orchestration. The results of my investigation into the thematic structure and programmatic content of Borodin's works (and the biographical material also) have enabled me to assess and evaluate Borodin's work as a whole. This I shall do in the final chapter.

In conclusion, may I make one observation. The reader will see that on several occasions I have compared the pattern of particular themes of Borodin with the sources from which he derived them, not according to rhythm or any given key, but according to the note sequence. The following will serve as an illustration:

Ex. 5

I am confident that the results of my research will vindicate the method I have used, providing an insight into the thematic structure of Borodin's works and into his personality as well.

I

Let us first of all take a close look at the Polka in D minor (*Hélène*), which we already know from Chapter 1. This piece has the symmetrical form usually found in works of this kind. The first section is in ternary form, and the principal theme is as follows:

Ex. 6

The eight-bar phrase constructed on this theme is twice repeated. The secondary theme consists of twelve bars and is of comparatively minor importance in that it does not contrast very markedly with the

---

[1] Nevertheless, I will pay some attention to Borodin's harmonic peculiarities, which, I trust, without going into the matter in great detail, will give us a better all-round picture of his creative profile.

principal theme. Then comes a recapitulation of the first eight-bar phrase, this time without repeat. The harmony is typical of such dances as the polka, and consists of chords built on a single bass line.

The trio, which is in D major, falls into two parts: the first of these is repeated and has the following theme:

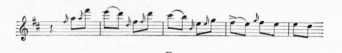

Ex. 7

The next three phrases have certain aspects in common with this theme; they constitute the second part of the trio. Then there is the conventional repeat (senza replica) of the first section, and finally a coda with a structure similar to the subject of the first section. It is worth saying that this polka is a lively and quite presentable work, possessing great clarity of form; there is no question but that it bears the mark of a great musical talent.

It is not difficult to see the influence of *Ruslan*, especially in the coda. Thus, we find an identical sequence of notes in the following motifs:

Ex. 8

The upper of the two is the basic theme of the coda to Borodin's polka; the lower motif is taken from Ratmir's aria 'Wondrous dream of impassioned love'.[1] Here is just one more instance (again, both motifs are transposed into the same key for convenience):

Ex. 9

---

[1] See the vocal score of *Ruslan and Ludmila*, Stellovsky edition, p. 85, bars 15–17 after the direction *Più moderato*.

In this case, the upper line is taken from the final bars of the polka, and the lower is from the same Glinka aria.[1] There is of course no possibility that Borodin could have been aware of these similarities[2]: but it is interesting to see that the conscious borrowings he made later follow the same pattern, that is, they take the tone-sequence and not the rhythmical form. In the theme of the trio we find leaps of a sixth, which play a significant part in Borodin's later work.

II

We now leave the only work of Borodin's childhood which survives in its entirety, and turn to the compositions of his early youth. Let us first of all take a look at the songs and ballads dating from his student days.

The three songs belonging to this period are: 'Why art thou so early, Dawn?' (in F sharp minor); 'The fair young maid no longer loves me' (in D minor); and 'Friends, hear my song'. They have a number of features in common. Their words are taken from obscure writers, all three poems have something of the pseudo-folk style and sentimentality prevalent in the twenties and thirties. Their theme is either unrequited love (as in the first two songs) or loneliness (as in the third song). On the whole, the music suits the loftier songs. The folk element in the songs is clearly present, but does not come through very clearly; it is obscured by the kind of treatment normally associated with nineteenth-century German music.[3] The harmonization for the most part revolves on the major and relative melodic minor. The number of deviations from this and modulations are insignificant. The accompaniments to the first two songs are reminiscent of the D minor polka, at least on the surface, and in the main consist of conventional rhythmic figures, in which bass notes and chords alternate.[4] The accompaniment of the third song is

[1] See the same edition of *Ruslan* as above, p. 83, bars 10–12 ff.
[2] As is generally known, this Polka was composed about 1842–3, i.e. precisely the same year as the première of *Ruslan*. We do not know whether little Sasha Borodin was present at one of the first performances, but it is quite likely that he heard Ratmir's aria at a private performance. In any case, these comparisons reveal that he was undoubtedly familiar with Glinka's brilliant opera during his childhood.
[3] The songs in D. Kashin's collection are rather like this, and Borodin might easily have known this anthology when he was young.
[4] This kind of guitar-like accompaniment is found, of course, in a richer, more developed form in some of his later songs, e.g. 'The Sleeping Princess', 'The Sea', and 'From My Tears'.

more interesting in view of the fact that it is polyphonic in character.[1]

All three songs, the first and third especially, have a sincere ring about them; and, even if they show little evidence of Borodin's touch of genius, at least one senses the presence of Borodin's humanitarian ideals. It is interesting to note that each of these songs attempts, even if unsuccessfully, to make use of Russian folk melodies.

The ballad 'The beautiful fisher-maid', to words by Heine, also belongs to this time. It is scored for voice, cello, and piano,[2] and the technique he uses is not very different from that of songs we have just been discussing. The composer clearly knows how to write for the cello. Some attempt at 'tone-painting' is made, in particular where the cello accompanies a reference to the sea by an arpeggio suggestive of the rolling sea. The theme, which has a number of variations, is not devoid of expressiveness and subtlety:

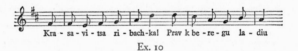

Kra - sa - vi - tsa ri - bach-ka! Prav k be - re - gu la - diu

Ex. 10

But, all the same, this ballad does not bear comparison with Borodin's later vocal works.

III

Borodin's development as a composer has something in common with that of Glinka. Like the great founder of Russian music, Borodin concentrated in his early days on works for various kinds of chamber ensemble. As far as we know, the only chamber work he completed while still a student is the G minor Trio, already referred to in Chapter 1. It is based on the melody of the song 'How have I offended thee?'

---

[1] It is interesting to note the first appearance of the ascending figure.:

Cello

Ex. 285

in this song, which describes a sad and desperate mood. It is met with similar significance in his other compositions up to the Third Symphony. There is a similar, though completely independent use of it in Tchaikovsky's opera *The Queen of Spades*, where it appears in Lisa's song just before she throws herself into the Winter Canal.

[2] There is another version of this song for voice and piano in D flat major. It is quite probable that the vocal part was arranged for the German words (see Chapter 2, where there is an account of a performance of *The Fisher-maiden* in Heidelberg).

The words of this song are quoted on the title-page of the Trio. Both the words and music are typical of a certain kind of popular song associated with various towns in Russia, and which served as a basis for many of Glinka's early ballads and those ballads written before his day.

The Trio is in one movement, and has six sections in all. The sixth section is an exact repetition of the first. All six sections are based on the theme of the song 'How have I offended thee?' which appears with various accompaniments and undergoes a number of variations.[1] The principal theme (in melodic G minor) is stated in the first section as follows:

Ex. 11

The theme is introduced by the first violin, and the second violin comes in (three bars later) with the theme in canon (one octave lower). The cello enters with a stretto in the fifth bar on D natural. The second part of the first section is derived from the main theme, and ends with a descending sequence and a chord on the tonic.

The second section (Nos. 2 and 3) is also in G minor, and is homophonic in structure. The first four bars of the principal theme are a melody in themselves; it is introduced by the first violin to an accompaniment consisting of harmonic figurations; this is followed by a phrase, which can be seen to be a somewhat free variation on a corresponding phrase in the first section.

The third section (Nos. 4 and 5), also in G minor, is in some respects an inversion of the second section. The first four bars of the principal theme are twice repeated by the cello, and this forms the bass line. The upper strings provide an accompaniment. The section ends with a passage which turns out to be an inversion of the corresponding part in the second section.

The fourth section (Nos. 6 to 11) is marked 'Risoluto e più vivo', and has a somewhat more complex structure, in that it introduces new thematic elements. The first part of this section is repeated and is in G minor. The accompaniment consists of complex harmonic figurations which have an harmonic sequence not far removed from the

---

[1] The first section of the G minor Trio cannot be regarded as a 'theme for variations' generally speaking, as the structure of the other parts is so different from the first.

note-sequence of the principal theme[1]; against this accompaniment the violins introduce a new theme[2]:

Ex. 12

There follows a G major section in the form of a short, independent intermezzo, which has no direct thematic connection with the principal theme. It is for the most part pizzicato. It has a number of chromatic features which in a way anticipate the chromatic turns found in the later 'mature' Borodin. In the last part of this fourth section the key reverts again to G minor. There is a reappearance of the first three-bar phrase of the principal theme, played this time by the second violin, and again later by the cello against a background of rapid semiquaver triplets. The concluding bars of this section are reminiscent of the final bars of previous sections.[3]

[1] An extremely free variation, part of the tonal scheme of this section of the main theme may be observed, for example, in both the first part (the second bar after the repeat mark) and the second violin part (from bar 6).

[2] As P. A. Lamm has already observed (in the preface to this Trio in the complete works of Borodin, Vol. V, No. 4, Moscow, 1946), there is a resemblance between this theme and the main theme of the first movement of his Second Quartet. This is obvious from the following:

Ex. 286

Apart from the other considerations (of which see below in the concluding remarks to Part Two of this book), I find it interesting to introduce this illustration here, as Lamm proceeded from the same comparison of consecutive notes as those which I set forth at the beginning of this chapter.

[3] In Lamm's foreword, referred to in the previous note, it is pointed out that in this part of the Trio there is some 'inconsistency' as regards mode, since there is hesitation between melodic minor and Dorian mode. It seems to me that in the case referred to, there is no accidental 'hesitation' but a definite artistic intention. Actually if we note

The fifth section (Nos. 12 to 21) is marked 'meno mosso' and is in G major. The first part of this section consists of fifteen bars and is made up of snatches of varied motifs from the principal theme. The remainder of the section is a polyphonic development of the initial four bars of the same theme. It is played twice in the key of G major against a contrapuntal background, and then in D major. It is then heard yet another four times in the minor, and a fifth time in D major; after that it comes twice more in the minor. Finally, the theme is played by each of the instruments in turn as a stretto, in C major. The section ends with a coda leading to the final G, in octaves.

The Trio ends (sixth section) with a complete repetition of the first G minor episode.[1]

IV

As the reader already knows, Borodin continued to write and play chamber music after he left the Academy. He became especially involved in this during his period abroad, in Heidelberg (1859–60;

down the appearances of one and the same motif in the passage under consideration we shall get the following tabular result:

Figures in the printed edition	No. of bars from the figure	Instrument and key	Mode
16	5	Cello: E minor	*Dorian* (without D sharp)
16	7	2nd Vn.: E minor	*Melodic minor* (with D sharp)
17	3	1st Vn.: B minor	Dorian (without A sharp)
17	5	Cello: B minor	Dorian (without A sharp)
18		D major	
19	4	Cello: D minor	*Dorian* (without C sharp and B flat)
19	6	2nd Vn.: D minor	*Melodic minor* (with C sharp but no B flat)

As my italics make clear, the passage shows symmetry in the alternation of modes—a circumstance which, in my view, confirms the theory of the composer's deliberate intention.

[1] Borodin's friend Shchiglev made a piano duet arrangement of this Trio, which was headed: 'Fantasia (on Russian songs) for two violins and cello composed by A. P. Borodin (written during the composer's youth). Arrangement for Piano 4 hands by M. R. Shchiglev.' Lamm, in the above-mentioned preface, speaks of an arrangement of this work 'for small orchestra' made by Shchiglev and even refers to a performance of it in this form in 1883, but the sources of his information are unknown to me. In Stassov's life of Borodin there is an account by Shchiglev (p. 12) of a performance of this Trio by a circle of music lovers in 1883, but there is no mention of its being given in orchestral form. (As a matter of interest, Stassov also erroneously states in the same book that Borodin was the conductor of this institution in 1883.)

1861) and in Pisa (1861–2); and this was a particularly fruitful period for Borodin. We shall briefly examine here two of the works he wrote in Heidelberg, but which were not published until quite recently: the String Sextet in D minor and the Piano Trio in D major. Unfortunately neither of these works has survived in its entirety.

We possess only two movements of the Sextet, an Allegro in D minor and an Andante in E minor. It is obvious from these two movements that Borodin was under the influence of German music at the time, Mendelssohn in particular. This is borne out by Borodin's own comment, later reported by Shchiglev.[1] The scoring of the Sextet shows clearly that Borodin knew how to write for string instruments.

The first movement is in sonata form, and the exposition has no repeat. The first subject is introduced by the first violin:

Ex. 13

This, in common with the motifs used as bridge-passages, appears in all six parts at some time or other. One motif of particular interest, though only of secondary importance in the work itself, betrays Borodin's interest in Russian folk-song[2]:

Ex. 14

The theme of the second subject is in F major:

Ex. 15

---

[1] See Stassov's *Life of Borodin*, p. 21.
[2] In examining the motif as it appears in its minor form:

Ex. 287

we notice that it has an inconsistent structure. In its first half, in harmonic D minor, it is very uncharacteristic of the Russian idiom, whereas its ending is completely in the style of Russian folk music.

and, although it is not particularly interesting from the musical point of view, it is not entirely without significance, as it contains features characteristic of Borodin's later works. The development section is extremely terse, and consists of the first subject in modified form, and 'the pseudo-Russian motif' given above, also modified. The re-capitulation is not an exact repetition of the exposition. The Russian motif this time appears fortissimo in the cello and in a minor key. The second subject is written in octaves and is played by first violin and cello, and not in F major, as before, but in D major. The coda is based on the 'motif' of the first bar of the first subject, and it is pre-ceded immediately by a passage in which each instrument plays the principal theme, alternately in major and minor.

The harmonic structure of the Allegro is not very complex. Of the various dissonances used, one is of particular interest:

Ex. 16

This dissonance occurs at the beginning of the exposition, and re-occurs a third higher at the start of the recapitulation.

The Andante of the Sextet is in E minor. The principal subject (the chief motif and 'response') is as follows:

Ex. 17

It appears first in the first violin part and is accompanied by the other instruments in chords. The form of the Andante is free. The first half is based entirely on the principal theme, and appears variously trans-posed. There is one motif of special interest:

Ex. 18

After this, the various instruments exchange fragments of the principal theme, now in the major key. This is succeeded by new thematic material. Here is a motif in B minor:

Ex. 19

and a miniature motif accompanying it:

Ex. 20

The Andante ends with a variant of the principal subject in B minor, tailing off into a morendo played by the cellos in octaves on a final B.

This work is not the only one from his Heidelberg period to show that Borodin had already begun to use the free juxtaposition of keys in his works.[1] This scandalized the musical purists, who were particularly horrified by similar transgressions in the B minor Symphony. The Sextet ends in B minor, and not E minor, as we might expect. This leads us to expect that the Scherzo, had he written one, would have been in B minor or B major.[2] Whether the Sextet ever had a programme, it is impossible to say, as we lack the necessary information. On the whole, the musical standard is high and the work is well-contrived,[3] but it does not give an impression of spontaneity. There is something cerebral and artificial about it, and the thematic material is not out of the ordinary.

Now let us take a look at the D major Piano Trio. We possess three movements of this work: an 'Allegro con brio'; a Romance (Andante)[4]; and an Intermezzo (marked 'Tempo di menuetto. Trio

---

[1] In the Cello Sonata and the Piano Trio.

[2] The theory that this Sextet was in not two but four movements has been expressed by Professor I. F. Belza (see his book *Borodin*, 1947, p. 48). This is confirmed by the nature of the ending of the second movement. The Finale was most probably in the key of D major.

[3] One has only to mention the skilful instrumentation of the coda of the Andante to substantiate this.

[4] This section is entitled *Romanza* in the manuscript. We have no idea as to how this curious title arose.

Piu lento. Menuetto da capo al-fine'). The work probably had a finale, though perhaps this never got written.[1]

The first movement (Allegro con brio) is in D major and is of considerable length, occupying some thirty-eight pages of the score. It is in sonata form. The first subject is introduced by the cello, accompanied by the piano[2]:

Ex. 21

This, in the course of the next twenty bars or so, is modified and developed. Then follows the bridge passage leading to the A major second subject; this is not especially interesting and is laid out as follows:

Ex. 22

The melody serves as basis for a somewhat extended section, in which the theme appears in the various instruments, undergoes various changes, and augmentation. After a general pause, and another brief passage, the exposition ends with phrases, based on a variant of the second subject, and then a modulation into A major.[3]

[1] In Findeisen's article, 'Le legs musical de Borodine' (*Révue Musicale*, 1927, No. 4, pp. 97–103), this Intermezzo is inaccurately referred to as a Scherzo.

[2] There is an interesting resemblance here between this theme and the Allegro theme in the D minor Sextet.

[3] At the end of the exposition, we find a passage (bars 137–40 incl.) which is filled with a succession of acute dissonances:

Ex. 288

and at this point, the editors have inserted a note to say that they have reproduced it 'exactly as in Borodin'. The manuscript from which this copy was taken was not written

Development. There is an extended development section, covering fourteen pages of the score, which leaves in no doubt about Borodin's technical accomplishments. This section is in the main constructed on the first and second subjects in various keys. First of all, there is an entry of the first subject in A major, D minor, and then A minor. The bridge-passage section appears in C major. After this, there is a modulation into A flat major by way of a phrase of the first subject, and the key signature changes. A variant of the second subject appears in this key. The development ends with yet another variant on the second subject, the one that concluded the exposition, with a key signature of 5 sharps.

The recapitulation is not worth detailed analysis. In accordance with the usual practice, the second subject appears in a different key, D major instead of A major.

The Allegro ends with a coda section which is built on fragments of the first subject.

by Borodin himself and (according to W. N. Rimsky-Korsakov) only the composer's corrections may be seen in it. Nevertheless, it seems impossible to impute these curiosities to the fault of the copyist, as exactly the same dissonances are encountered (a fifth higher) later (bars 467–70). On the other hand, these two instances are entirely out of keeping with the harmonies of the remainder of the piece and can only be regarded as 'eccentricities'. In considering that in similar figures, as, for example, in bar 128:

Ex. 289

there are no dissonances, it seems that we are here confronted with a slip of the pen on Borodin's part which was faithfully reproduced by the copyist. Without intending to be dogmatic on this question, I venture to suggest the following as the correct version:

Ex. 290

(We should also make a corresponding alteration to the passage in bars 467–70.)

The second movement of the Trio, the Romance, is in E major.
It is quite a lengthy movement and occupies twenty-one pages of the
score. First comes a section played by the piano, which includes a
statement of the principal theme, to the accompaniment of chords.

Ex. 23

In this excerpt, a letter X marks the beginning and end of the main
theme of the movement. The accompanying figures appear elsewhere
as different variants. From then on, the melody of the main theme
undergoes continual transformation; first on the piano, and later in
the strings. The second theme appears, after a short transition, at bar
26; it is in B major and is played by the violin[1]:

Ex. 24

This is followed by a counter-melody played by the cello.

The section following immediately upon this consists of twenty
bars in all, and is built on fragments of both themes with demisemi-
quaver accompaniment on the piano. Here we find melodic turns that
are characteristic of Borodin's later works, for example:

Ex. 25

[1] The entry of this theme is prepared by the music which developed the individual
fragments of the melody of the first subject.

There is a passage based on the following motif at the end of this 'development'[1]:

Ex. 26

It is derived from the second subject. After a short transition, for piano alone, we come to the recapitulation. Without going into detail, I should like nevertheless to mention that the second subject this time is in E major, and not in B major as before.[2] The same might be said of the 'development' when it appears for the second time. There is a coda to finish up with, built on motifs derived from the first subject and on an ascending arpeggio taken from the second.

The thematic and harmonic aspects of the D major Trio reflect the influence of Mendelssohn; perhaps the reader will have noticed this. However the influence is not as marked as in the D minor Sextet, to which Stassov gave the sub-title, 'à la Mendelssohn'.

Now on to the third movement of the Trio, the Intermezzo. The first section of this movement bears the indication 'Tempo di minuetto', and this heading is fully justified by the content.

The principal theme is as follows:

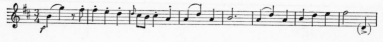

Ex. 27

It is played by the violin, with the other two instruments accompanying. There is much double-stopping in the string parts. In the eight bars which follow this, the theme is transposed a fifth higher into A major. The second section (bars 17 to 32 inclusive) is for the most part in the same key. In addition to variants of the principal theme,

---

[1] In one of the bars on p. 51 which uses this motive, there is the strange dissonance

$$B\sharp—G\sharp—B\natural—B\sharp—E'—E'''$$

which is probably either a misprint or a slip of the pen.

[2] It is interesting to observe that the beginning of the recapitulation has a different instrumentation from the opening of the exposition. The accompanying figures in bars 55–61 on p. 53 are played by the strings pizzicato as well as by the piano.

we encounter a new thematic element. The closing bars of the menuetto are as follows:

Ex. 28

They are based on this new element.

After the repeat, there follows something not unlike the development section of a movement in sonata form. The principal theme appears in a number of minor keys, chiefly B minor. There is an interweaving of variants in this theme, giving several bars of polyphonic imitation writing. The 'development' ends with a curious modulation into the original key. The first two sections of the menuetto are then played; the key is D major throughout, and there is no modulation to A major as before. The movement ends in D major (bar 118 to Fine), and then there is an abrupt modulation into C major, the key of the Trio section.

The tonality of the Trio section (Più Lento; 3/2; ♩=83) stands in sharp contrast to the preceding menuetto; but the abruptness is toned down by cadences which come later in the section. The trio is in free ternary form. The first section, which is in C major, is played by the violin and cello, and is built on the following theme:

Ex. 29

It is similar in some respects to the principal theme of the menuetto.[1] It is introduced by the violin, and the cello provides a contrapuntal accompaniment. At the same time, both instruments play open G's (in octaves), which act as a pedal note. The piano enters in the second section, accompanying a new theme which is somewhat reminiscent of the first subject in the Allegro con brio movement. The harmony tends towards F major and D minor. The third section comprises the first four bars of the repeat of the first section; this time,

[1] There is a similarity between the first three bars of the main theme of the Minuet, and the motif at the end of the second and beginning of the third bars of the theme of the Trio; also the motif of the last two bars of the same theme from the Minuet with the motif of the first half of the second bar of the Trio.

the piano accompanies throughout. The next three bars contain elements of the second theme; whilst the fourth bar concludes the section, and is identical with the ending of the first section. Then comes a modulation into D major, and the menuetto is played al fine.

The general impression of the D major Piano Trio is not strikingly different from that of the D minor Sextet, examined earlier. We cannot deny Borodin's technical facility, but his own particular individual stamp is altogether lacking. Nevertheless one may point to certain thematic elements which clearly foreshadow Borodin's later development.[1]

Borodin's Heidelberg period did not establish his individuality as a composer, but indubitably widened his musical horizon and heightened his technical proficiency.

V

Finally, we shall examine the works he wrote in Italy, in the spring and summer of 1862. The months that had elapsed between the time he had conceived his Heidelberg works and the time he wrote them down were very important in Borodin's musical development. In the summer of 1861 he had heard performances of *The Flying Dutchman*, *Tannhäuser*, and *Lohengrin*. He had heard Schumann beautifully played by his wife-to-be, and so became well-acquainted with his piano works and the E flat major Piano Quintet. Catherine herself tells us that Schumann's music had a powerful effect upon the impressionable Russian composer, who she thought had affinities with Schumann in his use of rhythm.[2] And now, while they were staying in Italy in 1861 and 1862, Borodin came to hear a great deal of music, both Italian and German classical. We are naturally curious to know how far all these impressions were reflected in his music. But, as we shall see, it is not easy to detect any definite influence.

Chronologically speaking, the first work belonging to this period is the Tarantella (Allegro molto vivo, in D major, 2/4 time signature) for piano duet,[3] probably conceived in April 1862. It was evidently

[1] One must point out that in the D major Piano Trio the unity of the thematic elements is more evident than in the Sextet.

[2] According to Catherine, Borodin's expression upon being introduced to the piano music of Schumann was: 'Your Schumann is so endless!' (see the unpublished part of Catherine's memoirs dictated by her to S. N. Kruglikov).

[3] This piece is often considered as being in the key of A minor, but that applies only to the middle section.

a kind of 'pièce d'occasion', which he wrote with Catherine in mind.[1]
When we take a closer look at this rather lengthy composition (24
pages long in the duet version) we cannot mistake the similarity with
the works of the 'Heidelberg' period, and of course the influence of
Mendelssohn. We need look no further than the first subject of the
'Tarantella' for a good illustration of this:

Ex. 30

This theme appears in various transpositions and undergoes a number
of variations. There follows a transition to the second subject:

Ex. 31

which reminds one of the 'camel train' episode in his *In the Steppes of
Central Asia* which he composed as late as 1880.[2] The second subject
is in A major, and the second time it appears it is accompanied by
harmonic figurations:

Ex. 32

and has a Russian folk flavour about it, very much more clearly
marked than in the 'Russian' motif which we noticed in the D minor
Sextet. After a comparatively short section, based on the second theme,

[1] My father, A. P. Dianin, used to tell me a story which might have some bearing on
the composition of the *Tarantella*. One night, during their stay in Pisa, Catherine saw
a tarantula on the wall of their flat. Needless to say, Borodin killed it immediately.

[2] See Chapter 7, below, for a section devoted to the sketch *In the Steppes of Central
Asia*.

the exposition ends with a passage which brings back the triplets of the beginning of the Tarantella.

The middle section of the piece (the 'development') has no key signature. The structure has nothing unusual about it. At the start the triplets of the first subject and variants appear in various keys (A minor, B flat major, and C major). The second subject is developed in the same way, but it is interspersed with phrases taken from the first subject. The key then returns to D major and the exposition is repeated but not bar for bar. The first subject is pitched one octave higher than previously, and the second subject is now conventionally in the fundamental key, not in A major as before, but in D major.

In the coda the thematic elements are dissolved into rising and falling harmonic figurations.

Before concluding our brief survey of Borodin's Tarantella, we ought to say that there are no radical differences in style between this and earlier works of the Heidelberg period. But the leaning towards Russian folk idiom in the second subject is not without significance, despite the fact that the work has an Italian title.[1]

Folk themes are used with even greater success in the C minor Piano Quintet, the second work he wrote in Italy. This was composed in May, June and the first half of July 1862.[2] It is quite likely that this work was inspired by the Schumann E flat major Piano Quintet, which he heard for the first time in 1861.[3] The Quintet is in three movements: Andante (C minor, 3/4, 2/4 time); Scherzo (A minor, Allegro non troppo, 2/4 time); and Finale (C minor and C major, 3/4 time).

The first movement of the Quintet is in the form of a rondo with two themes, the pattern being a–b–a–b–a. The first subject is introduced by the piano in octaves; the accompaniment is highly transparent:

Ex. 33

[1] I. Y. Katselnik, who wrote the Foreword to the published edition of the *Tarantella*, justifiably remarks on the composer's strong tendencies towards orchestral writing in the scoring of this piece.

[2] See extracts from Catherine's diary quoted in Chapter 2.

[3] See *Letters*, Vol. I, p. 305.

In the next section (a_1), the first subject is played first by the first violin, with the piano playing in counterpoint, then once again by solo piano, then by the cello, then by the second violin playing in E flat, and finally by the viola, this time in C minor, with the rest of the instruments in counterpoint. After a modulation into E flat, the second subject enters, also played by solo piano; it is four bars in length:

Ex. 34

In the following section (b_1) this theme is again played, but as three different variations, played by the first violin, viola, and cello in succession. The accompaniment here is considerably less contrapuntal than in the previous section.

The first subject now returns in the key of E flat. The whole of the third section (a_2) is built on this, and the scoring is very similar to that of the first section, although the subdominant keys derived from C minor and E flat are used.[1] A phrase on the cello, modulating into C major, is reminiscent of some of Glinka's Russian folk themes, and serves as a transition into the fourth section (b_2); once again the second subject is dominant, but, although it keeps the same series of variants as before, the keys are now a third lower (C major, G major the piano and the violin, and C major on the cello).

---

[1] The final motif in the last (partial) appearance of the first theme:

Ex. 291

is found, in a modified form, in the Finale of the Quintet, and in several later works of Borodin's.

The final section (a_3) takes us back to the first subject. This time, its first appearance is in C major (played by the violins) and then in A minor (first on the piano, and then on viola and cello). The key of A minor is maintained throughout, even in the coda, which is based on the second subject.

Scherzo. The key is for the most part A minor, and the structure has some likeness to that of the first movement. The themes are of no particular interest, and certainly in no way foreshadow the wonderful scherzo movements of Borodin's symphonies and quartets.

The first section (c_1) of the scherzo is based on the following theme:

Ex. 35

which brings to mind the principal theme of the Allegro of the Sextet. It makes its first appearance on the viola, and then (in C major) on the first and second violins, and finally, in A minor, on the cello.

The second section (d_1) introduces the second theme (in G major).

Ex. 36

This is played by the first violin with the rest of the instruments accompanying. The third section (c_2) follows after a brief transition; the first theme is heard again, first in G major and then in C major, and finally in A minor.

Then there is a very short development section which acts as a transition to the later sections; it is based on fragments of both themes. Next, the piano plays the (d_2) section solo, in C major; this brings in the second theme. The scherzo ends with the first theme, in C major, played by the viola, and a final cadence.

The trio as well is built on an alternation of the two themes, in major and minor. The first theme is given to the solo piano, in C major:

Ex. 37

and immediately after this comes the second theme, also solo piano:

Ex. 38

the next four bars (in the same 'choral' style) is a transition to G major.

The rest of the movement is fairly symmetrical in character. It consists of a threefold repetition of four passages, the first three of which are in a major key and based on the first theme; the fourth passage is in a minor key and is based on the second theme. The key relationships are as follows:

$$
\begin{array}{ll}
\text{First section:} & \left.\begin{array}{l} \text{G} \\ \text{G} \\ \text{C} \end{array}\right\} \text{major} \\
& \text{A minor;}
\end{array}
$$

$$
\begin{array}{ll}
\text{Second section:} & \left.\begin{array}{l} \text{G} \\ \text{G} \\ \text{G} \end{array}\right\} \text{major} \\
& \text{E minor;}
\end{array}
$$

$$
\begin{array}{ll}
\text{Third section:} & \left.\begin{array}{l} \text{E} \\ \text{E} \\ \text{G} \end{array}\right\} \text{major} \\
& \text{E minor.}
\end{array}
$$

At the end of the trio, the first theme is announced in E major. The trio ends on a dominant seventh in A minor. After this follows a straightforward repeat of the scherzo.

The *Finale* of the Quintet is in sonata form. It is much more interesting than the scherzo; there is such an abundance of material that the composer might be accused of 'polythematism' in places, but these shortcomings are amply compensated for by the grace and beauty of the principal theme.

The piano enters solo after an introduction, played by the strings alone:

Ex. 39

and plays the principal theme:[1]

Ex. 40

It is infused with Russian folk music and is tinged with a certain melancholy. Various thematic elements of a subsidiary nature are involved in the development of this theme. Very shortly after this, a phrase occurs which is a development of the introduction, and finally there is a free variation on the last motif of the theme. The principal theme then appears in the bass; this is succeeded by a shadowy bridge passage, played by the cello:

Ex. 41

This tends towards E flat minor[2] and is doubled by the rest of the strings. Thus ends the main section of the movement, which has great significance in the light of his later work.

[1] This duality in the statement of the main thematic elements (in this case Introduction *and* theme) is encountered in a number of Borodin's works of his maturity, and in a more developed form. It suffices here to recall, in this connection, the themes of the first Allegro of the Second Symphony, and the Moderato of the Third.

[2] Some slight disorder might be observed in the distribution and use of themes in the exposition of the Finale. For example, the theme of the transitional section is found on

The viola plays the second subject, which is in E flat major and slight compared with the first subject:

Ex. 42

After this, the second subject is played tutti, and then comes the sort of transition required by the conventions of sonata form. This passage is however extremely interesting, in that it contains a suggestion of Borodin's pizzicato leaps, which Mussorgsky called 'pecks':

Ex. 43

The exposition ends with a short 'concluding motif':

Ex. 44

several occasions leading directly into the theme of the second subject. This forces one to the conclusion that there is no separate transitional section, and that the passage in question should all be regarded as part of the second subject. On the other hand, if this is the case a great part of the second subject appears in the same key as the first subject. This would be very much at variance with Borodin's usual customs for this period. In addition to this, the motive which we recognized formerly as the second subject is repeatedly found by itself (i.e. in isolation from the transitional passage). In view of these last factors, I prefer to adhere to the original nomenclature as given in the text.

The development begins with a repetition of the introduction and the first subject, this time in E flat major, instead of C minor; this is played by the first violin over continuous notes held by the other strings. The next section is based on a juxtaposition of snatches from the principal theme and the bridge passage mentioned earlier. At the end of the development, the principal theme (in a modified form) is stated in C major, by the piano, first violin and viola in succession.

A transition above a sustained note leads to the recapitulation, which is an exact repeat of the exposition, except for a modulation into C major shortly after the first subject, and slight changes in detail later on. The Finale ends with a coda, in which the principal theme appears for the last time, played by the viola in C major. At the end of the coda the first violin plays a variant of one of the motifs of the main theme above a sustained C.

The C minor Piano Quintet is an important milestone in Borodin's development as a composer. We see the influence of the great romantic composers, Chopin and Schumann, but also signs of Borodin's own maturity.

The form of the Quintet is freer than that of his earlier compositions; the harmony is still tonal in character and not particularly rich in dissonances or any other departures from the norm.[1] There is much more of the Russian folk element in this than in any previous work; for the first time (in the first movement) we find the alternation: two bars of 3/4, two bars of 2/4, which is the equivalent of a 10/4 beat in disguise.[2] The influence of Glinka, which had been for some time

---

[1] There is a figure at the beginning of the Finale which is reminiscent of some of Borodin's 'unresolved seconds' of a later period:

Ex. 292

[2] In the first theme of the Andante may be observed an interesting double ornament (in the first bar) which connects it with the themes of the German classical Andantes, though the rest of this passage is very much in the style of Russian folk-song. There is always the chance that this inconsistency is intentional, but there is no way of proving this. We notice furthermore that there is a similarity between the theme of the Andante to which we have just referred, and the main theme of the Finale. It is possible that there is a hidden programme to the C minor Quintet, but without more details at our disposal, all our guesses are purely arbitrary.

eclipsed by that of Mendelssohn, is now visible once again in his themes and transition.[1]

Throughout the whole of this work one senses the composer's leaning towards the orchestra. Borodin himself saw that it would not be too difficult to orchestrate this quintet, and even took steps to do this, albeit somewhat tentatively.[2] His 'self-instruction' in the art of writing for chamber combinations was now complete. He was already unconsciously wanting to be a symphonist.

It was not until he met Balakirev that he was given the impulse to turn to symphonic composition. As a result of this meeting with Balakirev, Borodin became more consciously critical towards his own work.

---

[1] On p. 21 of his book on Borodin, Stassov follows the heading 'Quintet' with the word 'Glinka', but he gives no reason for this.

[2] In the foreword to the published Quintet, the editor, Lamm, informs us that in the first 6 pages of the score, Borodin has indicated the orchestration (viz. woodwind, trumpets, trombones) and in some places has added supplementary parts.

CHAPTER SEVEN

THE SYMPHONIES

THE FIRST SYMPHONY IN E FLAT MAJOR

I

In Chapter 3 I gave a brief account of how the First Symphony came to be written. It was seen that Balakirev's criticism was very important in determining the final shape of this work. Balakirev always acknowledged that the symphony was entirely Borodin's own work; yet it was a very long time (until the eighties at least) before he dropped the idea of introducing certain of his own alterations into the score of this symphony; he kept on making further suggestions to Borodin, and possibly even insisted on several modifications. However, Balakirev's 'last-minute' corrections did not appear in the printed score; they are not of interest, and add nothing of any importance to the work.[1]

Before Bessel published the symphony, Borodin himself made a number of alterations, which are easily seen if we compare the piano-duet arrangement of 1875 with the score published in 1882. The discrepancies cannot be accounted for solely by the argument that a piano version is bound to be different from an orchestral full score.[2]

---

[1] Balakirev mentions a number of 'corrections' in his letter to Borodin dated 1 February 1883 (see my book, *Borodin*, Russian 2nd ed., pp. 261–2). His pencilled suggestions as to further alterations are preserved in Borodin's original copy of the printed score. I reproduce on pp. 186–189 a comparison of the two versions of the end of the Trio of the E flat major Symphony Scherzo, made by Borodin and Balakirev respectively.

It is interesting to observe that Borodin willingly consented to the insertion of further corrections to the score even when it had been published in 1882, and at Balakirev's request posted them to the conductor of the Leipzig Musical Festival, Arthur Nikisch, so that they could be included in the symphony's performance in 1883. Borodin did this solely to please Balakirev, since as far back as the 1870s he had regarded the latter's continual alterations as unnecessary (see *Letters*, Vol. I, pp. 307–8).

[2] There are 1,792 bars in the score of 1882, whilst there are 1,817 in the piano-duet arrangement of 1875. I have compared the two scores in detail, but so far, my researches have not been published. (The most important changes apply to the first movement and were made by the composer before its publication.) Unfortunately, it is virtually impossible to make an exhaustive study of the evolution of the First Symphony, owing to the scarcity of material. Only part of the sketches of the original version of the score has been preserved, whilst the original manuscript score is presumably lost.

For my analysis of the First Symphony, I will use the composer's final version, as it appears in the printed score of 1882.

II

Borodin's E flat Symphony, like the Second Symphony, follows the classical tradition in having four movements.

The *first movement* begins with a slow introduction, marked Adagio (♩=40), in E flat minor. The theme of the introduction is based on Russian folk motifs, and has a melancholic, and even mournful character; the first half of the statement built around it is as follows:

Ex. 45

The second half of this complex statement uses the same theme transposed a fifth lower, but ends somewhat differently. The next passage acts as a transition, and includes the following motif:

Ex. 46

this is encountered later on in the symphony, and probably has some special significance in the work as a whole.[1] Then follows a transitional

---

[1] I notice that this motif, which is to be found several times in the E flat Symphony, has its origin in the pencilled sketch of the lay 'The Terrible Tsar Ivan Vasilyevich' which was taken down by Borodin from a wandering singer. The original sketch is preserved in the manuscript section of the library of the Leningrad State Conservatoire. In this sketch there is the following fragment:

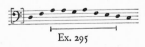

Ex. 295

I have underlined the part which is of interest to us and added the clef. The motif also appears with the addition of the last note (C) in the Trio of the Scherzo. A number of themes in the Second Symphony were compiled from the lay (e.g. the second subject of the first movement and the motif 'the commemoration of the dead' in the Finale).

Ex. 293

Ex. 293—*cont.*

Ex. 294

Ex. 294—*cont.*

modulation into E flat major. The mood brightens, and the sombre minor gives way to a lively, sunny Allegro (♩=184).

The horns and clarinets play a repeated staccato:

Ex. 46 (*a*)

and the timpani plays a motif from the second bar of the introduction:

Ex. 47

The ascending motifs of the third bar of the introduction are interwoven into this. The music grows louder. This passage of ascending motifs ends with a tutti forte chord (cf. Ex. 46 (*a*)) from the whole orchestra. The trombones then play the notes of the fourth bar of the introduction:

Ex. 47 (*a*)

followed by a powerful tutti, ending on a tonic triad.[1]

The tension dies down. The second violins play the first subject of the Allegro; this is identical with the first three bars of the theme of the introduction:

Ex. 47 (*b*)

---

[1] A number of striking harmonies are found at the beginning of the Allegro, unresolved dissonances in particular, though much of the harshness is mitigated by excellent orchestration.

But the harmonies are no longer minor, and the wistfulness has dissolved into a series of major motifs; in its new context, the theme conveys a glad, playful mood. The bridge passage, following upon this, is of no particular interest; it consists of a series of chromatic motifs, marked dolce in the strings, and then ostinato, which were first heard in the second bar of the introduction, but now pitched a semitone lower (D instead of E flat). A sustained G minor $\frac{6}{4}$ chord on the flutes and clarinets serves as a transition of the second subject:

Ex. 48

This is harmonized first in G minor and then in C minor (violas, cellos, and bass, forte). The theme is in a folk vein, and could be regarded as being in the Phrygian mode, though this would not tally with the actual harmonizations used.

The 'tail-piece' to the second subject is closely related to the latter:

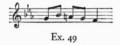

Ex. 49

This later acts as a sequence. The closing section of the exposition is very brief indeed and consists of repeated syncopated octave chords (on G), brought to a sudden conclusion by a tutti chord in G minor fortissimo.

The development begins with a statement of the first subject, in the original key of E flat major; a succession of chords leads into the key of A major. The music gathers force. The trumpets, trombones, and bassoons announce the first subject double forte in a slightly modified form (the interval is now a major second instead of a minor second). After this comes an alternation of the scale motif of the first subject with the second motif of the second subject. Against this is the timpani four-note motif, ostinato. At the end of the phrase, this ostinato changes to:

Ex. 49 (a)

Finally, the four-note ostinato reappears played double forte by the trumpets. After a series of chords gradually decrescendo, the second subject enters, and is played twice. There is a return to the key of E flat major. Then begins an interchange of motifs taken from the first and second subjects, ending on a tutti D flat major triad fortissimo. The development section ends with the bridge passage of the exposition; this is followed by an impressive 'coda' built on yet another transformation of the four-note motif.

The restatement of the first subject in the recapitulation is almost an exact repeat of the corresponding section in the exposition. The second subject however is comparatively more fully developed; its basic motif is played five times. Instead of a coda, there follows a rather extensive section, resembling the development. The first subject is played a fourth higher than in the development against a sustained horn pedal (C instead of G), and then the second subject enters as an oboe solo. This is followed by a reiterated phrase played by the various instruments of the orchestra in turn, and gradually the tension mounts (as in the middle section of the development). There is an accelerando. In a tremendous tutti (animato assai) the first motif of the first subject is heard in a totally different rhythm:

Ex. 49 (*b*)

The excitement dies right down to pianissimo, and this leads to a sunny, restful coda, marked Andantino (3/2 time; ♩=92). In contrast to the agitation and exuberance which has just passed, the cellos play the first subject and the two motifs of the second subject in augmentation. The first movement ends on transformed motifs of the first subject which gradually die away.

The *second movement* is a Scherzo, in E flat major, marked Prestissimo (3/8 time; ♩=144). It is one of the most delightful of Borodin's works. At the start of the Scherzo, we hear the main theme gradually ascending in the first violins:

Ex. 50

This is balanced by the descending motion of the second theme:

Ex. 51

The second theme marks the beginning of a passage which descends two complete octaves, during which time the tension grows and the texture becomes richer. The passage ends on a tutti motif as follows:

Ex. 52

The second appearance of this motif ends on characteristic octave leaps in the violas and violins[1]:

Ex. 52 (*a*)

This is followed by a sustained (*ff*) major third; the first 8 bars of the main theme are then heard in the bassoons in their lower register (in D major). The section ends with a further series of octave leaps in the strings, this time octave B leaps. After a short transition, the first theme re-enters. After a familiar sequence of notes on the timpani the

Ex. 52 (*b*)

Scherzo is repeated as far as the tutti motif (Ex. 52) with only slight alterations. The octave leaps make a further reappearance in the strings

---

[1] As the reader will remember, Mussorgsky nick-named these sequences 'nibbles'; they greatly pleased Liszt (see *Letters*, Vol. II, pp. 133 and 269. In the note on p. 269, I quoted all the instances appearing in the First Symphony, but following Stassov's terminology I restricted myself to only those cases which were played by the pizzicato strings.

(octave Gs) and the section ends with a first inversion in the minor, and then on the mediant alone, still minor.

The Trio, marked Allegro (♩=132), is constructed on a lovely Russian folk motif. The rhythm is not intended to be regular; the key is G sharp minor:

Ex. 53

After a modulation into D flat major, comes a nine-bar intermezzo which takes the form of a descending sequence based on the motif of the fifth bar of the theme given above (Ex. 53); this motif first appeared at the end of the introduction to the first movement[1] (Ex. 46). There is a sudden modulation into F sharp minor, and the principal theme returns, this time somewhat transformed. Very soon we are back to the original key of G sharp minor. There follows an exact repeat of the principal theme against a background of the familiar octave leaps in the strings. The Trio ends with a mighty tutti, based entirely on the principal theme. The coda consists of the descending motif of the fifth bar of the principal theme. There is a modulation into E flat major and then the traditional repeat of the Scherzo.

Instead of the last twelve bars of the Scherzo there is a coda, the opening of which is built on the motif of the third theme (Ex. 52). This is followed by a passage based on the descending second theme, and the coda ends with ascending chords in the woodwind suggestive of the first theme.

The *third movement* of the symphony is an Andante (♩=52) in Borodin's favourite key, D major. The strings and clarinets play sustained chords, while the cellos play the first subject:

Ex. 54

[1] For the editing of this part of the Trio, see note 1, p. 184.

The first part of the Andante ends with an unexpected entry of the motif from the introduction (Ex. 46), played 'pesante marcato forte' on the violas and cellos. This is followed by a cadence on the cor anglais and a sudden modulation into D flat major.

Against a 'sighing' ostinato on the clarinets and bassoons:

Ex. 55

there is a motif of Eastern origin, played first by the cellos and then by the violins:

Ex. 56

This is repeated in a slightly varied form, after which the cor anglais plays the beginning of the first theme. The key of D major returns, together with the first subject. There is a gradual crescendo to *ff*, and then a fairly rapid diminuendo. The Andante ends with repeated syncopated octaves on D, played by the horns and violas. Against this, fragments of the first subject are heard on the cor anglais and clarinet.

The *Finale* (Allegro molto vivo; ♩= 168) is in the key of E flat major, and is in sonata form, with a repeat of the exposition. It begins with a sprightly, boisterous principal theme, played by the strings:

Ex. 57

The second half of the sixteen-bar phrase, with which the Finale begins, is repeated (tutti). After this, the motif of the first bar of the theme is played by the different instruments of the orchestra, until the last bars of the section, when only the rhythm of the motif remains. The bridge passage begins on a tutti *ff* chord, and consists of a syncopated chromatic phrase against a background of complicated, modulating harmonies. There is a diminuendo towards the end of this section, followed by a forte phrase serving as a transition to the second subject.

The second subject is played by the first violins in G flat major. It is fairly lyrical in character and based on Russian folk motifs:

Ex. 58

The exposition ends with a phrase consisting of a repeated B flat in the rhythm of the opening of the first subject.

The *development* is quite lengthy, beginning with an alternation of two variants of the first and second subjects. The first subject is now as follows:

Ex. 59

while the second subject is more syncopated:

Ex. 60

Both themes are separated by bars incorporating the following rhythm:

Ex. 61

After the themes have both appeared twice, the first subject becomes dominant. There is an extended crescendo based on the rhythm of the latter, leading to a powerful C major chord. A descending passage of syncopated chords, recalling a similar section in the bridge passage of the exposition, leads to a quiet episode consisting of motifs of both subjects in alternation. There is another prolonged crescendo, again reminiscent of the bridge passage. At the start of this section, there are phrases of descending pizzicato leaps. The rest of the development section is not very different from the ending of the exposition.

A maestoso section takes the place of the usual recapitulation. The first subject is played *fff* at half the original speed. (Although there are no indications in the score to this effect, conductors, N. S. Golovanov in particular, have usually taken the maestoso rather slower than the tempo indicated at the beginning of the Finale.) After this solemn episode, there is a section which corresponds to the first section of the exposition, as far as the bridge passage. The latter this time leads to the second subject transposed a sixth higher than in the exposition, which is now in E flat minor. The symphony ends on a tremendous tutti and a direct return to the key of E flat major.

III

Although Borodin's E flat major Symphony lies on the whole within the bounds of accepted tradition, it nevertheless contains several unusual innovations. In addition to the freedom shown in the choice of keys (a characteristic feature of Borodin's cyclic works) and the original harmonies, there is a blend of contrasting styles which gives the whole symphony a rhapsodic character. Good illustrations of this are the 'Eastern' style of the slow movement and the slightly 'Schumannesque' character of the first subject of the Finale.[1] This can easily be explained, in my opinion, if we assume the existence of a programme for the Symphony which the composer never disclosed. We may base this assumption not only on the evidence offered by the symphony alone, but also on the composer's work taken as a whole.

If we allow for the existence of a 'hidden programme' in connection with this symphony, many aspects of the work acquire a special significance: (1) The origin of the first subject in a phrase of the Introduction; (2) the appearance of a single motif at the conclusion of the Introduction, in the middle section of slow movement, and in the trio section of the Scherzo; (3) the distortion of the first and second subjects of the Finale when they appear in the development; (4) the peculiar solemnity of the beginning of the recapitulation of the last movement; (5) the retention of the distortions of the second subject in the re-

---

[1] Many musicologists have commented on the similarity of the first subject of the Finale to several motifs encountered in the Schumann symphonies. This, of course, might not be mere coincidence. Borodin was perhaps trying to reflect in the Finale of his First Symphony 'The Five's' creative plans and aspirations. The Schumannesque nature of the main theme might easily represent an analogy between the activities of the followers of Balakirev and the deeds of Schumann's 'Davidsbündler' in their battles against the Philistines. (There is an interesting reference to this in a letter from Stassov to Borodin dated 8 August 1879, in which Stassov calls the composers of the New Russian Music School the 'Davidsbündler'. See the Russian 2nd edition of my book *Borodin*, pp. 230 and 316).

capitulation. All these details, which 'violate the rules', cannot possibly have a purely logical explanation.

But all this is only guesswork, and may of course be very far from the truth. I feel, however, that what I have to say next will be of use to the general listener, as well as to the musicologist. Let us look at the whole thing analytically. First of all, let us try to ascertain whether this programme (assuming its existence for the moment) was epic in character, or whether Borodin was trying to convey personal experiences and his own view of life. In pursuing this matter, we have to bear in mind that in all Borodin's works, those parts which are clearly epic in content are based on folk themes; whereas the lyrical elements are less obviously folk-based and much nearer to the Western-European classical and romantic tradition (Beethoven, Schumann, and Chopin).

The analysis which emerges is as follows:

In the *first movement* the music is constructed entirely on Russian folk motifs.

In the *Scherzo*, neither of the main themes is particularly Russian. But there is a folk-tune at the end of the Scherzo, and in the Coda. The theme of the trio is an exquisite old folk-song (a Russian round-dance).

In the *slow movement* the thematic material is essentially Eastern in character (with a tendency towards the Arabian or Persian idiom).

The first subject of the *Finale* is not at all Russian-sounding. But the second subject shows traces of folk influence.

If we consider the nature of the themes he used in this symphony, then the programme might be interpreted as a 'survey' of the new Russian ideal in music.

The introduction to the first movement is a kind of meditation on the boundlessness of Russia and the sad state of the people. It is the realization of Russia's creative potential which transforms the melancholy into gladness, at the beginning of the Allegro. The second subject is not unlike a round-dance and lends support to this idea. The conclusion of the first movement (Andantino) expresses a mood of quiet confidence and hopes for a better future.

The Scherzo contains the composer's own thoughts about music; while the trio reminds us of the vast treasure-house of Russian folk-song, the source of his inspirations.

The slow movement speaks of yet another of his favourite realms of musical exploration, the folk-lore of the East.

The last movement is the transition from dream to actuality, to the work of his friends in their efforts to establish the new music. The 'Schumannesque' character of the first subject symbolizes, perhaps, the work of the Balakirev circle as a whole, in that it is based on 'the new, unprecedented Russian music' and yet uses the techniques of the Western classical and romantic composers.[1] The second subject is more feminine in character, and stands for activity. The development shows both aspects interwoven. The maestoso section is a vision of the future recognition of Russian music.

IV

In his First Symphony, Borodin reached his maturity and established his own individual style. The themes he uses are memorable, and the listener cannot fail to be struck by the skilful and ingenious way in which he develops his material. The orchestration is brilliant and highly original. The symphony is indeed an important work in its own right.[2]

THE SECOND SYMPHONY IN B MINOR

I

Borodin's Second Symphony was written in 1870–1, and was probably orchestrated in 1876. He made a number of alterations to the score in the spring of 1879, shortly before its second performance in Petersburg.[3] The piano-duet version of the symphony was published by Bessel at the beginning of 1877, but the score and parts appeared in print only after the death of the composer. The original score was prepared for publication by Borodin himself, but the final editing fell to Glazunov and Rimsky-Korsakov.

Borodin himself tells us that his manuscript was 'covered with a mass of alterations and corrections in blue, red, and black pencil'. He wanted to go through the manuscript again before submitting it to the publishers, and to make 'a number of modifications and corrections, and so forth.'[4]

As far as I have been able to ascertain, the variant readings in the

[1] See the preceding note.
[2] For comments on the orchestration of the E flat Symphony, see Rimsky-Korsakov's memoirs (*Chronicle of my Musical Life*, 7th ed., p. 50), and also my book, *Borodin*, Russian 2nd ed., p. 243 (Liszt's opinions).
[3] See Chapter IV; also Rimsky-Korsakov's memoirs, 7th ed., p. 122.
[4] See *Letters*, Vol. IV, pp. 113 and 362.

later score are of only minor importance and are confined largely to the first movement; the latter was published during the lifetime of the composer.[1] As far as I know, a full comparison of all the printed and manuscript scores has not yet been made. In any case, we have no grounds for supposing the existence of radical differences between the composer's own final version and the printed score.

Whereas the First Symphony commanded the undivided attention of the composer, this was certainly not the case with the Second Symphony. In the early stages, Borodin was spending a certain amount of time on *Prince Igor*, and later, in 1872, he had to stop work completely on his symphony in order to concentrate on the Fourth Act of *Mlada*. The B minor Symphony did not suffer greatly, however, as a result of all this. There is a unifying spirit running through all three works mentioned, the result of a powerful urge to recreate in musical form the great scenes of Russia's heroic past. It is for this reason that we find certain similarities in the themes Borodin uses in these works.

II

The *first movement* of the B minor Symphony is in sonata form. It begins with a statement of the elemental 'archaic' principal theme:

Ex. 62

this is played unison by the strings. The pause notes are reinforced by the bassoons and horns. The theme is repeated a full tone lower. Then the flutes, oboes, and clarinets take over, playing a contrasting theme at a slightly quicker tempo, which adds a heroic, chivalrous flavour to the whole.[2]

Ex. 63

[1] In Borodin's letter to Catherine dated 3 February 1887, he says that his '2nd Symphony has been published in score,' but gives no further details. Therefore part of the score must have been 'in production' at the time (see *Letters*, Vol. IV, p. 231).

[2] There is a difference between the piano arrangement and the printed score in the appearance of this phrase. In the piano version it is written a tone lower in C major. We notice furthermore that the melody of the first and second bars of this phrase corresponds with a motif found in the First Symphony (Ex. 46).

The stark 'heroic' principal theme soon makes itself felt again, and is played twice in a slightly varied form. A short bridge passage follows, based on the motif:

Ex. 64

and ends in D major, leading to a repetition of the second theme, and eventually to the second subject, a tranquil, lyrical melody based on motifs of old Russian songs[1]:

Ex. 65

Later, the music assumes a sterner aspect; again motifs of the 'heroic' theme are heard. The exposition ends with a beautiful succession of sustained chords, which lead to the key of C minor.

The middle section of the first movement which might be regarded as the development begins with the first bar of the principal theme, which is repeated at a higher pitch. Then follows an ostinato motif, in 3/2 time, on the timpani: ♩ ♫ ♩ ♫ ♩ ♩ ♫, against which certain alternating motifs from the first and second subjects can be heard.

There is a crescendo and the rhythm on the timpani is established throughout the entire orchestra. The answering phrase (Ex. 63) makes

[1] Comparison between the first motif of the second subject and the sketches quoted above (in note 1, p. 185), together with the outline of the ballad 'The Nightingale', which is preserved in the same file, reveals that this motif was evolved from the melodies illustrated below. (The latter have been transposed for the sake of convenience into the same clef and key as that of the second subject):

Beginning of the theme of the second subject

Motif from the lay 'The Terrible Tsar'

Motif from the song 'The Nightingale'

Ex. 296

its reappearance, this time in D flat major (forte); after this comes the lyrical second subject in the same key. The development ends on a series of fragments from the first subject in various keys. The key returns to two sharps, and after a short transitional crescendo phrase the recapitulation begins.

The first subject is played at a somewhat slower tempo (meno mosso) and at half-speed ($\downarrow$ = $\uparrow$). There are no pause notes this time, but solemn, portentious chords. The first subject and the answering phrase are both repeated, and then the oboes play the second subject, in a slightly varied form and rather more compressed than previously. After an animated transition section built on snatches of the first and second subjects, the movement ends on a tutti, consisting of the 'heroic' principal theme played *fff* in half-time ($\downarrow$ = $\uparrow$).

The *second movement* is a Scherzo (Prestissimo) in the key of F major. The movement opens with the following chord played *fff* on brass and timpani:

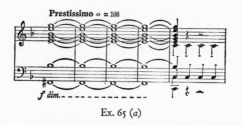

Ex. 65 (*a*)

which provides a modulation from B minor into F major, a very remote key. This was Balakirev's idea originally, and Borodin had already included it in the preliminary sketches of his symphony.[1]

The reiterated notes on the horn, playing C natural, begin at the fifth bar. The first theme is superimposed upon this, and is as follows:

Ex. 66

This theme is repeated, but between the repeats and after there is a descending phrase of no formal significance. After a brief transition,

[1] See Rimsky-Korsakov's memoirs, 7th ed., p. 109, and also note 5, p. 72, to Chapter IV of the present volume.

the second subject appears on the strings in the key of D flat major:

Ex. 67

The passage containing the second subject ends on a curious phrase consisting of descending leaps of a fourth. The first subject is heard once again, followed by the second subject, this time in F major. The Scherzo ends on a descending sequence of syncopated chords over a sustained F natural in the bass. A repeated A natural brings us to the Trio (Allegretto).

This section is based on a lovely melodic theme, not very different from that of the second subject of the first movement (Ex. 65)[1]:

Ex. 68

The Trio is monothematic in character and passes through various keys: D major, D flat major, G flat major, B flat major, and back to D major. After the Trio, there is a repetition of the Scherzo; a coda replaces the last thirteen bars, and has the following shape:

Ex. 69

The *third movement* (Andante) is in D flat major, and opens with a slow introductory phrase on the clarinet, accompanied by chords on

---

[1] In view of the similarity of this theme to the second subject, we may safely say that it, too, is based on the melodies illustrated in note 1, p. 201.

the harp. This is followed by a horn solo, playing the calm and warm principal theme[1]:

Ex. 70

But the mood soon darkens. There is a modulation into the relative minor (without change of key signature), and a new, restless woodwind motif makes its appearance[2]:

Ex. 71

[1] It is easy to show that the greater part of the first theme of the Andante is built on the motifs of the ballads mentioned above. This is clear from the following illustration. (I have transposed the folk-tunes into the same clef and key as the theme of the Andante):

Ex. 297

(Here (1) = the theme from the Andante; (2) = the motif from the ballad 'The Terrible Tsar'; (3) = motifs from the song 'The Nightingale'.)

[2] There are no accidentals in this theme, in which the note E plays an important rôle. One may consider it, therefore, as lying in the Phrygian mode (in the key of C).

There is yet a third thematic element (poco più animato) which creates
an impression of impending or inevitable danger[1]:

Ex. 72

There is a crescendo passage based on a rather characteristic phrase:

Ex. 73

The middle section of the Andante ends with a fragment of this phrase,
played *ff*. The key returns to D flat major. After a fresh appearance
of the second subject on the woodwind, the first subject returns once
more, making a triumphant entry against resounding chords in the
orchestra. After this we hear an oriental treatment of motifs taken
from the second and third themes, which fleetingly recall the struggle
that has just passed. The Andante ends on the clarinet and harp motif
with which the movement began.

The composer's directions are that the last movement should follow
without a break[2]; this is marked Allegro, and is in sonata form; the
key is B major.

The tone of the movement is bright and jubilant. First comes a
repetition several times of the opening bar of the main theme, interrupted by rapid passages on the harp in the style of the Russian zither
(gusli). Soon the main theme appears in its entirety:

Ex. 74

The bridge passage is not in any way remarkable, and is little more
than a repetition of the motif from the first bar of the main theme.
A sequence of repeated chords in syncopated rhythm appear at the
beginning and at the end of this section (♪ ♩ ♪ ♩).

[1] The motive from the end of the second bar up to the beginning of the fourth bar of
this phrase, corresponds with one of the leitmotifs of Prince Igor, for example, in his
aria in Act II at the words 'a happy feast of martial glory' (Belyaev vocal score, p. 170).

[2] The connection between the Andante and the Finale is provided by a concluding
sustained fifth of D♭–A♭ which is played by the second violins. This changes enharmonic-
ally into C♯–G♯ and leads immediately into the last movement.

There follows a modulation into two sharps, and the clarinet plays the second subject, which is rather like a Russian lyric song:

Ex. 75

The key is actually F sharp minor.

The exposition has no sharply delineated closing section, and ends on phrases built on motifs from the second subject.[1] ,

The development section has no key signature, and opens with a very characteristic new theme at a slower tempo than the rest of the movement (meno mosso); this theme in some respects is a free variation on the main theme[2]:

Ex. 76

[1] It would be incorrect to mistake the music following the second subject as a closing section, as then the modulation into another tonality and the playing of music in a new key would appear as the conclusion of the exposition.

[2] The phrase reproduced here is undoubtedly closely related to the theme which served as the basis for the Chorus of Idol Worshippers in Borodin's *Mlada*, and which was subsequently inserted into the Prologue of *Prince Igor*. Comparison of the themes

(Second Symphony)

(Prologue to Igor ⋆)

Ex. 298

shows that in the first bar, a B♮ and a C are added to the melody of the Second Symphony, which are missing from the Prologue to *Igor*, and that the notes at the end of the Prologue are missing from the beginning of the third bar of the phrase from the symphony. As in the Prologue to *Igor*, so in the chorus from *Mlada* the phrase below is seen to contain an interval of a semitone, and this feature remains constant throughout the development of the symphony. We observe that the theme of the Chorus of Idol Worshippers is probably based on one of the motifs from the lay 'The Terrible Tsar':

Chorus from
Mlada

Motif from the
ballad

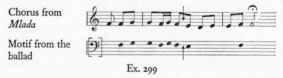

Ex. 299

(The arrow indicates the position of the semitone; we find the theme from the Prologue to *Igor* [vocal score, p. 9; bar 11, p. 10; bars 1–2] in the form given in the upper line.)

There is an *a tempo* and the theme is played in an ascending sequence, double time ($\flat = \flat$), which rises two full octaves. The development ends with a crescendo passage consisting of elements of the first and second subjects, and their variants. This is followed by the recapitulation.

There is a sudden modulation into the original key of B major. The first subject is almost exactly the same as it was in the exposition. This time, however, the bridge passage is based on the descending zither-like arpeggios, which in the exposition accompanied the first subject. The second subject is heard first in G sharp minor, and also in a modified form.

The final Coda is based chiefly on a motif rather like the answering phrase in the first movement (Ex. 63). Just before the movement closes, the opening bar of the main theme is repeated several times as a sequence.

III

We already have good reason to believe that the First Symphony followed some kind of programme. But in the case of the Second Symphony, we have no need to resort to the kind of guesswork we found necessary in dealing with the First Symphony. Although the programme was not given in the piano score edition, the main outlines at least were known to Stassov. The latter published the information he received directly from Borodin.[1]

Stassov tells us that Borodin had in mind a number of musical tableaux centred around the knights and heroic figures of ancient Russia. The first movement depicts an assembly of Russian knights. But what kind of assembly, one wonders? The music does not in the least suggest strife or preparation for combat.[2] The themes could equally represent the heroes or the setting. But at any rate the character

[1] See Stassov's article 'Twenty-five years of Russian art' in *Vestnik Evropy*, 1882.

[2] Stassov claims that the First Movement of the 'Bogatyr' Symphony represents a battle scene and that he always heard 'the clashes of swords' when listening to this movement (see V. Karenin's book, *Vladimir Stassov*, part 2, p. 412). Stassov's theories are purely subjective and we cannot dispute them; we can only observe that Borodin himself offered no such interpretation. I notice furthermore that I. F. Belza (in his brochure, *The Second [Bogatyr] Symphony of Borodin*, Moscow, 1951, p. 12) states that the answering phrase in D major evokes an impression 'of the sun playing on gilded shields and helmets'. The idea of D major being a 'gilded' tonality is in conformity with Rimsky-Korsakov's list of key-colours, and in one of my unpublished researches, I came to the conclusion that Borodin's associations of various colours with particular keys was more or less identical with that of Rimsky-Korsakov.

of the music is in keeping with the spirit of the programme; polyphony and the traditional classical treatment would be quite out of place here.

The second movement was left unexplained by the composer. The Scherzo could be intended to suggest a headlong chase, but it could equally well be a festive scene.[1] There is, one feels, something tender and feminine about the Trio theme. But all this is no more than speculation, since Borodin had nothing to say on the matter.[2]

According to Borodin, the third movement was to have depicted Bayan, the legendary minstrel who appears in the *Lay of Igor's Campaign*. The music is wonderfully evocative. Bayan and his zither (gusli) are there in the introductory bars; the first subject calmly opens Bayan's tale of dangers and struggles ahead (middle section),[3] and of their eventual triumph in victory (the first subject in the recapitulation). The total effect is powerful and convincing. The 'oriental' figures accompanying the repetition of the first subject suggest, perhaps, an incursion by nomadic raiders of the steppes.

The Finale is meant to depict 'the knights' feast, the sound of the gusli, and a jubilant throng of people'.[4] The programme here is quite detailed. The snatch of the first subject heard at the opening of the exposition and the strumming gusli represent the crowd and their heroes gathering for the feast. The theme is then heard in its entirety, and this is the beginning of the feast. The second subject is meant to represent the singing and conversation. The meno mosso passage at the start of the development and the ascending phrase based on it portray the ceremony of commemoration of the fallen and, possibly,

[1] The idea that the Scherzo of the Second Symphony represents games or some kind of amusement for the benefit of the Bogatyrs, was expressed by Professor Belza in the brochure I mentioned in the preceding note. Abraham states (on p. 42 of his book on Borodin) that the glittering sounds of the Scherzo are like sunbeams flashing from the helmets of (galloping ?—S. D.) warriors.

[2] There is a slight resemblance between the theme of the Trio, the song 'The Sea Princess', and the Nocturne of the Second Quartet in D major.

[3] Despite their complete independence from each other, the agitated mood of the second theme of the Andante has much in common with the second movement of Rimsky-Korsakov's *Sheherazade*. This analogy helps us to appreciate better the character of Borodin's Andante.

[4] The composer's programme and the music of the Finale clearly evoke an impression of pagan celebrations in the open country. This is splendidly illustrated in one episode where reference is made to bygone days (see text and note 2, p. 206). Therefore, I cannot agree with the picture of this feast as painted in M. Ilin and E. Sagal's book, *Borodin* (p. 336), in which they introduce the figures of Prince Vladimir Krasnoë Solnyshko and Princess Aprakseevna. The Finale is concerned with heroes, not potentates, and there are no social distinctions.

the libation offered to them. This rite would first be performed by one of the more prominent knights, and then by the crowd as a whole. The end of the development, the recapitulation and the coda are about the latter part of the feast. The close of the Finale marks the climax of the celebration.[1]

The whole character of the symphony is patriotic, and the composer is expressing his sincere admiration for the fortitude and spiritual integrity of the heroes of old, who saved Russia from her enemies, and thus laid the foundation for her future development. Borodin not only loved these great figures of the past, but was able to portray them faithfully in his music; he felt an instinctive affinity with this long-vanished epoch of Russian history.

IV

The Second Symphony aroused sharp criticism from more conservative musical circles. They found in it many violations of academic rules and tradition. They criticized the irregular sequence of keys exhibited by the various movements (B minor–F major–D flat major–

---

[1] Stassov's account of the programme of Borodin's Second Symphony has caught the attention of many Western European musicologists. Criticisms and opinions are found in French and English articles which show deep and considered understanding of the work in question. As well as this, one must mention a number of German musicologists who have also offered theories as to possible interpretations of the symphony, some of which are completely fantastic. In K. Nef's book, *Geschichte der Sinfonie und Suite*, for example, we are informed, with reference to Stassov's article, that the Second Symphony represents the mode of life ('Leben und Treiben') of the ancient Russian hero *Baysans*, who was something like a Minnesänger (p. 284). Willy Kahl in his article 'Die Russischen Novatoren und Borodin' (*Die Musik*, Vol. XV, 10 July 1923, pp. 733–8) also reproduces this. In connection with this sorry misunderstanding of the meaning and significance of the symphony, there are a number of critical articles dealing with its musical content. T. Kretschmar, in his book *Führer über den Konzertsaal* (1st part, 1887), suggests that the B minor symphony is not homogeneous. The first movement, he says, is of 'a peaceful atmosphere' featuring 'powerful natures'; later, the symphony 'revolves completely within the sphere of village life'. The Finale depicts 'some kind of rural incident' (eine Dorfgeschichte'). To confirm this, he asserts that the balalaika may be heard throughout the entire Finale ('Balalaika spielt beständig'). Obviously the author has never heard a balalaika and has confused its strumming with the imitation of the sounds of the gusli represented by the harp and pizzicato strings. In conclusion, I would like to mention some of the theories offered by the same musicologists as to the interpretation of the Andante. Nef finds that this is pervaded by a deep sense of melancholy, and that harmonically there is 'a mixture of major and minor'. Kretschmar considers that it resembles 'an evening meditation on the greatness of God' ('eine Abendandacht'), whilst Willy Kahl informs us that 'many of the diffuse melodic turns become completely comprehensible to us as the reflection of the basic religious mood of the orthodox Russian'. Further comment, I venture to suggest, is superfluous.

B major), the superabundance of themes in the first and last movements, and the liberties he had taken with his harmonies (unresolved seconds, etc.). This attitude towards Borodin's symphony was slow to change, and was even held by certain members of the 'Belyaev circle' long after its first performance. But today there is no doubt that the Second Symphony is among the great musical gems of Russian music. Its greatness is recognized not only in Russia, but throughout the entire world of music.

THE THIRD (UNFINISHED) SYMPHONY IN A MINOR[1]

I

The Third Symphony, of which only two movements are preserved, belongs to Borodin's last years. Apart from these two movements, published by Glazunov, there are only a few sketches for an Andante, and the account given by the person who claimed to have heard the Andante and Finale played by Borodin himself not long before his death.[2]

My purpose here is to attempt to restore the general outline of the symphony, and the ideas and emotions embodied in it, and to estimate the value of the work as a whole. This attempt will obviously involve a number of assumptions which might be questioned, but I hope that it will throw some useful light on Borodin's compositions, which have so far hardly been studied.

II

Borodin seems to have first thought of writing this symphony shortly after he had composed the D major Scherzo movement for the amateur chamber musicians who used to meet at Belyaev's. After hearing the Scherzo actually played, the composer very likely felt that it was not a chamber work at all, but more like a symphony; it could easily have reminded him of the scherzo movements of the First and Second Symphonies. At all events, Borodin made it clear that he intended to work it into his next symphony.[3] Two years later Borodin

---

[1] Part of the material reproduced here was given in my paper delivered on 22 April 1926 at a meeting of the Historical section of the department of music of the Russian Institute of the History of Art. The report was later included in the composition of the *Borodin* volume of the State Academy of Artistic Sciences which so far has not appeared.

[2] See Chapter V.

[3] Tchaikovsky heard of Borodin's intentions and was very much opposed to the idea. In all probability Tchaikovsky unfoundedly jumped to the conclusion that Borodin was

sketched a theme in C minor, marked Andante, after hearing the funeral dirges of the priestless sect at Pavlovsky which made a great impression on him.[1]

The light, fantastic Scherzo he had in mind was very different from the sombre Andante, which had a central motif something like Dies Irae.[2] The latter chant symbolized the vain yearning of these old believers for an eventual, saving miracle.[3] There could have been some basic idea underlying this 'flagrant contradiction', but as to what it was, we can do no more than guess. It was another two years before the composer shaped the principal theme of the first movement; this no doubt has some connection with the Scherzo he had already written and the Andante that he already had in mind.

Despite the fact that he simply had to finish his opera, he nevertheless concentrated entirely on this symphony from the time when he had sketched the first movement. He visualized the shape of the Andante, and, in a moment of inspiration, improvised the entire last movement. On the very day of his death, he was heard humming the theme of the Finale,[4] and was obviously working on the movement.

III

We turn now to an analysis of the structure of the Third Symphony. The *first movement* is marked Moderato Assai and is in sonata form. The first subject, with which the symphony opens, is as follows:

Ex. 77

It is in the key of A minor (Aeolian), and evokes a mood of quiet resignation. Later, when this theme is merged with other elements, it is

going to construct a symphony from a number of completely unrelated pieces composed at different times.

[1] See the music lists mentioned in Chapter V.

[2] See *Letters*, Vol. IV, p. 75.

[3] The sect of the old believers (the *bespopovtsi*) whose ritual music interested Borodin, taught that since the time of the Patriarch Nikon's reforms the lawful hierarchy had disappeared and therefore there could be no Holy Communion. This would last till the end of the world or till a miracle happened, which might be achieved through prayer.

[4] See Cui's obituary of Borodin which appeared in No. 66 of the journal, *L'indépendance Belge*, on 7 March 1887; also my book, *Borodin*, Russian 2nd ed., p. 343.

suggestive of autumn. This is followed by a second theme which is an answer to the first:

Ex. 78

The first section in fact consists of these two themes in alternation and in various forms. After the third repetition of the first two bars of the first subject (motif (i), (*a*), Ex. 77), a new motif makes its appearance:

Ex. 79

This is related to the second subject. The first section of the exposition ends with a phrase containing snatches of the first subject.

The bridge passage is marked poco più mosso, and is built around the answering theme (Ex. 78 (II)). The bridge section is interrupted by a motif from the first subject, the first bar of which is in the key of E minor, the second in E major; the rest of the section stays in the latter key. There is a return to a slower tempo (meno mosso), and the second subject enters:

Ex. 80

The folk origin of this theme is obvious.

We are actually in a position to examine the source, from which Borodin took the motifs for his second subject. If we compare Ex. 80 with the second line of the notes he made of the dissenters' tunes in 1884.[1]

Ex. 81

---

[1] See the music sketches quoted in note 1, p. 211.

we see that the motif marked (*a*) in Ex. 80 is a slightly adapted version of the first two bars of this religious tune. We notice also that motif (III) (Ex. 79) is connected with (D). This comparison shows that Borodin conceived his symphony as a whole, for we find in this particular case a thematic unity binding various motifs of the first movement and the Andante.[1] A point of psychological interest; this far from sombre theme has its origin in the old-believers' funeral dirges. Throughout the entire first movement an elegiac mood predominates, though this is none too obvious at first hearing.

The second subject first appears in the key of E major, and then in C major. There emerges yet another theme, in A major, which is important in the closing section of the exposition (the tempo is Animato):

Ex. 82

This occurs more than once and undergoes various modifications.

The rest of the exposition is light-hearted in character. The listener can easily imagine Russian country scenes. The A major theme (Ex. 82) at the very end of the exposition is reminiscent of a round-dance refrain, especially as it is played rallentando. In place of the usual cadence there is a typical Borodin sequence:

Ex. 83

The development follows, Animato. The first two bars of the first subject (Ex. 77) are heard in F sharp minor; this is followed by the A major theme (Ex. 82) in a somewhat modified form, against a syncopated accompaniment taken from the last bars of the second subject (Ex. 81). The sequence at the end of the exposition (Ex. 83) makes its reappearance, this time a full tone higher, followed immedi-

---

[1] For example, with the D♮ motif of the Allegretto. See below, section IV, sketch [4].

15

ately by the first two bars of the first subject (Ex. 78); on this occasion, the second of these bars (as previously) is in the major.

The succeeding bars of the development are at a rather slower tempo (Tempo 1, Moderato). The first subject is heard linked with the second subject; the former is first of all in G sharp minor, and then in F sharp minor.

The development ends with a descending passage based on motif (III, Ex. 79) and on a series of figures:

Ex. 84

The first of these is also found in the sketches made in 1884 and in the rough draft of the Andante.[1]

With the exception of stretto counterpoint in the opening bars, the recapitulation follows the exposition exactly until the sudden modulation into A major.

The bridge passage (based on motif II) leads to the second subject (Ex. 81) (Meno mosso); as in the exposition, this is heard in two keys, first in A major and then in F major. The statement of the final episode is exactly as it was in the exposition. The coda which follows (Sostenuto e tranquillo) is in the same tempo as the opening of the first movement. The mood of the coda is calm and leisurely; major harmonies predominate. The coda ends, as in the corresponding movements of the first two symphonies, with a section of the principal theme played in augmentation:

Ex. 85

The sadness of the principal theme still prevails, but now it is no longer so obvious and partly hidden by the peace and beauty of a landscape (perhaps the purple of an autumn sunset).

The D major Scherzo, which in the Glazunov edition follows the

---

[1] In the 2nd (b), 3rd and 4th lines of the sketches of 1884. In the beginning of the unison phrase [2] in the sketches of the Andante (see text below).

Moderato Assai, may be taken to be the second movement of this symphony.[1] This movement is first and foremost a scene of merry-making, in the true Russian folk idiom.

The Scherzo begins with an ostinato on a D major figure:

Ex. 86

This reminds one of the strumming of a rustic fiddler on three open strings of his instrument.[2] The main thematic elements are heard from the fourth bar onwards, in a passage consisting of sixteen bars in all. The music is built around three motifs:

Ex. 87

Ex. 88

The final motif of the passage is derived from the others:

Ex. 89

---

[1] The positioning of the Scherzo as the second movement is found in the majority of Borodin's cyclic productions belonging to his maturity (in the First and Second Symphonies, and in the Second Quartet). In this instance, it corresponds to the key system of the movements of the symphony, and probably gives an insight into the tonal structure of the symphony as a whole. Abraham also regards the quintuple Scherzo as the second movement of the Third Symphony (see his *Borodin*, p. 53).

[2] There is always the possibility that this deliberately simple piece is really a musical joke in disguise. The Scherzo was originally written for an amateur quartet ensemble organized by Belyaëv in his early days, and the players were not at their strongest in the question of purity of intonation and technique. It is interesting to remember Glazunov's account of his first acquaintance with this quartet as described by V. M. Belyaëv in his book, *Glazunov*, Vol. I, part 1, St. Petersburg, 1922, p. 58. Abraham has commented on the similarity of this piece to the introduction of the gopak from Mussorgsky's opera, *Sorochinsky Fair*. In this, Mussorgsky tried to give an imitation of Ukrainian village fiddlers (Abraham, *Borodin*, p. 54).

The first subject of the Scherzo is the four-bar phrase:[1]

Ex. 90

Next, Borodin introduced a rhythmical motif:

Ex. 91

this later acquires significance as an accompanying figure.

The first section of the Scherzo ends with a repeat of motif (IX). In places the harmony could be called gorgeous; it abounds in characteristic unresolved seconds. The predominant key is D major and the whole section is based on a major ninth (D–E).

At the end of this section, the tempo changes and becomes almost twice as slow. The second theme enters in F major (Sostenuto e pesante):

Ex. 92

The next section (which can be termed the second section) is in the tempo and rhythm of the first section. It is introduced by a chromatic motif:

Ex. 93

---

[1] This is quite feasible, as the theme is played frequently in different degrees throughout the movement. There is a slight inconsistency here, as the motifs which form this theme are split up into various fragments and are played sometimes apart, and sometimes in combination.

This motif is woven into an orchestral fabric, in the form of four-bar alternations. Then comes a C major motif:

Ex. 94

and variants of the rhythmical motif (X, Ex. 91). The thematic element (IXb, Ex. 88) also appears as an accompanying figure.

The transition to the third section includes a repetition of the second theme (XI, Ex. 92), which is in F major still, but with a rather different harmonization. The chromatic motif (XII, Ex. 93) provides a basis for the transitional phrase, leading to the third section.

The third section (in three flats) is built at first on theme (IX) played four times altogether. In the second half of this section there is yet another motif:

Ex. 95

This is related to certain thematic elements in the Andante.[1] The transition to the recapitulation is effected by means of motif (XII).

The fourth section of the Scherzo is a slightly different version of the second section, and is in A flat major. The movement ends with an appearance of the second theme, in B flat major, and the chromatic motif (XII) in which the minor second has been changed to a major second:

Ex. 95 (*a*)

The Trio section is in B flat major and contains material originally intended for *Prince Igor*—the 'Merchants' Tale'. It was the composer's own intention that Glazunov should carry out the necessary

---

[1] To the first and second bars of phrase [2]. If we do not take into consideration the possibility of an accidental resemblance (which is by no means impossible), then it seems that we must once again revert to the lists of 1884 and try to find some motifs which resemble those of the Scherzo. If this could be found, then the unity of the symphony would be guaranteed by the use of homogeneous elements throughout the various movements, differing basically in mood.

adaptation.[1] It would not be surprising if the movement, owing to its operatic origin, were disturbing the tragic in character. (It is the story of the battle of Kayala, where the Russian army was defeated and Igor captured.) But the Trio is not at all tragic in character. It has more the suggestion of a lyrical episode based on Russian folk motifs. The mood of the Trio, which is slower and more reflective, forms an excellent contrast with the Scherzo.

The themes of the Trio are somewhat similar to those of the Scherzo. There are a number of short motifs which are combined in various ways during the course of the Trio[2]:

Ex. 96

The first subject of the Trio is most likely the three-bar phrase heard at the beginning of this section:

Ex. 97

This is repeated in a number of different forms.

---

[1] See Rimsky-Korsakov's memoirs, 7th ed. (Moscow, 1955), p. 161; also V. M. Belyaëv's book, *Glazunov*, p. 112.

[2] The sequence of motifs seems to be fairly consistent:

(XV), (XVIa) (XVIa), (XVIIa)–(XVIIa)
(XV), (XVIb) (XVIIb) (XVIIb)

In the repeat, instead of a jump up of a fifth, the second bar (XVIa) has a jump of an octave.

In the poco animato section in the middle of the Trio there is a motif which is at least the germ of a second subject:

Ex. 98

The end of the Trio is based on motifs (XV) and (XVI).

The movement ends with a repetition of the Scherzo, but it is not an exact repeat in that it is more condensed and contains a number of modifications.

IV

We are now going to review the material and the various information we possess relating to the unwritten Andante. This comprises the following:

(1) The sketches for the Andante preserved in the Glazunov archives.

(2) Sketches of old-believers' songs made by Borodin in Pavlovsky in 1884.

(3) Dobroslavina's account of Borodin's performance of this Andante at her house. According to her, the Andante was a series of variations on a sombre theme, which the author called 'schismatic'.

We find records of these old-believer's chants in his notes of 1884. Naturally, the questions arise:

(*a*) Have the notes Borodin made in 1884 any connection with the sketches of the Andante which we possess?

(*b*) Does the material preserved in the archives support Dobroslavina's statement that the movement was in variation form?

The theme of the Andante is written at the bottom of the sketches of the religious tunes, and is a slight modification of the third line of these tunes, perhaps transposed from major to minor.

In the Glazunov archives in the Leningrad Conservatoire, we find the following eight sketches for the Andante:

Ex. 99

(The flats inserted in brackets were probably omitted by the composer.)

Ex. 99

Ex. 99—*cont.*[1]

Comparing these with the sketches of 1884 we find that:

(*a*) Sketch (1) (the second theme of the Andante) is thrown together with the first bar of the second line and the first two bars of the third line;

[1] The suggestions as to clefs in sketches [5] and [8], and as to keys in [5] and [7], are made as a result of comparing and identifying the individual melodies.

(*b*) Sketch (2) bears the indication 'Unison' and is based on tunes also marked unison (the second and third lines of the notes)[1]:

Ex. 100

(*c*) Sketch (4) has in its first bar the motif from the third bar of (1), and also a descending motif taken from the second bar of (2). Thus, here also, there is some connection with the notes of 1884;

(*d*) The bass line of (6) consists of a tune built on a $\frac{6}{4}$ chord found in the first line of the religious chants.

(*e*) in (5) and (8), the motifs:

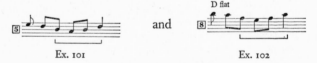

Ex. 101   and   Ex. 102

are probably variants of:

Ex. 103

[1] The insertion of the flats in sketch [2] seems to be essential when one takes into consideration the diatonic character of the melody beginning with the tenor clef. It is extremely probable that Glazunov did not know of the flat signs which determined the E♭ minor nature of phrase [2] on account of the lack of evidence as to the origin of the 'dissenters'' themes in the Andante.

which is taken from (2). If this is the case, then their affinity with the sketches of the religious chants is definitely established. In other words, Borodin used the sketches he made of these chants as the basis for the themes he intended to use in his Andante.[1]

It is not so easy, however, to find support for Dobroslavina's contention that the movement was in variation form. From the material at our disposal, we may make the following deductions:

(1) We have already seen that there are two themes[2] (in the strictest sense of the word) to the Andante. Thus, if the Andante was to have been in variation form, then we have to concede that the fundamental scheme underlying the variations must have included both these themes.

(2) A comparison of sketches (5), (7), and (8) shows that they are variants of a single phrase (or part of a phrase) but in different rhythms and keys.[3]

(3) Sketches (3) and (6) are sequences which could serve as connecting links between the variations. The remark on sketch (6): 'A major, double speed' is quite interesting, for it implies that section (6)

---

[1] It is impossible to establish definitely the first thematic element of the Andante. The most likely choice is the phrase headed 'Andante' found in the lists of 1884, in which case the opening of the movement (the beginning of the 'theme and variations'?) might have been something like this:

Ex. 300

One must mention that the presence or absence of the F♮ in the penultimate bar is difficult to decide. It is not in the original, but Borodin could easily have omitted it absentmindedly. It is quite possible that the Andante opened with the unison phrase [2] in the key of E♭ minor (like the introduction to his First Symphony), and that it was succeeded by another phrase similar to that produced above.

[2] The second theme here may be an answering motif, rather like the descending phrase following the first theme in the Moderato Assai movement of the symphony.

[3] One of these variants might possibly have been the original theme of the Andante.

was to have been repeated (first in C sharp minor, and then in A major).

(4) There are a number of short and fortuitous modulations. The keys of C minor, A flat major, E flat minor, C sharp minor, D flat major, A major and probably A minor and B flat major can be detected.

These details by no means run counter to the suggestion that the movement was in variation form, even though the word 'variation' does not appear in the sketches. The sketches exhibit many features characteristic of Borodin's later work; in particular, attempts at combining theme motifs in different ways.[1]

V

All things considered, it would seem that the Third Symphony is closer to those works of Borodin which are not purely epic in style; the First Symphony and the First Quartet, for example.

In the first movement, the first subject conveys a sense of resignation, and perhaps even a presentiment of death. The melancholy mood is there all the time, but it is alleviated to some extent by the autumnal landscape, the peasant songs, the radiance of the evening sunset.

In the second and third movements, this mood of sad reflection on life is replaced by scenes taken from actual life. The second movement is an idealized picture of simple joie de vivre; there is no reflection on life and its meaning. The Trio, although it is rather more reserved, is far from gloomy. The third movement (the Andante) would have stood in sharp contrast with the second. It was to have been compounded of funeral dirges ('Russian Dies Irae' as the composer called them), a fantasy on death and funeral rites, and on the futility of bargaining with death or trying to overcome it. (The closing variation of the Andante, according to Dobroslavina, 'was powerful and telling, permeated with a sense of impassioned despair.')

But what can we say about the last movement of this symphony,

---

[1] Thus, for example, if we provisionally call the motifs of the upper voice in [1] α in the second bar, β in the third, α′ in the fourth and β′ in the fifth; and the motifs from the first and second bars of [2] γ and δ respectively, then we get the following sequence of motifs:

In [1] . . . . (α) (β) (α′) (β′)
„ [2] (bars 1–2) . . . . (γ) (δ) . . (α′)
„ [4] (bars 1–4) . . . . (β) (δ) (β) (δ)

The theme of the Andante:

1884 (bars 1–4) . . . . (β′) (γ′)

the Finale which shook the composer to his very foundations, and which only one person was fortunate enough to hear. I think there can be little doubt that this movement embodied the antithesis of love of life and indignation at its brevity. In Borodin's mind, the whole question was resolved; the triumph of life, and the struggle to maintain life, despite the threat of personal extinction.

The tragic, premature death of the composer deprived us of the possibility of hearing and understanding this music.

THE SYMPHONIC SKETCH 'IN THE STEPPES OF CENTRAL ASIA'

I

In his Memoirs, Rimsky-Korsakov gives an account of how this work came to be written. Two otherwise obscure people, Korvin-Kryukovsky and Tatishchev, were in charge of the mis-en-scène for a festival performance in honour of the twenty-fifth anniversary of the reign of Alexander II; they were planning to include a series of tableaux depicting the most important events of his reign. They accordingly requested twelve Russian composers to write the incidental music. Borodin was asked to write music for a scene depicting the passage of a Central-Asian caravan, escorted by a guard of Russian soldiers.[1]

Borodin complied with this 'request', and the result was the sketch for orchestra, *In the Steppes of Central Asia*. The project, however, came to nothing; the producers 'disappeared' sometime in the jubilee year of 1880.[2] But the music written for the occasion gained recognition in its own right; especially *In the Steppes of Central Asia* which almost immediately became a regular item at symphony concerts and rapidly acquired great popularity both in Russia and abroad.[3]

II

In the Steppes of Central Asia is a splendid example of programme music, and is by no means unworthy of Borodin. The programme sequence is outlined in a simple and convincing manner.

[1] See Rimsky-Korsakov's memoirs, 7th ed., p. 124; also note 23, on p. 262.
[2] See p. 124 of Rimsky-Korsakov's memoirs.
[3] For details of the first performances, see Chapter V and the notes to it, and also Vols. III and IV of the *Letters*, together with pp. 265, 267, and 328 of the Russian 2nd edition of my book *Borodin*.

The work opens with high sustained notes on the flute, and harmonics on the first violins, giving a wonderful sense of space to the listener.

Ex. 104

Far away in the distance, we hear the refrain of a Russian folk-song.

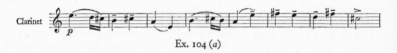

Ex. 104 (*a*)

This theme is repeated a sixth lower by a solo horn, in C major. Then comes the sound of chromatic intervals, representing the approach of the camel-train and horse-riders as they make their way through the desert[1]:

Ex. 105

A second theme is heard on the cor anglais. This is oriental in character, and is the song of the camel-drivers.[2]

Ex. 106

[1] Because of the effectiveness of the music representing the camel train, the symphonic poem later became known in France and Belgium as *The Camels* (*Les Chameaux*).

[2] As Abraham has justifiably observed in his book on Borodin (pp. 59 and 84), this oriental theme is undoubtedly connected in some way with the song of the Polovtsian

The Russian theme is now heard against a pizzicato accompaniment. There is a gradual crescendo building up to an orchestral tutti, in which the Russian theme is played twice *ff* in C major.

The chorus of Russian soldiers dies down, and again we hear the ponderous tread of the camels. The oriental theme and the Russian theme are played simultaneously, the former on the violins and the latter on the oboes. The two tunes are interwoven in an unforced and effective contrapuntal passage[1]:

Ex. 107

At the end of this passage the music dies away and the caravan recedes into the distance.

The 'tread of the camels' accompaniment returns; there is a steady diminuendo, and the Russian theme is heard on the first violins at half its previous speed, and is similarly repeated by the clarinet pianissimo. The 'tread of the camels' dies away, and once more we hear harmonics

girl in Act II of *Igor*. In an attempt to devise a counterpoint to the Russian theme in an 'oriental' manner, Borodin had to resort to one of the motifs from the song of the Polovtsian women:

Ex. 301

For the most part, figures 3 and 4 have the character of pipe music. He does not introduce any of the Arabian features which are to be found in the 'Polovtsian' song into the new theme.

[1] Borodin told my father that this combination of the two themes had greatly pleased Taneev and that the latter had asked him how he had discovered such a euphonious union. Borodin answered that he had written both themes simultaneously and had fitted each melody into the music in accordance with the programme. As a result of this conversation Taneev made use of Borodin's contrapuntal combination by way of an illustration in his book, *Strict Counterpoint* (p. 299). From a note to this example it is seen that the 'oriental' theme was grafted on to that of the Russian song (see the preceding note).

in the first violins; the Russian theme is heard for the last time on the flute. The work ends *pppp* in A major.

Ex. 107 (*a*)

It is easy to see that the work cannot be fitted into any classical framework. It is for this reason, as well as on account of its programmatic character and brilliant orchestration, that it stands closer to the symphonic poems of Liszt.

The work resisted any national or imperialist tendencies, and avoided any suggestion of 'the power of the oppressors.'[1] In this respect, his choice of a Russian folk-song is most significant, and gives the impression of being sung by Russian peasants in soldiers' uniform. The Russian theme in no sense overrides the oriental theme, but joins with it in counterpoint. There is no hint of victorious campaigns by the Russians against the Asiatics. Instead, we find a happy synthesis of the two national elements.[2]

Borodin arrived at a realistic solution to the problem confronting him. The Russian song here sounds as if it is actually being sung on the march, and not in the concert hall. The main theme is announced homophonically and is played unison and in octaves; there is nothing spurious about it. Polyphony is used only where it is unavoidable, and the composer never transgresses the bounds of realism into the sphere of naturalism. Even the ending is by no means a purely acoustic picture of sounds fading away in the distance. The whole thing is on a musical or psychological plane, and is much more than illustration pure and simple.

[1] See also Chapter V, n. 3, p. 128.
[2] This aspect of *In the Steppes of Central Asia* could be seen during its performance in concerts in the Near East. Academician A. N. Samoilovich told me that in the twenties the symphonic poem was very well received in Ankara, as the leading Turkish intelligentsia saw in this work an illustration of Soviet-Turkish friendship.

CHAPTER EIGHT

THE CHAMBER AND PIANO WORKS

THE FIRST QUARTET IN A MAJOR

I

As a young man, Borodin had gained much experience in the writing of chamber music. In the winter of 1874–5 he began to exercise his mastery of this genre on his first string quartet.[1] We know nothing of the circumstances which led Borodin to write this work; we do know however that it was not altogether to the liking of the 'left' of the Balakirev circle.[2] The fact that the work is dedicated to Rimsky-Korsakov's wife should not tempt us to think that it was inspired by her[3]; but it is quite possible that she suggested the idea to spite the more radical of Borodin's friends.

Work on the A major Quartet proceeded in fits and starts; the Scherzo was written last of all, in 1879.[4]

II

The quartet begins with a slow introduction (Moderato; ♩=84). The first violin introduces the following theme:

Ex. 108

[1] This mastery was acknowledged even by so hostile a critic as H. A. Laroche who grudgingly admitted Borodin's 'almost completely European technique' (*Russkii Vestnik*, October 1887, Borodin's obituary). For an account of the quartet players' admiration of this work, see my book, *Borodin*, Russian 2nd ed., p. 247 (letter of N. V. Galkin).

[2] See Chapter IV and also *Letters*, Vol. II, p. 89.

[3] I asked the late A. N. Rimsky-Korsakov if he could throw any light on the question as to why Borodin should dedicate the A major quartet to his mother, but despite his great knowledge of the circumstances of his parents' musical life, he could tell me nothing definite. One of the reasons might have been that the Rimsky-Korsakovs were strongly opposed to Stassov's attacks on the classical forms on the score of obsolescence, and were most sympathetic towards Borodin's efforts in this field.

[4] See *Letters*, Vol. III, pp. 64 and 300.

229

16

A polyphonic section follows, based on fragments and variants of this theme in various keys.

The tempo picks up, and the Allegro begins. It is a bright and sunny movement. The first violin plays the first subject[1]:

Ex. 109

There is a variant of this theme which follows:

Ex. 110

This gives way to a series of alternations, built around the variants (A) and (B), just quoted. After (B) has been heard for a second time, a chromatic motif is heard:

Ex. 111

---

[1] This theme was based on a motif from the finale of Beethoven's quartet in B♭ major, op. 130.

Ex. 302

Borodin stated that he had borrowed this theme from Beethoven in the title of his work, but he did not state which theme it was.

The bridge passage is based on this motif, both as a whole, and in snatches. A descending series of notes leads to the sombre second subject, which is played at a slower tempo:

Ex. 112

The exposition ends with a section based on the chromatic motif (Ex. 111), which provides a kind of frame for the second subject.

The development is almost devoid of any key signatures, although this by no means implies that the section is entirely in C major or A minor.

First we hear a variant (A) of the first subject, which is accompanied by a descending and rather mysterious passage in A flat major. Then follows the other variant of the first subject and motifs of the second subject which interweave to form a complicated pattern. The music becomes for a time a carpet of sound woven with considerable ingenuity from threads of all the themes so far encountered. Gradually the second variant (B) becomes predominant, and fugato is built upon it (in A minor) in which each entry is marked 'risoluto'. The fugato ends with the chromatic motif of the bridge passage, with its first five quavers altered, each having the form:

Ex. 113

The climax is reached, and the mood brightens once more. The key is now F major, and calm and optimistic motifs from the introduction are heard on the violins. In the lower parts, there is an interchange of phrases, built on the chromatic motif.

At the close of the development section, the music becomes more agitated and impassioned. Motifs from the second subject are heard against an accompaniment of elaborate, turbulent figures played by the viola and cello in different rhythms. There is a return to the key of A major, and the agitation dies away. Theme (A) returns and the recapitulation begins.

The beginning of the recapitulation is not substantially different from the corresponding section in the exposition. The first important change occurs with the second appearance of theme (A); it is an octave higher this time and the accompaniment is considerably livelier. The bridge motifs lead to the second subject, now in F sharp minor.

After a closing section similar to that of the exposition, there comes a rather extended coda, built on the various motifs of the first subject and on the bridge motif. The coda is embellished by prolonged trills on the first violin. After this, there is a gradual diminuendo ending on a peculiar cadence.

The Andante con moto (F sharp minor; ♩=72) is the most original movement of the quartet as regards its thematic content and structure. The main theme is heard at the start of the movement, and is in two parts:

Ex. 114

The development of the motifs of this calm section, which reminds one of a sad tale, is suddenly interrupted by a descending triplet passage (*ff* energico ed appassionato) played by the first violin, against a background of sustained chords:

Ex. 115

After this 'emotional outburst', the movement takes on an elegiac colouring. A new theme is introduced:

Ex. 116

The first two bars of this phrase is interwoven with the following chromatic ostinato:

Ex. 117

The end of the first part of the Andante is based entirely on this motif.

The middle section of the Andante (Fugato: Un poco più mosso) is also based on the chromatic ostinato motif just quoted. It is fugal in character, and the real fugato commences with the counter-subject, which enters on C sharp. Later comes a theme (with a contrapuntal counter-subject)

Ex. 118

in which the first two bars plus the first note of the third bar are the fugato subject (*a*); the remaining bars (*b*) are a transition motif, which comes again later with a slight change towards the end. (This latter motif is interesting in that it is a variant of the second and third bars of the principal theme (Ex. 114).) The counter-subject is marked 'misterioso *pp*' on the first two occasions on which it is heard.

Bearing in mind the fact that the fugato begins with the counter-subject, we should find the following table useful ('S' indicates the subject, and 'A' the counter-subject):

[I]	A′	.	.	.	C Sharp	.	.	.	Bass
	S′	.	.	.	F Sharp	.	.	.	Tenor
	A′	.	.	.	C Sharp	.	.	.	Alto
	S′	.	.	.	F Sharp	.	.	.	Soprano
[II]	S′	.	.	.	F Sharp	.	.	.	Tenor
	A′	.	.	.	C Sharp	.	.	.	Bass
	A″	.	.	.	B Natural	.	.	.	Soprano
	S′	.	.	.	F Sharp	.	.	.	Alto
[III]	A′	.	.	.	C Sharp	.	.	.	Tenor
	A′	.	.	.	C Sharp ⎫ stretto	.	.	.	Alto
	S′	.	.	.	F Sharp ⎭	.	.	.	Tenor
	A′	.	.	.	C Sharp	.	.	.	Tenor

The fugato ends in the key of D major.

The recapitulation begins double forte and is marked 'energico ed appassionato'. The main theme is heard again, and it is worth noting that the parts are inverted at the climax of the theme. The descending triplets at the beginning of the section are heard a second time and again a third time, and are marked più vivo. The movement ends with a restful coda built on snatches of the triplet passage and the chromatic ostinato.

The Scherzo is in one flat and is marked Prestissimo (3/8 time; ♩=114).[1] The basic motif (*a*) is as follows:

Ex. 119

First it provides a basis for the main theme, which is in the Lydian mode[2]:

Ex. 120

This theme and variants of it provide an ostinato accompaniment to the second subject:

Ex. 121

The section which develops this theme ends on a phrase compounded of motif (*a*) (Ex. 119), a *ff* triad in C major and a long pause (G.P.). The first theme (Ex. 120) is not heard again in its entirety. The Scherzo ends with a descending sequence based on motif (*a*).

The Trio section (A major and C major; Moderato; ♩=92) is built on the theme:

Ex. 122

[1] The Belyaev edition of 1894 has ♩=144.
[2] B flat is found in the accompaniment to the theme as well as B natural, in addition to other accidentals.

This phrase[1] is heard as a series of harmonics on the first violin. The viola plays simultaneously another motif, con sordino, which is not without significance:

Ex. 123

This is accompanied by a semiquaver passage on the second violin.

At the opening of recapitulation, the key returns to A major and the Trio ends with the themes heard at the beginning. The Scherzo is repeated in full.

The Finale begins with a short introduction marked Andante ($\downarrow$ = 58) in A minor. A wistful phrase with a major ending is heard; it is not very different from the first theme of the Andante:

Ex. 124

The first half of the second theme of the same Andante (Ex. 116) transposed into A minor serves as a counterpoint to this phrase. After a short cadence, the phrase is repeated (using the same counterpoint) a full tone lower. The introduction closes with the two-bar motif of the second theme heard already.

There is a short pause, and the main section of the last movement begins (Allegro Risoluto: A minor; $\downarrow$ = 112), the movement is in sonata form (the exposition is repeated). After three introductory sforzandos the energetic, bellicose first subject is played by the first violin:

Ex. 125

[1] For future reference, it should be pointed out that in the penultimate bar of this phrase the first two bars of the introduction appear in diminution.

235

The first few bars of the second theme of the Andante is played staccato by the viola and this acts as a counterpoint to the first subject. A short bridge passage in the form of a descending sequence leads to the second subject:

Ex. 126

The closing section is based, for the most part, on a combination of the thematic elements heard earlier in the movement.

The development section opens with a modulation into G minor (by means of a series of chords identical to the introductory chords of the exposition). The beginning of exposition appears in inversion and the first subject becomes a bass accompaniment, whilst contrapuntal fragments of the second subject of the Andante appear as the melody. A contrast is provided by the second subject in the bass; the violins bring in a new thematic element characterized by an already familiar rhythm:

Ex. 127

Later the second subject predominates, and the key of the exposition is re-established. The second subject and the first two bars of the second theme of the Andante are the melody this time, whereas the first subject appears in the bass. The development ends with a phrase in which the second subject of the Allegro is played *ff* in octaves in the bass, whilst the other parts (in the rhythm ♩♩ ♪) are taken from the bridge passage of the exposition.

The recapitulation does not differ materially from the exposition and ends with a coda. This is rather long and resembles the closing section of the exposition; it ends with transparent motifs from the second theme of the Andante, played in a major key.

III

We know nothing of the programme of Borodin's first quartet. But it is similar in character to the rest of Borodin's work; this makes it extremely unlikely that the quartet is merely a reflection of abstract musical ideas of a more or less tonal or emotional nature. We shall see that it is possible to make a number of plausible assumptions regarding the programme of the quartet by examining the sources of his themes. The Andante especially provides the necessary clue.

It is worth remembering that Borodin sketched the general outline of his first quartet during the winter months of 1874–5, that is, at the very time when he was helping Rimsky-Korsakov to compile material for his *Collected Russian Folk-Songs*. It stands to reason that he would have become acquainted with other anthologies which Rimsky-Korsakov was studying at the time.

It has already been mentioned in Chapter Four that Borodin paid special attention to the folk-song 'Song of the Sparrow Hills' in its many varied forms. This he found in Prokunin's collection, and he used versions of it in *Prince Igor*.

The first variant of the song as given in Prokunin's collections is as follows[1]:

Ex. 128

Comparison of this tune with the themes of the F sharp minor Andante shows that:

(1) The motif of the lower part of the first theme of the Andante (the first two bars) corresponds tonally with the first two bars of the folk-song[2]:

Andante: bars 1–2

'Song of the Sparrow Hills': bars 1–2

Ex. 129

[1] See Prokunin's *Collection of Russian Folk Songs* (ed. Tchaikovsky), 1872, Vol. 2, No. 64.

[2] For easier comparison, the motifs have been transposed into the same key.

(2) A single melodic phrase in the recapitulation of the Andante corresponds with the motif of bars 5–7 of the song:

Andante: bars 15–16

'Song of the Sparrow Hills': bars 5–7

Ex. 130

(3) The descending arpeggio in the second theme of the Andante has a tonal correspondence with bars 10–12 of the folk-song melody (with the exception of the position of the second semitone):

Andante: p. 23; bar 30

'Song of the Sparrow Hills': bars 10–12

Ex. 131

(4) There is a further correspondence between bars 11–13 at the top of p. 35 of the Andante and bar 13 and the beginning of bar 14 in the folk-song:

Andante: Fugato, p. 25; bars 31–32

'Song of the Sparrow Hills': bars 13–14

Ex. 132

(5) There is an almost exact tonal correspondence between the descending passage in bars 13–15 at the top of p. 35 of the Andante, and bars 14–16 of the folk-song:

Andante: ibid., p. 25; bars 33–34

'Song of the Sparrow Hills': bars 14–16

Ex. 133

I should also like to point out that the upper part in bar 1 of the first theme is possibly connected with bars 14–15 of the song. Also, further tonal correspondences can be found in the second Andante, the slow introduction to the last movement. This resemblance is easily seen in the melancholy phrase at the beginning of this introduction to the Finale:

(*a*) Finale: p. 36; bars 1–6
(*b*) 'Song of the Sparrow Hills': bars 5–8

Ex. 134

(The repetition of the note A at the point marked 'X' in the song is not found in the corresponding section of the Finale.) Thus we see that eleven out of a total of sixteen bars of the folk-song have some thematic relationship with the Andante and the introductory section of the last movement, either as separate motifs or in combination. It is also worth noticing that the descending, sobbing, triplet sequences, which interrupt the 'narrative' of the Andante three times in all, are built on scale-like figures very similar to the descending motifs in bars 10–12 and 14–18 of the folk-song.

To determine the significance of these correspondences to our satisfaction, we have to go to the text of the song. Here is the text in full:

O you hills, hills,
Vorobyevsky, Vorobyevsky,
Vorobyevsky, Vorobyevsky,
The hills gave birth
To a white burning stone
And from under the stone
Flowed a swift river.
By this same river
Is a thick clump of willows,
In this clump of willows
Sits a dove-coloured eagle.
And in his talons
Holds a black crow
but does not maltreat it
and asks:
'Tell me, tell me
Young, black crow!
Where have you been flying?
Where have you been flying?'
'Above the steppe I flew
in Saratov';

I saw in the steppe
A great wonder:
In a field lay
A white body,
Lay, lay the body
Of a young hero.
Three pipits hovered
Over the body;
The first pipit is
The hero's mother,
The second pipit
His beloved sister,
The third pipit
His young wife.
The mother weeps
Rivers of tears.
The sister cries
A stream of tears.
And the wife cries
A dew-fall.
When the red sun appears
the dew disappears.

If we compare the words of the folk-song with the scheme of the Andante, we may draw the following definite analogies:

(1) The first theme of the Andante is a duet consisting of two mournful, almost portentous themes. This corresponds to the 'conversation between the eagle and the crow' in the song.

(2) The fugato, built on chromatic motifs, is the imagined flight of the three 'pipits': the mother, the sister, and the widowed wife.[1]

(3) Finally, the turbulent streams of descending triplets, repeated three times in the Andante, represent the floods of tears for the dead hero.

Although we are unable to find in the Andante all the details of the crow's tale in the song, we are bound to admit that the composer wanted to allude to this old tale. It is even possible to maintain that this movement of the first quartet is a story of the misadventure of a lone man, and the lamentation of his kinsfolk. It is not a story as such, but more likely an allusion or suggestion of one.

The second theme of the Andante is a slight contrast with the fantastic introduction ('prophetic voices?') and the sombre fugato.

If we accept this interpretation of the Andante, we may now attempt an elucidation in a similar manner of the programme of the whole quartet.[2]

The first movement (Introduction) is the dawn of life illuminating the bright future opening up before a young man aspiring to be a knight.

The Allegro is the young man caught up in the whirl of life. Passions are inflamed and conflict arises. Reminiscences of the time when he first entered the lists. Preparations for battle (bold and care-free mood). (Recapitulation.)

Andante: In his imagination he sees the possibility of defeat as a lone knight. This produces an outburst of sympathy (the lyrical second theme). The gloomy vision of death evokes in his mind thoughts of his kinsfolk lamenting his downfall. (Fugato—the pipits, floods of tears.)

Scherzo: Myriad happy thoughts and intentions temporarily over-

---

[1] A characteristic feature: one of the motifs of the upper line in the first theme of the Andante (second and third bars) is repeated in the Fugato as an interlude immediately following the 'subject'. This might be intended as a means of underlining the character of the crow narrator when he is describing the pipits.

[2] I have no intention of trying to explain why Borodin used a theme of Beethoven as the first subject of the first movement. Obviously, the composer would have had some specific reason for this.

whelm the young man. For a brief moment, he recalls the glorious time of his entry into the lists. (In the Trio.)

Finale: Again we have the sombre picture in the Andante introduction. The hero is stirred to pity. Spurred on by this (and by love as well, perhaps; cf. the second theme of the Allegro Risoluto) the hero rushes to the assistance of those in distress.

THE SECOND QUARTET IN D MAJOR

I

This is among the few works written by Borodin at a single session. The work was completed by the end of August, not much more than two months after its first conception.[1]

The work was published posthumously; no doubt as a result of the heavy pressure of work at a time when Borodin was engrossed in many non-musical matters.[2]

II

The mood of the whole quartet is uniformly bright, and we do not find the sharp contrasts of the first quartet.

The first movement of the quartet (Allegro moderato; $\downarrow=84$) begins immediately with a statement of the first subject:

Ex. 135

The theme is then played by the first violin a fifth higher. The development of this theme is interrupted by a subsidiary theme, which

---

[1] See Chapter V; also *Letters*, Vol. III, pp. 187 and 190. In view of Borodin's many obligations in St. Petersburg, both academic and musical, and taking into account the date of the first performance of the D major Quartet, it seems highly improbable that he was able to work on it during the Autumn of 1881.

[2] A considerable interval passed between the completion of the First Quartet and its publication, the delay being caused by difficulties in preparing the piano arrangement. It is quite possible that the same thing happened in the case of the Second Quartet. For a long time, the composer intended to make the piano arrangement himself, but it was finally completed by S. M. Blumenfeld (see Chapter V).

bears some resemblance to the second subject. For convenience, we shall call this the intermediate motif:

Ex. 136

The bridge passage is built on a motif of the first subject. This is followed by the second subject; a lyrical, impassioned melody, with a slight suggestion of the oriental. The key is F sharp minor:

Ex. 137

Another theme interrupts the course of the second subject in its subsequent appearances:

Ex. 138

The final episode of the exposition (Animato) is based on an independent chromatic motif:

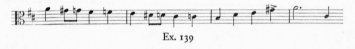

Ex. 139

The exposition has no repeat. The development (Tempo 1; keysignature of one flat) is comparatively short; it is built on the first subject, the intermediate motif, and the second subject. (The music derived from the second subject is confined to the end of the section.) The harmonies and modulations found in the development are serenely beautiful in the truly classical style.

The recapitulation is like the exposition, until the modulation into the key of G minor which follows close upon the intermediate motif. At this point we hear motif from the first subject, modified as follows:

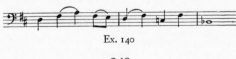

Ex. 140

The first movement of the quartet ends with a coda, which is first marked 'Animato' and later 'Tranquillo'. It is based on the chromatic motif heard at the close of the exposition.

The bright mood of the first movement is never destroyed by the occasional modulations into the minor. It reminds one of an animated conversation transfused with passionate but restrained feeling.

The Scherzo (Allegro; $\downarrow$ = 80) is in one flat. It is one of Borodin's most brilliant achievements. The principal theme (the first subject) appears on the violins:

Ex. 141

The tempo slackens to 'meno mosso' ($\downarrow\cdot$ = 60), and the violins play a second theme, in thirds, which resembles a waltz:

Ex. 142

The section ends with a passage based on motifs derived from the principal theme.

There is no Trio; but instead, a development section in the tempo of the first movement (Tempo 1)—the Scherzo is in free sonata form. In the recapitulation, the first fourteen bars are an exact repetition of the beginning of the exposition, but the rest is modified so that the second theme (meno mosso) is in A minor, and not D minor.[1]

The section following this is devoted to a development of the second theme. The movement has a final coda of thirteen bars length (Tempo 1). The harmony is far from conventional and the instrumentation is interesting. It is based on a single transformed motif taken from the first subject.

[1] This corresponds, to some extent, with the usual practice of sonata form.

The third movement is the famous Nocturne, in A major (Andante; ♩=60). The Nocturne opens with a beautiful sound of warmth and tenderness, and the main theme which enters very soon is slightly oriental in flavour:

Ex. 143

The tempo quickens to 'più mosso', and the restrained tenderness gives way to a passionate outburst in the second subject:

Ex. 144

A lengthy section follows in which the second subject undergoes various developments. The key is D minor. Motifs taken from the principal theme are woven into the texture. This ingenious interplay of motifs leads to the recapitulation and to the key of A major.

The main theme is once again in the cello, but the first violin plays the same melody in canon, one crotchet behind the cello, and an octave higher. The next section is based on motifs from the principal theme. The second subject has an episodic appearance; it is not heard in its entirety.

At the end of the nocturne, the principal theme is heard in the minor, in a slightly altered form. Then it appears in its original form on the first violin (in the aeolian mode) against a background of syncopated rhythms.

Ex. 145

244

A coda brings the movement to a close; this consists of a sequence based on the motif of the seventh bar of the principal theme.

The last movement of the quartet is in D major (the tempo varies between Andante, ♩=76, and Vivace, ♩=108). The mood of the Finale is one of high spirits and exhilaration. It provides a striking contrast with the preceding movements in both character and melodic content.[1] The movement begins with two themes played in succession. Together these go to make up the first subject:

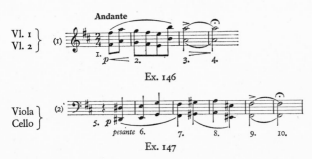

Vl. 1
Vl. 2 } (1)

Ex. 146

Viola
Cello } (2)

Ex. 147

There is an accelerando leading to Vivace. The bridge passage is sequential and based on a comparatively unimportant motif:

Ex. 148

The second subject is as follows:

dolce e espressivo

Ex. 149

and resembles a dance tune. It is in no way sharply distinct from what has gone before. The mood is bright. There is a quickening of the tempo and a return to Tempo 1. The exposition ends with motifs borrowed from the second subject, and finally the following motif.

Ex. 150

[1] This circumstance has already been observed by musicologists, e.g. see George Khubov, *A. P. Borodin* (Moscow, 1933), p. 123; also Abraham, *Borodin*, p. 138.

The development section is conventional. The coda is elaborate and quite lengthy.

III

The composer did not indicate whether there was a programme to his second quartet. The following considerations may throw some light on this matter.

Two factors will be considered:

(1) The nature of the music.

(2) The date of its composition, and matters relevant to this.

The quartet is not markedly Russian-folk in character, but rather tends towards the romantic and amorous. This leads one to suppose that the work arose out of Borodin's personal experiences. It is worth noting that Borodin composed the work in August, 1881, that is, twenty years exactly since he first fell in love with Catherine. If we take into account the fact that Catherine was highly sentimental and was fond of any kind of 'happy anniversary celebrations'; and if we bear in mind that the quartet is dedicated to her, then it is logical to assume that this work is a memento of his love for Catherine as a young man.[1]

If there is a programme to the D major Quartet, then the first movement might easily be taken for the growing love Borodin began to feel for Catherine during their walks in the vicinity of Heidelberg. The second subject certainly without any stretch of imagination, is an impression of newly-kindled love.[2]

The Scherzo fits in with the description of one of their walks, given by E. M. Braudo.[3]

The Nocturne is simply a love scene (in Heidelberg or Pisa?).

The last movement is definitely programmatical. If only we had some inkling of the nature of this programme, it would perhaps help to explain the difference in style between this and the other three movements.

The most likely assumption is that the Finale relates to their married life. Borodin could have been giving vent to his sense of

---

[1] See Chapter IV; also *Letters*, Vol. II, pp. 160–4.

[2] The oriental elements arise from Borodin's own predilections and his taste for the oriental.

[3] According to Braudo, 'in the second slyly flippant waltz-like theme of the Scherzo . . . Borodin, at his own admission, attempted to conjure up an impression of a light-hearted evening spent in one of the suburban pleasure-gardens of St. Petersburg' (p. 115). Unfortunately the writer gives no reference as to the source of this 'admission'. Braudo often visited my father to glean information about Borodin, but I personally never heard anything to that effect; perhaps he learnt this from Glazunov or Rimsky-Korsakov.

humour, and teasing his wife through the unusual medium of four stringed instruments.

I

Borodin was first and foremost a symphonist and devotee of the human voice. The works for piano are therefore very few in number. Borodin himself says that they were written 'for odd occasions'. The works we are about to consider include: (1) the four pieces he wrote as part of his 'Paraphrases'; (2) 'The Little Suite', and (3) the Scherzo in A flat major.

II

Borodin first conceived the idea of writing a set of 'Paraphrases' in the seventies (most probably in 1874). We know how they came to be written from a letter he wrote to Huberti. A young girl called Ganya, who later became his adopted daughter, asked Borodin to play piano duets with her. When he replied that he did not think she could play, she exclaimed: 'O yes I can: Look, I can play this!' and played the tune of 'chop-sticks' with two fingers (the 'dog waltz' as it is sometimes called).

The composer accordingly made up his own polka, a duet in which Ganya was to play the upper part ostinato.[1]

In addition to this, Borodin wrote three more pieces: a Requiem, a Funeral March, and a Mazurka. All except the last appeared in the first edition of the collection (in 1879), whilst the Mazurka was published posthumously in the final edition (1893).

The polka covers no more than two pages of manuscript. The form is of the symmetrical kind found in dances such as this. In addition to an introduction and coda, there is a triple middle section and a trio. By way of illustration, here is a part of the first section containing the theme:

Ex. 151

[1] See *Letters*, Vol. IV, pp. 221–2.

The second section is much less important; the key is G major. The trio section is in F major.

The Funeral March (in A minor) is very short (one page only in length) and has a single theme. The main theme, which is repeated in varied forms, is played against a soprano ostinato and is as follows:

Ex. 152

The Requiem (also in A minor) is a little more complicated in structure, and is considerably longer (two pages). First comes an 'organ prelude' of nineteen bars, played against the same soprano ostinato. This is followed by a vocal solo (with the Latin text of the Requiem written beneath it). Then a choir is heard in octaves; finally, the organ prelude returns *ff*. The motifs used in the 'chorus' are an adaptation of the vocal part of Stradella's 'Agnus Dei', which was originally in Borodin's library and is now in my possession.[1] The whole piece is extremely stylish, and the endless repetition of the ostinato does not appear in the least artificial.

The Mazurka (in C major; trio in F major) is of some interest as regards the relationship between the soprano ostinato and the second part. The ostinato ('cantus firmus') is written in 2/4 whilst the piano secondo is in 3/8. This produces a certain amount of rhythmical discrepancy between the two parts, which could present serious difficulties to 'the small pianists' for whom the work was intended.[2]

---

[1] Thus, for example, it is not difficult to observe that the motif in bars 8–12 which appears on p. 2 of Richault's edition of the 'Agnus Dei':

Ex. 303

served as the basis of the 'Requiem' movement in *Paraphrases* (transposed here into C minor):

Ex. 304

(*a*) is clearly based on bars 10 and 11 of motif (I) whilst
(*b*) is taken from bars 8 and 9.

[2] A similar instance is found in Rimsky-Korsakov's Minuet where the soprano ostinato is in 2/4 whilst the piano secundo is in 3/4.

The main section of the Mazurka is in C major and is sixteen bars long; the theme consists of an eight-bar phrase:

Ex. 153

The second eight-bar section is a free variation of this. Then follows a trio section (sixteen bars long) in F major. The theme is:

Ex. 154

After a repeat of the trio, the main section is heard once again.

The Mazurka is in the true Polish folk style; the accompanying fifths in the bass suggest the kind of music one hears in Polish country-dance ensembles.

These compositions are of interest not only for their technical perfection, but also for their genuine artistic quality.

III

The seven piano pieces belonging to the 'Miniature Suite' were composed in the early part of 1885 as a present to the Countess de Mercy-Argenteau. She was particularly anxious that Borodin should dedicate one of his works to her. Only four of the pieces were new; the last three—Rêverie, Sérenade, and Nocturne—had already been written during the previous decade.[1]

The music of the 'Miniature Suite' follows a definite programme, being sub-titled 'Petit poème d'amour d'une jeune fille'. Dobro-slavina (and the composer also) tells us that the programme was sub-divided under the following headings:

I. [Au couvent.]   Sous la voûte de la Cathedrale on ne pense qu'à Dieu.
II. [Intermezzo.]   On rêve la société.
III. [Mazourka.]   On ne pense qu'à la danse.

[1] We learn this from Stassov (*Borodin*, p. 53); but unfortunately, we do not know how these pieces came into being as the original, dated manuscripts are missing. Mr. David Lloyd-Jones has informed me that manuscripts of the 'Miniature Suite' and the Scherzo in A flat major are to be found in the Manuscript Section of the British Museum. Cf. A. N. Rimsky-Korsakov, *N. A. Rimsky-Korsakov. Life and Works*, Vol. III (Moscow, 1936), pp. 78–79.

IV. [Mazourka.]   On pense à la danse et au danseur.
V. [Rêverie.]   On ne pense qu'au danseur.
VI. [Sérénade.]   On rêve au chant d'amour.
VII. [Nocturne.]   On est bercée par le bonheur d'être aimée.[1]

The 'Miniature Suite' does not present a musical whole; the unity has to be looked for in the programme and in the resemblance between the various themes.[2]

[1] It is quite possible that Borodin had learned some detail of the Countess de Mercy-Argenteau's private life from Cui, and therefore had included this incident from her early youth.

[2] Comparison of the themes shows that there is a resemblance between them from the point of view of note-sequence. Despite the simplicity of the motifs, this is certainly not an accident. It is easy to see the similarity of the following:

Ex. 305

(which I have transposed into the same octave).

A motif from the Sérénade (VI) is perhaps also related to them:

Ex. 306

A major motif found on two occasions probably also has some connection:

Ex. 307

(In this instance, the second motif has been transposed into F major.)

The second group of themes is distinguished by a jump upwards of a major sixth:

Ex. 308

Let us examine each of the pieces in turn.

1. *In the Convent* (Andante religioso) (C sharp minor, C major) conveys a most vivid impression of a Roman Catholic service, though there are weak places here and there. The first section is devoted to a pianistic impression of the solemn tolling of the bell:

Ex. 155

The sound of the bells dies away. Children's voices are heard, first solo and then in chorus to the sustained notes of an organ[1]:

Ex. 156

There is a gradual build-up to a tremendous fortissimo. Then we hear the solemn, mournful chanting of a choir, again accompanied by chords on the organ.

The second section closes with the gradual diminuendo of the children's choir.

The third and last section is a straightforward repetition of the first.

and analogous to these is another motif with a leap of a minor sixth followed by a similar sequence of notes:

VI "Sérénade"

Ex. 309

[1] This theme is based probably on Stradella's 'Agnus Dei' which we mentioned in note 1, p. 248.

Ex. 310

2. *Intermezzo* (Tempo di minuetto; F major, F minor; 3/4 time).
Most important in this piece is the theme:

Ex. 157

The first section, based on this theme, is in the Lydian mode (but
without the B flat). The second edition has the same theme, this time
in F minor. The key returns to F major, but the section ends in B flat
major.

The middle section of the 'Intermezzo' (un poco meno mosso)
introduces a new subject

Ex. 158

variants of which appear first in D flat major, and then in F major.
After this, there is a repetition of the whole of the first part, exactly as
before.

3. *The First Mazurka* (Allegro; C major, G major, C major; Meno
Mosso; E flat major; 3/4 time) is nothing more than sheer revelling in
the dance form.

The first section is in ternary form. There is a very brief introduction, and then comes the first theme, which, as Gerald Abraham has
pointed out,[1] is a readaptation of the theme found in the posthumous
Mazurka of the 'Paraphrases'. Unlike the latter Mazurka the last eight
bars of the first section are in different in form from the first eight bars
(if we ignore the cadence). The accompanying harmonies are also
derived from the same piece. The second section has for its theme the
following:

Ex. 159

This phrase is repeated, but the last two bars are changed, and a
further two bars added. The third section is a repetition of the whole
of the first section.

[1] *Borodin*, p. 158.

The middle or second part of the Mazurka contains a short introduction, and a kind of ostinato motif which is heard four times in all:

Ex. 160

and this is based on a variant of bars five and six in the first main theme. There are various modulations (E flat major, E flat minor) around this ostinato. The section ends with a phrase not very different from the introduction.

The third section of the Mazurka is a literal repetition of the first, and ends with a six-bar coda.

4. *The Second Mazurka* (Allegretto; D flat major, A major, D flat major; 3/4 time) according to the programme indications, is the growing feeling of tenderness in the dancer towards her partner.

The first section is in the form of a dialogue on a single theme. This is stated in the first eight bars:

Ex. 161

The theme of the second part, as Abraham has already observed,[1] is taken from the trio of the posthumous Mazurka of the 'Paraphrases) with only very slight modification. The similarity is complete as far as the prima volta bar inclusive; this time however there is no full repeat, but instead the theme is played for six bars only, an octave higher than before. The second part ends with a transition passage which is quite incidental to the rest.

The third part is an exact repetition of the first part (though this would appear to conflict with the programme?).

5. *Day Dreams* (Andante; D flat major, C major). This delightful little piece remains one of a Chopin prelude. The main section is based on various capricious variations on an underlying theme. The following are good examples of this:

(1) A three-bar motif (bars 3–5 inclusive):

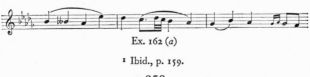

Ex. 162 (*a*)

[1] Ibid., p. 159.

and (2) the short motif:

Ex. 162 (*b*)

The piece ends with a repeat of the introduction.

6. *Serenade* (Allegretto; D flat major; 6/8 time). The opening bars of this piece are suggestive of guitar playing. Then enters the theme of the serenade:

Ex. 163

After this we hear a tune which is a free variation of the preceding theme.[1]

Ex. 164

The piece ends with the five bars heard at the beginning, the guitar imitation.

7. *Nocturne* (Andantino, G flat, F major, G flat major, C major). The composer apparently intended this movement to express 'the pleasant feeling when one is in love'. The most characteristic feature is the swaying, lulling harmonic texture, in which a G flat major chord in the bass is predominant; Borodin seems to have associated the latter with nocturnal darkness.[2]

In the first section, the 'lulling' figurations are confined to the upper parts; the bass consists of a descending chromatic passage. But in the next phrase, they appear in all the parts:

Ex. 165

This continues until the end of the first section.

[1] It is interesting to notice the melismata here which gives the motif a rather oriental character. (It is conceivable that this oriental element has some significance in the suite as a whole.)

[2] I recall at this point the harmony to the word 'night' in Igor's aria in Act II (the phrase, 'Night brings me neither comfort nor oblivion'), and also several harmonies in Konchak's Daughter's cavatina in the same act wherever there is any reference to night.

The second part (which consists of thirteen bars in F major) has a brighter theme, conveying a sense of blissful peace:

Ex. 166

The opening of the third part (two phrases in all) is an exact repetition of the first part. In the third and last phrase, a lyrical melody is heard in the left hand.

Ex. 167

It is interesting to observe that the notes which make up this phrase can be found in another guise in the first part of the Nocturne.

In its closing bars, the music gradually dies away, and the final bar (chord of G flat and B flat) has the dynamic marking *ppp*.

IV

The A flat major Scherzo is dedicated to Th. Jadoul. It was written about the same time as the 'Miniature Suite'. This piece was a token of Borodin's gratitude to Jadoul for his untiring efforts in disseminatng the 'new Russian music'.[1] It is sub-titled 'for orchestra'; but the composer left the work as a piano solo and apparently made no attempt to orchestrate it. It is for this reason that I am considering this piece in the chapter devoted to Borodin's piano works.[2]

[1] See *Letters*, Vol. IV, p. 109, fragment of a letter before No. 1080; also my book, *Borodin*, Russian 2nd ed., pp. 282 and 284.

[2] A number of musicians contemporary with Borodin considered that the pieces from The Miniature Suite were orchestral and had only been written for the piano by accident. Such is the opinion of Stassov (see p. 53 of his book). (I personally hold the view that this is rather on old-fashioned approach to piano music and to the potentialities of the piano. If one judges music according to Stassov's criteria, then one must regard many sections of Beethoven's piano sonatas as being 'orchestral'.) It was on these lines of thought that Glazunov was working when he published an orchestral arrangement of all eight pieces in 1889. He was probably guided by the fact that the A♮ major Scherzo contained the sub-title 'for orchestra'. Glazunov's arrangement of the pieces from the Miniature Suite is more of an elaboration than an orchestration, and apart from the changes of tonality of a number of items, he has introduced the A♮ major Scherzo into the suite by way of a Trio to the Nocturne (though this has no programmatic sense whatsoever.)

The Scherzo (Allegro Vivace; 12/8 time) begins with a short exposition in A flat major. The principal theme in this section is full of life, one might even say obtrusive:

Ex. 168

The two-bar theme is repeated three times, the third time an octave higher than before. This is followed by two bars based on the first bar of this theme, leading to a new section based on the chromatic motif:

Ex. 169

A phrase built on this motif leads to the second subject

Ex. 170

which is played three times in all. The exposition ends with a passage based on the chromatic motif just mentioned.

There is no Trio, but a development section instead (in B major and D flat major). The principal theme is announced immediately and is repeated with the rhythm somewhat altered. Then follows a short stretto on the second subject; after this, a phrase built on the chromatic motif, and a modulation into D flat major. In this D flat major section, motifs from the principal theme dissolve into repeated chords. The second subject is heard twice in the left hand and the development ends on a phrase based on the chromatic motif.

The recapitulation is like the exposition, except that the second subject is now in A flat major.

The piece ends with a coda closely resembling the D flat major episode of the development.

It is unlikely that the A flat major Scherzo follows a prescribed programme. But there is some justification for assuming that Borodin intended the work as a humorous portrayal of Jadoul and his friends; there was after all something comic, he thought, about their gallant efforts on behalf of a tired and beleaguered composer.

CHAPTER NINE

THE SONGS

We have already seen (cf. Chapter 3) that Borodin, upon completion of the First Symphony, turned his attention to the musical drama, *The Valiant Knights*. While it was to some extent a matter of chance that Borodin became involved in this opera-farce, it is nevertheless true that Borodin had a definite bent towards this kind of operatic writing. His work on this pastiche brought him into direct contact with a whole range of Italian and French operas. Borodin used his powers of discrimination, so that the whole enterprise enriched his understanding of vocal technique. From the first he had cultivated the style of Glinka and Dargomizhsky who had aimed at natural vocal expression and 'truth in sound'. It is not surprising therefore, that his first mature and serious vocal compositions should be of the highest technical and artistic standard.

To this mature period belong three works for voice and piano: The Sleeping Princess' (1867), 'The Song of the Dark Forest' (1867–8), and 'The Sea' (1870). The three songs have much in common in that they are all epic in character and extremely vivid. But they are more than this; each contains a secret programme. They reflect contemporary life and events. In them we find allegorical expression of the poet-composer's relationship to the past, present, and future of his country. The words, which are by the composer himself, are written in a fine, lucid Russian style.

Let us take a closer look at each of the songs in turn. The 'fairy-tale' for voice and piano, entitled 'The Sleeping Princess', is in A flat major, and is chronologically the first of the three. It was written roughly at the same time as the early numbers of *The Valiant Knights*. The mood is in sharp contrast with the humorous material he was getting together for Krylov's satire. The song is a Slav variant of the well-known French fairy-tale of the sleeping beauty (*La Belle au bois dormant*). On further acquaintance, however, this rather enigmatic and fantastic music leaves the hearer in no doubt as to its allegorical significance.[1]

The piece begins with dissonant seconds and mysterious C's (*sfz*) cutting through them. This evokes the power of sleep-making spells in the magic forest. It is against this background that the singer begins the tale of the sleeping princess:

Ex. 171

(*She sleeps, sleeps in the silent forest, The princess sleeps an enchanted sleep*)

The first ten bars, including the four just quoted, introduce the theme of 'the magic sleep'.[2]

A contrasting theme is heard, this time representing the flight of witches and wood-sprites. It begins with a slow ascending motif:

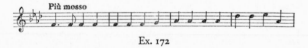

Ex. 172

A gradual descending movement follows immediately upon the climax of this phrase.

This second theme, in its widest sense, announces the arrival of the knight, who has come to the rescue of the sleeping princess. But the story-teller sees no signs of her awakening; a return to the musical motifs found at the beginning of the piece[3] suggests that the enchanted sleep will continue. At the end of the fairy-tale, we hear that 'no one knows how soon will be the hour of her awakening'. (According to

[1] Dargomyzhsky and Stassov claimed that Borodin's 'The Sleeping Princess' was 'simply a page from *Ruslan*'. See my *Borodin*, Russian 2nd ed., p. 193 (Stassov's letter to Borodin dated 28 December 1868).

[2] It is interesting to note that seconds are almost entirely absent from those parts not dealing with the magic sleep (in the section describing the arrival of the bogatyr, and the 'hour of awakening').

[3] The formal pattern is: A—B—A—B′—A—B″. [A= the theme of the magic sleep; B, B′ and B″= the contrasting theme and its ramifications.]

the composer, the clock will strike the notes C, F sharp, C, C, when the expected hour arrives.)

What did the composer of this wonderful song really have in mind when he wrote it?[1]

The 'Princess' can only signify Borodin's native land—Russia, which was still sleeping under the heavy spell of bondage and the oppressive 'bewitchment' of tsarist autocracy. At the time Borodin was writing his song, there was no organized revolutionary movement in Russia and not the least sign of one for years to come. But Borodin felt that Russia would have to awaken when the fateful hour struck, even though he viewed with scepticism the revolutionary groups and insurrectionists of his own day. He gave allegorical expression to these thoughts in the 'Sleeping Princess'.[2,3]

[1] See his letter to Catherine dated 14 February 1870 (*Letters*, Vol. I, p. 195).

[2] Mussorgsky, a man of warlike disposition, found elements of quietism in the tale of 'The Sleeping Princess' (which as a work he rated highly). He demanded that Borodin should omit the repetition of the word 'sleep', and on the latter's refusal to do so called him 'a sleepy soul' (see *Mussorgsky. Letters and Documents*, compiled and edited by A. N. Rimsky-Korsakov (Moscow-Leningrad, 1932), p. 262, letter to Stassov dated 23 July 1873).

[3] The free use of dissonant seconds in the accompaniment aroused strong indignation from the conservative critics. Laroche, their most prominent representative, expressed the opinion that Borodin had introduced these seconds in imitation of Liszt, mistaking the seconds of Liszt's trills as independent harmonic intervals. He further declared that it was impossible to convey to the unmusical reader 'the orgy of dissonance that rages in this song' (*The Voice*, No. 18, 1874). It is interesting to note that Laroche displayed a surprising ignorance in a field of music that was very dear to him, as can easily be established from examination of Taneev's book, *Strict Counterpoint* (dedicated to Laroche). On p. 94 of this book, the erudite author asserts that dissonant seconds in simple counterpoint (where stricter conditions apply than in homophony) 'are often encountered' in the old masters, and he produces as illustration of this an example from Palestrina (see Vol. XII of the complete works of Palestrina, Breitkopf and Härtel ed., p. 122):

Ex. 311

On the other hand, parallel seconds are found in choral folk-song as an imitative or onomatopoeic element. An interesting example of this is found in the Lithuanian song 'Sutartin':

Ex. 312

in which the female chorus sing of 'the little hawk' and 'imitate' its cries in a series of

The Songs

'The Song of the Dark Forest', on the other hand, is about the past. The song is highly suggestive of the times when the Russian people rose spontaneously against the tyranny of the tsar and his nobles. The tale is told by the forest itself. The words are:

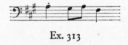

Kak zhi – va – la tam vo – lya   vo – liu sh-ka,   vol – na – ya

Ex. 173

(What liberty, what true freedom flourished there)

The story tells how a great force gathered in the forest, marched on a city, and put their enemies to death. The entire song, with the exception of the transitional phrase at the start of the 'piu animato' section, is built on a single refrain, which seems to follow the story-teller throughout. The music is of tremendous power. The forest murmur which appears at the beginning and end provides an 'objective' framework to the whole piece.[1] The listener feels that he is witnessing a series of events and a situation, which could not have been otherwise. Borodin is recalling the past so that others may experience it and sense the eternal struggle, which was acute even in those days of long ago.

The vividness and force of these 'reminiscences' give the song a positive value. Despite its epic form, the song is a veiled appeal to continue the struggle. When it recalls the struggles of old with the

---

parallel seconds (see the *Large Soviet Encyclopaedia*, Vol. 25, 2nd ed., article on the Lithuanian Soviet Socialist Republic, p. 272).

[1] We may make here a few observations as to the character of the music to 'The Song of the Dark Forest'.

(*a*) From the thematic point of view, there is undoubtedly a resemblance between the melody of this piece and the robbers' song 'Ei Ukhnem' [better known as 'The Song of the Volga Boatmen'—Tr.]

(*b*) We again encounter Borodin's favourite motif:

Ex. 313

As we saw in Chapter VII, this fragment was used by him as the second subject of the Andante of his Third Symphony. In this instance, the composer (who was near the end of his life) was strongly influenced by his sympathy for the 'dissenters' themes' upon which the Andante was based.

Muscovite tsars, the song is going nothing less than inciting the Russian people to brace itself for a struggle with the Throne.[1]

It is not easy to see the connection between the third song: 'The Sea', and the other two. The story is about a young man who is drowned while returning home to his country and his young wife, after having acquired a huge fortune.[2]

The song opens with a powerful introduction (G flat minor) in which we hear the roaring of the sea. The first theme is heard when the singer describes the seascape:

Mo - rĕ   bur - no   shu - mit_____

Ex. 174

(*The sea wildly roars*)

The theme of the fisherman provides a contrast to this simple motif and becomes interwoven with the undulation of the sea:

Po mo - riu   e - get plo - vets mo - lo - doy   i   ot - vazh - ny

Ex. 175

(*Across the sea there sails a fisherman young and brave*)

We can almost feel the young man fighting for breath as he struggles with the waves. This is accomplished simply by alternating the two themes just mentioned in modified form and in accordance with the demands of the narrative. The ballad ends with an account of the final stages of the struggle when the boat disappears beneath the waves. The sea is victorious.

There is a gloomy closing section (*p*) which expresses what the listener might feel at the tragic fate of this young man. The roar of the waves is heard till the very end but gradually dies away.

[1] As Lamm first pointed out, Borodin, realizing the artistic power and value of 'The Song of the Dark Forest' and appreciating the fact that it would be equally successful orchestrated, used its music for the seditious speech of Vladimir Galitski's at the end of the First Act of *Igor*. When he revised this Act he excluded 'the mob-scene' but preserved the scene with Galitsky. After Borodin's death, Glazunov made an arrangement of 'The Song of the Dark Forest' for male voice chorus and orchestra (1892–3).

[2] See Chapter IV and note 3, p. 68.

The three epic ballads we have just examined are shot through with a realistic awareness of the elemental might of the laws of nature and history. We should not mistake this for a simple lyric, even though the tone is far from callous. He loves life and feels strong enough to 'accept' these laws.

A truly live human being cannot confine himself to an epic frame of mind pure and simple. Experience shapes the soul. The songs 'Song of the Dark Forest' and 'The Sea' belong to a period when Borodin was experiencing the pangs of love which at one stage nearly led to a break-up of his marriage. The composer gave vent to his feelings in three romances: 'The Sea Princess', 'The False Note', and 'My songs are filled with poison'.

The first of the three, chronologically speaking, is 'The Sea Princess'; it was written early on in the love affair. To express his feelings he turned to the old story of a water-nymph luring her beloved into the depths of a river. The song is basically lyrical, but the epic mood recurs continually. (He uses the conventions of fable here, as in 'The Sleeping Princess', but for totally different reasons.)[1]

We first hear the appealing voice of the Sea Princess:[2]

Pri - di ko - mne noch - noi po - roĭ, o, put - nik mo - lo - doĭ!

Ex. 176

(*Come to me by night, young traveller*)

This is heard against a rich, exquisite harmonic background and series of successive seconds, so typical of Borodin. The refrain of the song is built almost entirely on this phrase, and variations of it.

Subsequent complications clouded this lyrical mood and were responsible for two rather more pessimistic songs: the laconic, disenchanted 'The False Note' (to words of his own composition), and the inconsolably impassioned 'My songs are filled with poison' (to words by Heine, in Russian translation).

In 'The False Note' we find a description of a woman's insincerity,

[1] According to E. G. Dianina, Borodin wished to dedicate his song 'The Sea Princess' to the first wife of K. E. Makovsky—the artist, E. T. Makovskaya. In the composer's eyes, 'she was just like a mermaid'. For some unknown reason, Borodin changed his mind and dedicated the song of K. E. Makovsky's sister A. E. Makovskaya instead.

[2] As seen from this example, in the music of 'The Sea Princess' one encounters the variant reproduced in note 1, p. 260.

concealed by her tender feelings, the superficiality of which she is nevertheless fully aware. The mood of the lover when he notices this insincerity is symbolized in the music by a repetition of a dissonant F natural in the accompaniment.[1] This acts as a pedal-note in the bass.

The romance 'My songs are filled with poison'[2] is a beautiful miniature, full of pathos. The composer has given a wonderful portrayal of a poet's hopeless passion for a woman who poisoned the life of her lover with 'fatal venom'. There is also the lightly ironical touch that one associates with Heine's more pessimistic verses. The song has a marvellously symmetrical form; and on closer inspection we find a most exact correspondence between the musical inflections and the text.[3]

The last of the romances belonging to this period is the setting of Heine's poem, 'Aus meinen Tränen' ('From my tears'), taken from the poet's *Buch der Lieder* in Russian translation. This composition did not spring spontaneously from the composer's mood, but should be included among those works which, to use his own terminology, were written 'for special occasions'. In all probability, Borodin wrote the romance for his sister-in-law, M. S. Stupishina, a very plain girl who was very attached to Borodin and unhappy in her private life.

Although this work cannot be compared with Schumann's setting of the same poem[4] (certainly it is not one of his more inspired works), nevertheless we cannot deny its high musical quality, the freshness of its harmony, and its fidelity to the text of the poem.[5]

[1] As the reader will probably recall, the singer L. I. Karmalina sent Borodin (through the medium of Balakirev) an additional four verses of five lines each, which she thought might be of use to him in the composition of 'The False Note'. Borodin thanked her courteously for her thoughtfulness but did not make use of the verses which were of a trivial nature (see Ch. IV and also *Letters*, Vol. II, pp. 22 and 202).

[2] One conservative critic found fault both with the title of this song and 'The False Note', making them the object of derision which we today can only regard with amusement, but which then raised the supporters of the 'Kuchka' to furious indignation (see Laroche's article in the journal, *The Voice*, No. 18, 1874; also Stassov's book on Borodin, pp. 44–47).

[3] One of the finest executants of this song was A. N. Purgold. Her rendering of it pleased the composer so much that he claimed that it had been written in collaboration with its performer.

[4] Several writers consider the absence of any strongly marked national German element in the song to be a failing. I cannot consider this objection to be justified, as the song was written to a Russian translation of the German text. Equally, music with a sharp Russian bias would be out of place here, and Borodin did not make this mistake.

[5] I have already discussed the method of determining the date of this composition (see Chapter IV, note 4, p. 72). A great deal of misunderstanding as to the date of this piece has arisen as the result of a rather misleading passage on p. 33 of Stassov's book on Borodin, where he asserts unjustly that the song 'is not distinguished by any

When he had finished this song, Borodin decided that it was time
to leave off vocal compositions for the time being, and devoted the
next ten years entirely to opera. His taste for epic was fully satisfied
by his work on *Mlada* and *Prince Igor*. His lyrical tendencies either
remained dormant or were directed into operatic writing.[1]

But Borodin returned to song writing in 1881 at a time when he
had dropped work on *Igor* which for the time being had become an
intolerable burden upon him. It was at this time that he wrote his
romances, 'For the shores of my distant homeland' and 'Arab
Melody', and the song 'At home among real people'.

The tragic song 'For the shores of my distant homeland' is a setting
of one of Pushkin's poems, and is among Borodin's most original and
beautiful compositions. He is completely sincere; he has not merely
written a musical situation but has actually lived through it himself.
In keeping with the classical character of Pushkin's poetry, he has
given the work a relatively simple harmonic texture. As Gerald
Abraham has rightly pointed out,[2] the piano accompaniment shows a
close resemblance to 'The False Note'. But there is an absence of
dichotomy, and no false note; in short, there is no excuse for incessant
dissonance. The harmony must not be florid or over-refined, for this
is a song of mourning; exuberance of harmony would be quite out of
place.[3]

The romance 'Arab Melody' was composed not long after this and
was the result of chance circumstances.[4] Borodin had been looking
through the Arabic Kasids in the Public Library with a view to adapting certain of their motifs, which he valued very highly, for his own
use, when he suddenly had the idea of writing an exotic love-song in a
most subtle harmonic setting.

Next came the comic song 'At home among real people', to words

---

outstanding qualities'. This is an excellent example of Stassov's tendency to criticize
any work which did not answer precisely to his preconceived ideas. Stassov was
suspicious of every work which did not possess a clearly expressed national element or
abound in harmonic innovations.

[1] See apropos of this, the section from Catherine's memoirs quoted in Chapter IV,
note 1, p. 102.

[2] See *Borodin*, p. 172.

[3] As I mentioned in Chapter V, the song 'For the Shores of a Distant Homeland'
produced an unfavourable impression on many of Borodin's friends when it was first
written. Stassov, in particular, suspected Borodin of an impending 'turn to the left',
and detected many resemblances in it to the works of Schubert. In this, he was probably
correct, but to write in the classical spirit was perhaps Borodin's deliberate intention.

[4] See Chapter V above and note 2, p. 118.

by Nekrassov. It is a complaint of poor people who feel they have not enough to live on; there is the man of means who pities them and at the same time gets a laugh out of them. The main tune reminds one of the 'town' songs of the time, not unlike limericks.

Oo liu - dei to vdo - mu___ chis - to - ta, le - po - ta,___ a oo
nas___ to vdo - mu tes - no - ta,___ du - kho - ta___

Ex. 177

The song is very like the rest of Borodin's humorous works.

The last two songs of Borodin are 'Pride', to words by A. K. Tolstoy, and 'Septain' (sometimes known as 'The Wonderful Garden'), also came into being quite by chance. The former was written at the request of A. A. Bichurina; and the latter was a present for the Countess de Mercy-Argenteau.

'Pride' is a splendid example of Borodin's musical wit. Tolstoy's satirical verses aimed at all smug self-satisfied nobodies were a labour of love for the composer who continually came into contact with such people in the course of his work. The words and the music are in the style of a solemn folk-epic. The main theme is as follows:

Kho - dit Spes na - du - va - iu - chis sbo - ku na bok pe - re -
- va - li - va - yas. Kho - dit Spes___

Ex. 178

(Pride goes by, puffed up, waddling from side to side. There goes pride!)

'Septain' was a setting of the poem of the same name by the French poet, Georges Collin. The words which are in praise of Mercy-Argenteau and her wonderful estate, are not of great interest. The main interest is Borodin's 'impressionism'; the rustle of leaves and the flowers in 'the wonderful garden'.[1]

Ex. 179

(*Wonderful garden*)

The music occasionally reminds one of 'The Sea Princess', although there are none of the consecutive seconds.

There is little to add to what we already know about Borodin's songs. These minor compositions are of considerable value both from the musical and ideological standpoints. They will continue to be performed and to bring pleasure to their listeners for many years to come.

[1] This song satisfied the composer himself. In a letter to Catherine dated 27 March 1886, he wrote: 'I am very pleased to hear that you like my *Septain* . . . I like it a lot' (*Letters*, Vol. IV, p. 188).

CHAPTER TEN

'MLADA' AND 'PRINCE IGOR'

It was inevitable that a composer of Borodin's genius would eventually turn to opera. He already had a marked taste for programme music, and a great love of song and vocal line. He was sufficiently a poet to be able to compose his own librettos. Thus, although Borodin himself felt he was first and foremost a lyricist and symphonist, he nevertheless made a significant contribution to opera.[1] Besides the operatic farce *The Valiant Knights*[2] and his *Tsar's Bride*, which never came to anything, he worked as we know on two operatic projects: the ballet-opera *Mlada* and the opera *Prince Igor*. We shall examine each of these works in turn.

THE BALLET-OPERA 'MLADA' (ACT 4)

I

I have already attempted in Chapter IV to give some explanation of how Borodin came to write music for *Mlada*, and how he used material compiled by S. A. Gedeonov from the history of the Baltic Slavs.

Borodin, it will be remembered, was allotted the fourth and last act of the opera. This act is a fantastic and tragic denouement.

The action takes place on the open square in front of the temple of Radegast, the god of the Baltic Slavs, and on the shores of a lake. The act begins with a pagan ritual, in which a chorus sings the praises of Radegast (No. 1). Yaromir, Prince of Arkona, one of the chief characters in the opera, demands an audience with the high priest.

He announces to the priest, who comes out to receive him, that he needs his 'words of wisdom'. He tells him that his bride, Princess Mlada, has died suddenly, and that he had it revealed to him in a nightmare that she had

---

[1] See *Letters*, Vol. I, p. 201.

[2] In discussing *The Bogatyrs*, I was obliged to restrict myself to the published material; to re-assemble the music scattered throughout the musical library of the Academic theatres would involve years of work. Historical details based on literary sources and my own investigations could easily be added to the biographical section of this book.

been poisoned by an 'evil witch'. Yaromir wants to get to the root of the matter. The high priest advises him to spend the night in front of the temple, and promises that he will have visions in which the ghosts of former princes will reveal to him 'the occult thread of his fate' (No. 2).

The priest leaves him and goes away. Yaromir sees four apparitions of these princes of bygone days.[1] Each apparition is accompanied by singing from the chorus. The latter gives the name of each spectre, and asks what each has to say to Yaromir. The reply is : 'Voyslava has poisoned Mlada. Take your revenge!' (No. 3).

Voyslava comes rushing in.[2] She declares: 'I have poisoned Mlada in order to win you, Yaromir!' Furious, he strikes her down (No. 4). As she dies, she calls on Morena, the goddess of the underworld, to avenge her death and to destroy peace on earth for ever (No. 5).

The goddess Morena appears, clothed in flames of subterranean fire. She invokes the elements, orders the destruction of the temple of Radegast, by way of funeral rites in Voyslava's honour, and sinks beneath the earth with Voyslava's corpse (No. 6). A storm arises. The waters of the lake burst into flood. The temple is destroyed. Yaromir is saved by clinging to the sacred stone. Beneficent spirits appear with the spirit of Mlada. Apotheosis (No. 7).[3]

To this scenario Borodin composed the most vivid music imaginable. The whole thing was written in a very short time and has all the spontaneity of an improvisation. A large part of this music (Nos. 1, 2, 3, 4, and some of No. 7) was later readapted for *Prince Igor*. The piano score has not yet been published. The most beautiful scenes are 'The Apparitions' and 'Yaromir and Voyslava's duet', but the finale also contains a great deal of fine music.

II

The psychological basis of the scene of the apparitions is their insistence that Yaromir must avenge Mlada's death. The first to appear is Attila, then Kii, Shchek and Koriv, all three together, then Chekh

---

[1] The writer of the scenario invited a motley company to act as Voyslava's accusers: Attila, King of the Huns; The King of the Slavs; the mythical Russian Princes Kii, Shchek, and Koriv, who were supposed to be 'the founders of Kiev'; Chekh, the personification of the Czech race, and the Princesses Wanda and Libuše.

[2] This is a typical operatic effect: Voyslava appears in person immediately her name is called. Neither she, nor Yaromir, nor the spectators are obliged to wait in vain.

[3] The file headed 'Libretto of Igor and musical sketches' also includes the libretto of the Fourth Act of *Mlada*. It is written in Borodin's handwriting and contains a number of underlined and corrected passages. Probably Krylov did not write the libretto of this act but left it to the composer.

and Samo, and finally Wanda and Libuše. But Borodin turned his naïve scenario into a musical scene of great epic force and verisimilitude. This impressiveness is gained by the use of an extremely simple framework. The music is composed of two elements: (1) In the prophetic scenes the choir has to sing 'They prophesy to Prince Yaromir' when each apparition makes its appearance, and then has to announce the names of the apparition. Here the choir sings in unison an ascending sequence consisting of alternate tones and semitones. The harmony uses the tonic minor, and the relative major and its minor, and a chord based on the preceding note, for example: (The apparition of Attila).

The chorus sings the notes: D, E, F, G, A flat, B flat; and the harmonic progression is: D minor, F major, F minor and E flat major.

(2) The choir sings a unison D at the point where the apparition reveals: 'Voyslava has poisoned Mlada. Take your vengeance!' and the harmony consists of a sequence of inversions of the dominant seventh chords in the keys of A major, C major, E flat major and G major.

These two elements are heard four times in all, and on each occasion the accompaniment modulates into a fresh key (firstly D major, then G major, then E flat major, and finally A flat major). Similarly, at each apparition's 'utterance', the dominant harmonies A, C, E flat, G, appear each time in a different order, and the connecting chord is never the same twice in succession. These extraordinary harmonic progressions, especially the modulations D–G–E flat–A flat, are wonderfully in keeping with the sense of suspense and mystery which pervades the entire scene. The modulations into more and more keys serve to emphasize the gradual build-up of anxiety, horror, and anger in Yaromir's soul. The scene may be naïve, but Borodin shows himself an inspired master of tone-painting; he is carried away by his subtle control of tone gradations, keys, and timbres.

The Duet of Yaromir and Voyslava is likewise a piece of great beauty and powerfully convincing.[1] The principal theme, later re-adapted for the trio of Act III of *Igor*,[2] sounds more natural in its original duet form. It is most characteristic of Voyslava, the dark, impassioned malignant devotee of Morena. Its use in *Igor*, despite its readaptation, seems strained and artificial by comparison.

[1] According to Stassov, the other composers involved in *Mlada*, Cui, Mussorgsky, and Rimsky-Korsakov, 'were all obliged to acknowledge the enormous superiority of Borodin, and bowed before their gifted friend in deep sympathy and admiration. The chorus to Radegast and the duet of Yaromir with Princess Voyslava amazed Borodin's acquaintances, and us in particular' (see Stassov's book on Borodin, p. 40).

[2] See the passage in the next section where I discuss the 'transplanting' of themes.

III

The Finale to Act 4 of *Mlada*, which was not completely recast for
other purposes by the composer, was later orchestrated by Rimsky-
Korsakov after Borodin's death and published by Belyaev.[1] Key
signatures are rarely used in this section. The introduction—the
appearance of Morena—is based on the leitmotif:

Ex. 180

and on the theme of invocation:

Ex. 181

(which incidentally is related to a number of Borodin's other themes.)[2]

The inundation and the destruction of the temple are portrayed by
wild, tempestuous music, based on the four-note sequence: C–B
natural–B flat–G flat, and on the theme of invocation.

The apparition of the benign spirits and the spirit of Mlada
(Andantino; A flat major) is built on the Mlada theme:

Ex. 182

Space does not allow me to make a detailed analysis of the Finale of
Mlada. A comparison of the latter with the other numbers of *Mlada*
will serve no useful purpose. It suffices to say that there is much fine

---

[1] There is one peculiarity in the Finale of *Mlada*. In Stassov's book, he says on p. 42
that this number was not completed by Borodin. The original manuscript has 14 April
1872 as its date of completion, and, strange to relate, this fact is supported by Stassov
himself in the same book (p. 90).

[2] The motifs of the first, second, and fourth bars of the 'theme of invocation' differ
(from the point of view of note-sequence) from the melody in the First Symphony.
In the examples Ex. 46, there is only a difference of two repeated notes (quavers which
form the first two notes of the melody) and a single note (of crotchet length).

music in it, and is particularly outstanding for the great beauty and lyricism of the apparition scene.

THE OPERA 'PRINCE IGOR'

I

Before proceeding to analyse such a great national opera as this, we should do well to bear in mind that both the music and the libretto are Borodin's, and that even the scenario owes much to his skill and assiduity. An examination of this opera should first take into account the composer's work on the libretto and the underlying dramatic conception.

There are many obvious and quite radical differences between Stassov's scenario, as set out in Chapter III, and the published libretto.

It is interesting to trace the various changes that Borodin made to the original scenario. As it happens, I am fortunate enough to have had in my possession a number of rough sketches that Borodin carefully kept in a special file, marked: 'The Libretto of Igor and matters pertaining to music generally.'[1] Until recently, this material has not been made available to musicologists. The headings on the separate paper covers were made partly by Borodin and partly by Rimsky-Korsakov.[2]

I shall also refer to Borodin's correspondence, as it appears in my edition, and certain personal communications which I believe to be authentic.

It seems that, at the outset, Borodin intended to keep strictly to Stassov's scenario. We know his initial reaction when he received Stassov's outline: 'Your project is so complete and detailed that nothing could be clearer. If I find I have to make any changes, these will be confined to abridgements.'[3] And this was by no means merely a polite expression of his gratitude to Stassov. After a certain amount of literary preparation, including the study of historical sources, and a summer spent in Kursk Province in a locality that reminded him of the countryside around Putivl, Borodin got down to work on the music

---

[1] In 1950 I gave it to the Glinka State Central Museum of Musical Culture. I analysed the material contained it in as far back as 1930; therefore I consider that I have priority in the consideration of these matters.

[2] The entries in Rimsky-Korsakov's handwriting were made during Borodin's life-time (probably in the spring of 1885), thus the editors of the opera obviously did not make use of the file after the composer's death. It was left in my father's possession.

[3] See *Letters*, Vol. I, p. 142.

for his opera; first came the so-called 'Yaroslavna's Dream' based on section 1 of Stassov's scenario. Borodin temporarily lost interest in the subject, and did not return to it for another four years, but this was in no way due to any dissatisfaction on his part with Stassov's plan.

When he resumed work on *Igor* in October 1874, the first task he set himself was to write the 'Polovtsian March'—No. 8 in Stassov's scenario, where it reads: 'Enter a crowd of Polovtsi returning from a campaign.' 'Yasoslavna's Lament' and the C major Final Chorus, written somewhat later, also follow the original plan very closely. The 'Lament' is No. 11 in Stassov's scenario, and the Final Chorus No.12.

The first version he wrote of Konchak's Daughter's arioso marks the beginning of the alterations, since it has very little in common with No. 5 of Stassov's plan. There is a fundamental change at the start of the scene in the Polovtsian encampment, and this is connected with Borodin's desire to modify Prince Vladimir's character which appeared rather unsatisfactory in Stassov's original. But the Polovtsian Dances he was writing at the same time in no way run counter to Stassov's scenario (cf. No. 8).

On the back of an unposted letter to Taneev, there is a sketch of the original scenario of the Third Act probably belonging to the spring of 1876. The original intention was that there should be two scenes. Scene 1 was to have taken place in Igor's tent, and was to have included the Duet of Vladimir and Konchak's Daughter ('Konchak-ovna alone better?') and the conversation between Igor and Ovlur (overheard by Konchak's daughter who is hiding there). It is now that Igor has decided to make his escape. After the entry of Igor there is a remark: 'music of spirits and nones.' Scene 2 would have included all the material in the present score, beginning with 'the dances of the guards'.[1] This sketch has some correspondence with No. 9 of Stassov's plan, and a very close correspondence with No. 10. Stassov, though, had intended these numbers for Act II.

In the summer and autumn of 1876, Borodin was taken up with the composition of those scenes dealing with Igor's return from captivity. These included Yaroslavna's aria 'How dreary is everything around me', and Igor and Yaroslavna's duet, both of which were later incorporated in Act IV. These scenes are very different from the scheme outlined in No. 11 of the original scenario. Igor makes no secret of his return to Putivl, and does not have any of the surreptitious discussions

[1] See *Letters*, Vol. II, p. 249.

originally intended, in which he schemes to regain the power usurped by Galitsky. The original version of the G major Chorus, composed probably in 1876 also, does however show a close correspondence to this. Here, Igor is simply greeted as the rightful prince. But the entire episode covering Igor's return to power was deleted by the composer (as well as Vladimir's attempts to seize control) who considered the whole thing to be completely out of place. (I ought to point out that 'The Welcome of the Prince' Chorus, which eventually was to form the epilogue of the opera, was at that time not yet excluded from Stassov's plan for No. 12 (the section including the return of Prince Vladimir with Konchak's daughter, and the chorus of praise, etc.). He decided upon the alteration at a much later date.)

The years 1877 and 1878 were not very fruitful as far as *Igor* was concerned. The numbers he wrote, however, do show that he was still revising the original plan (Vladimir's Cavatina is not in any way connected with Stassov's No. 5, and the scenes featuring Vladimir Galitsky, composed in 1878, have no counterpart whatsoever in the Stassov version).

In 1879 and 1880, Borodin introduced a number of innovations. By the summer of 1879 he had finished the scene involving Galitsky, and then he set about revising this particular section of the opera. The Merchant's Tale was excluded,[1] and there was a certain amount of reshaping of the Second Act, the extent of which is not known for certain. This was a result of his study of the Ipatevsky manuscript.[2] The beginning of the Finale of Act I is also very different from the corresponding passage in Stassov's version (the composer introduced an account of the Polovtsian attack on Putivl, and deleted the scene between Yaroslavna and Ovlur). Galitsky's attempt to seize power from Yaroslavna now appears in the final scene, in accordance with Stassov's indication for No. 4.[3]

In the early eighties, Borodin finally made up his mind to write a Prologue, and to exclude the last number of the scenario (No. 12) altogether. But he took the final C major Chorus from the latter and worked it into the Prologue. Borodin was to some extent driven to this by the superabundance of musical material now at his disposal.

---

[1] See *Letters*, Vol. III, pp. 68–69. As may be seen from the text of this letter, Borodin had the idea of leaving the merchants in the opera merely as walking-on characters, but later he decided to exclude them completely. As to the use of music from 'the merchants' tale', see Chapter VII, section III.

[2] See *Letters*, Vol. III, p. 67.

[3] Borodin called this part of the Finale 'the rebellion scene'.

Had he kept to the original scenario, he would have had to write not one opera, but two. As I have already mentioned in Chapter 5, this thought crossed Borodin's mind more than once.[1] It is just as well that Borodin never embarked upon such an undertaking, for, apart from the various technical and stylistic difficulties, the performance of such an enormous work would have been out of the question.

We are in possession of one rather interesting document, in which the composer made an outline of the opera as he visualized it in 1880. I am reproducing this in full, exactly as it appears in the original.[2]

(Cover.)

1st scene, prologue, heavenly warning.
2nd   ,,   'in captivity'.
3rd   ,,   at the house of [·] Prince Volodimir.[3]
              Crowd of Princes
              wanders   —18—19 m.

4   Yaroslavna's apartment
                    'Threat of the Gods'—32 min.
5   Flight [·]
6   Return.

[Contents of sheet of paper inside the envelope.]

Length   3 scene

Introduction and chorus 1–3 pag.	1 m.	
Soli and chorus, conclusion 6 pag.	1 m.	
Rec. of prince and chorus 1 m.		
Scene pag. 9 up to fem. chorus	1 minute	Whole scene less than 18 minutes.
Intr. and female chorus		
pag. 14	25 sec.	
Male 14–16 pag.	30 sec.	
Female 16–17 pag.		
(20 sec.) and rest up to Barrel	1 minute	

whole about 6 minutes	6 m.

[1] He probably intended to insert the first three acts of the score as it stands today (minus the prologue) into the first opera, which was to be called *Igor in Captivity*. The second opera, *Igor at Home*, would have consisted of the present Fourth Act, in a greatly modified form, plus a further act which would have corresponded to No. 12 of Stassov's scenario.

[2] The page numbers given in this table seem to refer to a rough piano sketch of *Igor*. This document is preserved in the Saltikov-Shchedrin Public Library in Leningrad.

[3] In another variant of the same sketch, instead of '3rd scene' is written 'Second Act'.

Song of Vlad. Galitsky 3½—4 min.   3–4 m.

Princely song	Introd. and	
	solo 1–3 p.	45 s.
	3–5 duet	45 s.
	5–7 chorus F maj.	45 s.
	8–10 solo	45 s.
	10–13 chorus	
	G maj.	45 s.
	up to end	
	About 4 minutes	

                                                                      4 m.

Scene of barrel   2 min.   2 m.

Scene with gudok

      player (s)   1 m. 30 s.

                                 (less !)   1 m. 30 s.

                    Finale p. 19–24

With omission 24 chorus after ⌒

in middle of ['] Young acolytes of the Prince ['']

      up to end   1 m. 30 s.   1 m. 30 s.

                      (less.)

[Reverse side of the sheet of paper.]

4 Scene   M.   S.

			M.	S.
	Introduction	1 m.	1	
	Dumka[1]	6 m.	6	
Scene with the girls	5 m.		5	
Duet with Vladimir Galits	6 m. + ...		6	
Little recitative of Yaroslavna	....			30 s.
Entry of Boyars	1 m. 5 s.		1	
Recit. Yaros.	45 s.			45 s.
Chorus 1st time	1 m. 45 s.		1	45 s.
Recit [·] few words—	5 s.			5 s.
Chorus 2nd time	1 m. 45 s.		1	45 s.
Ya. pag. 10 (recit) ½ minute +	....			30 s.
Ya. completes recit ½ minute	....			30 s.

---

[1] This is Yaroslavna's arioso (p. 77) which Borodin in a letter of 1869 called 'Yaroslavna's Dream'. The name 'dumka' was given to the arioso by the singer A. N. Molas.

Chorus Boyars Pag 15

up to end	1 m. 30 s.	....	1	30 s.
Rec Yar. p. 18	¾ m.	....		45 s.
p. 23	¾ m.	....		45 s.
Rec and entry of merchants		....	1	—
Vlad. Galits and [?][1]				
up to entry of women	2 m.	....	2	—
Women of Putivl	1 m.	....	1	

Whole Scene about 32 mins.[2]

With the exception of the Prologue, the whole opera was thoroughly revised two years later. The only thing he wrote for the opera during this time (sometime around November 1881) was the final version of Igor's Aria in the Second Act, (in B♭ minor, not C♯ minor) which was in no way counter to Stassov's original. Shortly after this, he reshaped the G major Chorus, 'The Welcome of the Prince', which eventually was to be the ending of the opera.

After completing the Prologue (in the summer and autumn of 1883) Borodin set to work on the final version of the opera. This was interrupted at various times for personal or domestic reasons, and his progress was slow. In the summer of 1884 he wrote part of the libretto for the eventual Third Act, the sketches of which show that he followed the Stassov scenario fairly closely (the middle of No. 10).

Early in 1885, Rimsky-Korsakov was given permission to get on with the editing of those parts of the opera that were already in existence; this included the Prologue, the first two scenes of Act I. He excluded the 'rebellion scene' from the finale of Scene 2. Rimsky-Korsakov notes that, according to sketches made by Borodin, the Third Act differed from Stassov's scenario in that it included Kon-

[1] Illegible in the original.

[2] The original copy of the sketch reproduced here was contained in the 'Libretto of Igor and Musical Sketches' referred to in note 1, p. 271. The probable date of the sketch is determined by (1) the mention of the 'entry of the merchants', although there is no reference to their 'tale'; this means that it could not have been written earlier than 1879. (2) The reference to Vladimir Galitsky's treason (and his appearance in the Finale of the fourth scene) which suggests that it was composed in 1880. Furthermore, we notice from a note in the text that instead of being divided into acts, it is divided into scenes. It seems that here there was some slight inconsistency in the composer's mind. There is a mention of dividing *Igor* into 4 acts in a letter of an earlier date (the summer of 1876) (see *Letters*, Vol. II, p. 109).

chak's praise of Igor ('What a fine fellow'!) and the proposal that his son Vladimir should marry his daughter (Konchakovna).[1]

In the latter part of 1886, Borodin sketched the Second Act. The numbers he had finally decided to include were: the Chorus of Russian Prisoners, the Polovtsian Patrol, the scene with Ovlur, and Igor's conversation with Konchak.

Of these scenes, only the last two are to be found in the original scenario. The Chorus of Prisoners and the Polovtsian Patrol are Borodin's own inventions. Ovlur's approach to Igor is not at all like his speech in No. 9 of Stassov; Borodin has left out the historical references, designed to 'raise Igor's spirits' and to incite him to escape.

Glazunov and Rimsky-Korsakov, who were of course the editors of the opera, published it without any further additions, and in strict adherence to the composer's intentions.

Here are a few points to sum up. What were the most important changes Borodin made to the original scenario in the course of his work on *Igor*?

(1) A number of characters, who appeared in the original, were excluded from the final version. These were: the two merchants, who brought news of the defeat of the Russian army; the equerry who tried to persuade Igor to escape[2]; the foreign confederates of Prince Galitsky (Venetians, Greeks, Moravians and Germans),[3] and the Gotfsky captive maidens held by the Polovtsi, who jangled gold stolen from the Russians and taunted them.[4]

(2) On the other hand, there are a few new characters: the gudok players Skula and Eroshka,[5] and a host of additional parts (the

---

[1] The rough sketch of Act III, drawn up by Rimsky-Korsakov in accordance with Borodin's directions, is preserved in the file 'Libretto of Igor and Musical Sketches'. At the end of this are written the words: 'music of the flood' which is found in a fragment of the scenario relating to 1876. This is a relic of a former idea relinquished by Borodin, in which he intended to use the music of the Finale to *Mlada* to illustrate the sudden flood of the Don, thus preventing the Polovtsi from pursuing Igor. (The composer found evidence for this fact somewhere in the historical sources. See Rimsky-Korsakov's memoirs, 7th ed., p. 171.)

[2] To be more precise, the rôle of Koniush was depicted by Borodin in accordance with the words of the Stassov scenario: 'The Russians surrounding the Prince . . . also encourage him to escape.' Borodin decided not to include this character some time during the 1880s.

[3] No. 3 of the Stassov scenario.

[4] No. 8 of the Stassov scenario.

[5] The names of the gudok-players are borrowed by Borodin from one of the manuscripts, as is revealed from the following note in the file, 'Libretto of Igor, etc.'; 'Skula

choruses of maidens in the First Act; the choruses of Polovtsian maidens, Russian captives, the Polovtsian patrol, the Polovtsian khans in Acts II and III; the chorus of peasants, and the chorus of welcome in Act IV).

(3) The speeches made by certain of the characters are very different from those in the scenario of 1869. For instance, in Konchak's Aria there are none of the reminiscences of his former campaigns with Igor; and the names and places mentioned are different. Comparable changes were made in the scene between Igor and Ovlur. Igor's Aria in its definitive form has no exact correspondence with those parts of Nos. 6, 8, and 9, where he gives vent to his feelings as a prisoner.

(4) Galitsky's seizure of power is omitted from the final version of the opera. Instead, Borodin inserted the 'heavenly warning' scene, in which Khan Gzak attacks Putivl (or more precisely, the distant echoes of this assault heard from Yaroslavna's apartment).

All these changes were made with the sole aim of transforming the scenario into the sort of epic that Borodin intended.

It will be remembered that Borodin had declared in 1876: 'A purely recitative style would go against the grain, and in any case I am not given to this kind of writing. . . . Song, and cantilena are more in my line, and I feel happier with more definite, and more concrete forms.' 'I am of the opinion that mere decoration, light-weight treatment, and details and minutiae of any sort are completely out of place in opera; everything should be written with bold strokes, with an eye on clarity, vividness and practicability as regards performance.'[1]

It was impossible then that the words and music of Borodin's opera should conflict. He was determined to cut out at the libretto everything that could be unimportant and 'distracting'.

He decided to avoid all unnecessary historical references and tedious enumeration of names, etc. The original chronicle contained much that was unsuitable for an epic opera, and had to be adapted accordingly; otherwise a great deal of colourless and shallow music would have resulted, or, at best, music that bore little relation to the text. But, in amending the dialogue, Borodin could not help but alter his

and Eroshka are taken from boyar Olstin Oleksich of the Chernogivsky Kovui who fled from the field of battle. Naturally both Kovui attached themselves to Vladimir Galitsky (illegible words) as opposed to Yaroslav Galitsky.' Borodin paid little attention to their national characteristics and depicted them as Russian gudok-players. (The *Kovui* were a tribe strange to Russia who lived on the territory of the Chernigovsky principality during the 12th century.)

[1] See *Letters*, Vol. II, p. 109 (letter to L. I. Karmalina dated 1 June 1876).

characters as well. He wanted an opera based on Russian and oriental folk-melodies, and thus deleted any national strains that might conflict with this; for instance, the foreign confederates of Galitsky, and the 'Gotfsky maidens'. If these had been introduced the opera would certainly have suffered from diffuseness.

Borodin's intentions went deeper than mere preoccupation with form. He wanted to bring out as clearly as possible the underlying idea of the Igor Chronicle; namely, Russia's sense of unity in her struggle against her enemies. To attain this, he excluded all elements of dissention and mob violence; these would have made for more colour, but would have destroyed the clarity of outline. We find, as a result of all this, that Borodin's characters are idealized versions of their historical prototypes, and that he managed to present a convincing picture of the struggle for a united Russia, which fired the imaginations of the heroes of the twelfth century. In addition to this, Borodin left the mark of his own personality on his characters, and imbued them with his own humanity.

The character of *Igor* is stronger and more restrained by comparison with Stassov's prototype. In the opera the aspect of the feudal lord is very much in the background.

Konchak, the enemy of Russia, is more sympathetic and courteous in Borodin's libretto. His ambition to conquer Russia is by no means toned down, but his fit of uncontrolled rage, indicated in No. 10 of Stassov's scenario, was omitted by Borodin. The composer pays great attention to Konchak's sense of chivalry.

Prince Vladimir (Igor's son) is little more than a traitor to his country in Stassov No. 5, but Borodin portrays him simply as a man of weak character, a slave to his passion. A pretext is brought in to explain his motives for wanting to remain in the Polovtsian encampment, namely, that Konchak's daughter would have raised the alarm if he had tried to escape with his father.

In his presentation of the negative characters, Prince Galitsky and the gudok-players, Borodin uses a light humorous touch. They are very different from the usual type of operatic villain.

In Borodin's libretto, the chorus plays a much more significant rôle, in accordance with the underlying principle of the opera.[1]

Borodin's recasting of Stassov's scenario was a very long process.

---

[1] See Stassov's letter to Borodin dated 8 August 1879 (in my *Borodin*, 2nd Russian edition, pp. 229–31) in which Stassov expresses his alarm at the number of 'massive choruses' in *Igor*. For Borodin's answer, see *Letters*, Vol. III, p. 76.

Borodin welded his musical numbers together to form an 'organic' whole.[1] Sketches of the libretto show that he changed not only the historical details, but often the complete personality of his characters.

When we examine the rough sketches of the libretto, we are impressed by Borodin's thoroughness in reshaping the text, rearranging word-order, and modifying the metre, etc. There are, for example, more than forty alterations to a single version of Yaroslavna's arioso in Act I, Scene 2 (this version is very close to the one in the published libretto). Ovlur's scene in Act II has at least sixteen corrections. The greatest number of alterations are to be found in Act I, Scene 1, and Finale; in the Chorus of Prisoners in the Second Act, in Igor's Aria, and in Igor's conversation with Konchak, also in Act II. Some of these changes are of course due to modifications of the original scenario.[2] For instance, names of certain princes and boyars were omitted from the Prologue,[3] as a result of Borodin's desire to keep the number of characters down to a minimum, and in some cases to shorten the scenes.

In the original sketch, the Prince's song in Act I, Scene 2, was begun not by Skula, but by Galitsky himself. The drunkards' barrel scene was to have been enacted by the gudok-players and servants of Prince Galitsky.

The action in Act I, Scene 2, between Galitsky and Yaroslavna, included his proposal that she should become his mistress.

A few alterations were made to Konchak's daughter's arioso at the start of the Second Act, in connection with the deletion of the projected scene in which Prince Vladimir returns from hunting.

Generally speaking, there are no violent clashes of personality or excesses of rage in the libretto of *Igor*. Borodin thought at first that his opera would lack the necessary dramatic intensity; he felt that any opera without a dramatic basis was bound to seem unnatural. It was these considerations which made him break off work on his opera for over four years.[4] When he returned to the task of finishing his opera, he realized that an epic opera would be, after all, a practical possibility.[5]

[1] See *Letters*, Vol. III, p. 70.

[2] I refer here only to minor alterations in the scenario. I have already discussed the major changes at the beginning of this section.

[3] With regard to these names, see above, Chapter IV.

[4] See *Letters*, Vol. I, p. 200.

[5] In a letter to L. I. Karmalina dated 1 June 1876 (*Letters*, Vol. II, p. 108), Borodin speaks ironically of himself as a poet in spirit, who nevertheless desires to 'realize (his) ardent dream—to write an *epic Russian opera*' (italics mine). The opera must be more akin to *Ruslan* than *The Stone Guest*; cantilena must predominate over recitative, etc.

In his opera, Borodin managed to bring a historical legend to life.[1] There remains one important question to answer with regard to the music. Is *Igor* purely rhapsodic, or does it contain symphonic elements? This question can only be answered after we have made detailed analysis of the themes.

II

Let us first examine those parts of *Igor* which take place in Putivl, and spend a little time on the choral numbers in particular. Chronologically speaking, the first of the choral numbers to be composed was the opening of Act I (featuring Skula and Eroshka). In all probability, this chorus can be traced to earlier sources; it is an adaptation apparently of earlier sources.[2] An examination of the main themes shows they are probably based on tunes taken from the ballads: 'The Terrible Tsar, Ivan Vassilyevich' and 'The Bird'. This is evident from the following comparison:

Ex. 183

Ex. 184

(Here, *I* is the theme from Igor; *T.T.* the tune from 'The Terrible Tsar'; *B.* the ballad of 'The Bird'.[3]

[1] Borodin jestingly refers to himself as 'the unsystematic Bayan' of *Igor*, i.e. a kind of rhapsodist (see *Letters*, Vol. II, p. 97). There is a grain of truth in this remark however —an indication as to the rôle of the composer in approaching his task.

[2] We have no definite information about this. It might be the final version of the chorus which (according to Stassov) represented the feast of the oprichniki originally destined for the projected but unwritten opera, *The Tsar's Bride* (see Chapter III above, and note 1, p. 53, to the same chapter).

[3] For the two themes quoted in the text, see p. 40 of the Belyaev vocal score. In the extracts from the ballads, as well as inserting the clefs I have transposed them all into the

The second theme appears in a slightly modified form in two choral numbers; firstly, in the Chorus of Praise in the Prologue[1]:

Ex. 185

Secondly, in the Chorus of Boyars in the Finale of Act I, Scene 2[2]:

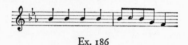

Ex. 186

These leitmotifs signify the people's respect for their prince, and their readiness to fight for him. The theme is varied according to the changes in mood of the populace. In Galitsky's scene, the motif is lacking in expression, for their leader has been defeated and things look black; but when Igor is being feted before his departure for battle, the motif is more pronounced and triumphant. When it comes a third time, in Yaroslavna's scene, it expresses her devotion to the princess and her willingness to sacrifice everything in defence of the town, and her confidence in her own strength.

The next chorus Borodin wrote was the 'Chorus of Praise'. This was later incorporated in the Prologue. The sources here are not so obvious, and the whole problem is much more complicated. At the time he was working on this chorus, Borodin knew at least two variants of the song 'The Sparrow Hills', published in Prokunin's collection, and he certainly made use of these.[3,4] Over and above this, however, there are a number of motifs from the Chorus of

same key (either from D minor or the Dorian mode of the original). I notice, in addition, that both these themes are found in contrapuntal combinations. In the first theme, a G has been introduced after B♮ in order to avoid a dissonance. These themes were composed separately as opposed to the themes of the symphonic poem, *In the Steppes of Central Asia.*

[1] See p. 2 of the vocal score.

[2] Ibid., p. 114.

[3] Borodin became familiar with the Prokunin anthology either in autumn or early winter 1875. This was probably due to Rimsky-Korsakov who had just begun work on his collection of Russian folk-songs and had studied the existing anthologies for a long time before this.

[4] See Chapters IV and VIII for a brief description of my discovery of the significance of the song 'The Sparrow Hills' in Borodin's choice of themes. See also the periodical *Vladimir*, III (1954), pp. 176-205.

Idolaters in *Mlada*, and even from the ballads mentioned above. (The introduction to the Prologue, and the boyars' replies to Igor in the same scene, are based on motifs 'transplanted' from *Mlada*.)

The monumental chorus of praise contains a fair number of themes. The first part (in C major) is built on motifs which again can be found in the ballads. I have already discussed the source of the first of these—the 'patriotic' motif. The probable origin of other motifs can be seen from the following comparison:

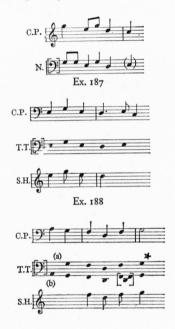

Ex. 187

Ex. 188

★ Here two motifs (a) and (b) from "The Terrible Tsar" are written on the same stave.

Ex. 189

The refrain 'Slava' could be from either of two sources:

Ex. 190

Ex. 191

(Here C.P. is the Chorus of Praise; N. the 'Nightingale'; T.T. the ballad 'The Terrible Tsar'; B. the ballad 'The Bird'; S.H. the song 'The Sparrow Hills'.)[1]

If we are willing to accept that the folk-song 'The Sparrow Hills' is probably the basis of the first part of the Chorus of Praise, we are forced to acknowledge the importance of its use in the first two bars of the second part (where it modulates into four sharps).

If we study carefully the example given below, we shall see that this motif (which we may from now on refer to as motif A) is not only woven into the melody, but even into the bass line. The theme incorporates an additional phrase (which we shall call R[2]):

Ex. 192

From this extract, it is clear that two variants of motif A (A' A'') form the basis of the second part of the Chorus:

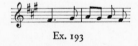

Ex. 193

[1] For The Chorus of Praise, see pp. 2–7 and 34–38 of the vocal score. The motifs reproduced above are all on pp. 2–3. Of the melody of 'The Sparrow Hills' see Chapter VIII. Where necessary, I have transposed all the motifs from the ballads and the 'Sparrow Hills' into the same key as the chorus. The clefs in brackets are also mine.

[2] Motif R also appears in the 'Chorus of Idol Worshippers' in *Mlada*. The original may be seen in Stassov's book on Borodin where it has the form:

Ex. 314

with the addition of motif R. The entire second part is built on the motifs A' and R; the conclusion reintroduces the theme of praise (E major, *ff*, p. 6, of the vocal score) and the 'patriotic' motif.

(In the middle of the Prologue comes the scene of the eclipse; the stage is gradually plunged into darkness, and all the characters, except Igor, are terror-stricken and vainly plead with him to abandon his plans for war. Here, the music is a recasting of that accompanying the apparitions in *Mlada*. I have given a detailed account of this in my article 'On the rôle of Borodin's sense of key-relationships' (printed in *De Musica*, Vol. 3, 1927); those who are interested should refer to this.)

The 'Chorus of Praise' is heard once more, in a somewhat modified form, at the close of the Prologue (op. 36 of the vocal score). Now motif A″ from the song 'The Sparrow Hills' occurs only in the bass line,[1] and follows the 'patriotic' motif.

Motif A″ might be said to have a tragic, mournful significance, when it appears in the Andante of Borodin's First Quartet (cf. Chapter 8). The same tone of sadness is maintained in *Prince Igor*, though Borodin's use of the motif here hardly seems justified by the spirit of the text. The only explanation is that it might be some kind of allusion of future disaster, some foreboding.

There are further traces of 'The Sparrow Hills' to be found in Act I, Scene 1, in the Chorus of Maidens, when they approach Galitsky and beg for the return of their dishonoured friend. As may be seen from the following comparison:

Extract from the
Chorus of Girls: p. 52

Bars 5–7 of the song,
'The Sparrow Hills',
transposed into G minor

Ex. 194

there is a close resemblance between the sequences. It is not impossible that the whole chorus evolves out of these two bars.

---

[1] As is seen from the following:

Ex. 315

P. 36
Its ending is changed here with a B♭ instead of a B♮, and A♭ instead of A♮.

The last number in Scene 1 sung by the chorus (the 'princely song'), is similarly derived. From the following example:

'Princely Song': p. 60

The ballad, 'The Bird', transposed into E major

Ex. 195

it is not difficult to see the resemblance between the two. Later in the scene, the notes underlined are most prominent (the same motif also appears in Borodin's First Symphony).

Let us now turn to the next choral number, in order of composition: the choruses in Act I, Scene 2. First, the Chorus of Maidens. On closer examination, we cannot fail to notice that it is a free variation of the choral theme in the previous scene. It is easy to see the source of the chorus in question:

Bars 2 and 3 from the Chorus of Maidens

Bars 5–7 of 'The Sparrow Hills', transposed into E minor

Ex. 196

An even closer comparison may be obtained by transposing the lower motif into E major. The relationship between these motifs proves that both choruses originate from the folk-song 'The Sparrow Hills'.

The second chorus of maidens (Allegro vivo, 5/4, C sharp minor) is also partially connected with these motifs, but, on the whole, it is an independent 'intermezzo' of considerable harmonic interest which gives a very vivid impression of the state of mind of the young girls.[1]

The tragic significance of motif A (taken from 'The Sparrow Hills)', and of yet another motif from the same song, becomes apparent in the course of the grandiose Finale to the second score of Act I, which was written some time after the women's choruses in this scene. At the beginning of this number (No. 6, p. 108) we hear the solemn, tragic

[1] The gradual rising of this melody and the presence of more poignant harmonies excellently illustrates the lessening terror of the girls as they approach the Princess to complain of her brother; as their indignation increases in enumerating the crimes of Galitsky and his 'young bloods', their fear proportionately disappears.

Chorus of Boyars (Andantino),[1] who have come to see Princess Yaroslavna with the news that the Polovtsi are approaching, that Igor has been wounded in battle and taken prisoner, and that the Russian army has been routed. The theme of this chorus is heard in the basses:

Ex. 197

This is built on motif A from 'The Sparrow Hills', on the very variant we considered earlier in connection with the second part of the Chorus of Praise.

This theme is played twice (in E flat minor and A flat minor), then a variant is heard based on almost exactly the same motif, namely on 'motif B'.[2]

Ex. 198

A further motif (motif T) is introduced, in the key of E minor:

P.109; bar 6
Bars 10–12 of
'The Sparrow Hills',
transposed into E minor

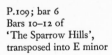 

Ex. 199

Comparison shows that this too is from the folk-song.

The tragic 'Motif T' gradually emerges as a leitmotif of hostile threats. It is sung at the close of the Finale to the accompaniment of the alarum (C sharp minor), which is giving the signal that the enemy have stolen upon the town unawares (F sharp minor). Later it is heard

---

[1] See vocal score, pp. 108–11.
[2] The original theme (illustrated above) is contracted to a single unit here. It almost becomes a separate motif.

in the orchestra (the alarum goes on sounding) in C sharp minor and in G sharp minor, the various motifs being woven together.[1]

The beautiful F sharp minor 'A cappella' Chorus in Act IV was also composed about the same time; here, as they go to work, the peasants are singing of their recent delivery from the threat of enemy attack.

To unravel the sources of the first eight bars of this chorus (the theme) is no easy matter. This smoothly-flowing, lyrical melody is the product not only of inspiration, but of much hard work. I shall not dwell upon this, but shall go ahead and put forward the most likely solution. The first thing we ought to bear in mind is that bars 2, 3, and 4 are heard in Yaroslavna's recitative, which follows this chorus (they accompany the words: 'happy songs are no longer to be heard here'); the important notes of the first bar are identical with the first bar of the recitative.[2] But this recitative was composed much earlier than the 'A cappella' Chorus[3]; it follows, then, that the first half of the theme of the latter chorus was taken from the recitative.

But bars 5 to 8 of the chorus are quite another matter. Before discussing this question, however, I should like to make a few introductory remarks. I mentioned earlier, in Chapter IV, that it was I. P. Lapin who first prompted me to make a comparison of 'The Sparrow Hills' with *Igor*; Borodin apparently told him that he wanted a copy of the folk-song, as he had forgotten it. Whether this is actually the case, or simply that Borodin was on the look-out for a new variant, does not really make much difference. The tune of 'The Sparrow Hills' which he heard in the village of Davydovo was certainly very different from the one in Prokunin's anthology. The question, then,

---

[1] See vocal score, pp. 117–24. It is interesting to note that 'motif T' appears again, in a modified form, in Act IV at the end of Yaroslavna and Igor's duet, where it accompanies Igor's words: 'My enemies I will crush':

Ex. 316

The fact that this motif is connected here with the idea of the enemy further confirms its significance in the mind of the composer.

[2] As to the motif underlying this bar, see section IV of this chapter devoted to the 'Polovtsian' themes.

[3] See Chapter IV, note 4, p. 95, and note 2, p. 110.

naturally arises: Is it this new variant that he used in the 'A cappella' Chorus? Unfortunately, we have no record of any note Borodin might have made of this tune. For this reason, we shall have to find a tune in the available collections similar to the theme of the Chorus. After several attempts, I at last succeeded in finding such a tune in L. Lineva's collection.[1]

The result of a comparison of this with bars 5 to 8 of the Chorus was as follows:

(*a*) 'A cappella' Chorus: bars 5–8.
(*b*) Bars 2, 3, and 4 of the variant of 'The Sparrow Hills' (Lineva), transposed into A major F♯ minor.

Ex. 200

It can be seen that there is a close correspondence.[2] Thus the theory seems tenable that a variant of the folk-song, other than Prokunin's version, was used in this chorus.[3]

[1] The following variant of the folk-song 'The Sparrow Hills', which I partly quoted in the text, is found in Lineva's work, *Great-Russian Songs in Folk-harmonization*, Vol. I (St. Petersburg, 1904):

Ex. 317

As Borodin obviously could not have consulted Lineva's anthology, he must have obtained a similar variant from a singer (I was told this recently by Lapin).

[2] We can see the resemblance between the Lineva variant of 'The Sparrow Hills' and the theme of the chorus of maidens from the comparison below:

(*a*) Motif from the theme of the chorus of maidens: p. 86.
(*b*) First two bars of the variant given in note above, transposed into E major.

Ex. 318

In view of the fact that the last chorus and the 'A cappella' chorus were composed almost simultaneously, it seems that Borodin must have made use of a variant similar to that of the Lineva version.

[3] If we make allowance for later changes to the recitative, 'How dreary is everything around me', then it is possible that the end of the 3rd and 4th bars of the melody of the

Let us now take a closer look at the final choral number of the opera, namely the Chorus in G major, otherwise known as 'The Welcome of the Prince'. The original version of this chorus was composed probably in the winter of 1876 and 1877, but was later revised by the composer. The concluding section of the opera was completely recast, and it may be for this reason that it is less interesting and flat by comparison with the Finale to Act I.

The scene begins with a short solo from Skula, the gudok-player, who already appears as a true follower of Igor. Skula invites everyone 'to drink to the health of our dear Prince'. His theme is as follows:

Skula's motif

Relevant fragments
from the ballad
'The Terrible Tsar'[1]

Ex. 201

and is obviously based on motifs of the ballads.

The theme introduced by the full chorus is:

Allegro marziale ♩ = 92

Ex. 202

It appears to be constructed from a repetition of the same motif in the form of a sequence; the rhythm is strikingly similar to that of the Chorus of Praise in the Prologue. If motif (I) forms the basis of the theme, then we are faced with an interesting situation, for this is no other than the motif of the first two bars of the folk-song 'The Sparrow Hills' (as it appears in the Prokunin collection), transposed into E minor:

Ex. 203

but in a different rhythm, and played backwards. Instead of the E natural (in brackets), the chorus has a G natural, but this is not so important in view of the fact that the key remains the same (E minor).

'A cappella' Chorus are built on a variant of bar 5 of 'The Sparrow Hills', as there is a similarity of their rhythmic structure.

[1] The second melody of the ballad is transposed up a fifth.

Here there is a 'musical surmounting', so to say, of the mournful aspect of the song, in keeping with events in the opera itself and the return of the prince from captivity.

After this, Skula and Eroshka invite the townsfolk to come into the citadel to give the prince the welcome due to him. The motifs here are variants of those previously used in Skula's solo. The chorus then rallies to this invitation.

The tempo then changes to 'Poco meno mosso' (♩=80). The boyars enter to pay their respects to Igor, and call on the towns-people to array themselves in their finest garments to celebrate the occasion.

The theme of this slower section is based on a modification[1] of the first two bars of the folk-song 'The Sparrow Hills' (as it appears in the Prokunin collection) and the F sharp minor theme from the 'A cappella' Chorus, which corresponds with another of the motifs of Lineva's version of the same folk-song. This may easily be seen from the following comparisons:

(a) Theme from the middle section of the Final Chorus.
(b) Bars 1–2 of the song 'The Sparrow Hills', transposed into F sharp minor.
(c) Theme of the 'A cappella' Chorus, based on the Lineva variant: bars 2 and 3 (in C sharp minor).[2]

Ex. 204

Here too, we find the 'fatalistic element' overcome; the mood brightens with a shift into the major (E major). In the middle section

[1] The change consists in the introduction of an extra note before the last note of the motif. (The extra note is in brackets.) This is a similar change to that seen in the bass parts in the example from the beginning of the second part of the chorus of praise. We find the 'motif of sorrow' in the same form at the end of the introduction of the Prologue (given to the basses).

[2] The melody given here is transposed up a fifth in relation to the motif of the 'A cappella' Chorus. The note in brackets appears in the chorus but is missing in the Lineva variant of 'The Sparrow Hills'.

the theme modulates through a series of keys, which may be summed up as follows:

Theme begins with the note:	Harmony:
F♯ (twice)	E major (twice)
C♯ (twice)	Lydian A major (twice)
changed ending	(with D♯)
D♯ (twice)	C♯ major (twice)
F♯ (twice)	E major (twice)
E (twice)	G major (twice)
theme changed and	
abbreviated	

There follows a return to the original key; the music of Skula's introductory solo is repeated, when both gudok-players invite everyone a second time to drink the health of the prince. Finally, the chorus is heard singing the first theme.

The opera ends with a coda in which Igor appears on the stage and bows to his people. In this coda there is an accompanying ostinato figure, based first on motifs from Skula's solo; this is followed up by chords, to give the effect of pealing bells. An identical sequence can be heard at the opening of the Finale of the second scene of Act I; we might almost call it 'the triumphant exit motif'[1]:

Ex. 205

There remains just one more chorus to be examined: the Chorus of Russian Prisoners in Act II. This was one of Borodin's last compositions; he played it to friends not long before his death, and Glazunov reconstructed it from memory.

[1] It is interesting to notice the differences and similarities between this coda and the coda of the Prologue. Both conclusions are built on ostinato motifs in the bass. In the coda of the Prologue there is a repeated motif (a fragment from the theme of the chorus to Radegast) which is sung by the boyars; it also appears in the introduction to express the people's sympathy and support for Igor. In the coda of the final scene there is a fragment from the theme of Skula, the gudok-player. In the one we have the representation of solemn affairs of state, in the other, an impression of popular rejoicing. The presence of the alarm bell in the finale to Act I and the peal of bells at the end of Act IV are also important. Both passages are based on similar rhythmic figures.

We need not make a detailed analysis. It suffices to point out that the theme is based on Lineva's version of 'The Sparrow Hills':

Ex. 206

The section underlined in the first bar is also to be found in the ballads (at the end of 'The Nightingale').

To conclude this analysis of the choruses in *Igor*, I should like to say that a thematic unity can be observed throughout, the most important melodic element being the folk-song 'The Sparrow Hills'.

III

We shall now make a brief study of the main characters of the opera in so far as they are reflected in the music.

I am convinced, after much thought on the matter, that Borodin uses his themes and motifs not so much to delineate his characters as to underline their moods and actions. This does not necessarily mean, however, that the composer has to use more than one leitmotif for each character, especially if his characters are properly integrated.

In the majority of the numbers in which Igor features, a descending motif is heard either in his part or in the orchestra, in a number of different rhythms:

(1) P. 23 (song)

(2) P. 169 (accompaniment)

(3) P. 180 (bar 4)

(4) Ibid. (bar 8)

(5) Ibid. (bar 12)

(6) P. 182 (bar 19)

(7) P. 193 [1]

Ex. 207

---

[1] This leitmotif is taken from the orchestral accompaniment to the duet of Yaromir

What was the composer's purpose in using this particular motif? Very likely, Borodin wanted to underline Igor's calm conviction, his firm belief in his duty as a patriot, and his readiness to undergo every kind of suffering for the sake of his country. Examples 3, 4, and 5 particularly support this idea—his conversation with Ovlur. Igor is saying that he has to save his native land. In Ex. 1, Igor summons his wife and breaks the news to her that he has to leave her to fight the foe. Example 2 expresses Igor's sadness and feeling of helplessness as a prisoner. In Ex. 6 and 7, in his conversation with Konchak, we find the outward calm masking his true feeling of wretchedness at his captivity.

The second motif associated with Igor is first heard in the Prologue, and again later, in the Second Act. It expresses his soldier-like gallantry, his readiness to meet the foe.

If we compare the well-known phrase from Igor's Aria in Act II: 'O grant me, grant me freedom', (p. 170), with the ballads, we find that it was from these that Borodin derived his themes[1]:

(a) *Igor*, p. 179.
(b) Ballad 'The Nightingale'
(c) Ballad 'The Terrible Tsar'

Ex. 208

and the High Priest in Act IV of *Mlada*. Borodin has used the descending tones of the first three bars (underlined in the following example):

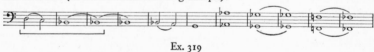

Ex. 319

A descending passage similar to that of Igor's motif may be found in the accompaniment on pp. 170, 172, 193, and 195 of the vocal score:

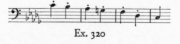

Ex. 320

(Starting on C in this case, but G and B♮ elsewhere.)

[1] The two motifs from the ballad 'The Nightingale' are transposed into D flat major. I have inserted the bass clef myself. The motif from the ballad 'The Terrible Tsar' has

'Mlada' and 'Prince Igor'

There is another theme, not so important, which reflects his thoughts around the possibilities of escape. The similarity of the following two fragments is worth considering:

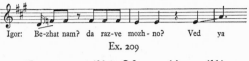

Igor: Be-zhat nam? da raz-ve mozh-no?   Ved   ya

Ex. 209

(Is escape possible? Of course it's possible)

Igor: Ya tai - no ·be - zhal

Ex. 209 (*a*)

(I fled in secret)

In the sketch of the scenario for Act III made in 1876, the conversation between Igor and Ovlur has a footnote: 'ninth'. It is evident that Borodin had some special harmony in mind, related to the idea of his escape. There are no less than seven instances of the use of ninths during their conversation in Act II. These are usually tremolos, in which the bass part descends tonally so that we have a resolution into a tenth. These harmonies represent Igor's growing indignation at Ovlur's suggestions.

There are some motifs connected with Igor which have no direct connection with his character.

At one point in the Prologue we find snatches of 'The Sparrow Hills' song in the same form in which it occurs in the E major section of the Chorus of Praise:

Ex. 210

Then there is another motif, in the same section, of two-fold origin:

Ex. 211

been transposed in the first instance into F minor. The second time it is untransposed. In the latter case, the note A♮ differs from the A♭ of the operatic phrase. The operatic phrase may not be a literal borrowing from the ballad, but a transposition into the key of F minor of the motif heard four bars earlier. (I have added the clefs myself.)

In those parts of Igor's Aria in which he reminisces about the times when he was with his wife, we hear one of Yaroslavna's themes, which we might label 'the theme of Yaroslavna's love and fidelity'. It is easy to see how he adapted this theme from *Mlada*:

(1) The first four bars of this theme are taken note for note from the 'spirit' motif of the poisoned princess:

Beginning of Yaroslavna's theme in Igor's Aria: p. 172

Theme from *Mlada*, transposed into D flat major

Ex. 212

(2) The next four bars of Yaroslavna's theme are a variant of the first four.

(3) The ninth and part of the tenth bar are based on the fragment indicated by the wavy bracket (Ex. 212).

This leads on to another motif connected with Yaroslavna, which symbolizes the mutual love and tenderness of husband and wife:

P. 173

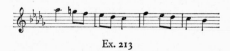

Ex. 213

This motif is used extensively in the scene where they are reunited and in their duet in Act IV.

The last theme directly relating to Igor is the duet theme. In accordance with the classic operatic tradition, both parts have the same theme, which conveys their happiness now that they are together once more[1]:

Ex. 214

This theme is first heard in the First Act, at the point in Yaroslavna's Arioso when she says: 'I often dream that my lover has returned' (phrase 1 of Ex. 214) and 'he holds my hands and calls my name'

---

[1] This theme is written in an abbreviated form.

(phrase 2). Thus, Borodin uses the same theme for the dream meeting, and the real meeting. (The keys and harmonies are different however.) The duet begins with the words: 'It cannot be . . . It is a dream'.[1]

Let us now examine the musical ideas associated with Yaroslavna. We shall begin with her arioso, in Act I, Scene 2. In this monologue the princess expresses her anxiety at the lack of any sort of news of her husband, and her sadness at being separated from him. She recalls her happy days which are now past, and is disturbed by the sinister dreams she has recently had. The main theme of the arioso is the phrase:

Ex. 215

In writing this, in 1869, Borodin probably made use of tunes from the ballads 'The Terrible Tsar' and the song 'The Nightingale'.[2] The first and final sections of the arioso are based almost entirely on this theme.[3]

[1] It is interesting to note that the theme of the duet, like the motif of the final chorus, is, in its own way, a kind of 'musical surmounting' of the doleful significance of 'The Sparrow Hills'. A fragment of this motif (bracket 1) is cut short by a joyful ascending modulation into the major. The mournful character of the motif in bracket 2 (which also stems from 'The Sparrow Hills') is neutralized to some extent by the rising sequence (with a major harmonization) which occurs in the following bars. In the duet, the appearance of grief is real; in the arioso (the account of the dream), it is only assumed.

[2] This is evident from the following comparisons:

(a) Yaroslavna's Arioso
(b) Ballad 'The Nightingale'
(c) Ballad 'The Terrible Tsar', transposed down a minor third

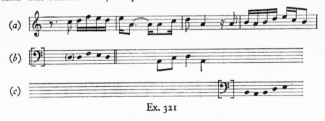

Ex. 321

[3] This melody acts as an episodic motif:

Ex. 322

It was introduced into 'the theme of Yaroslavna's love and faith' at a later date (1875).

In the middle section (key signature of 3 sharps) there is another theme of some importance; it is a free variation on the latter theme, and is as follows:

Ex. 216

We now pass to an analysis of the themes of Yaroslavna's Lament (in Act 4). Here, Borodin kept very close to the words of the Igor Chronicle, and recreated the atmosphere of Russian antiquity more successfully than anywhere else. Yaroslavna is lamenting the fate of her captive husband, and calls on the elements—the wind, the river Dnieper and the sun—and upbraids them for their neglect of her husband in refusing him help in battle. Thus we find idealism and human feeling side by side with animism, and echoes of past beliefs in inanimate nature. To achieve this, Borodin used a free variation form, based on two main themes (a sort of Rondo).

(1) The first theme, with which the introduction begins, may be called 'the theme of lamentation'. This is in the spirit of the peasant's funeral lamentation (in the Phrygian mode with a key signature of 2 sharps):

Ex. 217

This probably evolved from a shorter phrase, by means of a repetition of certain motifs in it. It is quite possible that the skeleton of this theme arose out of motifs 1, 4, and 5, and took shape in the following manner:

(*a*) Sections 1, 4, and 5 from theme 1 of the lament
(*b*) Motif from the ballad 'The Terrible Tsar', transposed down a minor third

Ex. 218

The theme is clearly derived from the ballad 'The Terrible Tsar'.

The ending of the first section of 'The Lament' is taken from the ballad 'The Bird':

The ballad of 'The Bird', transposed up a major third

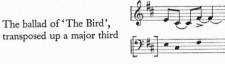

Ex. 219

Yaroslavna dreams of the time when she will see her husband again. She says she would like to fly 'like a cuckoo on the wing' across the Polovtsian steppes to tend her husband's wounds.

At the beginning of this section (the second section) we hear the theme of 'love and fidelity' again, which came in Igor's Aria in Act II, 'You alone, my dearest dove'. The end of section 2 (where she wants to tend her husband's wounds) is based on the theme:

Ex. 220

This theme is a free variation on the 'lamentation'. The bracketed notes also appear in Yaroslavna's arioso (where she confesses she cannot restrain her tears).

The third section is a repeat of the first (orchestra only). After it, Yaroslavna calls on the 'wild wind'. She reproaches the wind for not coming to the assistance of her husband. It consists of a song in three parts, the first and final sections being based on the theme:

Ex. 221

this is made up from the 'love and fidelity' theme (first bar) and the theme of 'lamentation' (second bar) and the beginning of the central theme of the arioso (A). The middle part of this section has the theme which concluded the second section.

The fifth section begins with a repeat of the lamentation theme. This is followed by a prayer to the River Dnieper to return to her her beloved husband. The principal theme here consists of a free variation on the 'lamentation' theme, with the addition of a motif heard in the arioso.[1] In the middle of this section we hear 'the cleansing of wounds' motif (from the second section); after this there is an elaboration of fragments of the theme of 'lamentation'.

In the sixth and final section, Yaroslavna turns to the sun. She is indignant that the kindly sun should have tormented Igor's friends with its scorching heat. The main theme here is that of 'love and fidelity'; in the middle of all this we hear the 'cleansing of wounds' motif. This also appears at the end of the section.

The 'Lament' ends with a phrase taken from the theme of 'lamentation'.

In these two major numbers, which feature Yaroslavna, she is portrayed as a loving, faithful companion of Igor, languishing over her separation from her husband. But in some of her phrases there are motifs which are not immediately associated with her. Here I shall take only examples derived from the folk-song 'The Sparrow Hills'. I have already mentioned the descending-scale motif in this song, which occur in Yaroslavna's part in the Finale of Act I.

We find the very same motif in the arioso (Act I, Scene 2)

Ex. 222

and in the Prologue (the words are: 'I have no strength to restrain my prophetic heart'):

Ex. 223

(As regards the position of the semitones, the phrase does not coincide completely with 'The Sparrow Hills'; the motif starts elsewhere in the

---

[1] I have in mind the motif

Ex. 323

the analogy of which is constantly encountered in the Arioso (pp. 77–84 of the vocal score).

scale.) Finally, we find this phrase in Yaroslavna's recitative in Act IV.[1]

We now turn to musical portrayal of Vladimir Galitsky—the rake and adventurer.

In presenting this character, Borodin stands out clearly as humorist and psychologist of considerable subtlety. Galitsky is portrayed most convincingly, and with a minimum of characterization. His entry leitmotif is primitive but appropriate, and may be referred to as the 'tempestuous' leitmotif:[2]

Impetuoso e vivo

Ex. 224

Vladimir Galitsky makes his worldly ambitions quite explicit to his followers in his well-known song, beginning with the words: 'If only I could honour gain, then on Putivl's throne I would reign.' The themes of the first and third part of this song are built up from motifs found in the ballads. This becomes apparent from the following comparison:

(*a*) Galitsky's Song: p. 45
(*b*) Ballad 'The Terrible Tsar': p. 1–2
(*c*) Ballad 'The Nightingale'
(*d*) Ballad 'The Bird'

Allegro moderato

Ex. 225

(Here, the tunes from the ballads are transposed into the same key.)

[1] At the words, 'Have the Polovtsi come upon us unawares?':

Ex. 324

[2] See p. 45 of the vocal score. This leitmotif is played a minor third higher (in F♯ minor) on pp. 96 and 105 (in the scene with Yaroslavna).

The middle section (the 'erotic') of this song introduces a second theme which probably originates from 'The Bird':

(a) *Igor*, p. 47.

(b) Ballad of 'The Birds', transposed into E flat minor

Ex. 226

Later we see his reactions when things are not turning out as he had expected. His reply to the maidens when they ask for the return of their friends is phrased as follows:

Ex. 227

and is closely linked with the theme of the chorus: 'The acolytes of the prince were on the prowl', at the beginning of Act I, Scene 1.

Galitsky's next appearance (Act I, Scene 2, p. 97) when he refuses Yaroslavna's request, plainly shows his rakish impudence. This theme, as we see below, could possibly have some genetic relationship with the tunes of the ballads:

(a) *Igor*, p. 97.
(b) Tune of 'The Terrible Tsar', transposed into E minor (the repeat of the tune is my own)
(c) Ballad of 'The Bird', transposed up a tone

Ex. 228

and is characteristic to the highest degree. It is interesting to note that the first motif (the one resembling 'The Terrible Tsar') is strongly reminiscent of the motif in Igor's Aria where we hear the emphatic words: 'I can redeem my own shame, and save my honour and glory', etc.[1]

Some of Galitsky's motifs in the Prologue are heard again later in the First Act; here Borodin throws into relief in a highly subtle manner his insincerity and immorality. The motif just quoted occurs at the point where Galitsky replies to Igor with the words: 'I am more than a little obliged to you.' The note sequence: F–G, F–G, F–G signifies Igor's kindness to him in defending him against this own father and brothers (p. 30); this is heard once again in the scene with Yaroslava, where Galitsky contemptuously demands that his sister should treat him with due respect. The 'magnanimous hero' of the Prologue proves to be nothing more than a worthless adventurer by the end of the First Act.

It now remains for us to take a closer look at the musical profile of Prince Vladimir, Igor's son.[2] His part, as befits him, is a small one, and he agrees with the historical data in having a weak and uninspiring character.

In his recitative at the beginning of Act II, his theme is a mere echo of his father's motif:

Theme from Vladimir's
recitative: p. 150

Igor's leitmotif,
transposed into C minor: p. 23

Ex. 229

This theme suggests Vladimir's kinship with his father, and yet, since it is a variant of his father's motif, emphasizes the difference between them. Igor's leitmotif is that of a calm and resolute nature, whilst Vladimir's variant is more passive suggesting his passion and impressionability.

Next comes Vladimir's monologue, in which he anticipates his

[1] We reproduce here both motifs for comparison:

Igor's Aria: p. 171
Galitsky's part,
transposed up a semitone: p. 97

Ex. 325

[2] Unfortunately, it is impossible to dwell upon the characters of Skula and Eroshka in detail. I trust that the brief references made to them above will be sufficient.

rendezvous with Konchak's daughter. It is a cavatina, and is built on two main themes as a rondo (A–B–A–B). The first theme has a marked Russian flavour:

Ex. 230

It is made up of variations and repetitions of the following fragment:[1]

Ex. 231

The second theme consists of two motifs, which might be considered as variants of a single rhythmical scheme:

Motif 1
(F major):
p. 153

Motif 2
(F major)

Ex. 232

The first is a kind of introduction, while the second is played a number of times and forms the main body of section B of the Cavatina.

It is worth mentioning that the second motif almost exactly reproduces one of the motifs of the Chorus of Praise, borrowed from the idol scene in *Mlada*. The prince's words of love are sung to this very same tune as Vladimir's, when he is about to go to war. Perhaps this is a reflection of Borodin's ironic attitude towards his young 'hero'.

There is nothing of particular importance in Vladimir's duet with Konchak's daughter, for the leading rôle is undoubtedly taken by the passionate, love-hungry princess.

To sum up, the use of leitmotifs is in direct proportion to the relative dominance of each individual character. Both Igor and Yaroslavna have motifs which characterize not only their personalities

---

[1] Similar melodies are found in, for example, the ballad 'The Terrible Tsar Ivan Vasilyevich'.

but even their moods, and states of mind. Galitsky has only one motif, and the expression of his moods is not clearly distinguishable from the general spirit of the choruses of his confrères. Prince Vladimir is a weak and passive character, and hence has no real motifs of his own, but relies on echoes of those of others.

IV

Our next concern is with those parts of the opera which feature the oriental, nomadic Polovtsi. It is extremely difficult to trace Borodin's sources, and there is much room for speculation. I shall therefore confine my study within the strictest limits, and shall consider only the probable sources.

Borodin began work on the 'Polovtsian' sections of his opera in the winter of 1874–5, and he had completed most of it by the end of 1877. In fact, the only sections which he did not finish in this period were Ovlur's scenes in the Second Act, and Igor's conversation with Konchak. It is quite certain that the composer considerably modified his approach to this oriental music during this comparatively long period. At first, apparently, he had no intention whatsoever of bringing out the national flavour in his Polovtsian numbers. For example, there is a rough copy belonging to this period with the heading: 'Material intended for Konchak's daughter or Yaroslavna, suitable for an impassioned, dramatic recitative.'[1] There is a whole 'supply' of music which Borodin considered suitable for two characters of completely different racial origin.

This sketch:

Ex. 233

could possible have been (with the exception of the two B's) the framework of Yaroslavna's theme:

Ex. 234

Several other tunes from this sketch appear in the final version of her recitative in Act IV, both in the vocal line itself, and in the orchestral

---

[1] The original of this remarkable sketch is preserved in the Saltikov-Shchedrin Public Library in Leningrad (Rimsky-Korsakov archive No. 118).

parts. On the other hand, the same motif was used in a slightly adapted form in Konchak's daughter's duet in Act II. We notice also that the melody of the Chorus of Peasants from the Fourth Act:

Ex. 235

and the opening of the Chorus of Prisoners: 'Fly away on the wings of the wind', in the Second Act

Ex. 236

are variants of the opening of Yaroslavna's recitative, given above, as it appears in Act IV. (It is most probable that the composer associated this motif with the mood of sadness.)

It is hardly conceivable, however, that Borodin could have got very far with his opera before coming into contact with folk-music material that would have lent itself to the general colour of his epic. But to incorporate the material that came to hand was no easy matter. Information about the music of the ancient Polovtsi, without going into the ethnography and history of this people, seemed hard to come by. The fact that Cui, a close friend of his, was opposed to any kind of 'ethnographical tendency'[1] in music did not help matters. At the same time, Borodin was determined to finish his 'oriental' numbers as quickly as possible, and this naturally did not leave much time for research into folk-lore collections.

It is no wonder then that the first numbers to the Polovtsian scenes of his opera (from the chronological point of view) contained pseudo-oriental music of an exotic nature, which was all he knew at the time.

Although we cannot discount the possibility of Borodin's 'oriental' music in these numbers being entirely spontaneous, there are nevertheless reasons to suppose that he drew on the experience of others:

(1) He had grown up with the music of Glinka's *Ruslan*.

(2) In the autumn of 1859, he heard Mussorgsky play his B flat major Scherzo, and was fascinated by the oriental motifs in the Trio section in particular.[2]

[1] It is quite possible that Cui's objections were one of the reasons for Borodin's wishing to conceal the fact that he had used Russian ballads and folk-songs in the composition of *Igor*, 'The Sparrow Hills' in particular.

[2] See *Letters*, Vol. IV, p. 298.

(3) In 1860 and 1861, during his stay abroad, he came by Salvador-Daniel's collection of Arabian folk-songs. It was Catherine Tolstoy who sent him a copy of them.[1]

(4) About the same time (perhaps in the summer of 1860), Borodin made a copy of L. Gottschalk's 'Le Bananier', based on negro melodies.[2]

(5) While in Paris (at the end of 1859 or in the winter of 1860–1) Borodin acquired two of Salvador-Daniel's songs, based on Algerian and Tunisian themes, published by Richaud.[3]

(6) Rimsky-Korsakov's symphonic suite *Antar* was very well known to him.

(7) At the end of the sixties, he became acquainted with Balakirev's romances on eastern themes, his sketches for *Tamara* and *The Firebird*, and his fantasy *Islamey*.

(8) It is probable also that before the end of the same period he heard Felicien David's symphonic ode *Le Desert*.

Borodin had therefore a fairly wide choice of material from which he could gain some idea of the different styles of Eastern music; for example the difference between Arabo-Persian and Tartar music. What particularly struck him was their similarity, and was impressed by the extensive influence Arabo-Persian music had had on other cultures.

In the early stages of his work on the 'Polovtsian' sections of his opera, Borodin no doubt felt it would be legitimate to make use of at least some elements of Arabian musical folk-lore. In actual fact, when taking a close look at the Second Act of *Igor* we notice that the refrain of the Polovtsian women's song:

P. 125

Ex. 237

[1] One may learn this from Rimsky-Korsakov's *Chronicle of My Musical Life* and from S. M. Lyapunov's notes to Rimsky-Korsakov's correspondence with Balakirev (*Muzikalni Sovremennik*, 1916–17, No. 1, p. 85, note 2). The date when Borodin received the Salvador-Daniel collection can be determined from data given in E. F. Tolstaya's reminiscences of Borodin.

[2] L. M. Gottschalk, 'Le Bananier', Chanson nègre, op. 5, Mayence, Schott. Borodin's original copy is now in my music library.

[3] Fço Salvador-Daniel, 'Soleima', Chanson Mauresque de Tunis, Sur le Mode Zeïdan. Paroles imitées de celles de la dernière Chanson de Mourakkich (l'Ancien). Paris, S. Richaud, Editeur.

Fço Salvador-Daniel, 'Heuss ed Douvo', Chanson mauresque d'Alger, Sur le Mode Meïa. Paroles imitées de celles de la Kacidah Arabe. Paris, S. Richaud, Editeur.

The copies of these two songs are now in my music library.

is taken, with only slight modification (omission of a C sharp, indicated with a cross), straight out of the Tunisian song 'Soleima' (bars 8–10):

Ex. 238

The same melody is found yet again in the same number in a different form

P. 125

Ex. 239

together with a rhythmical variant of the same melody, with an addition of several notes:

Ex. 240

This is the ending of the song of the Polovtsian girl, and of the Chorus of Polovtsian Women which follows.

The motif from the Arabian song, cited above, was originally earmarked for Konchak's recitative; in a note found in the file for the libretto we find the following sketches:

     Liu-bliu! ti smel i prav-di ne bo-ish-sya
(1) D C♯ C♯ B♭ A G A B♭ D C♯ B♭
     (I like you! You are brave and fearless.)

     za eto ved ya i liu-bliu teb-ya.
(2) G AB♭ B♭ B♭ B♭ D C♯ B♭ A
     (you know, I respect you for it.)

The following comparison shows that both were actually based on the song 'Soleima':

Konchak (1)

Soleima

bars 7 8 9

Konchak (2)

Soleima

bars 8 9

Ex. 241

(In these examples, the notes given as letters in Borodin's sketch are replaced by notes of quaver value, without any division into bars.)

Subsequently, Borodin made certain alterations to Konchak's recitative; in the score, the first of the phrases outlined above has the following shape:

Ex. 242

The second phrase was not included.

Although Borodin set out to avoid 'arabisms' in Konchak's parts in the Second Act, he did not manage to exclude them completely. The beginning of Konchak's song in Act III[1] (preserved thanks to Glazunov's memory) is obviously derived from the seventh bar of 'Soleima'[2]:

Ex. 243

Borodin used still another motif from the same song:

'Soleima': bars 13–14;
p. 3

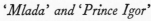

Ex. 244

[1] See Glazunov's note on his Editorial work on *Igor*. (Also in Belyaeu's book *Glazunov* (St. Petersburg, 1924), p. 124, the words: 'No. 19. Konchak's song. I remembered the first two bars.)

[2] This tetrachord in the song 'Soleima', which is found on the 12th degree of the tempered Moorish mode Zeïdan (= Arabic mode *Rehawi*), is encountered also in Tartar folk-songs, possibly as a result of Arabian influence.

which serves as the basis of[1]:

Igor pp. 202–206

Ex. 245

a motif appearing in the Polovtsian Dances.

He also probably made use of the Algerian song 'Heuss ed Douro' in the Polovtsian numbers. In particular, the cadence:

'Heuss ed Douro':
p. 2; bars 8–10
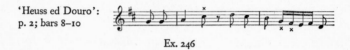

Ex. 246

might be the basis of the familiar phrase in Konchak's Aria:

Ex. 247

Gottschalk's 'Le Bananier' played an exceptionally important part in the formation of the themes for the Polovtsian numbers. One motif in particular:

'Le Bananier': p. 2;
bars 6–7

Ex. 248

and variants thereof[2]:

'Le Bananier': p. 3; bars 4–5

Ex. 249

'Le Bananier': p. 3; bars 5–6

Ex. 250

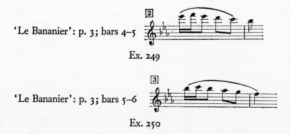

---

[1] Part of the melody in brackets corresponds with a motif from 'Soleima'.

[2] In this piece by Gottschalk, motifs [2] and [3] follow consecutively so that the final note of [2] becomes the first note of [3].

and a further related motif[1]:

'Le Bananier': p. 3; bars 4–5

Ex. 251

are of some importance. For example, motif (1) is used in Konchak's Aria as follows:

Ex. 252

Ex. 253

and appears in the 'Polovtsian Dances'[2]:

Ex. 254

The second motif, with a semitone between the third and fourth notes, is to be found in the Chorus of Women Prisoners:

Ex. 255

We also meet with it in the ballet scenes:

Ex. 256

The same motif is the unmistakable starting-point of the theme of the 'Polovtsian Patrol', written not long before his death:

Ex. 257

It is also possible to stretch the comparison to one of the motifs of the 'Dance of the Sentries' in Act III[3], which appears to be nothing

---

[1] Motif [4], indicated by a bracket, may be regarded as identical with motif [3] with the addition of a 'C' to the left, and the deletion of an 'F' to the right.

[2] The notes corresponding to the motif in question are marked by a horizontal bracket.

[3] According to Glazunov, this theme 'is found in a manuscript' (of Borodin). See *Glazunov*, p. 124.

more than a theme from the 'Patrol' in augmentation and transposed a fifth higher:

Ex. 258

The only other case, in which this motif (motif 2) appears, is in the opening of the Chorus of Polovtsian Maidens and the Song of the Polovtsian Women (cf. the notes in brackets):

Ex. 259

Motif (3) occurs in its original key, and almost unchanged, in Konchak's Aria[1]:

Ex. 260

In the same number, the motif reappears, this time rhythmically transformed[2]:

Ex. 261

It is also to be found in the Chorus of Women Prisoners in Act II:

Ex. 262

Lastly, we come across this motif in the final 'Moderato alla breve' with the following rhythmical shape:

Ex. 263

---

[1] The same motif is found: (1) transposed a fourth lower on p. 185 (bars 11–12 from the beginning of the Andantino) and on p. 188 (bars 16–17); (2) transposed a fifth higher on p. 191 (bars 21–22).

[2] This motif is found written a fourth lower on p. 185 of the vocal score (bars 6–7 from the beginning of the Andantino), and on p. 188 (bars 11–12).

Motif (4) may be found in the Chorus of Women Prisoners[1],[2]:

Ex. 264

It appears too in augmentation, at the end of the same chorus:

Ex. 265

In shaping his themes, Borodin transformed the borrowed motifs not only rhythmically, but melodically as well. There is no need to list completely all the variants of the four motifs; I shall single out only the most important:

(1) All the variants occur in the Chorus of Women Prisoners (cf. pp. 197–8; 212–19).

(2) Motifs (3) and (4) appear in Konchak's Aria, with the last note altered in each case.[3]

(3) In the Polovtsian Dances we find the first three motifs, with the first note lowered one tone in each case:

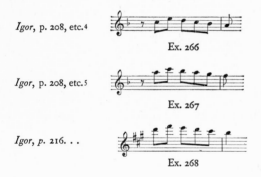

Igor, p. 208, etc.[4]

Ex. 266

Igor, p. 208, etc.[5]

Ex. 267

Igor, p. 216. . .

Ex. 268

[1] The notes corresponding to the motif in question are marked by a horizontal bracket.

[2] The same motif is found on p. 198 (bar 5), written a tone lower.

[3] See vocal score, p. 187 (bar 9), after the direction 'pochissimo'; p. 191 (bar 5), after the Poco più vivo; p. 187 (bar 1); p. 189 (4 bars before the Allegro moderato).

[4] On p. 208 of the vocal score (bars 12–13, 16–17); p. 209, transposed a fourth higher with a change in the position of the semitone, and on p. 211 (bars 18–19, 22–23), transposed down a fourth with a similar change in the position of the semitone.

[5] On p. 208 (bars 20–21, 24–25); p. 209 (bars 10–11, 14–15), transposed down a fourth with a semitone between the penultimate and final note, and on p. 211 (bars 26–27); p. 212 (bars 2–3), transposed down a fourth.

These motifs occur, with a different rhythm, and without the last note in the following:

Ex. 269

(4) Motif (3), transposed down a fourth, is of some importance in Ovlur's recitative (No. 14).[1]

(5) The following motif:[2]

Ex. 270

is one of the most important elements in the Polovtsian Dances; it is without doubt a melodic variation on the second example given as an illustration of the use of motif (2), besides being a variant of motif (2) from 'Le Bananier'.

(6) There is a motif in Konchak's Daughter's Arioso, which seems to be a free variation of motif (3):[3]

Ex. 271

In dealing with the Arabian and other exotic elements in the Polovtsian Dances, we have by no means exhausted Borodin's sources.[4] As the reader will remember (cf. Chapter IV), in the mid-

[1] See vocal score, p. 177 (bars 13–14); p. 179 (bars 4–5).

[2] The notes marked with a cross correspond with similar notes in the motif from the 'Polovtsian Dances' (see Ex. 269) quoted in the text. The note 'F' only serves as a connecting link and acts as a point of imitation.

[3] The main change here is that there is an additional semitone. This motif is found on p. 137 (bars 7–8) of the vocal score, p. 139 (bars 8–9), and on p. 140 (bars 1–2, 3–4). In the third and fourth instances, the motif is transposed a fourth higher.

[4] In view of the great influence of Arab culture on the life and art of Negro tribes, it is quite possible that there is a connection between the Negro motifs from 'Le Bananier' and the Arab melodies. As the celebrated expert on Arabian art, the late Professor E. Bertels justly observed in reply to my query, in order to determine the relationship between them, one would have to find out from what part of Africa the natives who introduced 'Le Bananier' originated, from whom L. Gottschalk in Louisiana drew his material. To arrive at an answer to this problem by means of comparison of the Arabian folk-tunes and the motives from 'Le Bananier' would only be possible after prolonged specialized investigation.

seventies Borodin was given some insight into the nature of the folk-music of the ancient Polovtsi by V. N. Mainov, the ethnographer, and P. Hunfalvy, the Hungarian ethnographer and explorer.[1] The information Borodin received was as follows:

(1) Polovtsian music (*a*) resembled the folk music of the Chuvash and Bashkirs, and not the refined music of the Arabs; (*b*) was based on a succession of harsh sounds, similar to those heard on the dudok.

(2) Since it was a fact that descendants of the Polovtsi were now in Hungary, the music of the Polovtsi might be taken as being that of present-day Hungary.

Mainov forwarded to Stassov a list of Hungarian folk collections, in particular, the title of a collection of Polovtsian folk-songs.[2] In addition to this, Stassov had asked him to let Borodin have some of the folk-tunes of the Finno-Ugrian peoples which Hunfalvy had recorded in Central Asia and in the Polovtsian districts of Hungary.[3]

These lists are not actually among Borodin's archive material, but it would be wrong to suppose on this account that he never used them. It is known however that the Public Library acquired a copy of one such collection (in 1877).[4]

Let us try to determine the extent of the ethnographers' influence on Borodin.

First of all, there is no doubt at all that Mainov's information about the differences between Arabian and Polovtsian music did give him food for thought. He wanted to keep the music he had already written for the Chorus of Prisoners, and to circumvent his ethnographical inaccuracy, even considered renaming his prisoners, 'Slaves from the other side of the Caspian'.[5] In Stassov's original scenario there is no mention of any such slaves of Konchak. This is yet another instance of the many innovations made in the scenario by Borodin himself.

Mainov's contention that the Turko-Ugrian folk-music at the time

---

[1] Unfortunately I could not discover whether this was before or after the composition of the Polovtsian Dances.

[2] See my *Borodin*, Russian 2nd ed., pp. 338–9.

[3] See Stassov's book on Borodin, pp. 36–37.

[4] According to letters which I received from the advisory bureau and administration of the Saltikov-Shchedrin Public Library in Leningrad, the following volume was ordered by Stassov in 1877: 'Törteneti, Bibliai és günyoros Magyar enekek Dallamai a XVI szàzadbol. A Magyar tudomanyos akademia megbizasabol meglejtve kazli Mátray Gábor. [Mélodies de Chant Hongrois historiques, bibliques et satyriques du XVI-mè siècle publiées par ordre de l'Académie Hongroise par M. Gabliel Matray.] Pesten, 1859.

[5] We remember Konchak's words: 'Do you see the prisoners from the distant sea? Do you see my beauties from beyond the Caspian?' (vocal score, p. 204).

of the Tartar invasions was in an exceedingly primitive state was taken seriously by Borodin, when he came to compose the male chorus of the Polovtsian Dances:

Ex. 272

The 'guttural pipe notes', mentioned in Mainov's letter, are clearly visible in many of the motifs in the Polovtsian sections of *Igor*; for example:

Ex. 273

all of which are vividly suggestive of pipes.

In order to determine the extent of Borodin's use of Hungarian folk-tunes, we shall have to make a comparison between Polovtsian themes and the Hungarian songs possibly known to Borodin. The most obvious procedure was to consult the folk-song collections in the Leningrad Public Library.

There were in all five collections of Hungarian songs in the Leningrad Library[1]; I asked my colleague N. V. Shelkov if he would kindly make a detailed study of them on my behalf, and to make a note of any that bore any resemblance to the Polovtsian tunes in *Igor*. Altogether, he found three tunes that were pertinent to the present enquiry.

[1] The titles of these five volumes are as follows:
  (1) The collection of Mátray Gábor referred to in note 4, p. 315.
  (2) 'Ungarische Volkslieder. Ausgewählt, Übersetzt und mit Benutzung der besten Bearbeitungen herausgegeben von Dr. Heinrich Möller.' B. Schotts Söhne, Mainz-Paris.
  (3) B. Bartók. 'Das Ungarische Volkslied, Versuch einer Systematisierung der ungarischen Bauernmelodien. Mit 320 Melodien.' Berlin-Leipzig, 1925.
  (4) B. Bartók. 'Acht ungarische Volkslieder. Nyole magyar népdal. Gesang und Klavier.' Universal-Edition. 1922.
  (5) 'Népszinházi müsorozat. A magyar nepszinhazban enekelt.' Budapest. Piznitzer-Trigyes. [100 songs in 12 music books.]

All three are taken from Béla Bartók's collection of 1925. Here they are, with their references:

(I) Muz.f.460 (d), *IV*. Szentegyházasfalu, Tankó Jozsefne; *V.*[1]

parlando

Ex. 274

(II) Muz.f.16 (B), *III*. Szegvar, Szarvas Pal; *V.*[2]

Ex. 275

(III) Bekésgyula, *III*. es Panna (18), 1906, 13.[3]

Ex. 276

Comparison reveals the following:
(1) It is not difficult to see a resemblance between Ex. 2 of the Hungarian motifs and Ovlur's leitmotif:

Ex. 2 transposed down a semitone

Igor: p. 177 ff.

Ex. 277

[1] See B. Bartók, loc. cit., music supplement, p. 5, No. 17.
[2] Ibid., p. 12, No. 47.
[3] Ibid., p. 26, No. 93ᵃ.

(2) In the same song we find a cadence of a minor third which occurs in the scene with Ovlur[1]:

Ex. 2 transposed
down a minor third

P. 181

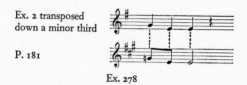

Ex. 278

(3) There is certain resemblances between parts of Ovlur's motif and fragments of the last two bars of Ex. 3. (For the sake of convenience, I have transposed the minor ending of Ovlur's leitmotif up a tone.)

Ex. 3 transposed
down a semitone

P. 177

Ex. 279

(4) After close examination, it would appear that Ex. 2 is identical with Konchak's daughter's motif in her duet in Act II[2]:

Ex. 2 transposed
down a fourth

P. 158

Ex. 280

[1] I have heard a number of criticisms of the comparison between the ending of example [2] and the theme of Ovlur as illustrated in the text. It has been asserted that in Hungarian folk-song the ending is always on the tonic, whereas in the scene with Ovlur the G♮ is a seventh and the E a fifth. I thing that this objection arises either through a misunderstanding, or from the fact that the composer did not have any definite harmony in mind when he borrowed the motif. Perhaps he did not know then where and how he would use the ending. In addition to this, Ovlur's theme cannot really be regarded as being in the key of A minor. It lies either in the Phrygian mode (in which case it is E minor minus the F♯), or in E minor (minus F♯ and F♮). The pedal point in the bass, A–E, does not affect the essence of this matter. These opinions are based on a misunderstanding of the process of 'transplanting' the melodies and from a tendency to criticize the music from a theoretical standpoint which is impossible in practice.

[2] In comparing the notes underlined in Konchak's Daughter's theme with the motif which appears in the sketch headed, 'Materials for Konchak's Daughter or Yaroslavna', we observe that these two themes differ only by one note which is unessential in the melodic outline.

(5) One of the sections of Konchak's Daughter's Arioso is based, in melismatic form, on motifs from Ex. 2:

Pp. 137–8

Ex. 2 transposed down a tone

Idem

Ex. 281

(6) Motif 1 seems to be connected with one of the melodies of Konchak's Daughter's Arioso:

Ex. 1 transposed up a semitone

P. 137

Ex. 282

As a result of these comparisons, the following points are to be noted:

(1) Béla Bartók's collection, from which these melodies were taken, was made in the twentieth century. Thus, although it is a systematic summary of Magyar peasant songs, it is by no means certain that Borodin had these songs at his disposal.

(2) Nevertheless, some of these Hungarian folk-tunes are so similar to the Polovtsian themes (for example, Ovlur's leitmotif, and one of the phrases from Konchak's daughter's duet in Act II, and some parts of her arioso) that the resemblances can hardly be regarded as coincidental.

(3) It seems then, that Borodin not only made use of Hungarian folk-songs but even consciously worked them into these numbers. In other words, our comparison supports Stassov's statement.

It is possible that Borodin's discovery of Hungarian folk-music led him to reconsider the numbers he had already written,[1] but it

---

[1] It is interesting to remember the following phrase from Rimsky-Korsakov's memoirs which relate to 1877 (3rd ed., p. 202): 'The charming aria of Konchak's daughter remained uncompleted; it was being altered, transposed and played in fragments in a variety of forms.' It is quite possible that the aria, originally composed in the beginning of 1875, was adapted here in accordance with the folk-lore material received later. (Its final formulation did not take place till the autumn of 1884.)

may nevertheless have confirmed him in his previous choice of material.

We have no definite information about any amendments or corrections, but I shall mention one interesting fact. One of the motifs taken from 'Le Bananier' is very similar to bars 3 and 5 of Ex. 3. This may be seen from the following comparison:

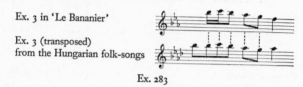

Ex. 3 in 'Le Bananier'

Ex. 3 (transposed) from the Hungarian folk-songs

Ex. 283

The motif of the Hungarian folk-song has the same notes as the motif from 'Le Bananier', with the exception of the last note. It would be foolish to exaggerate the significance of this, but it is nevertheless true that such comparisons are productive when dealing with Borodin's work as a whole. In this case, the composer might have seen that the original motif he chose from 'Le Bananier' was not far removed from the true character of Hungarian folk-music, or the music of the ancient Polovtsi.[1]

Here are a few conclusions. Our analysis of the Polovtsian numbers of *Igor* shows what an enormous amount of work Borodin put into

[1] If this is the case, it complicates the genealogy of Ovlur's leitmotif still further. Its origin seems to lie not only in fragments of the Hungarian song and the Algerian song 'Heuss ed Douro' but also (*horribile!*) in a motif from the ballad 'The Terrible Tsar Ivan Vasilyevich':

(*a*) Ovlur's leitmotif
(*b*) 'Heuss ed Douro': bars 4–6
(*c*) Motif from the ballad 'The Terrible Tsar', transposed down a minor third

Ex. 326 (*a*)

However this may be, the scene with Ovlur did not receive its final formulation till the last few months of the composer's life. I have seen two different sketches of the same scene by Borodin in the Rimsky-Korsakov archive of the Leningrad Public Library.

them. He knew nothing of Polovtsian folk-culture when he started work on the Polovtsian sections of his opera, and consequently made use of the 'accepted dialect' or oriental music. Yet, when he came by precise ethnographical information, he revised some of what he had already written, and composed a series of completely new numbers based on Hungarian folk-songs.[1] Through this work he became more and more master of his talent, but it did not stifle his spontaneity. Act II, in fact, shows the unmistakable marks of genius.

V

At the end of Chapter V, I explained that Glazunov and Rimsky-Korsakov put the finishing touches to *Igor* after the composer's death. Let us return to this matter, and decide how much of the published score of the opera is actually Borodin's own work. According to Glazunov, Borodin himself completed the Prologue, Act I, Scene 1, and the whole of Act IV. The short recitative of Yaroslavna in Act I, Scene 2 (before the entrance of the boyars) was the work of Rimsky-Korsakov, who was following the composer's strict instructions. Rimsky-Korsakov also wrote the concluding section of this scene, which had been left incomplete by the exclusion of a section involving a rebellion of Galitsky's supporters. As before, Rimsky-Korsakov used Borodin's own directions and material as far as possible, but introduced a new element—'the shrieks of women off stage'.

Most of the accretions to Act II are not very important: for example, the two-bar introduction to the Song of the Polovtsian Women, which was later added by Glazunov; the ritornello in the Chorus of Russian Prisoners, also the work of Glazunov. There are however two fundamental modifications made by Rimsky-Korsakov: (1) the addition of a contrapuntal line in the dance of the Polovtsian women; and (2) the introduction of a chorus which joins Konchak's daughter during her aria. These two additions are not at all necessary, and seem to me somewhat arbitrary. They are, though, so insignificant that their removal would hardly be noticed.

Act III, with the exception of the 'Polovtsian March', contains only Borodin's music, but had to be reconstructed by Glazunov and Rimsky-Korsakov from sketches left by the composer. At present,

---

[1] Borodin did not know then that the direct descendants of the Polovtsians, the Kumyk, lived (and still live) in the territory of Dagestan. Today this people has developed a national culture and is studying its native folk-lore. It would be interesting to compare the Kumyk songs with Borodin's Polovtsian music.

it is not easy to assess the degree of correspondence between the composer's intentions and the work of the editors. It is of course certain
that no one would have carried out this task of reconstruction better
than these two composers. Even so, one notices a certain strain and
artificiality in some places (especially in those passages 'transplanted'
from *Mlada*). It was certainly not Borodin who turned the 'Apparition of the Spirits' into the eclipse scene.[1]

What form did Glazunov and Rimsky-Korsakov's editing of *Igor*
take? One thing is certain; Rimsky-Korsakov treated the music of
Borodin and Mussorgsky quite differently. We have to be thankful
for the fact that it is entirely due to the efforts of Glazunov and
Rimsky-Korsakov that we are able to hear the opera performed; we
can therefore forgive them the minor changes and occasional trivialities they introduced. Borodin was a highly developed and experienced
composer, and for this reason his editors were not faced with the task
of rendering his work articulate. We ought therefore to regard the
opera, as it stands today, as entirely in the spirit of the composer's
original intentions.

Borodin's orchestration is quite another matter. We know that
Borodin was a master of orchestral technique, and that, when he was
writing a particular orchestral work, he always heard it as it would
eventually sound, and was never in the position of having to ornament
a piano score with suitable orchestral timbres. For this reason, the
compilation of a large orchestral score was for him 'an enormous piece
of mechanical drudgery' which he found great difficulty in finishing
on account of his many 'commitments'. Consequently, he did not get
as far as writing the score for *Igor*, but limited himself to a piano-duet
version with a few indications as to the eventual instrumentation he had

---

[1] I have in mind here the trio for Konchak's Daughter, Vladimir Igorevich, and Igor
composed by Glazunov, which was constructed in accordance with Borodin's intentions
on Voyslava's theme from *Mlada*:

Ex. 327

However, one must confess that there is a certain stiffness about this number which
Borodin would have removed by altering the theme. Glazunov decided to leave it
untouched.

in mind. The only numbers he orchestrated were those that were to be given a separate performance at various concerts, before the opera was finished. Here is a list of the numbers which he orchestrated himself:

(1) Introduction to the Prologue.
(2) The end of the Prologue, from the words, 'It is time for us to leave' (p. 31).
(3) Prince Galitsky's Recitative and Song.
(4) Scene with Yaroslavna and Maidens.
(5) Konchak's daughter's Cavatina.
(6) Prince Vladimir's Cavatina.
(7) Konchak's Aria.
(8) The Polovtsian Dances.
(9) Yaroslavna's Lament.
(10) Final Chorus.

These numbers are only a small part of the whole; the bulk of the orchestration was left to his editors, Glazunov and Rimsky-Korsakov. It would be idle to discuss the question of how far they modified the composer's intentions, for we shall never know. It is however impossible to discern any abrupt transitions between those passages orchestrated by Borodin and those not orchestrated by him. This is scarcely surprising, since Borodin, Glazunov, and Rimsky-Korsakov all belonged to the same period and even to the same school. They had known one another for a very long time and were in very close agreement on matters of orchestration. In the latter respect, Borodin was much closer to Rimsky-Korsakov than Balakirev, not to mention Mussorgsky and Cui.

VI

We are now in a position to discuss the unity of the opera. We may confidently assert that, from a purely musical point of view, *Igor* is more in the nature of a symphonic poem than a rhapsody compounded of mosaics.

The thematic content of *Igor* is derived from two sets of motifs: (1) motifs from the ballads and fragments of the folk-song 'The Sparrow Hills', which are the keystones of the Russian sections of the opera; and (2) motifs taken from Arabian, and kindred Hungarian tunes, used in the Polovtsian numbers.

There is some symmetry to be observed here: the Prologue and the end of Act IV have much in common from the musical point of view, while Acts II and III (in the Polovtsian encampment) make up the central section.

323

The unity of the whole is further strengthened by the use of leit-motifs, which not only identify particular characters, but even reflect their personal relationships with others, and the climate of events. As a good illustration of the latter, we might take the motifs derived from 'The Sparrow Hills' which appear in eight out of the twelve Russian choruses, and also in Yaroslavna's recitatives and in the duet from Act IV. These motifs reach their climax of importance when the dreaded enemy is mentioned or when foreboding of evil times to come is suggested. Sometimes they symbolize an inevitable chain of events, bringing destruction to individuals and even to entire peoples.[1]

We should add however that the underlying unity of the opera is not immediately apparent and can only be brought to light by analysis. There are two reasons for this: (1) the tune of 'The Sparrow Hills' could not be more simple, and the style of the other leitmotifs is not at all Wagnerian; and (2) the opera is divided into separate numbers, which makes it impossible to sense the unity directly.

Borodin had written *Igor* specifically as an operatic epic. He had wanted his opera to be stylistically similar to *Ruslan*. We have to admit that Borodin achieved this, especially in his use of arioso and cantilena in place of recitative, and in his extensive use of the chorus. Like Glinka, he also wanted 'the voices to take first place, and the orchestra second', but I venture to suggest that this intention was not completely realized; in many of the numbers (for instance, 'The Polovtsian Dances') the vivid and powerful orchestral writing is the centre of attraction; though there is nothing of Wagner's subjugation of voices to the level of 'speaking instruments'.

But, although there are similarities between *Igor* and *Ruslan*, there are also great stylistic differences. Borodin's opera belongs essentially to his later period and, in this respect, is closer to those of Rimsky-Korsakov's operas that were written at about the same time: the *May Night*, and more especially, *The Snow Maiden*. There are also to be

---

[1] If in *Ruslan* this 'fatal' force is personified by the legendary figure of Bayan who sings how 'fate threatens destruction with terrible carnage' to the bogatyr, then in *Igor*, Bayan is relegated to the chorus and orchestra, while 'fate' appears in the form of the mournful song about the weeping mountains, of the dead body of the bogatyr lying in the steppe and the relatives bewailing him. The song 'The Sparrow Hills' hints at the tragedy about to overtake the warriors as they embark upon their campaign against the Polovtsi; it is heard as the basis of the solemn 'slava'; it is heard in the chorus of boyars, prophesying the impending defeat; it features in the chorus of prisoners who at home are perhaps reckoned as dead. In a different way, the same melody is heard in the plaintive 'A cappella' Chorus telling of the destruction of the towns and villages, whilst finally it appears in a disguised fragmentary form in the concluding G major chorus.

found certain traits in common with the styles of the innovators, Wagner and Dargomyzhsky; Borodin keeps up a close metrical correspondence between words and music, and allows neither distortion of speech nor needless repetition.

Borodin was a true product of his age, in that he subscribed to musical realism. He always did his utmost to portray his historical characters realistically and convincingly. Since it would have been out of the question to employ the archaic language of the Igor epic poem, he fabricated a style of speech which was not out of keeping with original idiom of the Chronicle, and yet not banal or stilted.

What is the fundamental idea behind the opera? Its character seems to be largely determined by the original Igor Chronicle. This work *The Lay of Igor's Campaign* had been composed as a protest against the internecine strife of the princes, a plea for the establishment of national unity within Russia. The hero of the Chronicle is just such a prince, in his struggle to preserve the common weal, and to end petty conflicts between neighbouring princes. Their common task was to defend the growing national community from the marauding Polovtsian hordes.

Borodin was a great patriot; a man who cherished the history of his people. He did not find the spirit of the Chronicle in any way alien. He broadened the scope of the original, and cut out all trivial and unnecessary detail, whilst at the same time giving the main characters a bolder outline. He even strengthens the idealized traits of the main character, and Igor becomes 'the knight-errant of the Russian national ideal'.

Igor is not simply a patriotic, but a heroic opera, a tale of glorious exploits. Igor's very first words are: 'Let us away now to fight the enemies of Russia', whilst his final words, at the end of the duet with Yaroslavna, tell of his intention of summoning all Russia to his aid, of gathering a massive army, and of smashing the ranks of all those who infringe Russia's territories. Yet Borodin is not callous in his attitude to other races, even when he is patriotic and glorifies his hero. The Polovtsi in the opera are by no means 'the spawn of Hell'. The composer is not on their side, but he understands them and finds in them many redeeming features.

The end of the opera, in accordance with history, is not a scene of triumph.[1] The chorus, welcoming Igor on his return from

---

[1] Borodin wrote in the file 'Libretto of *Igor* and Musical Sketches' (as the result of his study of the original manuscript) that 'nowhere was there any mention of a decisive victory over the Polovtsians'.

captivity, does nothing more than express hopes of better times to come.

The composer, an epic poet of music, sings in his opera of the struggle for national unity. There is a prophetic strain too in the opera in the form of the fatal motifs of 'The Sparrow Hills', which are woven into the texture of the music, reminding the listener of the inevitability of things.

CHAPTER ELEVEN

A FEW GENERAL CONCLUSIONS

I

At the beginning of Chapter VI, I put forward a few suggestions as to the origin of Borodin's themes. He uses the language of folk-song throughout, and yet we never hear whole folk-tunes in his work; we have to conclude from this that he constructed his own folk-themes from an assortment of motifs actually taken from folk-music of different regions.[1] I am convinced that whenever he was constructing his folk-themes, Borodin kept the melodic line of borrowed motifs but altered the rhythm and tonality.

I hope that my analyses in Chapters VII, VIII, IX, and X will have supported my thesis. The majority of his themes are taken from the ballads, which are on the whole a-rhythmic, and from the songs 'The Sparrow Hills', 'Le Bananier', and the Arabian songs, which have been rhythmically transformed and shifted into different keys.

With this fact established, we are now in a position to consider Borodin's method of constructing folk-themes.

My critics, and those who hold to the view that there is no point in analysing themes sprung from the mind of a genius, will by this time be smiling to themselves. They may think that I am naïve enough to visualize a 'struggling composer' copying various bits of motifs from one source to another, and trying out ways of piecing them together until they come right on paper. Nothing could be further from my mind. One has only to compare this distorted picture with the true one, given us by Catherine and Stassov in their memoirs; here the picture is of an inspired man in the throes of composition, his eyes sparkling with intensity, completely lost in a world unknown. My reader will easily recognize the stupidity of such

---

[1] This is almost self-evident. The situation is outlined by Rimsky-Korsakov: '[Melodies in the folk-spirit] . . . must of necessity contain turns and phrases which are found in genuine folk-melodies. Can two works resemble one another as a whole if no component part of the one resembles any component part of the other? It may be asked: if no single particle of the created melody resembles any single particle of the original folk-song, can the whole created melody recall folk-creation?' (see *Chronicle of My Musical Life*, 7th ed., p. 137).

accusations, and will see that my view of Borodin is by no means distorted.

The ballads and songs may have suggested to Borodin an authentic form of musical language (the byliny language, for example) in which he found a suitable vehicle for his ideas. He had a prodigious musical memory, and could always remember folk-tunes he had written down without having to refer to his notes.[1] The individual turns of phrase in a longish ballad such as 'The Terrible Tsar' might perhaps have become associated deep in the composer's mind with some intonation of the voice or with some visual image.[2]

Borodin's instinct could have been his sole guide in all this, but it is impossible to rule out the possibility that he did compile his themes consciously from sketches already made. Like all composers who have been steeped in the classics and who have mastered the art of counterpoint, Borodin knew how to make the most of his material and how to secure the best combinations of sounds.

It is worth remembering that he was constantly combining simple elements and complex structures in quite another field—in chemistry. The handling of symbols and formulae (chemical, mathematical, or otherwise) leaves a mark on one's way of thinking. 'Combinatory' activity can be applied in any direction, in music as in chemistry, and it does not necessarily stand in the way of the creative urge and inspiration.

The 'allegorical' content of several of Borodin's themes is somehow related to his flair of parody, and musical humour in general. Borodin was always sensitive to his critics, and for this reason might easily have preferred to conceal his more intimate thoughts under the cloak of parody or allegory, especially in those works where no programme is indicated by the composer himself.

We can now draw our conclusions about the way in which Borodin used derivative motifs in his compositions. It is already clear that he

---

[1] By way of an illustration of this, may I quote the following story. On 10 July 1884, during his visit to the dissenters' chapel, Borodin made a note of those melodies which interested him, and at the end of this list wrote down the theme of the Andante which was evolved from them. He gave this list to E. A. Guseva, who was with him at the time, with instructions 'to look after it well'. After this, he never asked for the list again and it remained in E. A. Guseva's hands until the 1920s. Nevertheless, as is seen from the sketches preserved in the Glazunov archive, he used the contents of this list in the composition of his Third Symphony.

[2] Even extremely short motifs might have some sense or significance for the composer. (One need only remember the motif of four notes which served Beethoven as the foundation of the first movement of his Fifth Symphony.)

strove to preserve the melodic outline of borrowed motifs and yet at the same time played about with the rhythms. Borodin had a great gift for rhythm, and had acquired a vast knowledge of the various folk rhythms, which often dispensed with regular conventional metre altogether. In other words, folk metres are not fixed, like those of printed music.

His reverence for the melodic structure of folk tunes is the natural outcome of his further and deeper acquaintance with folk music, a reverence which stems from Glinka and eventually culminated in a national Russian music, which supplanted the Russo-German idiom prevalent at the time. His firm grasp of the melodic structure of folk-song provided him with a basis on which he could erect the harmonic structure of a full-scale composition.[1]

II

It now only remains for us to consider Borodin's achievements as a composer. We are of course aware that Borodin ranks as one of the most representative and gifted members of the 'mighty Handful', who took over and developed the ideas and methods of the two founders of Russian music—Glinka and Dargomyzhsky. Balakirev was the composer who brought them together, and it was he who guided 'the Handful' from the very outset. This group aimed at a synthesis of the technical achievements of European music and the melodic characteristics of Russian and oriental folk music. They grew up with the musical ideas of the leading composers of the West: Schumann, Berlioz, and Liszt.

Their approach received no encouragement from the official patrons of the Court, who were opposed to folk music, and they were as revolutionary as Gogol and Pushkin had been a generation earlier when they put Russian literature on a truly popular footing.

A study of Borodin's works, both early and late, reveals not only his great talent but his fine technical mastery as well. He was more than a creator of beautiful and original musical ideas[2]; he could cast

---

[1] Here, of course, one must remember that we are dealing with a composer who thinks 'within the bounds of tonality'. As regards the fixing of definite tonalities to given works, one often has to take into consideration the tonal plan as a whole (especially in large-scale compositions), as opposed to the individual tonalities of separate motifs.

[2] It would be interesting to make a general survey of the characteristics of Borodin's themes, and by that reveal some of the secrets of his mode of composition. As it is impossible to do this, we must content outselves with Borodin's own opinion. He expressed the view that every composer has, in essence, one basic musical theme, the development of which is seen in his various compositions. Despite the fact that this

A Few General Conclusions

them into the most exquisite of art forms.¹ Those 'critics' who have
found fault with so-called formal imperfections in his work have
failed to see that Borodin was breaking away from academic convention.

Borodin's harmony contains many innovations, and is not over-
respectful of the traditional rules for resolution of dissonances; it is
not surprising that he angered those who were more orthodox than
himself. He nevertheless kept within the bounds of established
tonality.²

He was a great master of the orchestra. Without augmenting the
size of his orchestra to anything comparable with that used in Wagner's
Ring, he managed to achieve dramatic and acoustical effects of
tremendous power. He had a most exceptional command of the timbres
of the various orchestral instruments and families.

Although Serov has called all the members of 'the Handful' 'Ruslanists', Borodin and Rimsky-Korsakov were actually closest to Glinka
in their compositions.³ Like Glinka, Borodin had a leaning towards
programme music, and the folk-music of Russia and the Orient.
Borodin's major works are similar in spirit to *Ruslan*, though not at all
derivative. Borodin was a great lover of fantasy, but, generally
speaking, his music is nearer to the realists.

Very few of Borodin's works are lyrical or subjective, and even his
humorous works, although satirical, never relate back to his own
personal feelings.

The general mood of his music is optimistic. He loves life in all its

would hardly seem to apply in Borodin's case, it shows that he found in his own thematics
one fundamental idea, a striving for thematic unity. One might mention in passing that
he had one favourite tonality—D major, and if one takes into consideration his youthful
productions its use, together with that of D minor, assumes an even greater importance.

¹ Analysis of Borodin's composition (beginning with the works of the Heidelberg
period) shows that he was a complete master of sonata form. He adhered to it far more
closely in his youthful productions than in his later compositions. He displayed a
thorough command of counterpoint in his First Quartet, the skill of which even such an
enemy as Laroche could not deny.

² Certain contrasts of tonality in the movements of Borodin's symphonies and chamber
works might be regarded as exceptional dissonances for the time (as, for example, the
leap of a tritone in the transition from one movement to another in a cyclic production).
One is not struck so forcibly by such features in our modern freedom of creation, but
there are no reasons for considering these peculiarities as imperative or even interesting.
(In the 'Bogatyr' symphony, the contrast between the tonalities of B minor in the first
movement and F major in the Scherzo has a certain 'programme' significance.)

³ This kinship found external expression throughout Borodin's musical life. The first
of this childhood compositions contains an imitation of one of the themes form *Ruslan*,
whilst his last great composition, *Prince Igor*, is dedicated to the memory of Glinka.

various manifestations. Yet he never falls into naivety or false joie de vivre. He is always conscious of the fateful inevitability of natural and historical laws, and is keenly aware of the misery and afflictions of his fellow men. His sympathies are with the poor and oppressed,[1] but we never hear the voice of protest in his work.

I have one interesting document in my possession which throws into relief his attitude towards life and death. We already know that the words and the tunes of 'The Sparrow Hills' had a very powerful effect upon Borodin. Apparently he intended to use some of its themes yet again in another work, probably a cantata. The composer sums up the basic idea of this work in a couplet derived from Schiller's 'Das Siegesfest':

> 'Let the dead [man] sleep peacefully in his tomb,
> Whilst the living revels in life.'[2]

This is the composer's philosophy as it appears in his greatest work.

Borodin's compositions are few, but their artistic value is considerable. They will never fail to delight.

[1] We need only remember the end of 'The Sea' and the song 'From the Shores of a Distant Country' and many pages of *Igor*.

[2] The sketches of these verses were written on the back of a postcard dated 12 June 1881. They are preserved in the file, 'Libretto of Igor', etc. I reproduce here one of the most connected sketches, concluding with the couplet of Schiller which I mentioned above*:

> On the forgotten field of battle
> Stand the burial mounds
> Sullen, dumb:
> The graves of ancient knights,
> Who have laid down their lives
> In battles with the enemy—
> Death is their reward—
> They guard . . .
> And above them
> Brightly shines
> The sun with tender care
> And with grass and flowers
> Paints [the field] of death
> As if to say it wants the world:
> Let the dead [man] sleep peacefully in his tomb
> Whilst the living revels in life.

Without quoting the other sketches, I noticed that in one of them is a mention of 'the willow' which is mentioned in the text of 'The Sparrow Hills'. All these illustrations serve to confirm the deep impression which the words and melody of this folk-song produced upon the composer.

* The original Russian is written in unrhymed free verse. I have made a literal line-by-line translation. The punctuation, which is absent in the original, has been suggested by Dianin.—[TR.]

APPENDIX A

LIST OF BORODIN'S WORKS

Year of composition	Title	Present situation of original manuscripts	Notes
	1. OPERAS		
1867	*The Valiant Knights.* Farcical opera, in five acts. Words by Krylov. (Unpublished.)	T.B.A.K.T.* A sketch of the finale to Scene 5 is to be found in the Library of Music Manuscripts, Stanford University.	Cf. Otto E. Albrecht, *A Census of Autograph Music Manuscripts of European Composers in American Libraries,* Philadelphia, Univ. of Pennsylvania Press, 1953, p. 47.
1867–8	*The Tsar's Bride.* Opera based on the drama by L. A. Mey (fragments). (Unpublished.)	Not preserved.	Cf. V. V. Stassov, *A. P. Borodin,* Muzgiz, 1954, p. 33 and p. 71.
1869–70, 1874–87	*Prince Igor.* Opera in four acts, with Prologue. Libretto by Borodin. Dedicated to the memory of Glinka. (Pub. by Belyaev, 1889.)	G.P.B.* Several sketches in G.I.T.I.M.* Five extracts from the published score are in the Library of Congress (U.S.A.). Polovtsian Dances (the piano score) in the G.T.M.M.K.* Various sketches in the L.G.K.* and in private hands.	Ibid., p. 47.
1872	*Mlada.* Ballet-opera in four acts. Act IV, libretto by Krylov. Scenario by S. A. Gedeonov. (Finale pub. by Belyaev.)	Original manuscripts of Nos. 2–8 in G.P.B.* Sketch of No. 2 in I.R.L.I.*	Nos. 5–8 were pub. by Belyaev in Rimsky-Korsakov's transcription. The autograph MS. of No. 1 is untraceable.

* See list of abbreviations at the end.

Year of composition	Title	Present situation of original manuscripts	Notes
	2. SYMPHONIC WORKS		
1862–7	Symphony No. 1 in E flat major. Adagio (E flat minor)— Allegro (E flat major). Scherzo: Prestissimo (E flat major); Trio: Allegro (G sharp minor). Andante (D major). Allegro Molto Vivo (E flat major). Dedicated to Balakirev.	Arrangement for piano duet in the G.T.M.-M.K.* A variant of the first movement is in the G.P.B. Sketches of the score are in the N.I.I.T.M.K.*	Final draft of the full score is missing. Full score pub. by Bessel in 1882, and parts in 1883. Piano duet transcription pub. by Bessel in 1875.
1869–73, 1876	Symphony No. 2 in B minor. Allegro Moderato (B minor). Molto Vivo (F major); Trio: Allegretto (D major) Andante (D flat major). Allegro (B major) Dedicated to Borodin's wife.	Fragments in L.G.K. Complete final draft of the score in G.P.B.	Score pub. posthumously by Rimsky-Korsakov and Glazunov. Pub. by Bessel in 1887. Piano duet transcription pub. by Bessel in 1877.
1880	*In the Steppes of Central Asia.* Allegretto con moto (A minor—A major). Dedicated to Liszt.	G.P.B. Piano-duet version, and full score (pub. by D. Rahter in 1882). Original manuscripts in the G.T.M.M.K. Sketches for themes in the L.G.K.	
1882, 1886–87	Symphony No. 3 in A minor. Moderato Assai (A minor—A major). Vivo (D major). Trio: Moderato (B major). Andante (C minor ?). Finale.	Scherzo (5/8, without trio) in the G.P.B. Sketches in the L.G.K. and in S. A. Dianin's possession.	Unfinished. The first and second movements ed. by Glazunov, pub. by Belyaev in 1888. The second movement was adapted for string quartet: 'Les Vendredis'.
	3. CHAMBER MUSIC		
1847	Concerto for Flute and Piano (D major—D minor).	Not preserved.	Unpublished. Cf. Stassov, op. cit., p. 6

* See list of abbreviations at the end.

Year of composition	Title	Present situation of original manuscripts	Notes
1847	First String Trio in G major (for 2 violins and cello) on themes from the opera *Robert the Devil* (Meyerbeer). (Unpublished.)	Not preserved.	Ibid., p. 6.
1852–6	Second String Trio in G major ('The Grand Trio') (for 2 violins and cello): 1. Allegro (G major). 2. Andante (D major). 3. Scherzo (unfinished).	Three movements in the N.I.I.T.M.K.	Score and parts pub. by Muzgiz, 1949.
1852–6	(?) Quartet for Flute, Oboe, Viola and Cello, in D. 1. Allegro (D major). 2. Adagio (B minor). 3. Menuetto (Moderato) (D major); Trio (un poco meno mosso, D minor). 4. Finale. Rondo (D major).	N.I.I.T.M.K.	Score and parts pub. by Muzgiz, 1949. As has been shown by G. Golovinsky (cf. 'Sovietskaya Muzyka' 1954, No. 7, p. 113) the first and fourth movements are transcriptions of Haydn's Piano Sonata, op. 93.
1853–4	Quintet for 2 violins, viola, and 2 cellos, in F minor. 1. Allegro con brio (F minor). 2. Andante ma non troppo (A flat major). 3. Menuetto (F minor); Trio (F major). 4. Finale (F minor—F major).	Score in N.I.I.T.M.K.	The coda of the last movement is missing. Score and parts pub. by Muzgiz, 1960.

Year of composition	Title	Present situation of original manuscripts	Notes
1855	Third String Trio (for 2 violins and cello). Set of variations on the theme of the folk-song: 'Chem tebya ya ogorchila'. G minor. Dedicated to P. I. Vasilyev.	N.I.I.T.M.K.	Score and parts pub. by Muzgiz, 1946. A transcription for piano duet by M. R. Shchiglev, in N.I.I.T.-M.K.
1850–60 (?)	Fourth String Trio (for 2 violins and cello) in G major. Single movement. (Unpublished.)	N.I.I.T.M.K.	
1860	Sonata for Cello and Piano, in B minor. (Based on a fugue of J. S. Bach from the first sonata for unaccompanied violin.) 1. Allegro (B minor). 2. Pastorale (Andante dolce F major). 3. Finale: Maestoso-Presto (B minor—B major). (Unpublished.)	Fragments in N.I.I.T.-M.K. (beginning of first movement), and in private hands.	
1860–1	Sextet for 2 violins, 2 violas and 2 cellos, in D minor. 1. Allegro (D minor). 2. Andante (E minor). 3. & 4. (?).	40 pages in N.I.I.T.-M.K. Sketch for introduction to Finale (D major) in the G.P.B.	Score. Muzgiz, 1946. The last two movements are missing, but must have been written. Cf. I. Belza, *A. P. Borodin*, Muzgiz, 1947, p. 48.
1860–1	Piano Trio in D major. 1. Allegro con brio (D major). 2. Romance. Andante (E major). 3. Intermezzo. Tempo di minuetto (D major); Trio (C major).	N.I.I.T.M.K.	Muzgiz, 1950. It is likely that there existed a fourth movement.

Year of composition	Title	Present situation of original manuscripts	Notes
1862	Piano Quintet in C minor. 1. Andante (C minor). 2. Scherzo. Allegro non troppo (A minor). 3. Finale (C minor —C major).	G.P.B.	Parts and score pub. 'Iskusstvo', 1938.
1874–9	String Quartet No. 1 in A major. 1. Moderato. Allegro (A major). 2. Andante con moto (F sharp minor). Fugato, un poco piu mosso (D minor). 3. Scherzo. Prestissimo (F major). Trio. Moderato (A major). 4. Finale. Andante; Allegro Risoluto (A minor—A major). Dedicated to Rimsky-Korsakov's wife.	Sketches in G.P.B. and L.G.K.	Score pub. by D. Rahter, 1884. Piano duet transcription pub. by D. Rahter, 1887.
1881	String Quartet No. 2 in D major. 1. Allegro Moderato (D major). 2. Scherzo (F major). 3. Nocturne. Andante (A major). 4. Finale. Andante-Vivace (D major). Dedicated to Borodin's wife.	G.P.B. Sketches in the L.G.K.	Score pub. by Belyaev in 1888. Transcription for piano duet by S. M. Blumenfeld.
1886	*Spanish Serenade* (Serenata alla spagnola) for string quartet in B flat major. Dedicated to Belyaev.	G.P.B. Sketches in the L.G.K.	Score, parts and piano-duet arrangement pub. by Belyaev in 1887. Incorporated into a collective quartet *B–la–f*, pub. by Belyaev.

Year of composition	Title	Present situation of original manuscripts	Notes
1882	Scherzo for String Quartet in D major (5/8).	G.P.B.	Later incorporated into Third Symphony and 'Les Vendredis' under the title of 'Russian Scherzo'.
	4. WORKS FOR PIANO		
1843, 1846 (?)	*Polka ('Hélène') in D minor for piano duet.*	N.I.I.T.M.K.	Pub. Muzgiz, 1946.
1849 (?)	*Fantasia on a theme of Hummel.*	Not preserved.	Pub. by Gedrim, 1849. For information relating to these works, cf. 'Severnaya Pchela', 25 November, 1849.
1849 (?)	Study: *Potok* (Le Courant).	Not preserved.	
1851–2	Fugues for Piano.	Not preserved.	Also cf. Stassov, op. cit., p.22.
1852	Scherzo in B minor.	Not preserved.	Unpublished.
1852–5 (?)	Pot-pourri on a theme from Donizetti's opera: *Lucrezia Borgia*—A major. (Unpublished.)	G.P.B.	The preserved MS. might conceivably be the piano part of a chamber composition.
1861	Allegretto in D flat major, for piano duet. (Unpublished.)	N.I.I.T.M.K.	An adaptation of the Trio of the 3rd movement of the F minor Quintet.
1861 (Aug.)	Scherzo in E major for piano duet. (Unpublished.)	G.P.B.	
1862	*Fugue.* (Unpublished.)	Not preserved.	Cf. Stassov, op. cit., p. 34.
1862 (?)	*Tarantella* in D major, for piano duet.	Autograph copy (last page missing) in G.P.B. Copy of latter (complete) in N.I.I.T.M.K.	Pub. Muzgiz, 1938. Preface by S. L. Ginsburg (based on I. Y. Katselnik).

Year of composition	Title	Present situation of original manuscripts	Notes
1870 (?)	*'Ey ukhnem'*—transcription of a folk-song ('The Volga Boatmen') for piano duet (sketch).	G.P.B., L.G.K.	Unpublished.
1874 (?)–1878	Polka, Marche Funèbre, Requiem and Mazurka, for piano duet.	G.P.B. Sketch of the Polka in N.I.I.T.M.K. Sketch of Requiem in L.G.K.	Pub. D. Rahter, 1879. Nos. 2, 3, 12 and 14, pub. by Belyaev, 1893. The Polka, Funeral March, Requiem, and Mazurka were included in the collected anthology of *Paraphrase*.
1879 (?)	*Pièce* in E flat major for piano duet (fragment).	G.P.B.	Unpublished.
1885	*The Miniature Suite.* 1. *Au Couvent.* Andante Religioso. C sharp minor. 2. *Intermezzo.* Tempo di minuetto. F major. 3. *Mazurka.* Allegro. C major. 4. *Mazurka.* Allegretto. D flat major. 5. *Reverie.* Andante. D flat major. 6. *Sérénade.* Allegretto. D flat major. 7. *Nocturne.* Andantino. G flat major. Dedicated to Mercy-Argenteau.	G.P.B. : corrected proofs, with composer's corrections. British Museum : autograph (Nos. 2, 3, 4, 5, 6, and Scherzo).	Pub. by Bessel, 1885.
1885	*Scherzo* (Allegro vivace) in A flat major. Dedicated to Jadoul. (Pub. by Bessel, 1885.)		There is mention of an orchestral version on the title page, though this was of course never realized. Glazunov orchestrated this as No. 7 (Finale) for the *Miniature Suite*.

Year of composition	Title	Present situation of original manuscripts	Notes
	5. VOCAL COMPOSITIONS		
1852–5 (?)	*Why art thou so early, Dawn ?* Folk-song arrangement. F sharp minor.	G.P.B.	Pub. Muzgiz, 1947. In a preface to this edition Prof. Lamm writes: 'The autograph is very rough, and the interpretation approximate.'
1852–5 (?)	*Merciful God.* Folk-song, anonymous. E major.	N.I.I.T.M.K.	Unpublished.
1853–5 (?)	*The fair young maid no longer loves me.* With cello obligato in D major.	N.I.I.T.M.K.	Pub. by Muzgiz, 1947.
1853–5 (?)	*Friends, hear my song.* Anonymous. Voice and piano with cello obligato in E minor.	N.I.I.T.M.K.	Pub. by Muzgiz, 1947.
1854–5	*The beautiful fisher-maiden.* Words by Heine. D flat major. Also arr. with cello obligato. Dedicated to A. S. Shashina.	N.I.I.T.M.K.	Pub. by Muzgiz, 1947.
1867	*The Sleeping Princess.* Words by Borodin. A flat major. A fairy-tale for voice and piano. Dedicated to Rimsky-Korsakov.	G.P.B. G.T.M.M.K.	Pub. by Jurgenson, 1870. Score and parts (orchestrated by Rimsky-Korsakov) pub. by Jurgenson, 1904.
1867–8	*Song of the Dark Forest.* Words by Borodin. F sharp minor. Dedicated to L. J. Shestakova.	G.P.B. G.T.M.M.K.	Pub. by Bessel, 1873. Also called *An Old Song.* Score and parts, ed. Glazunov, pub. Bessel in 1893, for male chorus with piano.

Year of composition	Title	Present situation of original manuscripts	Notes
1868	*The Sea Princess.* Words by Borodin. Ballad for voice and piano. F major. Dedicated to A. E. Makovskaya.	G.P.B. G.T.M.M.K.	Pub. by Bessel, 1873.
1868	*The False Note.* Words by Borodin. D flat major. Dedicated to Mussorgsky.	G.P.B. G.T.M.M.K.	Pub. by Jurgenson, 1870.
1868	*My songs are filled with poison.* Words by Heine. Ballad for tenor and piano. E flat minor. Dedicated to Cui.	G.T.M.M.K.	Pub. by Jurgenson, 1870.
1869 (Dec.) –1870 (Feb.)	*The Sea.* Words by Borodin. Ballad for tenor and piano. G sharp minor. Dedicated to V. V. Stassov.	G.P.B. G.T.M.M.K.	Pub. by Jurgenson, 1870. In 1884, Borodin wrote an orchestral version of the accompaniment, but he was not satisfied with it (MSS. in G.P.B.). Work orchestrated by Rimsky - Korsakov, and in 1904 pub. by Jurgenson.
1870–1	*From my Tears.* Words by Heine (Russian translation by Borodin [?]). Ballad for voice and piano. B major. Dedicated to M. S. Stupishina.	G.D.M.C.	Pub. by Bessel, 1873.

Year of composition	Title	Present situation of original manuscripts	Notes
1881	*Arab Melody.* Words by Borodin. Ballad for voice and piano. F major.		Pub. by Belyaev, 1889. Based on original folk-melody. Cf. *Esquisse historique de la musique arabe aux temps anciens avec dessins d'instruments et quarante melodies notées et harmonisées par Nicolas Christianowitsch,* Cologne, 1863, p. XIX Cf. also: A. N. Dmitriev 'History of Borodin's opera *Prince Igor*', *Soviet Music,* 1950, No. II, p. 84.
1881	*At home among real people.* Words by Nekrassov. Song with piano or orchestral accompaniment. F major. Dedicated to D. M. Leonova.	Orchestral score in G.P.B. Rough sketches and fragments in L.G.K.	Score and parts pub. by Belyaev, 1890. Ed. with piano accompaniment (G. O. Dutsch), pub. by Belyaev, 1890.
1881	*For the Shores of a Distant Homeland.* Words by Pushkin. Ballad for voice and piano. C sharp minor. Dedicated to Borodin's wife.	G.P.B.	Pub. by Belyaev, 1890.
1884	*Pride.* Words by A. K. Tolstoy. Ballad for voice and piano. F major. Dedicated to A. A. Bichurina.	G.P.B. Copy of autograph with composer's comments in L.G.K.	Pub. by Belyaev, 1890.
1885	*Septain.* Words by C. J. (in French). Ballad for voice and piano. D flat major. Dedicated to Mercy-Argenteau.	Rough sketches in L.G.K.	Pub. by 'Veuve Muraille', 1885, Liège. Also appeared in Russian translation under title, *The Wonderful Garden,* pub. by Bessel, 1887.

23

Year of composition	Title	Present situation of original manuscripts	Notes
6. WORKS FOR CHORUS, AND SEVERAL VOICES			
1862 (?)	*Slava Kirillu! Slava Methodiu!* Words anonymous. For male voice choir with piano accompaniment. C major (unfinished). (Unpublished.)		
1868–71 (?)	*Serenade in honour of lady by four cavaliers.* Words by Borodin. Humorous quartet for four men's voices with piano accompaniment in D flat major.	N.I.I.T.M.K. Manuscript copy by Belyaev in the G.P.B.	Pub. by Belyaev, 1889. A musical joke on N. N. Purgold. The four cavaliers were Mussorgsky, Borodin, Rimsky-Korsakov, and Stassov
(?)	*Misera me, barbara sorte.* Words anonymous. Duet for tenor and base with piano accompaniment. F minor (unfinished). (Unpublished.)	N.I.I.T.M.K.	
7. MUSICAL JOKES AND IMPROVISATIONS LEFT UNFINISHED			
1866 (?)	*Southern Night.* A parody on a ballad by Rimsky-Korsakov. Musical joke for piano.		Cf. M. Y. G. (Goldstein, M. Y.), 'Something new about Borodin', *Russian Musical Gazette*, 1899, No. 38.
1867	60 Variationen über ein böhmisches Thema für das Pianoforte componiert und Hern Mily Balakireff zugeeignet von A. Borodin.	L.G.K.	Humorous work on a pseudo-Czech theme, proposed by Balakirev. Only one variation actually composed (cf. *Letters of Borodin*, Muzsektor Gosizdata, 1928, (I), pp. 93–94)

Year of composition	Title	Present situation of original manuscripts	Notes
1870s (?)	Waltz on the theme of Varlaam's Song from *Boris Godunov* (Mussorgsky). Musical joke for piano.		
	Quadrille on motifs from the *Maid of Pskov* (Rimsky-Korsakov) Musical joke for piano.		Cf. Goldstein's article quoted above.
	A musical joke for piano on a motif of a well-known ballad: 'Gusar, na sabliu opirayas'.		
	Lancer. In church modes.		
1874	*Kuchki.* Humorous waltz for piano.		Cf. *Letters of Borodin*, II, p. 242.

LIST OF ABBREVIATIONS

G.D.M.C.—*Gosudarstvenni Dom-Muzei P. I. Chaikovskovo v Klinu* (The State Museum at Tchaikovsky's House, Klin).

G.I.T.I.M.—*Gosudarstvenni Institut Teatra; Muziki v. Leningradë.* (The State Institute of Theatre and Music in Leningrad).

G.P.B.—*Gosudarstvennaya Publichnaya biblioteka imeni M. E. Saltikova-Shchedrina v Leningrade* (The Saltikov-Shchedrin State Public Library, Leningrad).

G.T.M.M.K.—*Gosudarstvenni Tsentralni Muzei Muzikalnoi Kulturi imeni M. I. Glinki v Moskvë* (The Glinka State Central Museum of Musical Culture, Moscow).

L.G.K.—*Leningradskaya Gosudarstvennaya Konservatoriya imeni Rimskovo-Korsakova* (The Rimsky-Korsakov Leningrad State Conservatoire).

M.U.Z.G.I.Z.—*Gosudarstvennoe Muzikalnoë Izdatelstvo* (The State Musical Publishing House).

N.I.I.T.M.K.—*Nauchno-issled. institut teatra, muzyki i kinematografii (Leningrad)* (The Research Institute for drama, music and the cinema, Leningrad).

T.B.A.K.T.—*Tsentralnaya Muzikalnaya Biblioteka Akademicheskikh Teatrov* (The Central Musical Library of Academic Theatres).

APPENDIX B

BORODIN'S BIRTH CERTIFICATE, AND
A FURTHER NOTE ON BORODIN'S ANCESTRY

Borodin's Birth Certificate[1]
taken from the 'Len. Gubzagsa' Archive
on 7 February 1925.

No. 1369.

[On the reverse side:—]

The Panteleimonovsky Church in St. Petersburg.[2]

1833

No. 83 Male sex	On 31 October (O.S.) a son *Aleksandr* was born to Porfiry Ionovich Borodin and his wife Tatyana Grigoryevna[3] by their first marriage, who both belong to the household of retired Lieutenant Luka Stefanovich Gedianov.[4] Baptism was administered by the Rev. Aleksei Maksimov. Deacon Vasilii Krylov was present at the christening.	Date of baptism 15 November	Godparents: Sergei Konstantinovich Antonov[5] Assistant to the superintendent of works at the Winter Palace, Hof-intendant's Department. Ustinya Konstantinovna,[6] wife of Vladimir Petrovich Gotoutsev, official in the War Office at St. Petersburg.

At the Head Gubzagsa Office: [Signature.]

Keeper of Records: A. BRONZOV.

[Public Records Office, Admin. Section, Len-Gubispolkom.]

---

[1] At the time when I started work on my biography of Borodin, I thought it desirable as far as possible to base my study on the documentary evidence then available.

When I began to go through the relevant documents, then kept in the archive section of the Army Medical Academy, I detected an error, common to all the previous biographies, relating to Borodin's date of birth. This had always been given as 1834, but the birth certificate record (Documents File No. 346) gave 1833.

But I was not satisfied with this particular document, and decided to examine the original register in which Borodin's birth was recorded. I was able to do this owing to the cooperation of Professor A. Bronzov, the then keeper of records in the Leningrad Registry of Births [and Deaths].

He produced at my request a copy of the original birth certificate.

[2] The christening of Borodin in the Panteleimonovsky Church (on what was formerly Panteleimonovsky Street, now Pestel's Street) supports my own finding that the actual birthplace was a house at the corner of Gagarinsky Street and former Sergievsky Street. This house is situated quite near Panteleimonovsky Street.

[3] Porfiry Ionovich and Tatyana Grigoryevna Borodin were not Borodin's real parents; they were serfs of Luka Gedianov. Borodin was thus legally born as his serf.

[4] The real father of Borodin.

[5] Sergei Konstantinovich Antonov (b. 1804), was Borodin's uncle on his mother's side.

[6] Ustinya Konstantinovna Gotovtseva (*née* Antonova, died 1870), was Borodin's aunt.

344

Appendix B

In examining the documents relating to Borodin's ancestors on his father's side, one is struck by the strong contrast between the details of these documents and the early pages of Stassov's biography of Borodin. According to the documents, the Gedeanov family, i.e. Borodin's paternal ancestors, are of Tartar origin. In the Stassov biography, however, it is stated that Borodin descended 'by his father from a family of Princes of Imeretia'.[1] In the French biography by Habets, which is based largely on material taken from Stassov and published in Paris in 1893, there is an additional piece of information evincing the composer's 'natural' musical talent, for in the arms of his 'ancestors', the Imeretian Tsars, it is alleged that there is a musical instrument—David's psaltery.[2] Tiuneev, who was the first to draw attention to this (in a note in *Russkaya muzykalnaya gazeta*), held that Stassov's statement about Borodin's Imeretian ancestors should be regarded as fallacious. However, there are a great many considerations to be taken into account. First of all, there is the testimony of Borodin himself who often spoke of his Georgian (Imeretian) origin to his friends, my parents, and to A. N. Kalinina.[3] This is further confirmed by the facial features of Borodin and his father, both of whom are lacking in characteristic Tartar traits.

There are two probable solutions:

(1) One may either accept the theory that the forebear of Borodin's ancestors on the male side—the Tartar Prince Gedea—descended from the Imeretian Bagratides and ruled over a group of the Northern Caucasian Tartar nomads, in which case one of the Gedeanovs must have abandoned Christianity and become a Mohammedan; or

(2) One may look for ancestors of Imeretian origin on the female side who were connected with the Gedeanovs by marriage.

The first of these theories, in any case, does not explain the clearly Georgian features of Borodin and his father.[4] The Gedeanovs had lived in the Muscovite dominions (in Moscow and in the Vologda region) for many generations (from the sixteenth to the eighteenth centuries) and had contracted marriages with Russian women; as Luka Stepanovich was eight generations removed from Prince Gedea, and Borodin nine generations, it is surprising that the Georgian characteristics should have been so strong.

The second theory seems much more plausible. During the seventeenth and eighteenth centuries, members of the Georgian royal families often

---

[1] Stassov: *Alexander Porfiryevich Borodin. Evo zhizn, perepiska i muzykalnie stati*, St. Petersburg, 1889, p. 1.

[2] Examination of the coat of arms of the Gedeanov Princes reveals nothing resembling this. The arms are typical for noble families whose origin goes back to converts from Islam.

[3] A. P. and E. G. Dianin repeatedly told me of this. A similar story was handed to me by A. N. Kalinina's niece, S. M. Einwald.

[4] The two resembled each other very strongly. Sometimes (according to my father) Borodin would even dress up as his father for a joke.

visited Russia seeking asylum from Turkish or Persian aggressors. They frequently stayed in Moscow. In the reign of Peter the Great, who summoned the Russian nobility for state service from the furthermost corners of the land, the Gedeanov Princes might easily have been brought from their Vologda patrimony, and in this way a union arranged between the Russianized Tartar family, on the one side, and one of the Imeretian Princesses on the other. This could easily have happened to Borodin's grandfather, Stepan Antonovich Gedeanov, who died in the seventies of the eighteenth century, or to his great-grandfather, Anton Stepanovich, who died before 1734. Unfortunately, an objection to this otherwise feasible theory is the fact that no mention of any union of this nature is to be found in the Gedeanov documents known to us. This is all the more strange, for Luka Stepanovich, who was greatly concerned about the confirmation of his coat of arms and princely title, would surely have made much of his descent from the Imeretian rulers. On the other hand, the marriage (assuming that it ever took place) might have been morganatic and hence kept secret, or finally it might have been a love match not legalized by marriage with the consequent adoption of the offspring. Details of this nature would have been unbecoming in Luka Stepanovich's appeal for recognition, but would inevitably be preserved in the family traditions, echoes of which are found in Borodin's own words. After studying minutely the deeds of the Department of Heraldry 'concerning the princely titles' of descendants from the Georgian and Imeretian rulers, I was unable to discover, as with the other genealogical records dealing with the Bagratides, any details or evidence relating to Prince Gedeanov. I then determined to investigate the history of the last Tsar of Kartalintsi and his ancestors who had settled in Moscow in the seventeenth century and who also (usually) bore the name of the Imeretian princes. This line died out in the eighteenth century, and, as there were consequently no heraldic records, I had resort to a printed biography of one of the members of the family—The Tsarevich Alexander, which I found in the Naval archives. I discovered that the Kartalintsi Tsar Archil Vakhtangovich fled to Moscow following the Mohammedan invasion during the reign of Alexei Mikhailovich, taking with him his children, his son Alexander, and his daughter Darezhana. His son Alexander Archilovich, the 'Imeretian Tsarevich', was the same age as Peter the Great and often used to take part in his 'mock' military battles, becoming the Master of Ordnance in his army at a later date. During the Swedish war Alexander was captured at Narva and died in captivity from consumption. We gather that his sister, Darezhana, died in 1740.[1] It is also stated that 'the Imeretians' of this line 'possessed estates in the Province of Ekaterinoslav'. This last factor may possibly be connected with the story of Borodin's grandfather,

---

[1] I tried to prove this fact, which I unearthed in one of the encyclopedias, by means of the *S. Petersburgskie vedomosti* for the year 1740, but I was unsuccessful.

Appendix B

Prince Stepan Antonovich Gedeanov, being in the town of Bakhmut in the Province of Ekaterinoslav in the year 1734.[1] The idea of a marriage between Stepan Antonovich or his father and one of the Imeretians of the 'Kartalintsi' line instantly suggests itself. Furthermore, it is interesting to note Luka Stepanovich's love of the name 'Alexander'. He christened his son Alexander (Borodin), his daughter Alexandra, and yet another infant was given the same name. It is conceivable that he should wish to preserve the memory of Alexander Archilovich, but on the other hand, this fact might simply be explained as another instance of the use of the name 'Alexander' which was very fashionable among a certain section of the Russian nobility during and after the reign of Alexander I.

[1] The phrase 'The Ekaterinoslav Province' is used only as an indication of the geographical situation of these three estates, as the province did not then exist as such.

APPENDIX C

Art = *Iskusstvo.*

Autobiographical Notes = *Avtobiograficheskie zapiski.*

Balakirev's Correspondence with Stassov = *Perepiska M. A. Balakireva s V. V. Stasovym.*

Chronicle of My Musical Life = *Letopis moei muzykalnoi zhizni.*

Fifty Years of Russian Music = *Pyatdesyat let russkoi muzyki v moikh vospominaniyakh.*

Former Years = *Starye Gody*

History of the Academy of Military Medicine = *Istoriya Voenno-Meditsinskoi Akademii.*

Journal of the Russian Society of Physical Chemistry = *Zhurnal Russkogo Fiziko-Khimicheskogo Obshchestva.*

Literary Archives = *Literaturny arkhiv.*

Le Messager de l'Europe = *Vestnik Evropy.*

Moscow Gazette = *Moskovskie vedomosti.*

Moscow Necropolis = *Moskovskii Nekropol.*

Musical Chronicle = *Muzykalnaya Letopis.*

Musical Contemporary = *Muzykalnii Sovremennik.*

My Reminiscences of My Brother = *Moi vospominaniya o brate.*

Naval Archives = *Voenno-morskoi sbornik.*

News of the Affairs and Successes of the Bible Society = *Izvestiya o deistviyakh i uspekhakh Bibleiskogo obshchestva.*

Northern Bee = *Severnaya Pchela*

Northern Messenger = *Severny Vestnik.*

Proceedings of the Academy of Science = *Byulleteni Akademii Nauk*

Russian Messenger = *Russkii Vestnik.*

Russian Musical Gazette = *Russkaya muzykalnaya gazeta.*

St. Petersburg Gazette = *S.-Petersburgskie Vedomosti*

Soviet Music = *Sovetskaya Muzyka*

The Voice = *Golos.*

INDEX OF BORODIN'S WORKS

Allegretto in D flat major, for piano duet, 35, 337

Arab Melody, song, 118, 264, 341

At Home among Real People, song, 118, 123, 125n., 130, 264, 341

Beautiful Fisher-maiden, The, song, 15, 29, 162, 339

Concerto for flute and piano, 333

Fair Young Maid no longer Loves Me, The, song, 15, 161, 339

False Note, The, song, 55, 68, 79, 139, 262–263, 264, 340

Fantasia on a theme of Hummel, for piano, 12, 337

For the Shores of a Distant Homeland, song, 122, 264, 331n., 341

Friends, hear my Song, song, 15, 161, 339

From my Tears, song, 72, 79, 161n., 263, 340

Fugue, for piano, 337

How Early art Thou, Dawn, song, 161, 339

In the Steppes of Central Asia, symphonic poem, 113–114, 117, 120, 128–129, 134, 135, 140, 144, 175, 225–228, 281–282n., 333

Kuchki, humorous waltz for piano, 85, 343

Merciful God, song, 339

Miniature Suite, The, for piano, 140, 141, 142–143, 249–255, 338

Misera me, barbara sorte, duet for tenor and bass, 342

Mlada, opera, Act IV, 75–77, 86, 87, 89, 123n., 132, 137, 200, 206n., 264, 267–271, 277n., 283, 284n., 285, 293n.–294, 296, 304, 322, 332

Musical joke for piano, on a well-known ballad, 343

My Songs are Filled with Poison, song, 55, 68, 262–263, 340

Paraphrases: Polka, Marche funèbre, Requiem and Mazurka, for piano duet, 102, 107, 247–249, 252, 338

Piano Quintet in C minor, 39, 40, 41n., 130n., 176–183, 336

Piano Trio in D major, 29, 32, 35, 166, 168–174, 335

Pièce in E flat major, for piano duet, 338

Polka (*Hélène*) in D minor, for piano duet, 10, 12n., 159–161, 337

Pot-pourri on a theme from *Lucrezia Borgia*, for piano, 337

Pride, song, 21, 140, 265, 341

Prince Igor, opera, ix–x, 32, 48, 58–65, 66, 69, 76n., 77, 85–88, 89, 90–91, 93–94, 95–96, 97, 100, 102, 103, 104–106, 107–112, 113, 114n., 116, 118, 119, 121, 123, 125n., 129, 132, 133, 134–135, 136, 137, 139, 141–142, 145, 146–147, 148, 149, 150–151, 155, 156, 200, 205n., 206n., 208, 217–218, 226n., 237, 254n., 261n., 264, 267, 269, 271–326, 330n., 331nn., 332, 341

Quadrille on motifs from *The Maid of Pskov*, for piano, 343

Quartet in D major, for flute, oboe, viola and cello, 334

Quartet No. 1, for strings: *see* String Quartet

Quartet No. 2, for strings: *see* String Quartet

Quintet in C minor: *see* Piano Quintet

Quintet in F minor: *see* String Quintet

Scherzo in A flat major, for piano, 141, 143, 247, 255–256, 338

Scherzo in B minor, for piano, 337

Scherzo in D major, for string quartet, 337

Scherzo in E major, for piano duet, 35, 337

Sea, The, song, 67, 68–69, 136, 137, 161n., 257, 261–262, 331n., 340

Sea Princess, The, song, 55, 79, 141, 208n., 262, 266, 340

Septain, song, 143, 265–266, 341

Serenade in Honour of a Lady by four Cavaliers, for men's voices, 342

Sextet in D minor: *see* String Sextet

Slava Kirillu, for chorus, 342

Sleeping Princess, The, song, 54, 58, 68, 139, 140, 141, 161n., 257–259, 262, 339

Sonata in B minor, for cello and piano (based on a fugue of J. S. Bach), 27, 168n., 335

Song of the Dark Forest, The, song, 54, 58, 79, 257, 260–261, 262, 339

Southern Night, a parody on a ballad by Rimsky-Korsakov, for piano, 342

Spanish Serenade, for string quartet, 149, 336

String Quartet No. 1 in A major, ix, 83n., 85, 87, 89, 93n., 100, 108, 109, 117, 118, 140, 224, 229–241, 330n., 336

String Quartet No. 2 in D major, 121, 125, 130, 150, 164n., 208n., 215n., 241–247, 336

String Quintet in F minor, for 2 violins, viola and 2 cellos, 334

String Sextet in D minor, for 2 violins, 2 violas and 2 cellos, 29, 32, 35, 166–168, 174, 175, 335

String Trio No. 1 in G major, on themes from *Robert the Devil*, 12, 334

String Trio No. 2 in G major, 334

String Trio No. 3 in G minor, variations on a folk-song, 15, 27, 162–165, 335

String Trio No. 4 in G major, 335

Study: *Potok (Le Courant)*, for piano, 12, 337

Symphony No. 1 in E flat major, x, 41, 45, 46, 54, 56–57, 58, 74, 88, 96, 102, 115, 117, 127, 130–131, 133–134, 140–141, 144, 145, 150, 184–199, 200, 207, 210, 215n., 223n., 224, 270n., 286, 333

Symphony No. 2 in B minor (*The Heroic (Bogatyr)*), x, 44, 57, 58, 69, 70, 72, 73–74, 76n., 77, 79, 82, 83, 89, 96–97, 98, 101, 106–107, 117–118, 134, 144, 145, 148, 149n., 168, 185n., 199–210, 215n., 330n., 333

Symphony No. 3 in A minor, 130, 135, 137, 138, 148, 150–151, 152, 155, 210–225, 260n., 328n., 333

Tarantella in D major, for piano duet, 38–39, 174–176, 337

Transcription of a folk-song (*The Volga Boatmen*), for piano duet, 338

Trio in D major: *see* Piano Trio

Trio in G major: *see* String Trios

Trio in G minor: *see* String Trio

Tsar's Bride, The, opera, 53–54, 66, 267, 281n., 332

Valiant Knights, The, farcical opera, 21, 47–53, 257, 267, 332

Variations on a Bohemian theme, for piano, 342

Waltz on the theme of Varlaam's song from *Boris Godunov*, for piano, 343

GENERAL INDEX

Abraham, Prof. Gerald, xi, 208n., 215nn., 226n., 245n., 252, 253, 264
Alekseev, P. P., 32, 33, 34n., 55–56, 73n., 147n.
Alexander II, Tsar, 46n., 117, 119, 225
Alexander III, Tsar, 126, 130
Alexandrov, Dmitri S. (Borodin's half-brother), 6n., 7n., 8n., 10 and n., 12, 16n., 17, 99, 126n., 128n.
Antonov, Sergei K., 6 and n., 9nn., 344
Antonova, Avdotya K. (Borodin's mother), 6–8, 9, 10, 11, 12, 13, 16, 17n., 18, 19, 23, 26, 27, 28; death of, 80; 83n.
Antonova, Ustinya K.: see Gotovtseva, U. K.
Antwerp, 143, 144
Asafyev, B. V., 48, 68n., 151n.

Baden-Baden, 34, 115
Balakirev, Mili, 20; Borodin meets, 40; 43, 53, 54, 55, 64, 65, 67, 71, 72n., 74, 79, 83, 87, 92, 114n., 127, 263n., 323, 342, 348; influence of, 41–42, 43, 183, 184, 307, 329; mental crisis of, 73; and Borodin's 1st symphony, 56, 115, 131, 184, 333; and Borodin's 2nd symphony, 70, 74, 75, 202; and Borodin's songs, 68; and the Borodin Scholarship, 156; and the Free Music School, 66, 71, 121–122, 123n., 126, 131
Balaneva, Elena (Borodin's adopted daughter), 104, 108
Bartók, Béla, 316n., 317, 319
Beethoven, 22, 37, 39, 84, 85, 111n., 126n., 198, 230n., 240n.
Belinsky, V. G., 21, 43
Belyaev, M. P., 130, 144, 146–147, 149; and Borodin's memorial, 155; 210, 215n., 336, 342; publisher of Borodin's works, 234n., 270, 281n., 332, 333, 336, 338, 341, 342

Belza, Prof. I. F., 168n., 207n., 208n., 335
Belzmann, Ekaterina E., 7nn., 16, 81
Berlin, 19, 24, 40, 78, 98, 119, 143
Berlioz, Hector, 22, 66, 112, 329
Bernard, Claude, 31
Bertels, Prof. E., 314n.
Berthelot, M. P. E., 19, 26
Bessel (music publisher), 79, 81, 103, 122, 143, 146–147, 184, 199, 333, 338, 339, 340, 341
Bible Society, The, 5–6, 348
Bichurina, Anna A., 130, 140, 265, 341
Blaramberg, P. I., 114n., 128
Blumenfeld, S. M., 134, 146, 150, 241n., 336
Borodin, Catherine (Ekaterina), 9, 10; Borodin meets, 33–34; 35; illness in Heidelberg, 36; in Italy with Borodin, 36–40; 41; their marriage, 42; 44, 45, 46, 54, 55, 64, 66, 67; and Prince Igor, 69; 72, 74, 75, 77–78, 80, 81, 93n., 95, 99, 100, 103–104, 105, 108, 115, 122–123, 124, 128, 131, 134, 137, 138, 151; peculiar way of life of, 83, 86, 88, 121, 127, 135; illness of in Moscow, 147–148; and death of Borodin, 155; in Moscow, 70–71, 73, 85, 89, 98, 101, 116, 132, 133, 136, 139, 142, 144, 150; death of, 156; on Schumann, 174; and Borodin's Tarantella, 175; and 2nd String Quartet, 246; 266n., 327; works dedicated to, 333, 336, 341
Borodin, Porfiry I., 8, 344
Borshchov, Ilya G., 24, 25
Bortnyansky, D., 38
Botkin, Prof. Sergei, 40
Bourgault-Ducoudray, Louis A., 143
Braudo, E. M., 15, 58, 122n., 142n., 246
Brugger, Anna P., 26, 27, 28
Brussels, 19, 145

Bülow, Hans von, 120, 145
Bunsen, R. W., 24, 26
Butlerov, A. M., 13n., 35, 67, 113

Chopin, Frédéric, 33, 81, 84, 114n.,
    125n., 134; influence of, 182, 198
Collen, Georges, 143, 265
Collen, Paul, 139
Cui, Cesar, 40; Borodin meets, 43; 54,
    55; *Ratcliffe*, 55, 57; 71, 74; *Mlada*,
    76, 269n.; 82, 91; and *Prince Igor*,
    94; 98; Paraphrases, 102; 114n.;
    and Mussorgsky's death, 119; 129,
    141, 145; *The Caucasian Prisoner*,
    141, 145; 211n., 250n., 306, 323, 340

D'Albert, E. F. C., 134
Damrosch, Leopold, 117
Dargomizhsky, Alexander, 54, 57, 141,
    154, 257, 285n., 325, 329; *The Stone
    Guest*, 54, 93, 280n.
David, Felicien, 307
Davydkovo, village of, 70, 72n., 73
Davydov, K. Y., 134
Davydovo, village of, 100, 101; fire at,
    103; 104, 105, 108, 109, 110, 115, 288
Denier, portraits by, 4n., 5, 7n., 9
Dianin, Alexander P., 8n., 13, 16n.,
    56n., 78n., 79, 81n., 84, 85, 86n., 88,
    89n., 93n., 96n., 97 and n., 100 and
    n.; Borodin's private assistant, 101;
    103, 104, 105nn., 110nn., and *Prince
    Igor*, 116; 120, 126n., 128n., 130n.,
    132n., 137, 142n., 144n., 147, 148n.,
    149, 150n., 151n., 152, 156; and
    Borodin's *Tarantella*, 175n.; 345n.
Dianin, Fyodor P., 101, 103
Dianin, Nikolai P., 53, 100, 101, 103
Dianin, Prof. Pavel A., 100, 103, 108,
    146
Dianina, Elizaveta (Liza), vii, 7n.,
    16nn.; Borodin's adopted daughter,
    72, 73, 75; 82, 83n., 84, 85, 101,
    108n., 122n., 128n., 132n., 142n.,
    153n., 156, 262n., 345
Dmitriev, A. N., x, xi, 53, 341
Dobroslavin, Prof. Alexey P., 40, 75,
    109n., 110

Dobroslavina, Marya V., 75n., 96, 146;
    and Borodin's death, 153; 154; 249;
    and Borodin's 3rd symphony, 150–
    151, 219, 223, 224
Dumas, J. B. A., 31
Dupont, Auguste, 145
Dutsch, G. O., 133, 139, 341

Elena, Grand Duchess, 43, 66, 71
England, 19
Erlenmeyer, E., 26, 99

Fedorov, Fedor A., 11, 12, 13
Filippov, T. I., 117, 122, 126n., 156
Findeisen, N. F., 7n., 16n., 169n.
Florence, 38
Frankfurt-am-Main, 19
Fribourg, 28

Galkin, N. V., 118, 125n., 126n., 229n.
Gavrushkevich, I. I., 14, 15, 16n.
Gebel, Franz Xavier, 14
Gedeonov, S. A., and *Mlada*, 75–77,
    123n., 267, 332
Gedianov, Prince Luka Stepanovich
    (Borodin's father), 3–10, 21, 344–
    346
Gedianov, Prince Stepan Antonovich,
    3, 346, 347
Gedianov Princes, The, 2–4, 345–347
Glazunov, Alexander, 126, 134, 139,
    141, 146, 149 and nn., 152; and
    Borodin's unfinished works, 155;
    and Borodin's 2nd symphony, 199,
    333; 255n., 261n., 338, 339; and
    Borodin's 3rd symphony, 151n., 155,
    210, 214, 215n., 217–219, 222, 333;
    and *Prince Igor*, 155, 277, 292, 309,
    311n., 321–323
Glebov, Igor: see Asafyev, B. V.
Gleichenberg, 78
Glinka, Michael, vii, 15; Borodin's
    admiration for, 21, 22; 24, 40, 71,
    87, 93, 124n., 129, 145; influence of,
    158–161, 162, 163, 177, 182–183, 257,
    280n., 306, 324, 329, 330; 332
Gogol, Nicolai V., 24, 55, 329
Goldstein, M. Y., 84, 97, 342, 343

Golovinsky, G., 334
Gotovtseva, A. V., 127, 130n.
Gotovtseva, Marya V., 10, 17, 18
Gotovtseva, Ustinya K., 6, 9n., 344
Gottschalk, Louis M., 307, 310, 314n.
Graz, 45, 78n.
Gungl, Johann, 11
Guseva, Elena A. (Borodin's adopted
    daughter), vii, viii, 5n., 7n., 8n.,
    16n., 104, 108, 115, 126n., 135, 138,
    328n.
Guseva, Marya A., 17n., 115, 147

Heidelberg, 23, 24–29, 30, 31, 32,
    33–36, 99, 162; works composed in,
    165–174, 175, 176, 246, 330n.
Heine, Heinrich, 15, 72, 162, 262, 263,
    339, 340
Helmholtz, Prof. H. L. F., 26
Hérold, L. J. F., 52
Herzen, Alexander, 26, 37, 43
Hummel, J. N., 12, 38, 39, 81
Hunfalvy, P., 86–87
Hunke, I. K., 14, 15

Ilynsky, V. N., 126, 146
Imeretian Princes, The, 4, 19, 345, 346
Ippolitov-Ivanov, M. M., 106n., 122n.,
    126
Italy, 30, 31, 32, 36–40; works com-
    posed in, 174–183

Jadoul, T., 134, 135, 139, 140, 141,
    143, 255, 256, 338
Jena, 78, 97, 98, 99, 120, 134
Jurgenson (publisher), 68, 117, 339, 340

Kabat, Ivan I., 19
Kahl, Willy, 209n.
Kalinina, Anna N., 54, 55, 128, 131,
    133, 142, 345
Karamzin, N. M., 86, 132n.
Karenin, Vladimir, 79n., 84n., 86n.,
    87n., 207n.
Karlsruhe, 29
Karmalina, Lydia I., 22n., 79, 83, 87n.,
    88, 92n., 94, 95n., 97, 263n., 278n.,
    280n.

Katselnik, I. Y., 176n., 337
Kazan, 80–81
Kekulé von Stradonitz, F. A., 65, 67,
    99
Khilovo, 46
Kirchhoff, Prof. G. R., 26
Kitarry, M. Y., 28
Kleineke, Christian I., 9 and n.
Kokorev, V. T., 19
Kretschmar, T., 209n.
Kruglikov, S. N., 9, 128, 156, 174
Krylov, V. A., *The Valiant Knights*,
    47–53, 257, 332; *Mlada*, 76–77,
    268n.
Kudashev, Prince N. I., 34, 64
Kulomzin family, the, 84, 85, 88

Lamm, Prof. P. A., 10n., 15n., 41n.,
    50, 53, 164nn., 165n., 261n., 339
Lamoureux, Charles, 139n., 140
Lapin, I. P., 109, 289n.
Laroche, H. A., 229n., 259n., 263n.,
    330n.
Laub, Ferdinand, 34
Leichtenberg, The Duke of, 67
Leipzig, 120, 131, 143, 144
Leningrad (*see also* St. Petersburg):
    Conservatoire, 53, 185n., 219
    Public Library, 316, 320n.
    Saltikov-Shchedrin Library, 274n.,
        305n.
    State Institute of Drama and Music,
        28n.
Leonova, Darya M., 113, 114n., 118,
    119; Jubilee concert, 123–124; 341
Lesnoye, suburb of St. Petersburg, 5,
    127, 131
Liège, 135, 136, 140, 141, 143, 145
Lineva, L., 'Great-Russian Songs in
    Folk-harmonization', 289, 291, 293
Liszt, Franz, 22, 44, 82, 87; Borodin
    meets, 98–99; 101, 102–103; and
    Paraphrases, 107; 112, 114n.; in
    Magdeburg, 119; 125n.; and *In the
    Steppes of Central Asia*, 120, 134n.,
    333; and Balakirev, 126n.; 138, 143,
    193n., 228, 259n., 329
Lithuania, 24, 259n.

Litvinenko, Ganya (Borodin's adopted daughter), 104, 105, 121, 247
Lloyd-Jones, David, 249
Lodyzhensky, Anna N.: *see* Kalinina, A. N.
Lodyzhensky, Ivan N., 54
Lodyzhensky, Nicolai, 54, 73, 120, 121, 128, 134
Lomakin, G. Y., 46n.
'Luischen', 10, 11, 16
Lukanina, Anna N., 75, 78, 101, 152
Lukash, Elizabeth, Nikolai and Sergei, 8n., 9n., 28,
Lyadov, Anatol K., 102, 106, 124, 134, 149
Lyapunov, S. M., 307n.
Lysenko, K. I., 32, 33

Magdeburg, 119
Mainov, V. N., 33, 86, 87, 315, 316
Makovskaya, Elena T., portrait of Borodin by, 69; 262n.
Makovsky, Konstantin E., 69,146,262n.
Mannheim, 34
Marko-Vovchik: *see* Velinskaya-Markovich
Marsick, Pierre J., 143, 145
Mendeleev, Dmitri I., 24–25, 28–31, 32n., 80
Mendelssohn, Felix, Borodin's enthusiasm for, 11, 20, 22, 100; influence of, 166, 172, 175, 183
Menocci (violinist), 37, 38, 39
Mercy-Argenteau, Countess of, 16n., 135, 136, 137n., 139, 140, 143; Borodin visits, 143; Borodin burns letters from, 152; works dedicated to, 249, 250n., 265, 338, 341
Meshchersky, Prince Ivan and Prince Peter, 6
Meyerbeer, Giacomo, 47, 49n., 50–52
Miropolskaya, M. A., 84, 93
Moscow:
Bolshoi Theatre, 47–48, 107
Mme. Borodin born in, 33n.
Borodin in, 41, 45, 46, 64, 67, 70, 78, 81, 89, 95, 101, 103, 105, 118, 120, 128, 136, 144, 146, 147, 148, 150

cholera in, 70
Exhibition of Industry and Fine Arts, 1882, 128, 129
Golitsyn Hospital, 33n., 89, 120, 133, 148n.
Mussorgsky, Modeste, Borodin meets, 18; 19–20, 40–41, 43, 54, 73, 81, 88, 90, 105; death of, 118, 122; memorial to, 145; 154, 181, 193n., 259n., 306, 322, 323, 340, 342, 343; *Boris Godunov*, 53, 73, 79, 83, 141; *Khovanschina*, 114n., 117; *The Marriage*, 55; *Mlada*, 76, 269n.; *Sorochinsky Fair*, 124n., 215n.

Naples, 32–33
Napravnik, Edward, 96–97, 106, 117
Navashin, S. G., 135–137
Nef, K., 209n.
Nekrassov, Nikolai A., 118, 123, 124, 125n., 265, 341
Nicholas I, Tsar, 5, 21
Nikisch, Arthur, 119, 131, 184n.

Offenbach, Jacques, 50–52
'Old Believers' (bes-popovtsi), 137, 211, 213, 219

Pacini, Giovanni, 38
Paris, 19, 25, 31, 32, 140, 143
Passek, T. P., 26, 32
Pasteur, Louis, 31
Pavlovskoye, 135–139
Peter the Great, 346
Petersburg: *see* St. Petersburg
Pisa, 36–39, 166, 175n.
Prokunin, 'Collection of Russian Folk-Songs', 93, 236n., 237, 282, 288–291
Protopopov, Alexei (Borodin's brother-in-law), 46,71, 80,122, 127,133
Protopopova, Ekaterina A. (Borodin's mother-in-law), 33n., 89, 101, 104n., 105, 128, 132, 133, 147, 148
Purgold, Alexandra N., 54, 263n.
Purgold, Nadezhda N.: *see* Rimsky-Korsakov, N. N.

Pushkin, Alexander S., 122, 264, 329, 341

Ramenskoye, suburb of Moscow, 142, 147, 148
Razumovsky, D. V., 118
Regnaud, H. V., 31
Riedel, Karl, 103, 115, 120, 131, 134, 144
Rimsky-Korsakov, Andrey N., vii–viii, 92n., 229n., 249n., 259n.
Rimsky-Korsakov, Nadezhda N., 54, 74, 90–91, 134, 229, 336, 342
Rimsky-Korsakov, Nikolai A., 18n., 40 and n., 41; Borodin meets, 43; 44–45, 48, 54, 66, 67, 70, 72n., 73, 79, 80, 82, 85, 90–91, 93–94; conducts Borodin's 1st symphony, 96; conducts Borodin's 2nd symphony, 106–107; conducts fragments from *Prince Igor*, 105–107, 111–112; and *Prince Igor*, 106–109, 118n., 141–142, 146, 155, 271, 276, 277 and n., 319n., 321–323; conducts *In the Steppes of Central Asia*, 113–114, 128–130; and Mussorgsky's death, 119; 121, 127, 131, 149 and n., 152–153; edits Borodin's 2nd symphony, 199; 202n., 207n., 208n., 218n., 225, 248n., 307 and n., 327n., 330, 333, 339, 340, 342, 343; *Antar*, 119, 129, 307; Collected Russian Folk-Songs, 93, 237, 282; *The Maid of Pskov*, 53, 55, 73, 79, 111n., 114n.; *A May Night*, 93, 324; *Mlada*, 76, 269n., 270, 332; Paraphrases, 102; *The Snow-Maiden*, 122, 141, 324
Rimsky-Korsakov, W. N., 170n.
Rome, 31
Röntgen, Julius, 150
Rossini, Gioacchino, 25, 47, 50–52
Rotterdam, 28
Rozhnovo, village, 84, 85, 88, 100
Rubinstein, Anton, 83, 84, 129
Rubinstein, Nicholas, 117
Russian Musical Society:
Moscow branch, 117, 128, 129

St. Petersburg branch, 43, 54, 56, 65, 66, 71, 96, 117, 118, 125n., 130; Borodin elected Director of, 134; resigns, 144; von Bülow conducts at, 145

St. Gotthard, 30
St. Petersburg:
Borodin's father in, 5–8; his mother's houses in, 11, 13, 18; Borodin in, 14, 17, 40, 42, 46, 55, 64, 70, 73, 78, 80, 81, 85, 89, 91, 101, 105, 110–111, 118, 121, 130, 132, 139, 144–145, 147, 148; Borodin's death in, 154; Mme. Borodin in, 46, 72, 73, 83, 86, 101, 122, 134
Academy of Physicians, The, 7n.; Borodin enters medical faculty of, 12–13; graduates at, 16; 23, 32; becomes Zinin's assistant in, 40; Borodin's flat in, 42, 44, 72, 75, 81, 89–90, 101, 132, 133; 43, 46, 55, 88, 93, 110, 122, 147, 152; fancy-dress balls at, 75, 153–154
Academy of Sciences, The, 17, 65, 348
Chemical Society, The, 55, 67, 78, 105, 113
Circle of Music Lovers, The, 115, 117, 121
Conservatoire, The, 73, 134, 152n., 156
Free Music School, The, 45n., 56, 66, 71, 94, 96n., 105–107; concert of Russian operatic music in, 111–112; 121, 123n., 126, 131
Second Military Hospital, Borodin's appointment at the, 16–18
Women's Medical Courses, 78, 88, 91, 101, 122, 126–127, 130, 132, 144
Saint-Saëns, Camille, 143
Sainte-Claire, Deville E. H., 31
Salvador-Daniel, Francesco, 32, 307
Samoilovolich, A. N., 2nn., 228n.
Savich, Valerian, 31, 32
Schiller, 331
Schubert, Franz, 264n.

Schumann, Robert, 20, 22, 33, 84, 263; influence of, 174, 176, 182, 197n., 198, 199, 329
Sechenov, I. M., 24, 25
Sennarmon (chemist), 31
Serov, Alexander, 14; *Rogneda*, 47, 48, 51; 57, 330
Severtsev, Nikolai A., 24
Shashina, Adelaida, 15, 339
Shcherbachev, friend of Stassov's, 82, 86n., 91
Shchiglev, Mikhail, 11, 12, 13–14, 15, 21, 35n., 91, 115; dispute with Circle of Music Lovers, 121; at Borodin's funeral, 154; 165n., 166
Shelkov, N. V., x, xi, 316
Shestakova, Liudmila, 70, 72, 90, 91, 97, 130, 339
Shonorov, Dr. V. A., 85
Sokolovo, village, 111n., 115, 116
Soligalich, town, 19
Sorokin, Prof. Ivan, 17, 18, 26, 34, 36, 70, 75n., 82
Staraya Ruza, village, 95
Stassov, Vladimir, 7n., 8n., 10n., 11n., 12n., 14n., 15n., 16n., 17n., 18n., 19n., 28n., 31n., 33n., 40, 41 and n., 42; meets Borodin, 43; 53, 54, 56n., 66, 68 and n., 69, 75n., 76, 77, 82, 83, 85, 86, 87, 88, 90–91, 92n., 95n., 102, 105, 106nn., 107, 116; and Mussorgsky's death, 118; 123, 127, 128, 132n., 133n., 134, 144, 146; and Borodin's memorial, 154–155; his biography of Borodin, 155–156; 165n., 166n., 172, 183n., 193n., 197 n., 229n., 249n.; and Borodin's *Miniature Suite*, 255n., and *Mlada*, 269n., 270n.; 327, 333, 337, 340, 342,

345, 348; and *Prince Igor*, 58, 64, 90–91, 93, 94, 271–277, 279, 281n., 319; and Borodin's 2nd symphony, 79, 207, 209n.; and Borodin's songs, 258n., 259n., 263n., 264n., 269n.
Stradella, Alessandro, 248, 251n.
Stupishina, M. S. (Borodin's sister-in-law), 71, 72, 89, 263, 340

Taneev, Sergei I., 93, 227n., 259n., 272
Tassinari (chemist), 36, 37
Tchaikovsky, Peter I., 34n., 64, 93, 118, 162n., 210n.
Tolstaya, E. F., 32, 307n.
Tolstoy, A. K., 265, 341
Tolstoy, F. M., 56
Turgenev, Ivan S., 32, 83–84, 101

Vasilyev, Peter K., 14, 335
Vasilyev, Vladimir K., 14
Velinskaya-Markovich, M. A., 26, 32
Viardot, Pauline, 101
Viareggio, 39

Wagner, Richard, 34, 120, 174, 324, 325, 330
Weimar, 98, 99, 119, 120, 143
Weissheimer, Vendelin, 115
Würzburg, 35
Wurtz (chemist), 26, 31

Yurevich, Marya, 8 and n.

Zhitovo, village, 120–121, 127, 131
Zinin, Prof. Nikolai N., 13, 16, 19, 23, 26, 28, 31, 35, 40, 67, 82, 88, 97; death of, 113; memorial to, 130, 141

Schumann, Robert, 20, 22, 33, 84, 263; influence of, 174, 176, 182, 197n., 198, 199, 329

Sechenov, I. M., 24, 25

Sennarmon (chemist), 31

Serov, Alexander, 14; *Rogneda*, 47, 48, 51; 57, 330

Severtsev, Nikolai A., 24

Shashina, Adelaida, 15, 339

Shcherbachev, friend of Stassov's, 82, 86n., 91

Shchiglev, Mikhail, 11, 12, 13–14, 15, 21, 35n., 91, 115; dispute with Circle of Music Lovers, 121; at Borodin's funeral, 154; 165n., 166

Shelkov, N. V., x, xi, 316

Shestakova, Liudmila, 70, 72, 90, 91, 97, 130, 339

Shonorov, Dr. V. A., 85

Sokolovo, village, 111n., 115, 116

Soligalich, town, 19

Sorokin, Prof. Ivan, 17, 18, 26, 34, 36, 70, 75n., 82

Staraya Ruza, village, 95

Stassov, Vladimir, 7n., 8n., 10n., 11n., 12n., 14n., 15n., 16n., 17n., 18n., 19n., 28n., 31n., 33n., 40, 41 and n., 42; meets Borodin, 43; 53, 54, 56n., 66, 68 and n., 69, 75n., 76, 77, 82, 83, 85, 86, 87, 88, 90–91, 92n., 95n., 102, 105, 106nn., 107, 116; and Mussorgsky's death, 118; 123, 127, 128, 132n., 133n., 134, 144, 146; and Borodin's memorial, 154–155; his biography of Borodin, 155–156; 165n., 166n., 172, 183n., 193n., 197 n., 229n., 249n.; and Borodin's *Miniature Suite*, 255n., and *Mlada*, 269n., 270n.; 327, 333, 337, 340, 342,

345, 348; and *Prince Igor*, 58, 64, 90–91, 93, 94, 271–277, 279, 281n., 319; and Borodin's 2nd symphony, 79, 207, 209n.; and Borodin's songs, 258n., 259n., 263n., 264n., 269n.

Stradella, Alessandro, 248, 251n.

Stupishina, M. S. (Borodin's sister-in-law), 71, 72, 89, 263, 340

Taneev, Sergei I., 93, 227n., 259n., 272

Tassinari (chemist), 36, 37

Tchaikovsky, Peter I., 34n., 64, 93, 118, 162n., 210n.

Tolstaya, E. F., 32, 307n.

Tolstoy, A. K., 265, 341

Tolstoy, F. M., 56

Turgenev, Ivan S., 32, 83–84, 101

Vasilyev, Peter K., 14, 335

Vasilyev, Vladimir K., 14

Velinskaya-Markovich, M. A., 26, 32

Viardot, Pauline, 101

Viareggio, 39

Wagner, Richard, 34, 120, 174, 324, 325, 330

Weimar, 98, 99, 119, 120, 143

Weissheimer, Vendelin, 115

Würzburg, 35

Wurtz (chemist), 26, 31

Yurevich, Marya, 8 and n.

Zhitovo, village, 120–121, 127, 131

Zinin, Prof. Nikolai N., 13, 16, 19, 23, 26, 28, 31, 35, 40, 67, 82, 88, 97; death of, 113; memorial to, 130, 141

Pushkin, Alexander S., 122, 264, 329, 341

Ramenskoye, suburb of Moscow, 142, 147, 148
Razumovsky, D. V., 118
Regnaud, H. V., 31
Riedel, Karl, 103, 115, 120, 131, 134, 144
Rimsky-Korsakov, Andrey N., vii–viii, 92n., 229n., 249n., 259n.
Rimsky-Korsakov, Nadezhda N., 54, 74, 90–91, 134, 229, 336, 342
Rimsky-Korsakov, Nikolai A., 18n., 40 and n., 41; Borodin meets, 43; 44–45, 48, 54, 66, 67, 70, 72n., 73, 79, 80, 82, 85, 90–91, 93–94; conducts Borodin's 1st symphony, 96; conducts Borodin's 2nd symphony, 106–107; conducts fragments from *Prince Igor*, 105–107, 111–112; and *Prince Igor*, 106–109, 118n., 141–142, 146, 155, 271, 276, 277 and n., 319n., 321–323; conducts *In the Steppes of Central Asia*, 113–114, 128–130; and Mussorgsky's death, 119; 121, 127, 131, 149 and n., 152–153; edits Borodin's 2nd symphony, 199; 202n., 207n., 208n., 218n., 225, 248n., 307 and n., 327n., 330, 333, 339, 340, 342, 343; *Antar*, 119, 129, 307; Collected Russian Folk-Songs, 93, 237, 282; *The Maid of Pskov*, 53, 55, 73, 79, 111n., 114n.; *A May Night*, 93, 324; *Mlada*, 76, 269n., 270, 332; Paraphrases, 102; *The Snow-Maiden*, 122, 141, 324
Rimsky-Korsakov, W. N., 170n.
Rome, 31
Röntgen, Julius, 150
Rossini, Gioacchino, 25, 47, 50–52
Rotterdam, 28
Rozhnovo, village, 84, 85, 88, 100
Rubinstein, Anton, 83, 84, 129
Rubinstein, Nicholas, 117
Russian Musical Society:
    Moscow branch, 117, 128, 129

St. Petersburg branch, 43, 54, 56, 65, 66, 71, 96, 117, 118, 125n., 130; Borodin elected Director of, 134; resigns, 144; von Bülow conducts at, 145

St. Gotthard, 30
St. Petersburg:
    Borodin's father in, 5–8; his mother's houses in, 11, 13, 18; Borodin in, 14, 17, 40, 42, 46, 55, 64, 70, 73, 78, 80, 81, 85, 89, 91, 101, 105, 110–111, 118, 121, 130, 132, 139, 144–145, 147, 148; Borodin's death in, 154; Mme. Borodin in, 46, 72, 73, 83, 86, 101, 122, 134
    Academy of Physicians, The, 7n.; Borodin enters medical faculty of, 12–13; graduates at, 16; 23, 32; becomes Zinin's assistant in, 40; Borodin's flat in, 42, 44, 72, 75, 81, 89–90, 101, 132, 133; 43, 46, 55, 88, 93, 110, 122, 147, 152; fancy-dress balls at, 75, 153–154
    Academy of Sciences, The, 17, 65, 348
    Chemical Society, The, 55, 67, 78, 105, 113
    Circle of Music Lovers, The, 115, 117, 121
    Conservatoire, The, 73, 134, 152n., 156
    Free Music School, The, 45n., 56, 66, 71, 94, 96n., 105–107; concert of Russian operatic music in, 111–112; 121, 123n., 126, 131
    Second Military Hospital, Borodin's appointment at the, 16–18
    Women's Medical Courses, 78, 88, 91, 101, 122, 126–127, 130, 132, 144
Saint-Saëns, Camille, 143
Sainte-Claire, Deville E. H., 31
Salvador-Daniel, Francesco, 32, 307
Samoilovolich, A. N., 2nn., 228n.
Savich, Valerian, 31, 32
Schiller, 331
Schubert, Franz, 264n.